Computational Models of Mixed-Initiative Interaction

Edited by

Susan Haller

University of Wisonsin-Parkside, Kenosha, USA

Alfred Kobsa

German National Research Center for Information Technology, St. Augustin, Germany

and

Susan McRoy

University of Wisonsin-Milwaukee, Milwaukee, USA

Reprinted from *User Modeling and User-Adapted Interaction*
Volume 8, Nos. 3–4, 1998; Volume 9, Nos. 1–2, 1999

Kluwer Academic Publishers

Dordrecht / Boston / London

A C.I.P. catalogue record for this book is available from the Library of Congress.

ISBN 978-90-481-5171-4

Published by Kluwer Academic Publishers,
P.O. Box 17, 3300 AA Dordrecht, The Netherlands.

Sold and distributed in the U.S.A. and Canada
by Kluwer Academic Publishers,
101 Philip Drive, Norwell, MA 02061, U.S.A.

In all other countries, sold and distributed
by Kluwer Academic Publishers,
P.O. Box 322, 3300 AH Dordrecht, The Netherlands.

Printed on acid-free paper.

Table of Contents

User Modeling and User-Adapted Interaction **8:** 167–170, 1998.
© 1998 *Kluwer Academic Publishers.*

Preface

SUSAN HALLER[1] and SUSAN McROY[2]
[1]*Computer Science and Engineering Department, University of Wisonsin–Parkside, Kenosha, WI, USA. e-mail: haller@cs.uwp.edu*
[2]*Department of Electrical Engineering and Computer Science, University of Wisonsin–Milwaukee, Milwaukee, WI, USA. e-mail: mcroy@cs.uwm.edu*

In a problem-solving situation, the information and abilities needed for the task at hand are often distributed among the collaborators. As a result, direction and control of the interaction shifts among the participants. If future computational systems are to collaborate effectively with users to solve problems, they must have the ability to take and relinquish control of the problem-solving process and the communication about it. The theory and the mechanisms that underly these behaviors are the topics of this special issue of *User Modeling User Adapted Interaction* on computational models for mixed initiative interaction.

Systems capable of mixed initiative interaction must include mechanisms for recognizing when to lead or take control of an interaction and when to relinquish control to collaborators. They must be able to take the current locus of control into account when interpreting utterances and actions and formulating responses. From the perspective of user modeling, one way of tailoring an interaction to an individual is to vary the amount of initiative exhibited by the system for each user. Adapting initiative in response to individual user needs and preferences is yet another challenge to building mixed initiative systems.

The contributors to this two-part issue discuss theoretical models of mixed initiative as well as implementations that exhibit mixed initiative behavior. The focus of the first part is on specifying the nature of mixed initiative – defining initiative and control, recognizing who has initiative, and simulating mixed initiative. The focus of the second part is on illustrating the utility of mixed initiative by presenting an array of applications, including tutoring, scheduling of meetings, and information retrieval, in which mixed initiative plays an important role.

The first article provides an introduction to the issue of what mixed initiative is and why it is important. Cohen et al. present four theories of initiative that classify and sythensize early work on mixed initiative. They discuss the circumstances under which each theory is valuable – a discussion which naturally leads to whether it is necessary to model initiative at all and whether different models of initiative are needed for different types of problem-solving activities. The survey of early work in mixed initiative also provides useful background for the other work discussed in this issue.

The next two articles present computational models of mixed initiative. Chu-Carroll and Brown describe a predictive model for determining who will have the initiative during the course of a dialogue, where initiative with respect to solving the task is distinguished from initiative in the dialogue about it. The determination of who will have initiative is based on the current distribution of initiative across participants in the dialogue, in combination with a set of observed cues. Guinn provides a prescriptive model that explains how mixed initiative can be achieved by a system, including how agents should decide who should be in control of constructing a plan for the next subgoal in a planning problem. In this context, dialogue is a by-product of agent collaboration where no single agent has all the information necessary to solve the planning problem. In contrast to the theory of Chu-Carroll and Brown, dialogue initiative is the same as task initiative.

The last article in the first part discusses the development of a software agent that provides human-computer mixed initiative assistance. Rich and Sidner describe COLLAGEN, a program that manages a collaboration between an application and a user, mediating between a software interface agent and the user by tracking the attentional state and collaborative intentions of each participant. The COLLAGEN agent's mixed initiative capability results from the representation and use of the discourse state and the collaboration model.

The second part of this issue begins with a discussion of simulations of computer dialogues, by Ishizaki, Crocker and Mellish, in which initiative is mixed. Their results suggest that the utility of mixed initiative may be a function of the type task–in their experiments, mixed initiative dialogue proved to be in inefficient for solving hard problems. Previously, it has been shown that the utility of mixed initiative also depends on the abilities of the agent who is allowed to take control.*

The remaining articles of this issue discuss different applications of mixed initiative. Lester, Stone, and Stelling present their work on an interactive tutoring system. In such systems, efficiency of problem solving is not as important as engaging the learner's interest and enhancing learning. In the authors' system, initiative changes depending on the learner's state of knowledge. For example, at the beginning the agent takes control to introduce the problem. Once the learner begins to solve the problem, the system allows the learner some control. However, the system will retake control when the learner has difficulty or requests assistance and then release control when the learner is ready to continue with the learning exercise. Cesta and D'Aloisi present an application of mixed initiative to the design of a personal assistant. In such systems, usability and trust are important concerns. The

---

* Performance issues for mixed-initiative interaction have been studied previously in the context of expert-client dialogs (Whittaker and Stenton, 1988), in collaborative planning (Burstein and Mc-Dermott, 1986; Veloso, 1996; Ferguson et al., 1996) and in collaborative problem-solving (Walker and Whittaker, 1990; Smith and Hipp, 1994; Guinn, 1996; Rich and Sidner, 1996; Rich and Sidner, 1997). This work suggests that efficiency can be improved by allowing the initiative to shift to the agent with the best knowledge of a particular subproblem.

authors discuss the design of an interactive meeting agent that gradually increase its degree of initiative as the user develops trust in the agent's reliability.

Stein, Gulla and Thiel discuss the mixed initiative aspects of an information retrieval system. In such systems, there is often no well-defined model of the task that can be drawn upon to focus the interaction. Users may refine or change their goals during the problem solving process. They argue that a system can best support this exploratory style of problem-solving by explicitly managing a mixed initiative interaction. In contrast, Hagen describes an acoustic user interface to a database. She argues that initiative tracking and control is an emergent property of her approach. In the last article, Green and Carberry describe a computational mechanism for taking the initiative to include unsolicited information during response planning. In their approach, discourse plan operators are supplemented with stimulus conditions to motivate the inclusion of unsolicited information. Stimulus conditions are evaluated with respect to the user model, the discourse context, and anticipated effects of the planned response.

Examination of the different domains and genres of human-computer interaction exposes the need for new theories and mechanisms for controlling the progress of the interaction itself in a way that is efficient and productive. We trust that you will enjoy this special issue on computational models for mixed initiative interaction. As guest editors of the special issue, we welcome your feedback.

Acknowledgements

This effort was partially funded by the National Science Foundation, under grants IRI-9523666 and IRI-9701617. We would like to extend special thanks to Alfred Kobsa, editor of UMUAI, for his assistance and advice in putting together this issue.

References

Burstein, M. and D. McDermott: 1986, Issues in the development of human-computer mixed-initiative planning. In: Gorayska and Mey (eds.): *In Search of a Humane Interface*. North Holland, pp. 285–303.

Ferguson, G., J. Allen and B. Miller: 1996, TRAINS-95 Towards a mixed-initiative planning assistant. In: *Proceedings of the Third International Conference on AI Planning Systems (AIPS-96)*. Edinburgh, Scotland, pp. 70–77.

Guinn, C.: 1996, Mechanisms for mixed-initiative human-computer collaborative discourse. In: *Proceedings of the 34th Annual Meeting of the Association for Computational Linguistics*. Santa Cruz, CA, pp. 278–285.

Rich, C. and C. Sidner: 1996, Adding a collaborative agent to graphical user interfaces. In: *Proceedings of the 9th ACM Symposium on User Interface Software and Technology*. Seattle, WA, pp. 21–30.

Rich, C. and C. Sidner: 1997, Segmented interaction history in collaborative interafce agent. In: *Proceedings of the International Conference on Intelligent User Interfaces*. Orlando, FL, pp. 23–30.

Smith, R. and D. Hipp: 1994, *Spoken Natural Language Dialog Systems: A Practical Approach.* Oxford University Press, New York.

Veloso, M.: 1996, Towards mixed-initiative rationale supported planning. In: A. Tate (ed.): *Advanced Planning Technology.* AAAI Press, Menlo Park, CA, pp. 277–282.

Walker, M. and S. Whittaker: 1990, Mixed initiative in dialogue: An investigation into discourse segmentation. In: *Proceedings of the 28th Annual Meeting of the Association for Computational Linguistics.* Pittsburgh, PA, 70–78.

Whittaker, S. and P. Stenton: 1988, Cues and control in expert-client dialogues. In: *Proceedings of the 26th Annual Meeting of the Association for Computational Linguistics.* Buffalo, NY, pp. 123–130.

Authors' vitae

Susan M. Haller
Computer Science and Engineering Department, University of Wisconsin–Parkside Kenosha, WI, USA 53144.

Dr. Susan Haller is a professor of Computer Science and Engineering at the University of Wisconsin–Parkside. She received her B.S. from Cornell University and her doctorate from the State University of New York at Buffalo under the supervision of Dr. Stuart Shapiro in the area of interactive natural language generation. Her research interest is in interactive natural language processing in human-computer interfaces. She is a member of the Natural Language and Knowledge Representation Research Group at the University of Wisconsin–Milwaukee.

Susan W. McRoy
Department of Electrical Engineering and Computer Science, University of Wisconsin–Milwaukee, Milwaukee, WI, USA 53211.

Dr. Susan McRoy is a professor of Computer Science at the University Wisconsin–Milwaukee and the Association Director of Decision Systems and Artificial Intelligence Laboratory. She received her doctorate from the University of Toronto and her B.S. from the University of Michigan. Her research interests include Artificial Intelligence, Human-Computer Communication, Computational Linguistics, and Information Retrieval. Dr. McRoy has developed computational methods for effecting robust, yet flexible communication between people and computer systems. She is also investigating techniques for addressing information overload, for example, by dynamically tailoring an interaction to the needs of individual users.

User Modeling and User-Adapted Interaction **8:** 171–214, 1998.
© 1998 *Kluwer Academic Publishers.*

What is Initiative?

ROBIN COHEN, CORALEE ALLABY, CHRISTIAN CUMBAA, MARK
FITZGERALD, KINSON HO, BOWEN HUI, CELINE LATULIPE,
FLETCHER LU, NANCY MOUSSA, DAVID POOLEY, ALEX QIAN and
SAHEEM SIDDIQI
Department of Computer Science, University of Waterloo, Waterloo, Ontario, Canada N2L 3G1

(Received 27 November 1997; accepted in revised form 10 June 1998)

Abstract. This paper presents some alternate theories for explaining the term 'initiative', as it is used in the design of mixed-initiative AI systems. Although there is now active research in the area of mixed initiative interactive systems, there appears to be no true consensus in the field as to what the term 'initiative' actually means. In describing different possible approaches to the modeling of initiative, we aim to show the potential importance of each particular theory for the design of mixed initiative systems. The paper concludes by summarizing some of the key points in common to the theories, and by commenting on the inherent difficulties of the exercise, thereby elucidating the limitations which are necessarily encountered in designing such theories as the basis for designing mixed-initiative systems.

Key words: Initiative, discourse, goals and plans.

1. Introduction

The term 'initiative' has been used in discussing mixed-initiative interaction and mixed-initiative AI systems (Haller and McRoy 1997, Allen 1994), although there hasn't been a clear definition of the term itself. This paper presents four distinct answers to the question 'what is initiative?'.[1]

In order to provide some common grounding for the theories which are presented, each description is restricted to focus on the following:

- providing a brief, 'working' definition of initiative;
- extending this to a deeper representation for initiative, which provides the basis for determining which party in an interactive discourse has the initiative;
- some commentary on why it is important to distinguish who has the initiative, according to this definition – i.e. some indication of the possible value of this representation, the potential application areas for this definition;
- some commentary on whether it is worthwhile to try to model initiative.

---

[1] As will be seen in Section 3, the different theories which are developed demonstrate a range of focus on the concerns of discourse and of goals and plans.

Each of the theories presented in the paper will offer a different opinion as to the importance of modeling initiative. In particular, each one will provide a different kind of focus for the study of initiative. After the theories are presented, we will perform an analysis of the inherent differences, commenting on the circumstances under which each theory can be ideally suited to assist with the development of a mixed-initiative system.

2. Background

The theories presented in this paper compare and contrast with previous research on initiative and mixed-initiative systems. This section presents a brief outline of this related work, as background.

2.1. A LINGUISTIC APPROACH TO INITIATIVE

Perhaps the earliest investigations into initiative and the design of mixed-initiative dialogue systems was presented in the papers of Steve Whittaker and his colleagues (Whittaker and Stenton 1988, Walker and Whittaker 1990). The latter paper builds on work of the earlier one, so we will focus on it here in our discussion.

This work aims to model mixed-initiative discourse using an utterance type classification and rules for transfer of control between participants. In fact, shifts in control are associated with linguistic constructions used and there are different kinds of shifts distinguished – seized and negotiated. The model described in the paper therefore assists in analyzing initiative patterns in discourse.

Utterances are classified according to certain types, with associated control rules,[2] as follows:

- assertion: speaker control, unless response to a question;
- command: speaker control;
- question: speaker control, unless response to a question or command;
- prompt: hearer control.

There is also a claim that shifts of control do not occur until the controller indicates the end of a discourse segment by either abdicating (e.g. saying 'OK') or producing a repetition/summary. In addition, the noncontroller can simply seize control by issuing an interruption.

This then leads to a study of when interruptions occur which is characterized as happening due to one of two possible problems. The first, information quality, is involved when the listener has doubts about the truth or concerns about the ambiguity of a statement made by the speaker. The second, plan quality, occurs when

---

[2] Speaker control means that the participant who makes the utterance has control afterwards. Hearer control means that the participant who hears the utterance has control afterwards.

the listener finds that the goal being proposed by the speaker either presents an obstacle or is unclear. The conclusion is that when plans are succeeding, prompts, repetitions and summaries are used to signal a move to the next stage of the plan, but when there are obstacles, then interruptions take place.

Walker and Whittaker also examine the difference between task-oriented and advice-giving dialogues. Overall, the conclusions are that different control patterns exist in different types of discourse, that there are linguistic constructions which signal control shifts and that there are clear reasons for control shifts.

2.2. DESIGNING MIXED-INITIATIVE AI PLANNING SYSTEMS

Mixed-initiative interaction has been considered in the design of collaborative AI planning systems. Two position papers have been written (Allen 1994, Burstein and McDermott 1996), which outline the usefulness of dialogue as a metaphor for the design of these systems and which discuss the decisions which must be addressed when allowing users and systems a more active role in the problem solving process. As described in (Burstein and McDermott 1996): 'The overall objective of research on mixed-initiative planning (MIP) is to explore productive syntheses of the complementary strengths of both humans and machines to build effective plans more quickly and with greater reliability.' They also make clear the motivation for this research. 'Our larger interest in mixed-initiative planning systems grows out of some observations of the strengths and weaknesses of both human and automated planning systems as they have been used... Humans are ... better at formulating the planning tasks... Machines are better at systematic searches of the spaces of possible plans...' The papers then focus on the changes required in order to construct MI planning systems. Again to quote Burstein and McDermott 1996: 'We begin by taking apart current notions of AI planning techniques to examine where they will need to change... in order to fit into the world of collaborative problem solving.'

The position papers then go on to present in more detail some of the specific issues which must be addressed when constructing an MI planning system. Allen sees the three main issues as designing mechanisms to: maintain control (directing the focus of the planning, since different agents will have the initiative at different times); register the shared context (since different views will have to be merged); and to achieve efficient communication (for instance, allowing abstractions of plans to provide a common view of the planning process). Burstein and McDermott have a somewhat different taxonomy of issues. However, they reach similar main conclusions: that the key to effective design lies in productive solutions to dialogue-based task management, to context registration and to information management, often by developing flexible, interactive visualizations of plans and support information. In addition, Allen has perhaps a stronger claim – that viewing MI planning as a dialogue is the most appropriate framework within which MI planning systems can be compared and evaluated, in order to advance that field. These researchers are therefore contributing to our understanding of initiative by demonstrating the design concerns which must be addressed in developing systems which allow for mixed initiative between users and system.

There has also been some work on specific AI planning systems which can in fact be described as mixed-initiative. Examining these systems leads to insights into the challenges in actually producing a working model of cooperation and coordination between the users and the system. Two projects described below are TRAINS-95, a transportation scheduling system (Ferguson et al. 1996) and Veloso's work on case-based military force deployment planning (Cox and Veloso 1997, Veloso et al. 1997).

The work on TRAINS-95 leads to the general conclusion that the plan reasoning requirements in MI systems are different from traditional planning and that an interactive, dialogue-based approach to plan reasoning is effective. In MI planning, operators are constructed from incompletely specified initial situations and the goals of the plan may be poorly specified, requiring changes. This is due to the role being played by the human, who is knowledgeable in the domain but not necessarily in the representation and reasoning required by the automated planner. The planning which takes place in this MI system is conducted via communication between the user and system; a significant portion of the communication is actually directed at establishing the state of the world and at clarifying the current situation, rather than specifically refining the plan at hand. This again provides evidence for the usefulness of modeling the underlying dialogue which drives the planning process.

In Veloso's case-based planning system for military applications, there were similar observations that humans may not have a precise understanding of the automated planner and how it works. Her solution has been to allow users to express themselves more freely (so not requiring them to learn the details of the planning system) and then to convert some of the human directions into a level of detail appropriate for the planning system to address. For example, humans may specify goals in terms of actions, whereas the system works primarily with state conditions. A preprocessor is built which automatically transforms the action representation into a state representation. Similar solutions are developed for the problems of users viewing actions at a more abstract level of detail and for users including subgoals along with higher level goals. Again, the main conclusions to draw by examining these specific projects which admit mixed initiative is that there are indeed differences in the views between humans and system, which must be identified and addressed.

2.3. EVALUATING THE BENEFITS OF MIXED-INITIATIVE DESIGN

Two researchers who have examined both the design of mixed-initiative systems and the means for evaluating the benefits of setting the initiative levels of a system are Guinn (1993; 1996) and Smith (1993). Both believe that the level of initiative in the system should mirror the level of initiative in the task being solved by the system. So, there is a clear focus on the current goals and plans in operation. Guinn is interested in who will control how the current goal will be solved. A primary design decision is to have a participant ask a collaborator for help if it is believed that the collaborator will have a better chance of solving the goal. Then, the basis for deciding who is best able to control a goal is determined in terms of a probabilistic examination of the search space of the problem domain. Guinn then conducts experiments to measure the benefits of what is termed a 'continuous' mode of dialogue initiative and a 'random' mode. (There are other modes described, but these two are the ones compared most closely). The random mode simply assigns control to one of the agents involved in a random fashion, whenever there is a conflict. The continuous mode allows for true mixed initiative, as follows. The more knowledgeable agent, defined by which agent's first-ranked branch is more likely to succeed, is initially given the initiative. If that branch of the plan solution fails, then a comparison is made with other agents to assign initiative to the one most likely to succeed with the goal. Experimental results show that there is significant pruning in the continuous model, resulting in more efficient problem solving.

Smith (1993) is concerned with modeling spoken dialogue in human computer interactions. He conducted experiments comparing two main designs – one where the computer has complete dialogue control (directive) and one where the user has control and can interrupt any desired subdialogue at any time (declarative). (The cases where the computer has control but can allow minor interruptions and where the user has complete dialogue control are included, for completeness, but are not highlighted in the experimental evidence). The conclusion is that the declarative mode has some significant gains, in that users will gain experience and take the initiative more frequently, resulting in a decrease in average completion time and a decrease in the average number of utterances. However, there will also be an increase in the number of non-trivial utterances and the elapsed time for subjects to respond, which suggests that the variable initiative is primarily of benefit to experienced users.

What these researchers provide is some basis for evaluating systems which incorporate mixed initiative, in comparison with models which do not. In addition, they provide one point of view of linking initiative to goals and plans.

There has also been recent work by Walker (1997) which in fact suggests that in certain circumstances it is more efficient to have the system in control, than to allow for freer input from the user. Her comparisons of system initiative (SI) and mixed initiative (MI) were conducted for an application of spoken assistance to users on the subject of electronic mail and it is certainly possible that the domain and sophistication of the system have an influence on the success of allowing for more mixed-initiative interaction.

2.4. WHETHER TO MODEL INITIATIVE

Although there are various opportunities for measuring the potential benefits of mixed initiative in the design of AI systems, one question which can be asked is whether it is actually necessary to model initiative in order to design an MI system. Miller (1997) ultimately argues that one can design systems effectively without a concrete model of initiative. Traum (1997) also contributes to the debate by trying to label initiative as a concept related to obligation amongst participants and related to who is in control; he is not certain that it is important for participants to realize who has the initiative, rather than simply modeling their collaborators' mental states. These points of view can be seen as distinct from the position of researchers such as Walker and Whittaker (1990) and Guinn (1993; 1996), who show the value of designing systems to follow a certain allocation of initiative to participants.

2.5. INDIVIDUAL EFFORTS IN DESIGNING MI SYSTEMS

The theories presented in the upcoming section had as background the general positions on initiative summarized in this section. They also took as a starting point an examination of several mixed-initiative systems, as outlined in (Haller and McRoy 1997). Some of the work described below is more at the level of a position paper on how to design a system, derived from experience with existing systems, rather than a specific MI design. Some of the work reported in these papers has now been expanded for inclusion in this special issue. We indicate below the cases where expanded versions exist and comment further on how our work contrasts to this work, in the Discussion section of our paper. The individual research examined as background for the theories we develop include the following.

- Shah and Evens (1997) and Freedman (1997) from the CIRCSIM-Tutor tutoring environment. This work allows for student initiative, classifies various forms of expression from students and from tutors, and comments on how a tutor can handle student initiatives, using a tracking of agenda items in an overall plan.
- Carberry (1997) who continues to argue for allowing more interaction from students during tutoring sessions.
- Lester and his colleagues (Lester et al. 1997) on the use of pedagogical agents doing tutoring, commenting on when these agents should intervene and the form/mode of communication which is most effective. Lester et al. (1998) provide a description of extended work by the authors.
- Chu-Carroll and Brown (1997) who distinguish task and dialogue initiative and provide a list of linguistic cues for both kinds of control shifts, primarily to guide response generation. Chu-Carroll and Brown (1998) provide a description of extended work by the authors.

- Kortenkamp et al. (1997) on allowing mixed-initiative design for robotics applications, indicating the levels at which humans can intervene, and the potential benefits of this intervention.
- Sibun (1997) on the desirability for tracking what, who, where, when, why and how, when determining the degree of initiative in systems, including allowing for several participants at once.
- Lee (1997) on the need to identify deception and mistaken beliefs, in order to determine how to manage mixed-initiative dialogues.

These papers are only a subset of those addressed at the recent symposium on mixed-initiative interaction. All the same, they indicate the diversity of applications which are being studied as candidates for MI design.

2.6. OTHER REFERENCES FROM THIS SPECIAL ISSUE

There are other papers in this special issue which are worthwhile to draw into our discussion of the comparative value of the individual theories of initiative. For completeness, we briefly summarize these papers in this section, indicating why they are potentially relevant to our topic. These papers include:

- Rich and Sidner (1999) who discuss the design of a collaborative interface agent that works on a plan with its user and communicates via a kind of dialogue.
- Stein et al. (1999) who analyze dialogues arising in the context of information retrieval and reveals when initiative can be taken.
- Cesta et al. (1999) who look specifically at interface agents and ties the opportunities for initiative to features in specific user models.
- Ishizaki et al. (1999) who examine the efficiency of mixed-initiative dialogues in a route finding application.
- Green and Carberry (1999) on the generation of responses to yes/no questions and when to take the initiative to provide additional information.

Since this work did not form the initial motivation for the design of the theories, whenever these papers are referenced, it should be understood that they were considered subsequent to the formation of our theories. In addition, we make further reference to related work in the analysis phase of our paper, Section 4.

3. Theories of Initiative

The theories presented in this paper can be briefly described as follows. The first argues that initiative should be equated with control over the flow of conversation, so that the metaphor of conversation is important in designing mixed-initiative systems. The second theory takes quite an opposite point of view, focusing narrowly on viewing initiative as controlling how a problem is being solved, therefore aimed at the level of goals and plans. The third theory, to some extent, combines the points of view of the first two by suggesting that initiative in a conversation occurs when one participant seizes control of the conversation by making an utterance which presents a goal for the participants to achieve. The fourth theory has elements of control, conversation and goals, but develops a unique set of terminology for distinguishing different cases when participants have the initiative. This theory discusses when a participant takes the first step in an entire 'process' underlying the conversation. It also distinguishes between different strengths of initiative and allows for one participant to be active in more than one conversation at the same time, therefore playing a different role with respect to each. Utterances can also play a role in more than one 'process' simultaneously.

Although we will provide a more detailed analysis and comparison of the theories in Section 4, it is worth noting the following. The theories have a natural progression in thought, from the least complicated perceptions of initiative as a control of the conversation (Theory #1) or simply as a control of the task (Theory #2), to more complex arrangements, where initiative controls both dialogue and task (Theory #3) and where initiative must be distinguished further, allowing for different strengths of initiative and for multiple threads within a dialogue to be tracked simultaneously (Theory #4). In our Discussion section, we will provide some preliminary thoughts on the characteristics of application areas which make each of the particular theories most useful. It is also important to note that for one of the theories, Theory #2, the description is presented as a coherent theory but there is an adjoining argument that one need not have a definition of initiative in order to model mixed-initiative systems. This is the theory which focuses on tracking who controls the current task, so that the position that formal modeling of initiative is not a requirement for system building coincides well with comments from others in the area of planning such as Miller (1997).

3.1. INITIATIVE AS CONTROL OVER THE FLOW OF CONVERSATION (THEORY #1)

3.1.1. Introduction and Definitions

In order to develop a definition for initiative, one approach is to draw on dictionary definitions as a basis for this discussion. The dictionary definition of *initiative* is '*n*. ability to initiate things, enterprise; first step; power or right to begin', whereas *initiate* is defined as '*v.t.* originate, begin, set going' (Oxford 1984). This definition of initiative is actually quite close to how artificial intelligence researchers view initiative.

Therefore, for the purposes of this theory, the following definition is proposed:

> *Initiative is control over the flow of conversation.*

The terms in this definition that need to be discussed are *control* and *flow*.

Control is the more straightforward of the two terms. Control is '*n*. power of directing or restraining, self-restraint; means of restraining or regulating. . .' (Oxford 1984). Basically, it is a characteristic of the flow of conversation – the flow is controlled by one of the participants.

Flow is the crucial term in the proposed definition of initiative. The definition of flow as a verb lends insight into exactly what is meant in the proposed definition: '*v.i.* glide along as a stream, move like liquid; gush out;. . . move smoothly and steadily' (Oxford 1984). Flow, in our definition, is the movement of the conversation, through a subject or series of subjects.

3.1.2. *Expanded Definition*

In a mixed-initiative system, a designer should allow a certain amount of initiative for each participant in the collaborative discourse. In line with the definition outlined above, the ability of a participant to take the initiative in a conversation simply means that the participant can change the direction or topic of the conversation, or take the lead in discussing the current topic. Only one participant can have the initiative at any given time.

The definition presented in this section with its concept of *flow* places no restrictions on when the flow can change; a participant can in fact interrupt in the middle of a conversation in order to take the initiative. It is therefore useful to examine other work on initiative and interruption. Walker and Whittaker (1990) identified four situations where a participant will interrupt, and these situations can be grouped into two categories: information quality and plan quality. Interruptions due to information quality are:

- Listener believes assertion P and believes assertion P is relevant and either believes that the speaker doesn't believe assertion P or believes that the speaker doesn't know assertion P.
- Listener believes that the speaker's assertion about P is relevant but ambiguous.

Interruptions due to plan quality are:

- Listener believes assertion P and either believes that assertion P presents an obstacle to the proposed plan or believes that assertion P has already been satisfied.
- Listener believes that an assertion about the proposed plan is ambiguous.

[13]

In addition, we identify three more situations where a participant will interrupt the current conversation:

I. When the listener knows or tries to induce the meaning of the speaker before the speaker finishes.
II. When the listener has another more important goal that he/she believes needs to be satisfied before the current goal.
III. When the listener is no longer interested in the current plan.

In situation I, the listener can interrupt the speaker and respond immediately. This increases the efficiency of the conversation. It also increases the clarity if the speaker is repeating him/herself. In both situations II and III, the listener interrupts the speaker in order to change the current plan. In general, initiative should increase flexibility, efficiency and clarity of a conversation.[3]

In this theory, control is defined as the management of the direction of flow. Before discussing flow in more depth, the meaning of *direction* must be clarified. There are five types of direction:

1. Go forward: continue along with the plan towards a goal. (e.g. prompts such as 'yes', 'no', 'ok', 'that's right', or additional information or comments that lie along the path towards the goal that the speaker is following.) When a participant issues a simple prompt or supplies responses which simply help to retain the current flow, this does not constitute a shift in initiative.[4]
2. Change direction: discard or temporarily suspend the current plan and change to a new plan or topic. (e.g. 'But...', 'What if...', 'On the other hand'.) The participant who proposes the new direction has the initiative. This can lead to a subplan or actually change to another plan.[5]
3. Stop or pause: temporarily or permanently discontinue the current conversation and plan. (e.g. 'Let me think.', 'Wait a sec.') There is no change in possession of initiative. If the pause becomes lengthy, then the initiative is possessed by no one, and the next speaker with a new contribution to the conversation takes the initiative again.
4. Close or repeat: refine the conversational details before continuing. (e.g. repetition, summary.) When the speaker repeats him/herself or summarizes the previous conversation, then as in (Walker and Whittaker 1990), this shows

---

[3] Note that in cases where the speaker 'disagrees' with the listener's interruption, the speaker may then choose to take back the initiative. We do assume that all interruptions constitute a change of initiative.

[4] Prompts and simple responses may indeed allow the current flow to go forward, but the participant who utters them is not controlling the conversation.

[5] Temporarily suspending a current plan may be considered somewhat distinct from interrupting to completely change the direction of a plan, as in situations II and III. Both constitute a change of initiative.

that the speaker has nothing new to say, and so the listener has the initiative. This is true if the listener takes the initiative, i.e. the listener goes forward along the plan or changes direction of flow. Otherwise, if the listener has no contribution (such as another pause or simple prompts or another repetition), then no one has the initiative and the next speaker with contribution to the conversation takes the initiative again.

5. Interruption: unexpected seizure of control. The listener has the initiative because the listener interrupts the speaker and takes the initiative explicitly. In some cases, the interrupted flow is continued by the interrupter. In other cases, the interrupted flow is terminated or put on hold, and another flow begins with the same participants.

The flow of a conversation is a high level concept borrowed from network resource management (Lin and McKeown 1997). A party can belong to zero or more flows and s/he can only participate in the flow(s) of conversation that s/he belongs to. A flow can have one or more participants in it. (One participant is the case where an interlocutor talks to him/her/itself.) Flow is especially important if the conversation has more than two participants. For every flow of conversation, one of the flow's participants has the initiative. So, if there are three conversations going on in a room, three people have initiative. It is possible that these three people are actually the same person, who has the initiative in all three flows.

For example, if A and B are discussing one idea, while A and C are discussing another idea, and the two ideas are independent, then clearly, when A is talking to B, C should not participate. Similarly, when A is talking to C, B should not participate. Here the concept of flow plays an important role. Denote the conversation between A and B as flow F1; similarly, denote the conversation between A and C as flow F2. Both of these flows can be active concurrently. Whenever F1 is active, only the participants in F1 (A and B) can become involved. Either A or B has the initiative in flow F1. A or B can leave flow F1 and thereby end their participation in that particular conversation. Similarly, when flow F2 is active, either A or C has the initiative. In order to manage such issues, flow management functionality is needed in the system.

How does initiative change hands? A participant can take the initiative by successfully changing the topic or direction of the conversation. To demonstrate what is meant by initiative in this theory, we have used some dialogue examples taken from related work and specified which participant is in charge at any given point in the conversation.

Example 1 (Circuit helper) (Smith 1993)

1. C: This is the circuit fix it shop. How may I help you?
2. U: I want to fix a circuit.

3. C: What is the ID of the circuit?
4. U: Rs111.
5. C: I am familiar with that circuit. The LED is supposed to be displaying
      alternately flashing one and seven.
6. U: The LED is off.
7. C: What is the switch at when the LED is off?
8. U: The switch is down.
9. C: Put the switch up.
10. U: Okay.
11. C: Put the knob to one zero.
12. U: Okay.

In Example 1, C is in charge of the conversation throughout and has the initiative;
the user doesn't get to take the initiative at all. To explain, C first controls the flow
of the conversation and starts on the initial plan of helping to fix the circuit. This
plan goes forward as U responds, but U does not have control over the flow of
the conversation. What U supplies are additional comments which lie along the
path that the speaker is following. C continues to take control of the flow in line
3, by introducing the new subtopic of the ID of the circuit. U provides a simple
response, but still does not attempt to control the new flow. C goes on to a new
subplan, considering the behaviour of the LED and goes forward on that subplan
through to the end of the conversation, retaining the initiative, as U only issues
simple responses or prompts (such as 'Okay').

Example 2 (TRAINS-95) (Ferguson et al. 1996)

1. M: I need to get to Detroit, Syracuse and Montreal.
2. S: Ok. [highlights three cities]
3. M: Let's send the trains from Chicago to Detroit.
4. S: OK. [draws route] But the terminal at Toledo is delaying traffic due to bad
      weather. Trains will take an additional five hours to move through there.
5. M: That's ok. Now let's go from Atlanta up to Syracuse.
6. S: Please tell me a route to use to get from Atlanta to Syracuse.
7. M: Go via Charleston and Pittsburgh.
8. S: OK. But traffic through Cincinnati is being delayed due to construction.

In Example 2, the initiative switches between the system and the user quite frequently. For the first three statements, the user is in control since she initiates the
topic and goes forward on it by giving further instruction, while S simply issues a
prompt. After the system draws the route, it takes control of the flow of conversation by suggesting a change in plan. Then the user takes control of the conversation
again in line 5, suggesting that the plan proceed from Atlanta. This constitutes

discarding S's suggestion and returning to the original plan. However, S asks for more input on that plan in line 6, and so controls the flow of the conversation and has the initiative. M makes a move to go forward with the current plan in line 7, so has the initiative and in line 8, S has the initiative once more since it suggests a change in the current plan.

3.1.3. *Discussion of the Value of the Definition*

The strictness of the definition of initiative in this theory in fact narrows the scope of systems that can be classified as mixed initiative. In order for there to be mixed initiative in a system, all participants must be able to take control of the flow of conversation. Many of the artificial intelligence systems that have been studied in mixed initiative research would not actually meet this criterion. For example, in many tutoring systems, the student does not have the capability to control the movement of conversation through a given topic or a series of topics. Mixed-initiative tutoring systems can be designed, however, to allow for more active participation on the part of the user (e.g. Lester et al. 1999, Lester et al. 1998, Carberry 1997 and Freedman 1997) and our definition would therefore be applicable to these kinds of systems. In a similar fashion, while there are some advice giving models which do not require the system to share the initiative with the user at all (e.g. Haller 1996), there are also systems such as van Beek et al. (1993), which aim to elicit clarification from users during the advice giving and therefore are quite well suited to this theory of initiative.

In many task-oriented dialogues, the system has the initiative, as defined in this theory, for the entire dialogue (e.g. the circuit fixing case of Example 1). Yet there are task-oriented systems (such as the TRAINS system of Example 2) which allow all participants to take the initiative (as discussed for planning in Allen 1994) and in fact allow the initiative to change hands frequently.

Finally, the theory is also applicable to multiparty conversation with specific topics being addressed (referred to as 'small talk' in Sibun 1997). The concept of flow can be used to maintain the consistency of the conversation, by assigning each participant to individual flows which have a particular subject.

3.1.4. *Summary of Theory*

The definition of initiative presented in this theory basically equates initiative with control. However, the definition specifies exactly what needs to be controlled in order for a user to have the initiative. The flow of conversation is the object to be controlled.

Flow is defined here as the movement of the conversation through a series of topics. A conversation which consists of many subtopics can be viewed as many mini-conversations and each mini-conversation focused on a specific topic is a flow. Since a flow is the movement of a conversation, there can be many directions of movement. This theory has identified five types of directions. This then provides for flow management, namely using the current type of direction in the conversation to identify who possesses the initiative. Only systems where both participants change the control of flow can be truly labelled as mixed-initiative systems.

3.2. INITIATIVE AS EXERCISING POWER TO PERFORM A TASK FOR SOLVING A PROBLEM (THEORY #2)

3.2.1. *Introduction and Definitions*

The theory presented in this section is concerned with initiative as it manifests itself in collaborative problem solving interactions. It shall be argued that initiative is best identified with the behavior exhibited by the dialogue participant who is currently *taking the lead* in the problem solving process.

Only the case where the participants demonstrate initiative in order to solve the domain problem is considered in this theory. Initiative that is taken to satisfy personal, non-problem related, goals are ignored. Within this context, initiative may defined as:

Initiative is the exercising of the power or ability of a dialogue participant to suggest (or perform) a plan (or task) which is instrumental to the solving of the problem at hand.

Although solving a problem is the activity each dialogue participant is ideally attempting to do, the position taken here is that it is the initiative holder who is currently controlling how the solution is being formulated or realized. In contrast with Theory #1, there is no concern with the direction of the conversation and utterances which do not constitute a proposed solution to a task do not result in initiative being taken.

3.2.2. *Expanded Definition*

In this theory, when dialogue participants take the initiative, they then become the active leaders in the problem solving process. They are either *eliciting information* from the other agents regarding a potential solution (i.e. a sequence of steps), or perhaps they are *delegating tasks* that must be done in order to realize a subgoal. When the other dialogue participants follow the initiative, they play a more passive, supporting role. They are to *perform the tasks* requested of them from the initiative holder, and they *provide the requested information*.

Communication amongst the participants relates to the steps being proposed, and thus the initiative followers may also be *requesting information* and *requesting tasks* to be done on behalf of the initiative taker. Furthermore, the initiative followers *scrutinize the solution* as it is being formed: they look for ambiguities, inconsistencies or even mistaken beliefs. As long as a set of steps are being followed by the dialogue participants, the dialogue participant who suggested them is referred to as the initiative taker, and the others are referred to as the initiative followers.

The definition for initiative presented in this theory is in fact a strong one. The participant who initiates a direction to the problem solving has the initiative and retains it, unless a competing solution is proposed and this proposal is not rejected (an initiative shift) or there is no clear direction present (the initiative is dropped and no one has the initiative). If another participant makes a proposal which is rejected, then there is no shift in initiative (this does not constitute presenting a solution). The focus is on the problem solving aspects of the dialogue only, to track where the initiative with respect to the task currently lies. Although this theory is motivated by Chu-Carroll and Brown (1997) and its discussion of the term 'task initiative', the aim is to adopt a constrained view of task initiative which merely tracks successful task proposals.

If we continue with the viewpoint of a collaborative problem-solving dialogue, we can consider the circumstances under which initiative will shift.

(i) The initiative taker can no longer proceed in attempting to solve the problem.
   This may come about because a dialogue participant is no longer capable of leading the problem solving process, or perhaps has determined with the rest of the participants that another is best able to continue.

(ii) Another participant detects invalidity and proposes a correction.
   In this case, the initiative shifts as another participant suggests a new and improved version of the current steps being pursued.

(iii) An alternative has been suggested which must be considered with respect to the current proposed steps; based on the merits of the new proposal, initiative may or may not shift.
   In this case we have the participants engaging in a debate as to which solution path to follow. If the current initiative holder has been allowed to proceed, then the initiative does not shift. However, if the participant with the alternative succeeds in getting the other participants to follow his initiative, then he takes the initiative and there is an initiative shift.

From the rules above, it can be seen that there may be cases in which determining who should take the initiative next may lead to disputes. The rules above do not provide any mechanisms to resolve such disputes, as such rules may depend heavily on the application domain. To examine the theory in more detail, consider Example 3, from the course advising domain.

Example 3

1. S: I want to take NLP this semester. I don't have the prerequisite.
2. A: You can take AI this semester, and NLP in the summer.
3. S: I have a co-op term in the summer.
4. A: Is the job in town?

5. S: Yes.
6. A: Great, NLP will be offered as a night-course this summer!
7. S: Er, I'm really not comfortable taking a course while I work. Can I take NLP and AI simultaneously this semester?
8. A: I'm not really sure. I'm afraid I don't have the authority to let you do that. The student handbook clearly states, however, that AI is a prerequisite and not a corequisite for NLP.
9. S: Thanks. I'll check with the professor.

In line 1, the student simply establishes the problem. There has been no demonstration of initiative yet, let alone an example of a dialogue participant taking the initiative. Next, the advisor responds with a possible solution, namely taking the two courses back to back in subsequent semesters. The student states that this is not feasible due to an upcoming co-op term. At this point the advisor has taken the initiative: a solution has been proposed and the other dialogue participant, in this case only the student, has considered it. The advisor continues to pursue the solution until the student devises a possible solution on her own in line 7. In the next utterance, the advisor contemplates the solution, but is of no help. The student has taken the initiative, and maintains it for the rest of the dialogue. Overall, this example has demonstrated two examples of a dialogue participant taking the initiative, and one initiative shift occurring on lines 6 and 7. The initiative shift occurred based on rule iii mentioned above.

Consider another example, assuming the same utterances for lines 1 through 6, but changing lines 7 to 9 (labelled below as Example 3b).

Example 3b

7. S: Er, I'm really not comfortable taking a course while I am working.
8. A: I am not really sure what I can do for you.
9. S: Thanks, I'll think about it.

The analysis of this scenario is that the advisor will keep the initiative until line 7 and in line 8 will lose the initiative according to rule i. In this case, the scenario will conclude with nobody having initiative.

Next, consider the dialogue in Example 4 which demonstrates a dispute in a possible solution to a problem.

Example 4

1. A: We need to get to Ottawa fast.
2. B: We can take Highway 7. There are more places to stop.
3. A: How about Highway 401? The road conditions are better, and the speed

limit is higher.

4. B: You're right, but the 401 is a bit of a round about way to get to Ottawa. How about taking Highway 8 that runs through both Highway 401 and Highway 7? It's right before the 401 veers away from Ottawa, so we can save about 40 minutes by turning onto Highway 8 and heading north to Highway 7.

5. A: Great, let's do that! How do we get to Highway 8 from 401?

Line 1 establishes the problem and alternative solutions are disputed from lines 2 to 4. The net effect of the dispute is B gaining the initiative, as in line 5 A begins to contemplate B's solutions.

3.2.3. *Discussion of the Value of the Definition*

As seen from the examples in Section 3.2.2, this theory is applicable to domains like advice giving where one participant is an expert and another is not and where the overall task is advising the student. The theory is also applicable to task-oriented collaborative planning environments, such as transportation planning systems.

The notion of initiative presented in this theory contrasts with those proposed in other papers. Traum (1997) and Miller (1997) consider initiative as what a participant does when it's his dialogue turn. A dialogue participant can either pursue personal goals, in which case he holds the initiative, or he may react to what another participant has said or done, in which case he does not hold the initiative. This is similar to the view put forward in this theory, that the initiative taker is the one pursuing his own ideas on how best to solve the solution, while the initiative followers are simply reacting to the initiative taker. However, when participants are pursuing conflicting, or mutually destructive goals, then this does not constitute taking the initiative in this theory.

The presented notion of initiative also differs from that of Walker and Whittaker (1990), Whittaker and Stenton (1988), and Ferguson et al. (1996) who consider initiative as control over the dialogue. In this theory, initiative is considered as taking over control of the problem solving process. Establishing control of the conversation does not constitute a change in initiative unless it is done in order to seize control of the problem solving process. Consider, for example, line 3 in Example 3. The student makes an assertion that he has a co-op term in the summer. According to the rules presented by Walker and Whittaker, the student has taken the initiative, as an assertion has been made. However, according to the model of initiative presented in this theory, initiative remains with the advisor.

As mentioned earlier, the theory also compares with Chu-Carroll and Brown (1997), which includes a concept of task initiative. However, Chu-Carroll and Brown also model dialogue initiative, and consider a participant who offers information towards a possible goal as having this dialogue initiative. In the theory presented in this section, we would simply continue to assign the (task-oriented) initiative to the participant who proposed the original goal.

3.2.4. *Summary of Theory*

This theory focuses on tracking control of the problem solving activity in goal-oriented collaborative dialogue. There is also an important implication for considering whether we need to model initiative explicitly. As described above, taking the initiative is the process of providing solutions. The participants who are best able to pursue the solution would take the initiative. In fact, a model such as Guinn's (1993; see also 1996, 1998) could be used to provide algorithms for determining which agent should be controlling the task at the moment and taking the initiative. In the theory presented in this section, agents already reason in terms of goals and solutions, thus there is no need to introduce the concept of 'initiative' into their reasoning process. Therefore, one could argue (as in Miller 1997) that we do not need to model initiative explicitly. One possible concession, however, is that, in certain domains, it is in fact important to be tracking when the initiative is shifting in dialogue, in order to optimize the problem solving process, (for example with collaborative agents as in Rich and Sidner 1998). The point of this theory is that it is not always necessary to do so.

3.3. INITIATIVE AS SEIZING CONTROL OF A CONVERSATION BY PRESENTING A GOAL TO ACHIEVE (THEORY #3)

3.3.1. *Introduction and Definitions*

In this section, we develop a theory which models both control of the conversation and control of the task. We consider the ultimate goal of a mixed-initiative system to be performing tasks by modeling conversations, where participants actively participate in the dialogue to make useful contributions in order to achieve a goal. In order to identify when such conversations occur, we need to carefully define what initiative is in a precise and unambiguous manner.

When two or more participants attempt to solve a problem, it is generally believed that an interactive discussion, where each participant actively directs the conversation, is more beneficial than one where only a single participant guides the work. When a participant shows initiative, we recognize that the participant is actively contributing to the conversation. This belief leads to the need to identify the occurrence of initiative within a discussion. By identifying when initiative occurs and who takes the initiative, we can recognize if a discussion is truly interactive and then use these interactive discussions as the basis for creating an artificial system which can interactively solve a problem with others. This is the viewpoint of mixed-initiative AI systems adopted in developing this theory. Moreover, we attempt to define initiative in an unambiguous manner that will hopefully simplify the identification of initiative within a conversation.

Initiative in a conversation occurs at an instant in time when a person seizes control of the conversation by making an utterance that presents a domain goal for the participants to achieve.

In contrast with Theory #1, this theory models not only control of the conversation but also presentation of domain goals. In contrast with Theory #2, this theory models not only control of a task but also control of the conversation. In fact, it allows initiative to shift when a goal is simply proposed for consideration, directing the attention of dialogue participants to the goal (so not tied to having a solution.) Moreover, in contrast with Chu-Carroll and Brown (1998) this theory does not track task and dialogue initiative separately (see Section 4 for more discussion).

There are several important points that must be distinguished in this definition of initiative. First, we must recognize that control of a conversation does not imply initiative. However, when initiative does occur, the one who took the initiative also has taken control of the conversation. In other words, in this particular definition initiative implies control, but control does not imply initiative.

As an example, consider the dialogue in Example 5.

Example 5

1. A: How do we get to the CN Tower?
2. B: Go south on highway 404 until you reach the Gardiner expressway. Go west on the expressway and follow the signs.
3. A: How far along the expressway do we need to go?
4. B: About 5–6 kilometers. It is well marked, so you should not have any problems.
5. A: OK. Thanks.

In this conversation, person A is proposing goals while person B is solving them. So, person B has control over the conversation while the solution is being presented (after line 2). However, since B is simply solving the goal, no initiative (by B) is demonstrated. Although solving a problem is related to task oriented behaviour, it does not constitute 'proposing a new goal and directing the dialogue towards this goal', so does not constitute initiative, in this theory. In contrast, Theory #2, which is focused more precisely on the task and not the dialogue, would interpret the example as follows. In line 2, B proposes a solution and takes the initiative. B retains the initiative afterwards, since neither of A's statements indicate grounds for an initiative shift.

There is a second important distinction of the definition of initiative presented in this section. We assume that there is an overall domain goal driving the mixed-initiative system and are restricted to systems with this characteristic. Then, any goal arising in a discussion must be relevant to the main goal of the discussion,

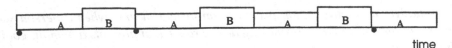

Figure 1. One Pattern of Initiative.

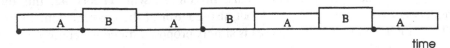

Figure 2. A Second Pattern of Initiative.

unless it is the start of the conversation. This restriction avoids random utterances which do not help in achieving the main goal.

3.3.2. *Expanded Definition*

Defining when initiative occurs allows us to identify when a conversation is interactive or not. It also allows us to characterize the quality of the interaction when a conversation is interactive. We can illustrate this point by viewing a conversation diagramatically over an interval of time.

In Figures 1 and 2, the boxes marked A represent an interval of time while A controlled the conversation and similarly for the boxes marked B. The circles represent occurrences of initiative. As you can see from Figure 1, initiative always occurs when A is in control of the conversation. Therefore, Figure 1 illustrates a conversation which is not interactive because only one participant ever takes the initiative. Figure 2 illustrates an interactive conversation where both A and B take initiative. These figures also illustrate how control can shift from one participant to another, but this shift does not in any way imply that any initiative has been taken. For instance, in Figure 1, B has control of the conversation three times but never takes any initiative because any time she makes an utterance she hasn't started a new goal (unless you start a goal, by the definition presented here, you have not taken any initiative). Figures 1 and 2 also emphasize a fundamental distinction between initiative and control: initiative is a discrete event happening at a single point in time, while conversation control is a continuous one, happening over an interval in time.

The model presented in this section essentially characterizes an interactive conversation along three dimensions: initiative, dialogue control, and goals. All three domains are tied together. By the definition presented in this section, initiative requires the creation of a goal and seizing control of the dialogue. A person controls the dialogue when they direct the conversation in order to try to reach the goal.

One aspect of the definition that may not be completely clear is why initiative is tied to the creation of a goal. In order to explain this requirement, consider the conversation in Example 6.

Example 6

> John: How do you make a cake?
> Sally: Get two eggs, flour, butter, sugar,...

By our definition, John took initiative by proposing the goal of making a cake. Sally did not take any initiative even though she achieves the goal by giving John the answer. We do not recognize that Sally has taken initiative because clearly this conversation is not interactive in any way. In other words, there is no inter- action in trying to achieve the goal, since Sally just gives John the answer. From this conversation, we can recognize that in order for an *interactive* discussion to achieve a goal, it is required that no single participant know how to completely solve the problem. Each participant may possess a part of the solution which they may volunteer. But the parts they miss represent subgoals that they are proposing to the group that hopefully another participant may help achieve. For example, consider this conversation:

Example 7

> John: Do you know how to program the VCR?
> Sally: No, but I read that you can get it from the on-screen menu selection.
> John: I think you have to use the remote for that.
> Sally: I'm not sure. Let's see.

In Example 7, neither John nor Sally has the solution to the goal of programming the VCR, but they are clearly interactively trying to achieve the goal. The definition presented in this theory recognizes John as taking initiative by proposing the main goal. Sally takes initiative by proposing an implicit subgoal of having to figure out how to bring up the on-screen menu selection. So using this theory of initiative we can recognize the conversation in Example 7 as a mixed-initiative discussion.

This definition can identify an *interactive* conversation because it requires the creation of a goal (and subgoals) and therefore implies an inability to reach the goal by any single participant. Since no single participant can reach the main goal, interactive discussion is required. Of course, by this definition a conversation that does not achieve any goal can still be considered a mixed-initiative conversation as long as more than one of the participants took initiative by proposing a goal. Yet we do recognize that there is a problem in identifying when a goal has been created.[6] This concern is really a problem of implementation and is dependent on how broadly a goal is defined. Almost any conversation can be seen as a mixed-initiative one if a goal is defined broadly enough.

---

[6] As Lee (1997) points out, in real conversations people may even be deceptive, so that their goals remain hidden.

3.3.3. *Discussion of the Value of the Definition*

Since modeling initiative can be viewed as an attempt to make systems more flexible in their ability to solve problems and to thereby increase the possibility of reaching their goals, it would be advantageous to try to make them interact with humans as smoothly as possible. In fact any mixed-initiative model should be general enough to encompass any language. For instance, a conversation could be held using the language of mathematics. The definition of initiative presented in this section elegantly handles these concerns because of its simplicity, requiring only that the presentation of a goal drives the control of the conversation.

This theory also has a narrow focus, considering the task of defining initiative as distinct from some of the other theorizing regarding initiative which other researchers attempt. Guinn, for example (1993; 1996; see also 1998), discusses as well how to direct problem solving by supplying strategies as to who should solve a particular goal, and how to model another participant's knowledge. In (Guinn 1996), the model of initiative indicates that 'when an agent A1 asks another agent A2 to satisfy a goal G, agent A2 gains initiative over goal G and all subgoals of G...'. The definition presented in this section would place the initiative with agent A1, which makes some sense since the participant proposing the goal is presumably required to solve a goal, and control should be left with this participant until the goal is solved or abandoned.

In addition, there is some benefit in forgoing a strong focus on linguistic theory. Walker and Whittaker (1990) set stringent rules stating how different responses should be interpreted in different contexts. However, it may be important to consider whether these rules still hold when dealing with different cultures and/or individual people. For example, North Americans may be comfortable with being interrupted while other cultures may find it extremely rude and insulting; thus, having only one interpretation for each conversation fragment (question, prompt, etc.) could lead to difficulties. Rather than focus on a linguistic classification, this theory concentrates on the analysis of the goals of the participants.

As mentioned, this theory is intended to model truly interactive conversation, where participants are controlling dialogue by directing the conversation towards a particular goal. In strict expert/novice applications (e.g. certain problem solving or intelligent tutoring systems) only one participant proposes goals to be addressed. The initiative would not shift in these applications and there would really be nothing to track (in this theory) except initiative or the lack of it from one party. In applications where the participants are more 'equal partners' (e.g. collaborative problem solving systems such as Rich and Sidner 1999), truly interactive discussion occurs. When no single participant can solve the goal of the conversation alone, collaboration is required and mixed-initiative conversation occurs, whether or not the goal is actually solved. Note as well that the theory is not really relevant to domains where goals are not clearly stated. An example could be agents designed to engage in 'small talk'. Since goals are not easily identified, there is nothing for this theory to track. Hence, it is not applicable.

3.3.4. *Summary of Theory*

In summary, this theory has presented a definition of initiative which states that initiative occurs at an instant in time when a person seizes control of a conversation by making an utterance that presents a goal for the participants to achieve. This definition was developed with the aim of making it simple to recognize interactive discussions and in turn model such initiative within a computer system.

The definition used in this theory differs from previous ones in that we do not make initiative synonymous with dialogue control (as in Theory #1) and we view initiative as a discrete occurrence. We leave it up to the system designer to determine how broadly he wishes to define a goal and thus allow him to choose the level of the interactions that he wishes to model.

3.4. A PROCESS-BASED MODEL OF SCALED INITIATIVE (THEORY #4)

3.4.1. *Introduction and Definitions*

Allen uses the term *mixed initiative* to describe AI systems which should 'be able to interact in a way that is convenient and effective for a human' (Allen 1994). The term implies that the human agent as well as the system agent are allowed to take the initiative at various points in the dialogue. In order to provide a more fine-grained theory of initiative, we introduce two new concepts. The first concept is process. A process is defined as 'a finite set of turns in an interaction'. As we will define later, processes are goal-oriented. A participant then has the initiative in an interaction *if she takes the first turn in a process.*

The second concept that we introduce is the *strength* of initiative. Notice how the three situations below have qualitative differences in initiative.

Example 8

1. A: I wish I knew how to split up the work of peeling this banana.
2. B: Yeah.
3. A: What do you think we should do?
4. B: I don't know. It's a tough problem.
5. A: Sure is. I'm so confused.
6. B: Me too. Maybe the waiter has an idea.
7. A: I hope so, I'm getting hungry.

Example 9

1. A: So, how should we split up the work of peeling the banana?
2. B: I don't know. What do you think?

3. A: We need a plan.
4. B: I know we need to split this up somehow.
5. A: Yes, you're right. We need something sharp.
6. B: A cleaver?
7. A: Good idea! That way we can split it up evenly.
8. B: Then we can each peel our own half.

Example 10

1. A: Need to split up the work of peeling this banana. I have the plan. You grab the bottom of the banana and hold it steady. Then I grab the top of the banana and pull hard. That's how we'll do it.
2. B: No! I think I'll just peel the banana myself. That would be way more efficient.

These three dialogues seem to exhibit different strengths of initiative. The degree of initiative shown by both participants in Example 8 is lower than that of Example 9, and both are lower than that of Example 10. We will return to this point in Section 3.4.2.2. We will want to apply our model to a broad range of domains (such as planning, conversation, etc.); therefore, we will refer to the term 'conversation' as a set of utterances or a set of actions. The term 'participants' will also be used to refer to either humans or systems.

We will begin by further developing the concepts of processes and strengths of initiative. Both of these terms are complex and are introduced in order to be able to address a wider range of possible dialogues, such as multiple conversations managed by two participants. We therefore acknowledge that the definitions for the concepts are at a preliminary stage. We provide a somewhat deeper discussion of these terms in connection with our presentation of related work in Section 3.4.3.

3.4.2. *Expanded Definition*

In order to expand on the definition in Section 3.4.1, this section further develops the concepts of processes and different strengths of initiative by defining the terms and applying them to several mixed-initiative domains.

3.4.2.1. *Processes*

Recall the definition for initiative as the first step in a process. We shall define a process as a sequence of turns $t_1, \ldots, t_n$ where each turn is composed of utterances. In this theory, processes are not defined in terms of topics and goals alone, since goals and subgoals are related hierarchically and it would then be difficult to determine which level of goals defines a process. Defining processes in terms of sentences is also seen as problematic. First of all, not all utterances are grammatical phrases (such as backtracking thoughts, filler sentences, and utterances made by non-native speakers), so it would be impossible to define a process in terms of syntax alone. Perhaps we could simply delete these utterances, but then we could mistakenly delete important information. Secondly, if an utterance is ungrammatical or near-grammatical, we still have no problem figuring out who has the initiative in the conversation. This is compelling evidence that initiative is not directly or purely dependent on linguistic terms. Defining processes in terms of turns can address the aforementioned problems. In particular, since initiative is the first step in a process, initiative is t_1.

A process can have one or more turns. If one participant asks a question and another participant simply answers that question, then both of these turns will be grouped as one process. (Note that answering a question is acknowledging another participant's request for information. Similarly, repetitions and summaries only repeat previous ideas. Therefore, none of these start a new process.) On the other hand, one turn can be categorized into more than one process. If a turn should belong to more than one process then we can duplicate that turn and group the duplications into the appropriate processes. Consider the conversation in Example 11.

Example 11

1. A1: Are you going to school this term?
2. B1: Yes, I am taking five courses.
3. A2: How are you liking the courses?
4. B2: They're fine right now.

Here, the first process would consist of turns A1 and B1, while the second process would consist of turns B1, A2, and B2. The turn B1 is categorized into two processes because speaker B not only answers the Yes-No question but volunteers information on the same topic.

A process can have one or more speakers since a process can have one or more turns. Consider a situation where a boss is explaining a project to her employees, Jen and Cindy. The boss's explanation may take one or more conversational turns, but all the turns in the explanation make up a single process. Jen might then begin a new process by asking the boss to clarify the problem specifications. The boss could complete this second process by responding with the requested information.

However, there is only one initiator per process, which is defined to be the speaker or the performer of t_1. Since each utterance has a goal (otherwise the speaker would not have said it), then each process has a higher goal, and the role of the initiator is to establish the goal among the speakers for that process. Hence, processes are goal-oriented. By this definition, a conversation is a set of processes, $P_1, \ldots, P_n$, each contributed to by one or more participants.

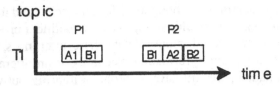

Figure 3. A graphical representation of processes.

Figure 3 shows a graphical representation of the dialogue in Example 11. In this example, A1 starts the conversation so it is the initiator of process one, P1. Because B1 answers with a 'Yes', it does not provide initiative, so it belongs to the same process as A1. However, B1 also volunteers extra information, which indicates initiative for a new process, so B1 is the initiator for P2. A2 then follows up on that new information, so it belongs to the same process as B1. Finally, B2 is an answer to A2 so it belongs to that process as well. For this theory, the graphical representations are useful to help track utterances which belong to more than one process.

Note as well that in our figure, P1 and P2 are separated. Technically, processes need not be separated because it implies that there is a time lapse between them, but this is a style of representation which we have consistently adopted – separating the processes for ease of reading.

What if there are several conversations taking place simultaneously? Sometimes participants may be carrying on multiple conversations at the same time through verbal or non-verbal means. Here, the term conversation is equated with the term topic, so that when a conversation shifts in topic, we will call it a new conversation. Therefore, when the participants are talking and performing actions at the same time, we can refer to these as two conversations, or two topics.

Consider the following scenario: a dentist and his assistant are casually talking about their favourite dog and cleaning a patient's teeth at the same time. The conversation about the dog obviously involves verbal communication, but it can include non-verbal communication such as body gestures[7] as well. On the other hand, cleaning someone's teeth also needs verbal communication such as asking the assistant to apply suction or holding the jaw apart. These are done by actions as well as verbal requests. Hence, the first topic is the conversation about the dog, and the second topic is the conversation about cleaning the patient's teeth.

What if we represent these two conversations as embedded processes? There is little motivation behind this since the two topics are not related. In addition, as mentioned above, we do not want to have embedded processes because then the concept of process will be confused with the concept of goal or topic. The alternative solution is to have disjoint conversations with sequential processes (see Figure 4): Process PX represents the conversation about the dog and QX represents the conversation about cleaning the patient's teeth.

---

[7] Note that every body gesture can be translated into an equivalent linguistic expression.

topic

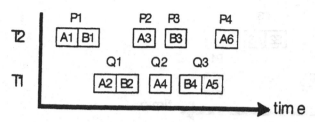

Figure 4. Disjoint Processes.

topic

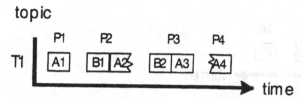

Figure 5. Interrupting process on the same topic.

How do we represent interruptions? If speaker A interrupts speaker B, then speaker A is really just creating another process. However, this new process can belong to the same topic or to a different topic. The following graphs (Figures 5 and 6) represent these two situations respectively.

In both cases, P3 is the process initiated by B2 to interrupt P2, and P2 followed up with A4 thereafter. Note that in both cases, P2 was interrupted and it was followed up on afterwards. (The process labelled as P4 in both figures is the continuation of P2). We will refer to processes of this type as 'closed processes'. This need not be the case. Not all processes are closed since after an interruption, participants often forget what the previous process was or time constraints disallow the process to be followed. Processes of this type are called 'open processes', shown by the graph below (Figure 7). This graph shows that P2 was interrupted by P3, but it was never followed up on in the conversation so it remains open.

One special case of interruptions is arguments. Often, when participants in a conversation argue about something, they do not wait for the other participants to finish and simply speak at will. To represent this, the processes initiated by these participants will overlap each other (see Figure 8).

Here, A1 starts P1 and B1 starts P2, and so forth. One interesting note is that although these processes do interrupt each other, they do not need to be broken and followed up later on. B1 can interrupt A1 while A1 continues to talk and A2 can interrupt B1 while B1 continues to talk. This way, even though A1 and B1 are being interrupted, they can still finish up the process. If a participant does get interrupted and the process is broken, then it would look something like P3 interrupted by P4.

topic

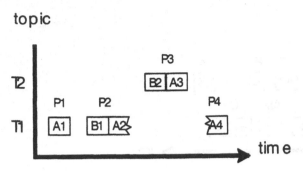

Figure 6. Interrupting process on a different topic.

topic

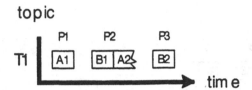

Figure 7. An open process.

3.4.2.2. *Strengths of Initiative*

In this theory, we take the position that initiative is not a property that is either present or absent in a turn. Instead, initiative can be present in many different degrees or strengths. All turns are assigned a degree of initiative, though not all turns have strong enough initiative to start a new process. This idea is different from Freedman (1997) because she talks about different degrees of student interaction whereas we characterize different degrees of initiative exhibited by each turn. This is also different from the levels of initiative used in Smith (1993). Smith refers to the level of initiative in an entire application – strong control by one party, free control amongst parties, etc. For the theory presented in this section, strength of initiative refers to how strongly a participant is in control, when he or she does have the initiative. Some processes demonstrate a stronger form of initiative than others so it is possible to place the types of initiative in an order from weak to strong.

Although initiative is the first turn of a process, each turn actually has some level of initiative. One idea for future work is to introduce a threshold which once crossed causes the beginning of a new process.[8] This idea differs from the concept of initiative in discourse developed by Walker and Whittaker (1990). In their model, utterances such as prompts or assertions in response to questions have no initiative. In the theory presented in this section, such utterances have weak initiative. Consider Example 12 with speakers *A* and *B*.

---

[8] In the remaining discussion, we speculate on how strengths of initiative can be modeled. The theory presented here would still propose only labelling the participant taking the first turn in a process as the one with initiative. The role of weaker labels of initiative is left open.

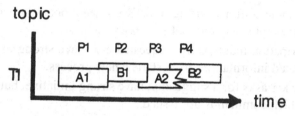

Figure 8. Overlapping processes.

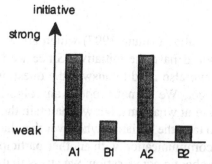

Figure 9. A graphical representation of strengths of initiative.

Example 12

1. A1: What colour do you think the sun is?
2. B1: I don't know...
3. A2: How about red?
4. B2: Sure.

In this example, speaker *A* demonstrated a high degree of initiative, first by introducing a new topic (the colour of the sun), and then by suggesting an answer. Speaker *B*, on the other hand, demonstrated a very low level of initiative. We can compare the degree of initiative present in each turn with a graph (as in Figure 9).

Now consider Examples 8, 9, and 10 from Section 3.4.1. In the first dialogue, both participants took turns saying very little and not deciding anything. Thus in that dialogue, we would assign a fairly low degree of initiative to the turns taken by each participant. In the second dialogue, both participants worked towards a solution and thus each participant exhibited 'more than half strong' initiative. Finally, in the last dialogue, where A made a decision and B argued, both participants exhibited strong initiative.

What decides degrees of initiative? Typically, turns have strong initiative if they contain utterances which would result in a transfer of control to the speaker, under Walker and Whittaker's (1990) 'Rules for the Allocation and Transfer of Control'. Certain properties of turns suggest stronger initiative.

- A turn that results in a topic shift has strong initiative, since it not only begins a new process, but a new topic (sequence of processes) as well.
- Turns which give information that was not requested also have strong initiative, since the unrequested information often starts a new process.
- Turns in which the speaker asks for a suggestion have strong initiative, but not as strong as turns in which commands are issued.
- Turns in which the speaker has more intent or certainty have stronger initiative than turns delivered less assertively.

Some systems have in fact preallocated initiative (Traum 1997) which allows the system to figure out which participant should have the initiative. Since we have discussed different strengths of initiative, we also need to answer the question of how much initiative each participant can get. We do not propose any algorithm which decides who should have the initiative at what time, but we maintain the position that all participants should be able to take the initiative whenever they have a goal which can only be obtained through communication with another participant. Although this could potentially result in a chaotic conversation, we stress that this is an important point because participants need to be able to direct attention to the source of problems that may come up (Carberry 1997). A participant can get the initiative by interrupting or waiting. If the participants are co-operative, then each participant should ideally wait until initiative is available, so that there are few interruptions.

3.4.3. *Discussion of the Value of the Definition*

This theory is applicable to collaborative planning systems, where initiative is still the first step of a process and (similar to conversation) a process is a set of turns which have the goal of modifying the current plan in some concrete way. This coincides well with the view of Allen (1994), who says that initiative changes from one agent to another in plan-oriented environments as agents take control of the dialogue.

Consider Example 13, where a hockey coach is explaining a game strategy to her player. The player's goal is to get the puck deep in the opposing team's end of the ice. The initial plan is to carry the puck in over the blue line but it doesn't seem to be working.

Example 13

1. Coach (A1): When you get to the red line, dump the puck in.
2. Player (B1): Okay, but I never remember to do that.
3. Coach (A2): Well, I'll yell for you to do it, and then your centre and wing will be skating in fast to beat the other team's players to the puck.

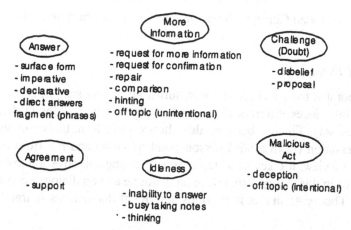

Figure 10. Types of student initiative.

In A1, the coach is initiating a new process (P1) by modifying the current plan. She is suggesting what to do to help the player invade the other team's zone. In B1, the player first continues P1 by saying 'okay', and then initiates another process (P2) by indicating a problem with this new plan. Finally, the coach completes process P2 in A2 by giving a solution to the problem. A2 starts a new process (P3) by explaining the next step in the plan.

Tutoring systems are another area of application for this theory. Initiative on the part of the student would mean that the student begins some process. The communicative goals from Shah and Evens (1997) can be recast to be viewed as the types of possible initiators of processes in a tutoring system, as in Figure 10.

In this figure, different types of student initiatives have stronger or weaker degrees of initiative. In order of decreasing strength, they are Challenge and Malicious Act, More Information, Answer and Support, and finally, Idleness. If strength of initiative is modeled, this may be correlated with these types of student initiative, when interpreting tutoring dialogues.

The theory presented in this section can also be applied to the mixed-initiative robotics domain described by Kortenkamp et al. (1997). In this domain, humans interact with a layered robot control software system in order to get a robot to perform some complex task. This task is accomplished by a mix of high-level robot commands called *operators* and low-level robot commands called *skills*. Interacting with the robot control system ultimately involves negotiating the robot's execution of a mix of operators and skills. Thus, all interaction with the control system can be broken down into turns which negotiate the execution of single commands. These turns form the processes of this domain. In addition, the authors present what they call a 'scale of control' of possible human/computer interaction styles, which is somewhat similar to our scale of initiative. For example, Teaming allows equal levels of initiative and control of the interaction between the computer and human, whereas Guided Control allows the human to have high initiative and control.

3.4.4. *Summary of Theory*

This theory incorporates the concepts of topic, turns, goals and sentences. In addition, the theory introduces different degrees of initiative which helps to define initiative more precisely. Finally, because this theory models initiative in view of the entire conversation (from a third person point of view) and not from each participant's point of view, it takes us a step closer to giving initiative a universal definition. The focus in this theory is therefore on dialogue and on dialogue control, but contrasts with Theory #1 in that it provides additional distinctions in tracking the initiative.

4. Discussion

In this section, we offer some initial analysis of the relative benefits of the theories described in this paper. We begin with an overview of the differences between the theories. We then include a comparative analysis of the theories on a common set of sample dialogues. Next, we discuss more generally the range of mixed-initiative applications currently being developed, to comment on the differing characteristics of these application areas, which make one or another working definitions of initiative more useful. Finally, we discuss some of the other papers in this volume more specifically, to comment on the potential value of the theories for the application areas which are discussed in these other papers.

It is important to note that the primary aim of this paper was to simply present a set of differing points of view, with respect to the definition of initiative, in order to include each separate theory as a useful starting point for someone with an aim of designing a mixed-initiative system. Our position is that depending on the application area and the community of users which it involves, each theory may be more or less appropriate to use as a starting point. Nonetheless, we will offer some preliminary insights into how the theories compare and how mixed-initiative application areas differ, in this section.

4.1. OVERVIEW OF THE COMPARISON OF THE THEORIES

Theory #1 focuses on tracking the control of the conversation. In addition to allowing for different flows of control, it is general enough to be applicable to both task-oriented and progressive tutoring systems. While simple prompts do not result in a change of initiative, in a spirit similar to (Walker and Whittaker 1990), many other kinds of comments in a dialogue will indeed result in a participant having the initiative. Of all the other theories, Theory #4 is perhaps closest in spirit to Theory #1, since it is also focused on modeling the structure of the underlying dialogue. This theory has additional features which allow for varying strengths of initiative and for the grouping of turns into processes. It is this latter feature which sometimes results in a labeling of an entire segment with one participant's initiative and which sometimes results in one utterance operating in two distinct processes, where different participants have the initiative. Both of these theories are also quite directed at tracking the goals underlying a discourse. Theory #4 considers a process to be a goal-oriented set of turns and Theory #1 allows for a participant to gain the initiative when a new subgoal is proposed.

Theory #2 and Theory #3 focus on the goals underlying a conversation and do not perform any dialogue modelling. They have somewhat different treatments of utterances used towards the solution of the plan being discussed between participants. Both of these approaches in fact contrast nicely with the work of Chu-Carroll and Brown (1997; see also 1998) on task vs. dialogue initiative. Theory #2 models something similar to task initiative and treats cases of dialogue initiative as situations where no one has the initiative. Theory #3 would treat cases where a participant is offering information towards a plan and actually contributing towards a new direction for the plan as a situation where initiative has shifted to this participant. So, certain cases of dialogue initiative are considered together with the cases known as task initiative.

4.2. COMPARING THE THEORIES ON A COMMON SET OF DIALOGUES

In this section, we extract some of the sample dialogues which were introduced in the paper and show how they would be analyzed by each of the four theories. A table is included for each example which shows who has the initiative at each step of the dialogue, according to each of the theories. A '−' indicates that no one has the initiative, and square brackets show utterances grouped into one process, for Theory #4. The table identifies the example to be analyzed by referring to its number, providing a descriptive title and including the starting words in each line.

Table I shows the analysis of the four theories on Example 1. The analysis of this example according to Theory #1 was presented in Section 3.1.2 and is summarized here. C initiates a plan to help the user in line 1. This plan continues forward and a subplan of finding the ID is started, which continues forward to a subplan of determining the behaviour of the LED. The subplan to address the LED is then carried forward, to the end of the dialogue. All the utterances from U in this example are either simple responses or prompts (e.g. 'Okay'). As discussed in flow type 1), neither case constitutes taking control of the flow of the conversation, so that there is never a shift of initiative to U. C continuously moves forward on the flow of the conversation and has the initiative throughout.

According to Theory #2, the first line where a solution to a problem is introduced is line 5. Here, C is proposing that they work on fixing the LED. This constitutes taking the initiative, as a solution to fixing the circuit is proposed, namely addressing the LED. C has control of the problem solving (being the expert)

Table I. Analysis of Example 1 (Circuit Helper)

			Theory #:	1	2	3	4
1	C :	This is the...	Line # : 1	C	–	–	C
2	U :	I want	2	C	–	U	
3	C :	What is	3	C	–	C	C
4	U :	Rs111	4	C	–	–	
5	C :	I am familiar	5	C	C	C	C
6	U :	The LED is off	6	C	C	–	
7	C :	What is the	7	C	C	C	C
8	U :	The switch	8	C	C	–	
9	C :	Put the switch	9	C	C	–	C
10	U :	Okay	10	C	C	–	
11	C :	Put the	11	C	C	–	C
12	U :	Okay	12	C	C	–	

and continues to hold this control by offering steps for solving the problem (fixing the LED and thus the circuit).

According to Theory #3, the goal of fixing the circuit is proposed in line 2 by U, so directs the dialogue to focus on this goal, and U has the initiative. C has the initiative in line 3, because he proposes using the ID of the circuit to help fix the circuit (a new goal, which is a subgoal of the first one). The statement in line 4 does not propose any new goals. C proposes investigating the LED in line 5; U's response in line 6 contributes no new goals, so no one has the initiative. But C proposes investigating the switch in line 7 and so has the initiative once more. After line 7, no one has the initiative, since neither party is proposing a new goal; the current goal is being solved or simple prompts are supplied and neither of these cases constitutes taking the initiative.

According to Theory #4, the dialogue breaks into six processes, where in each case C has the initiative. U always responds to C's questions/commands without volunteering more information, so U never starts his/her own process. In terms of strength of initiative, C's utterances are consistently strong and U's are consistently weak.

For this example, there is a definite similarity between Theory #1 and Theory #4 (with the latter including a grouping into processes). Theory #2 is similar only in the fact that it allows the participant with initiative to retain it; but, C only gets the initiative by virtue of presenting a solution to a problem (a focus on task). Theory

#3 is concerned with cases where new subgoals are being proposed and assigns initiative to the participant who initiates these goals, at this point in time. There is therefore no prolongment of initiative with the current participant, as in the other theories.

Table II. Analysis of Example 2 (TRAINS).

				Theory#:	1	2	3	4
1	M:	I need to go	Line#	1	M	–	M	M
2	S:	OK.		2	M	–	–	
3	M:	Let's send		3	M	M	M	M
4	S:	OK. But the...		4	S	M	S	S
5	M:	That's ok		5	M	M	M	M
6	S:	Please tell		6	S	M	–	S
7	M:	Go via		7	M	M	–	
8	S:	OK. But traffic		8	S	M	–	S

Table II shows the analysis of the four theories on Example 2. The analysis of this example according to Theory #1 was presented in Section 3.1.2 and is summarized here. M initiates a plan to go to the 3 cities in line 1, so has control over the flow of the conversation and has the initiative. After a simple prompt by S, m continues to go forward on this plan. In line 4, S changes the direction of the plan by suggesting disadvantages and so has control over the flow of the conversation. This is followed by M, then S, then M each going forward on the original plan, followed by S suggesting a change of plan.

According to Theory #2, M first proposes a solution in line 3, so this is where initiative is first exhibited. M controls the plan for the remainder of the dialogue and keeps the initiative. In line 4, S makes some comments but does not propose a solution and its ideas are not accepted by M, who retains the control and has the initiative.

According to Theory #3, M suggests a goal to be addressed in line 1 and thus has the initiative. Raising this goal indeed directs the participants to continue a dialogue focused on resolving this goal. No one has the initiative in line 2, since no one is proposing a goal. M clearly suggests a goal in line 3 (a subgoal of the one in line 1) and then S takes the initiative in line 4, by adding new information. This asks M to re-evaluate the subgoal of sending trains, implied in line 3. M has the initiative in line 5, working on a new subgoal of going from Atlanta to Syracuse. Initiative is not occurring after line 5, since S simply indicates that it does not know how to solve the goal and M only helps to solve the goal which has already been proposed (so no new goals are introduced).[9]

---

[9] It is worth re-iterating that the interpretation of examples according to Theory #3 is dependent on the accompanying representation of goals.

According to Theory #4, the first two lines are interpreted in a very similar way to those of Theory #1; simple responses do not constitute taking the initiative and the first two lines form one process. M has the initiative in line 1, taking the first step in the process of addressing the plan of travelling to the 3 cities. A second process is started in line 3, focused on sending the trains from Chicago to Detroit. In line 4, S provides a response to M's suggestion, so this is part of that process, but S also includes additional information, so a new process starts at this point, with line 5 included as the response to S's suggestion. In line 5, M initiates a process regarding Atlanta. S starts a new process in line 6, discussing how to work out the required route. This process continues to the end of the dialogue, with M offering a simple response and S coming back with a quick 'OK'. A final new process begins in line 8, with the additional information from S about Cincinnati. Most of these turns have a high degree of initiative, since so many initiate new processes. The exceptions are the simple acknowledgement of S in line 2 (very low initiative) and the response by M in line 7, which can be labelled as moderate initiative.

For this example, Theory #1 and Theory #4 are somewhat similar, with Theory #4 breaking the analysis into processes. The places where S controls the flow according to Theory #1 (lines 4, 6 and 8) are all places where S initiates a new process, according to Theory #4. There is also a distinction between the theories in line 7. Theory #1 allows M to have the initiative, by offering a response which sets the flow of the conversation going in a particular direction. Theory #4 still treats this as a response to a question, with no 'new' information, so that it is included within the process initiated in line 6, and no change in initiative occurs. Theory #3 allows both M and S to have the initiative at the beginning of the dialogue. But this theory assigns initiative to the participants who propose new goals only, so that no one has the initiative when no new subgoals are being discussed. So, while there are changes to the direction of the dialogue after line 5, there are no recorded instances of initiative. Theory #2 perhaps contrasts most sharply with the rest. Like Theory #3, there is a focus on the task at hand, but the strict interpretation of having initiative rest with the participant who controls the problem solving results in M taking and retaining the initiative throughout.

Table III shows the analysis of the four theories on Example 7. According to Theory #1, John initiates a plan to program the VCR in line 1, Sally goes forward on that plan by trying to work with the on-screen selection and then John goes forward by proposing the use of the remote. In line 4, Sally merely prompts and pauses without a new contribution, so that John retains the initiative.

According to Theory #2, a solution to the goal of programming the VCR is first proposed by Sally in line 2. Sally retains the initiative afterwards, since no competing solutions are accepted. (John's proposal in line 3 is a suggestion and not an accepted solution).

According to Theory #3, John makes the suggestion of programming the VCR in line 1, so directs the dialogue towards this goal and has the initiative. Sally takes

Table III. Analysis of Example 7 (the VCR).

				Theory#:	1	2	3	4
1 John:	Do you	Line#	1		J	–	J	J⌉
2 Sally:	No, but I		2		S	S	S	S⌐⌡
3 John:	I think you		3		J	S	–	J⌉
4 Sally:	I'm not		4		J	S	–	S⌐⌡

the initiative in line 2, by proposing a subgoal (using the on-screen menu). After this, the conversation is unsettled and no one has the initiative. John is offering a solution to using the on-screen menu, but is not suggesting a new subgoal and there are clearly no new goals in line 4.

According to Theory #4, John starts trying to program the VCR and Sally answers his question, so that this is one new process. Sally also offers additional information in line 2, to start another process. John moves onto the topic of using the remote, starting a new process which includes Sally's simple response that she is not sure. In saying 'Let's see', Sally is leading into a new area of discussion and starts a final new process. Each turn here starts a process and therefore has high initiative.

In comparing the theories, we see that Theory #2 allows S to retain the initiative after proposing the main goal. The other theories agree on the analysis for the first two steps of the example–they allow both participants to have the initiative, since all three theories consider the new proposal made by Sally as the basis for an initiative shift. After this, Theory #1 assigns John the initiative and considers Sally's last remark as only a small prompt. According to Theory #4, this is indeed the 'response' to John's utterance in line 3, so that the two turns are grouped into one process, but Sally is offering some new information at the end of the dialogue ('Let's see'), so is initiating a new process as well. Theory #3 considers the conversation after line 2 to be unsettled, so that no one has the initiative. It is worth noting that Theory #3 does not always result in no one having the initiative, when plans are being discussed. As we have seen in Example 2, since Theory #3 is not restricted to modeling the participant who is the primary controller of the plan, there are examples where this theory will show a shift in initiative, whereas Theory #2 will not.

4.3. COMPARING THE RANGE OF MIXED-INITIATIVE APPLICATION AREAS

In the presentation of each separate theory, application areas where the definition would apply were discussed, including a range of different applications, from task-oriented dialogues to tutoring systems.

First, this paper begins to provide insight into the important differences between some of these application areas. For instance, in general it is difficult to make a definition of initiative that is valid for both task-oriented dialogues and for tutoring dialogues. Although some tutoring systems have been designed to allow for rather little initiative on the part of users, there are clearly some current proposals which are aimed at allowing students to take charge (e.g. Carberry 1997, Lester et al. 1999). But then, tutoring dialogues are significantly different from ordinary conversation in many ways. They do not obey Grice's maxims (Grice 1975) against asking people questions for which you already know the answer, or telling them things they have heard before. Another difference is that the tutor's plan often changes in the middle of a turn. Typically, the tutor acknowledges a correct answer representing the successful termination of the old plan, and then starts to introduce a new remediation plan. A major advantage of the definitions provided in this paper is that they separate the initiative from control of the turn (see Theory #1 on control vs. flow, Theory #3 on control vs. initiative and Theory #4 on the definition of process) and allow the initiative to change in the middle of a turn. Each of these theories can therefore be applied to tutoring domains.

In contrast, there are certain domains which are completely task-oriented. As discussed in Section 3.2.4, with Theory #2, one point of view is that at times it is not important to even model initiative, in order to construct a mixed-initiative planning-oriented system. Yet, in certain task-oriented domains, the modeling of initiative may be quite valuable, as well. For example, if a rule such as 'the agent who currently has the initiative is expected to continue' is applicable, then one could conclude that the participant who is taking the initiative is signaling a willingness to take control of the problem solving process; others will look to that participant for further direction. Systems may need to model initiative in order to capture such expectations. Although Theory #2 is exclusive to task-oriented domains, each of the other theories is also applicable for these kinds of domains. In some sense, Theory #2 takes a very strong interpretation, associating initiative with the participant who is controlling the current plan. Theory #1 models the changes in initiative at the level of dialogue, providing a finer distinction for tracking the participants. Theory #4 allows for more than one participant to have the initiative concurrently, by tracking the individual processes which make up the dialogue. It also acknowledges that some participants may be exhibiting only weak initiative. Finally, Theory #3 takes the position that for task-oriented dialogues, deciding which participant should ideally control the task is not the concern of a theory to define initiative.

In considering the range of application for the four theories, it is also worth noting that the theories are general enough to address systems with more than two participants. Theory #1 simply tracks the current flow of control, regardless of which dialogue participant takes the initiative to direct it. Any participant who elects to interrupt the flow is allowed to have the initiative from that point onwards. Theory #2 is focused on collaborative environments and allows open disputes regarding a possible plan of action, amongst any number of participants. The participant whose plan is ultimately in control then has the initiative. For applications such as expert systems and some advising domains, when there is an imbalance in the status amongst participants, then the participant with the expertise is also the one who sets the plan in motion and who has the initiative, according to the theory. For Theory #3, more than two participants may propose goals. Finally, for Theory #4, there is quite an open declaration that multiple processes may be operating within a dialogue, allowing for multiple parties to be participating.

4.4. COMPARISON TO THE OTHER PAPERS IN THIS VOLUME

The other papers in this volume present a wide range of possible application areas for designing mixed-initiative systems. Examining each paper more closely provides additional insight into the suitability of each of the theories for particular application areas.

There are some papers which are clearly focused on designing tutoring systems, examining both student and tutor initiative during the tutoring session (Lester et al. 1999). In the discussion of Theory #1, there is in fact an argument that it is important to allow this shift of initiative to take place, as a more beneficial approach to designing tutoring systems.

There are also papers directly concerned with task-oriented domains, such as work on expert/apprentice collaboration by Guinn (1998). These task-oriented applications can be addressed by all of the theories, as explained in Section 4.3, with the choice of definition desirable depending on the richness of the planning dialogues and the potential need to identify the initiative holder.

Other papers in the volume are focused on collaborative problem solving applications. For example, Chu-Carroll and Brown (1998) focus on the TRAINS-91 corpus, which has two parties collaborating on transportation planning, Cesta et al. (1999) have agents and user working together in order to settle on a schedule for the user and Rich and Sidner (1999) operate in the domain of travel planning. The latter two papers also consider the system which is operating as a kind of interface agent for the user. These kinds of applications have a definite goal-oriented characterization but do not restrict one participant to be the dominant controller.

All of the theories presented here will allow for this arrangement amongst participants. Theory #2 will not consider a participant who does not actually control the underlying plan as exhibiting initiative, in its analysis. Theory #3 will focus on the main goals in the dialogue, factoring out background discussion as cases where no one has the initiative, but will assign initiative to a participant who is proposing a new subgoal. Theory #1 and #4 continuously track changes in the conversational structure. While some of the theories also track dialogue shifts (Theory #1 and #4), this does not preclude them from being applied to task-oriented domains. Once more, which theory to select depends on the reasons why a designer may wish to be modeling the initiative and how rich the kind of interactions may be.

Stein et al. (1999) allow for both agent and user to take the initiative, but are concerned with assisting a user to perform information retrieval. This is more of an advice-giving setting rather than a purely collaborative planning effort, perhaps. More importantly, the paper focuses on the nature of the dialogue between the two parties, towards the ultimate satisfaction of the user's goals. Focus on dialogue also occurs in other papers in the volume, notably Green and Carberry (1999) and Ishizaki (1999). All three of these papers, therefore, would be most concerned with a theory such as Theory #1, which clearly focuses on analyzing the control of the flow of the conversation.

In addition, Stein et al. mention that if the direction of the dialogue is not changed, then there is no initiative change. This seems especially in line with the point of view of Theory #1. This paper also mentions that initiative changes start new dialogue segments. It is therefore possible that Theory #4's concept of 'process' may be of interest as well.

Green and Carberry develop a model which determines when a participant should contribute more than was his obligation in a particular discourse turn. Providing additional information in a response is in fact treated differently in the four theories described here, and so is interesting to examine as another way of comparing the theories. Theory #1 proposes that the participant offering the information has the initiative if that person is controlling the flow of the conversation. Theory #3 has the participant showing initiative if the new information is directly relevant to the current goal. Theory #2 suggests that in order for initiative to shift the new information should in fact be proposing a solution. Finally, Theory #4 allows the participant to have the initiative in all cases – the new information constitutes beginning a new process.

Ishizaki et al.'s work is particularly interesting, in that it includes a few ideas which are also addressed within Theory #4. These include a discussion of sequencing and embedding constructions in dialogue, situations where a boss is 'in control', allowing a participant to both respond and initiate a new segment and allowing for multiple turns to occur within one segment.

5. Conclusions

To conclude, we first reiterate that the main purpose of the paper was to present differing viewpoints on how to define initiative, each of which has a somewhat different scope and level of detail. Developing these theories has lead to some general insight into what initiative can be construed to be and highlights the reasons why it is quite possible for differing viewpoints to have emerged in the field.

There are clearly some recurring themes in the proposals outlined in the paper– that initiative has something to do with control, with goals and with conversational turns and that initiative may provide some insight into interruptions, plan failures, differences in beliefs among participants, the lack of interactivity among participants and the degree of commitment towards problem solving among participants.

There are also clearly some new proposals which extend other existing theories. The first theory proposes three new reasons for interruptions, beyond those catalogued in (Walker and Whittaker 1990). The third theory suggests that there is value to a simpler modeling of goal control, than the one presented in (Guinn 1993, Guinn 1996). The fourth theory introduces at least three new directions for modeling initiative. The first is to develop a context, separate from the notion of utterances or topic or goals – something which they refer to as a process. The second is to model varying strengths of initiative amongst participants who are said to have the initiative. The third is to allow for the modeling of more than one conversation, for each participant.

Clearly, no one theory presented here is comprehensive, in itself. In other words, there is no clear 'winner' or 'loser' amongst the theories. Section 4 presents some insights into the applicability of each of the specific theories. It is important to note, as well, that the aim of the paper was to provide descriptive theories rather than operational algorithms for analyzing interactions which label the initiative among the participants. There is sufficient ground to be covered in this first step– trying to gain an understanding of initiative and its potential use in the design of systems. As future work, it might be possible to evolve a toolkit for designers of mixed-initiative systems, with more specific suggestions for how to integrate the theories into some kind of experimental testing phase within the design process.

Nonetheless, the theories presented here clearly show that different users may exhibit different levels of initiative in an interaction; only by modeling the users directly, including tracking their specific utterances in the interaction, can one properly model the level of initiative among discourse participants. There is therefore an important relevance to user modeling, as part of the process of interpreting initiative.

More importantly, we feel that there is inherent value in presenting these theories, as part of the ongoing discussion of initiative and as part of the ongoing enterprise of designing mixed-initiative systems. This paper provides a clear basis for discussion in the future, with concrete, differing proposals. Since each theory has, as well, discussed its applicability to particular application areas, it is also possible for potential designers to evaluate whether the theory presented does indeed provide the necessary starting point, for their system. In all, we are one step closer to appreciating the nuances of the term 'initiative' and the enterprise of designing mixed-initiative AI systems.

Acknowledgments

The authors acknowledge the valuable feedback provided by Toby Donaldson and Peter Vanderheyden. In addition, we are very grateful to Wendy Rush for technical assistance in preparing this paper, and to Arthur Hills and Kim Martin for technical assistance as well. We also want to thank the reviewers for their valuable comments. In particular, two of the key arguments presented in Section 4.3 arose directly from comments from the reviewers. Finally, we are indebted to Susan Haller for her careful reading of the final versions of the paper, and to Susan McRoy and Alfred Kobsa for their assistance in the reviewing process. This work was partially supported by NSERC (the Natural Sciences and Engineering Research Council of Canada).

References

Allen, J.: 1994, Mixed-initiative planning: position paper. *ARPA Planning initiative workshop*, http://www.cs.rochester.edu/research/trains/mip/

Burstein, M. and McDermott, D.: 1996, Issues in the development of human-computer mixed-initiative planning. In Gorayska and Mey, eds., *In Search of A Humane Interface*, North-Holland; pp. 285–303.

Cesta, A. and D'Aloisi, D.: 1999, Mixed initiative issues in an agent-based meeting scheduler; *User Modeling and User-Adapted Interaction* **9**(1–2).

Carberry, S.: 1997, Discourse initiative: its role in intelligent tutoring systems. In Haller, S. and McRoy, S. (eds.), *Working Notes of AAAI97 Spring Symposium on Mixed-Initiative Interaction*, Stanford, CA, pp. 10–15.

Chu-Carroll, J. and Brown, M.: 1998, An evidential model for tracking initiative in collaborative dialogue interactions. In this issue.

Chu-Carroll, J. and Brown, M.: 1997, Initiative in collaborative interactions – its cues and effects. In Haller, S. and McRoy, S. (eds.), *Working Notes of AAAI97 Spring Symposium on Mixed-Initiative Interaction*, Stanford, CA, pp. 16–22.

Cox. M. and Veloso, M.: 1997, Controlling for unexpected goals when planning in a mixed-initiative setting. *Proceedings of 8th Portuguese AI Conference*, Coimbra, Portugal, pp. 309–318.

Ferguson, G., Allen, J. and Miller, B.: 1996, *TRAINS-95*: Towards a mixed-initiative planning assistant. *3rd Conference on AI Planning Systems*, Edinburgh, Scotland.

Freedman, R.: 1997, Degrees of mixed-initiative interaction in an intelligent tutoring system. In Haller, S. and McRoy, S. (eds.), *Working Notes of AAAI97 Spring Symposium on Mixed-Initiative Interaction*, Stanford, CA, pp. 44–49.

Green, N. and Carberry, S.: 1999, A computational model for initiative in response generation; *User Modeling and User-Adapted Interaction* **9**(1–2).

Grice, H.P.: 1975, Logic and Conversion, in P. Cole and J. Morgan, eds., *Speech Acts (Syntax and Semantics, v.3)*, New York: Academic Press, pp. 41–58.

Guinn, C.: 1998, Principles of mixed-initiative human-computer collaborative discourse. In this issue.

Guinn, C.: 1996, Mechanisms for mixed-initiative human-computer collaborative discourse. *Proceedings of ACL96*, Santa Cruz, CA, pp. 278–285.

Guinn, C.: 1993, A computational model of dialogue initiative in collaborative discourse. *AAAI93 Fall Symposium on Human-Computer Collaboration*, Raleigh, NC, pp. 32–39.

Haller, S.: 1996, Planning text about plans interactively. *International Journal of Expert Systems, Special Issue on Knowledge Representation and Inference for Natural Language Processing*, L. Iwanska (ed.), **9**(1), 85–112.

Haller, S. and McRoy, S., eds.: 1997, Computational models for mixed initiative interaction. *AAAI97 Spring Symposium* Working Notes, Stanford, CA.

Ishizaki, M., Crocker, M. and Mellish, C.: 1999, Exploring mixed-initiative dialogue using computer dialogue simulation. *User Modeling and User-Adapted Interaction* **9**(1–2).

Kortenkamp, D., Bonasso, P., Ryan, D. and Schreckenghost, D.: 1997, Traded control with autonomous robots as mixed initiative interaction. In Haller, S. and McRoy, S. (eds.), *Working Notes of AAAI97 Spring Symposium On Mixed-Initiative Interaction*, Stanford, CA, pp. 89–94.

Lee, M.: 1997, Belief ascription in mixed initiative dialogue. In Haller, S. and McRoy, S. (eds.), *Working Notes of AAAI97 Spring Symposium On Mixed-Initiative Interaction*, Stanford, CA, pp. 95–97.

Lester, J., Stone, B. and Stelling, G.: 1999, Lifestyle pedagogical agents for mixed initiative problem solving in constructivist learning environments. *User Modeling and User-Adapted Interaction* **9**(1–2).

Lester, J., Callaway, B., Stone, B. and Towns, S.: 1997, Mixed initiative problem solving with animated pedagogical agents. In Haller, S. and McRoy, S., *Working Notes of AAAI97 Spring Symposium on Mixed-Initiative Interaction*, Stanford, CA, pp. 98–104.

Lin, S. and McKeown, N.: 1997, A Simulation Study of IP Switching. *Proceedings of SIGCOMM 97*, Stanford University Technical Report CSL-TR-97-720.

Miller, B.: 1997, Is explicit representation of initiative desirable?. *Working Notes of AAAI97 Spring Symposium on Mixed-Initiative Interaction*, 105–110; Stanford, CA.

Oxford Dictionary of Current English, New York: Oxford University Press, 1984.

Rich, C. and Sidner, C.: 1998, COLLAGEN: A toolkit for building collaborative interface agents. In this issue.

Shah, F. and Evens, M.: 1997, Student initiatives and tutor responses in a medical tutoring system; in Haller, S. and McRoy, S. (eds.), *Working Notes of AAAI97 Spring Symposium On Mixed-Initiative Interaction*, Stanford, CA, pp. 138–144.

Sibun, P.: 1997, Beyond dialogue: the six W's of multi-party interaction. In Haller, S. and McRoy, S. (eds.), *Working Notes of AAAI97 Spring Symposium On Mixed-Initiative Interaction*, Stanford, CA, pp. 145–150.

Smith, R.: 1993, Effective spoken natural language dialogue requires variable initiative behaviour. *AAAI93 Fall Symposium On Human-Computer Collaboration*, 101–106; Raleigh, NC.

Stein, A., Gulla, J. and Thiel, U.: 1999, User-tailored planning of mixed-initiative seeking dialogues. *User Modeling and User-Adapted Interaction* **9**(1–2).

Traum, D.: 1997, Views on mixed-initiative interaction. *AAAI97 Spring Symposium On Mixed-Initiative Interaction*, Stanford, CA, pp. 169–171.

van Beek, P., Cohen, R. and Schmidt, K.: 1993, From plan critiquing to cooperative response generation. *Computational Intelligence* **9**(3), 132–154.

Veloso, M., Mulvehill, A. and Cox, M.: 1997, Rationale-Supported mixed-initiative case-based planning. *Proceedings of AAAI97*, 1071–1077; Providence, RI.

Walker, M.: 1997, Performance Models for Dialogue Agents. Invited talk, *AAAI97*, Providence, RI.

Walker, M. and Whittaker, S.: 1990, Mixed-initiative in dialogue: an investigation into discourse segmentation. *Proceedings of ACL90*, Pittsburgh, PA, pp. 70–76.

Whittaker, S. and Stenton, P.: 1998, Cues and control in expert-client dialogues. *Proceedings of ACL88*, Buffalo, NY, pp. 123–130.

Dr. Robin Cohen

Computer Science Department, University of Waterloo, Waterloo, Canada N2L 3G1.

Robin Cohen is a Professor of Computer Science at the University of Waterloo. She completed a Ph.D. in 1983 in the Computer Science Department at the University of Toronto, under the supervision of Ray Perrault. She has been at the University of Waterloo since 1984. Her research interests include discourse, plan recognition and user modeling. She has been involved with research on increasing user involvement in plan recognition and is currently working with students on the topics of modeling turn-taking, increasing user involvement in interface agents and studying the role of user involvement in information extraction.

The remaining authors

Computer Science Department, University of Waterloo, Waterloo, Canada N2L 3G1.
Coralee Allaby, Christian Cumbaa, Mark Fitzgerald, Kinson Ho, Celine Latulipe, Fletcher Lu, Nancy Moussa, David Pooley, Alex Qian and Saheem Siddiqi were all graduate students in the Computer Science Department at the University of Waterloo, at the time that this paper was written. Bowen Hui was a undergraduate student in the Computer Science Department at the University of Waterloo.

User Modeling and User-Adapted Interaction **8**: 215–253, 1998.
© 1998 *Kluwer Academic Publishers.*

215

An Evidential Model for Tracking Initiative in Collaborative Dialogue Interactions

JENNIFER CHU-CARROLL and MICHAEL K. BROWN
Bell Laboratories, Lucent Technologies, 600 Mountain Avenue, Murray Hill, NJ 07974, U.S.A.;
e-mail: {jencc,mkb}@bell-labs.com

(Received 13 November 1997; accepted in revised form 28 April 1998)

Abstract. In this paper, we argue for the need to distinguish between *task initiative* and *dialogue initiative*, and present an evidential model for tracking shifts in both types of initiatives in collaborative dialogue interactions. Our model predicts the task and dialogue initiative holders for the next dialogue turn based on the current initiative holders and the effect that observed cues have on changing them. Our evaluation across various corpora shows that the use of cues consistently provides significant improvement in the system's prediction of task and dialogue initiative holders. Finally, we show how this initiative tracking model may be employed by a dialogue system to enable the system to tailor its responses to user utterances based on application domain, system's role in the domain, dialogue history, and user characteristics.

Key words: Initiative, control, dialogue systems, collaborative interactions.

1. Introduction

Naturally-occurring collaborative dialogues are very rarely, if ever, one sided. Instead, initiative of the interaction shifts among dialogue participants in a primarily principled fashion, signaled by features such as linguistic cues, prosodic cues, and in face-to-face interactions, eye gaze and gestures. Furthermore, patterns of initiative shifts between participants may differ depending on the task the participants are attempting to accomplish, on the roles they each play in this task, and on their experience in interacting with each other in current and previous dialogues. Thus, in order for a dialogue system to successfully collaborate with its user on their interaction, it must be able to dynamically track initiative shifts during their interaction by recognizing the user's cues for initiative shifts, and by providing appropriate cues, when necessary, in its responses to user utterances.

To illustrate merely one of the many decisions that a dialogue system must make when generating responses to user utterances, consider the following dialogue segment between a bank teller and a customer where we show three possible responses that the teller may provide in response to the customer's question:

(1)   C: *I need some money.*

(2)   *How much do I have in my 6-month CD?*

(3a) T: *You have $5,000 in that CD.*

(3b) T: *You have $5,000 in that CD, but that CD will not mature for another 3 months.*

(3c) T: *You have $5,000 in that CD, but that CD will not mature for another 3 months. However, you have $3,000 in another CD that will be available next week.*

In response (3a), the teller directly answers the customer's question. In (3b), the teller conveys her belief in the invalidity of the customer's proposed plan, while in (3c), she conveys the invalidity of the proposal and proposes an alternative solution. Given that all three alternative responses are reasonable continuations of the dialogue, the question that comes to mind is *what criteria should a dialogue system adopt to select one response over the others given a particular circumstance?* Existing cooperative response generation systems (e.g. (van Beek, 1987; Pollack, 1990; Chu-Carroll and Carberry, 1994)) are able to select response (3a) versus (3b)/(3c) based on whether or not the customer's proposal is in fact valid; however, to our knowledge, no existing model is able to distinguish between responses (3b) and (3c), and to determine the circumstance under which each response is appropriate. We propose to approach this decision-making process from an initiative point of view, i.e., by viewing the difference between the alternative responses as a difference between the levels of initiative exhibited by each dialogue participant. This model then allows a dialogue system to select an appropriate response based on how initiative is distributed among the participants.

In the rest of this paper, we argue that most existing models of initiative conflate two types of initiatives, which we call *task initiative* and *dialogue initiative*, and show how distinguishing between these two types of initiatives accounts for phenomena in collaborative dialogues that previous models were unable to explain. In particular, we show that the distinction among responses (3a)–(3c) in the above dialogue can be modeled by the distribution of these two types of initiatives between the dialogue participants, i.e., the teller having neither task nor dialogue initiative in (3a), having dialogue but not task initiative in (3b), and having both task and dialogue initiatives in (3c). We discuss our evidential model for tracking initiative shifts between dialogue participants during their interaction using a set of cues that can be recognized based on linguistic and domain knowledge alone, i.e., not considering physical cues such as gesture and eye gaze. We demonstrate

(1)   the performance of our model by showing that it can correctly predict the task and dialogue initiative holders in 99.1 percent and 87.8 percent of the dialogue turns (compared against manually labeled initiative shifts), respectively, in the TRAINS domain in which the model is trained, and

(2) the generality of the model by showing that its application in various other collaborative domains consistently increases the accuracies in the prediction of task and dialogue initiative holders by 2-4 and 8-13 absolute percentage points, respectively, compared to a simple prediction method without the use of cues.

Finally, we illustrate the usefulness of such an initiative tracking model by showing how it may be incorporated into a dialogue system to allow the dialogue system to vary its responses to user utterances based on the factors that affect patterns of initiative shifts, such as the application domain, the system's role in the dialogue, the dialogue history, and individual user characteristics.

2. Related Work

2.1. VIEWS OF INITIATIVE

Previous work on mixed-initiative dialogues focused mainly on tracking and allocating a single thread of control among dialogue participants (Novick, 1988; Whittaker and Stenton, 1988; Walker and Whittaker, 1990; Kitano and Van Ess-Dykema, 1991; Smith and Hipp, 1994; Guinn, 1998; Lester et al., 1999). However, these researchers differ in terms of what they consider to be *initiative*, and the circumstances under which an agent is considered to have the initiative in a dialogue. Novick considered a dialogue participant to have the initiative if he controls the flow and structure of the interaction (Novick, 1988). Whittaker, Stenton, and Walker (Whittaker and Stenton, 1988; Walker and Whittaker, 1990) equated initiative with control, and argued that as *initiative* passes back and forth between the discourse participants, *control* over the conversation gets transferred from one participant to another. Kitano and Van Ess-Dykema (1991) considered an agent to have control of the conversational initiative if the agent makes an utterance that instantiates a discourse plan based on her domain plan, i.e., if the agent makes a task-related proposal. Smith and Hipp considered initiative in dialogue to be a representation of the control of the task (whose goals currently have priority), and argued that the level of initiative in the dialogue should mirror the level of initiative in the task (Smith and Hipp, 1994). Guinn considers an agent to have initiative over a mutual (task) goal when the agent controls how that goal will be solved by the collaborators (Guinn, 1996; Guinn, 1998).[1] Finally, in their work on mixed initiative problem solving, Lester et al. (1999) equate initiative with the control on problem solving.

More recently, researchers have come to the realization that simply tracking one thread of initiative does not adequately model human–human dialogue interactions. Novick and Sutton (1997) analyzed the earlier views of initiative and proposed

---

[1] Guinn provides definitions for both *task initiative* and *dialogue initiative*, but argues that when an agent holds the task initiative, he must also hold the dialogue initiative.

a multi-factor model of initiative, including *choice of task, choice of speaker,* and *choice of outcome.* Choice of task determines what the conversation is about, choice of speaker models turn-taking among dialogue participants, and finally, choice of outcome allocates the decision or action necessary to achieve the task. Jordan and Di Eugenio (1997), on the other hand, argued in contrary to Whittaker, Stenton, and Walker's view that *control* and *initiative* are equivalent. Instead, they proposed that *control* should be used to describe a dialogue level phenomenon, and that *initiative* should refer to the participants' problem solving goals. Cohen et al. (1998) presented alternative theories of initiative. In one of their theories, they argued that theories of initiative that model merely the flow of the conversation or the task-level actions in collaborative problem solving are problematic because of their inappropriate mixing of *initiative* and *conversational control*. As a result, they proposed a theory that follows Jordan and Di Eugenio's distinction between initiative and control. Rich and Sidner (1998) distinguish between *global initiative*, which is concerned with whether or not a dialogue participant has something to say, and *local initiative*, which addresses problems local to a discourse segment such as turn-taking and grounding. In their interface agent, however, they focus mainly on modeling global initiative. In Section 3, we motivate our view of initiative, which consists of modeling *task initiative* and *dialogue initiative* (Chu-Carroll and Brown, 1997a). Note that although our distinction between task and dialogue initiatives is similar to Novick and Sutton's choice of outcome and choice of task, as well as to Jordan and Di Eugenio's initiative and control, these ideas were conceived independently.

2.2. ANALYSIS AND USE OF INITIATIVE

Previous work on mixed-initiative interaction can loosely be grouped into three classes. First, some researchers have developed models that capture mixed-initiative behavior in dialogues. Novick developed a computational model that utilizes *metalocutionary acts*, such as *give-turn, clarify,* and *confirm-mutual*, to explain issues such as turn-taking, negotiation of reference, and confirmation of the mutuality of knowledge in mixed-initiative dialogue interaction (Novick, 1988). In addition, Kitano and Van Ess-Dykema extended Litman and Allen's plan recognition model (Litman and Allen, 1987) to explicitly track the conversational initiative based on the domain and discourse plans behind the utterances (Kitano and Van Ess-Dykema, 1991).

Second, some researchers have investigated the causes of initiative shifts in mixed-initiative dialogue interaction and their effect on the structure of discourse. Whittaker and Stenton (1988) devised rules for allocating dialogue control based on utterance types, which included *assertions, commands, questions,* and *prompts.* They then analyzed patterns of control shifts by applying their rules to a set of expert-client dialogues on resolving software problems. They noted that the the majority of control shifts are signaled by *prompts, repetitions,* or *summaries,* while in the remainder of the cases, control shifts as a result of *interruptions*. Walker and Whittaker (1990) subsequently utilized the control allocation rules devised by Whittaker and Stenton to perform

(1) a comparative study of the cues used to signal control shifts in different types of dialogues (advice-giving dialogues and task-oriented dialogues), and
(2) an analytical study of control segmentation and the structure of discourse by analyzing the distribution of anaphora with respect to control segments in advice-giving dialogues.

Third, some researchers have taken into account the notion of initiative in dialogue interactions and have developed dialogue systems that vary their responses to user utterances based on their models of initiative. Smith and Hipp (1994) developed a dialogue system that varies its responses to user utterances based on four dialogue modes, *directive*, *suggestive*, *declarative*, and *passive*. These dialogue modes characterize the level of initiative that the system has in a dialogue, and affect the topic selection in the system's response generation process. For instance, in the *directive* dialogue mode, the system has complete dialogue control and will not allow interruptions from the user to other subdialogues. Thus, during topic selection, the system simply pursues its current goal without regard for the user's focus. However, in their system, the dialogue mode is determined at the outset and cannot be changed during the dialogue. Guinn (1996; 1998) subsequently developed a system that allows change in the level of initiative based on each agent's competency in completing the current subtask. Guinn employs a probabilistic model for evaluating competency based on the likelihood of each agent's path for solving the goal being successful. The initiative setting of the dialogue is then based on the result of this competency evaluation.

Our work overlaps with work in classes two and three above. We investigated potential cues that trigger initiative shifts, and developed a model that tracks the distribution of task and dialogue initiatives between participants during the course of a dialogue based on the combined effect of a set of observed cues. The long term goal of this work is to incorporate our initiative tracking model into a dialogue system in order to allow the system to tailor its responses to user utterances under different circumstances.

3. Task Initiative vs. Dialogue Initiative

3.1. MOTIVATION

As discussed in the previous section, most existing models of initiative focus on tracking a single thread of initiative, often considered to be the *conversational lead*, among dialogue participants during their interaction. However, we argue that merely maintaining the conversational lead is insufficient for modeling complex behavior that affects a dialogue system's decision making process during response generation. We illustrate this argument by analyzing in further detail the dialogue segment shown in Section 1 using a model of initiative that tracks only the conversational lead, such as that of Whittaker and Stenton (1988).

In utterances (1) and (2), C states her goal and requests for information as part of formulating a plan to achieve this goal; thus C has the conversational lead at this point in the dialogue. In utterance (3a), T provides a direct response to C's question; hence the conversational lead remains with C. On the other hand, in utterances (3b) and (3c), instead of merely answering C's question, T takes control of the dialogue by further initiating a subdialogue to correct C's invalid plan of attempting to withdraw money from an immature CD. However, existing models for initiative, when adopted by a dialogue system, cannot distinguish between situations when it may be more appropriate to provide a response such as (3b) and those when a response such as (3c) may be more desirable. A comparison between (3b) and (3c) shows that the two responses differ in the level of involvement that T has in the agents' planning process. More specifically, in (3b), T merely conveys the invalidity of C's proposal, while in (3c), T further actively participates in the planning process by explicitly proposing what she believes to be a valid plan for achieving C's goal. Based on this observation, we argue that, in a collaborative problem-solving environment, it is necessary to distinguish between *task initiative*, which tracks the lead in the development of the agents' plan, and *dialogue initiative*, which tracks the lead in determining the current discourse focus (Chu-Carroll and Brown, 1997a). This distinction then allows us to explain T's behavior from a response generation point of view: in (3b), T responds to C's proposal by merely taking over the dialogue initiative, i.e., changing the discourse focus to inform C of the invalidity of her proposal, while in (3c), T responds by taking over both the task and dialogue initiatives, i.e., taking the lead in the planning process by suggesting an alternative plan which she believes to be valid. In other words, by modeling both task and dialogue initiatives, a dialogue system is able to determine the appropriate distribution of task and dialogue initiatives for each dialogue turn, and thus tailor its responses to user utterances based on its model of initiatives.

An agent is said to have the *task initiative* if she is directing how the agents' task should be accomplished, i.e., if her utterances directly propose *actions* that she believes the agent(s) should perform. The utterances may propose *domain actions* (Litman and Allen, 1987) that directly contribute to achieving the agents' goal, such as *'Why don't we couple engine E2 to the boxcar that's at Elmira, and send it to Corning.'*[2] On the other hand, the utterances may propose *problem-solving actions* (Allen, 1991; Lambert and Carberry, 1991; Ramshaw, 1991) that contribute not directly to the agents' domain goal, but to how they will go about constructing a plan to achieve this goal, such as *'Let's look at the first [problem] first. I think they are separate.'* An agent is said to have the *dialogue initiative* if she takes the conversational lead in order to establish mutual beliefs between the agents, such as mutual beliefs about a piece of domain knowledge or about the validity of a proposal. For instance, in response to agent A's proposal of sending a boxcar to

---

[2] The majority of the examples in this paper are taken from (Gross et al., 1993).

Corning via Dansville, agent B may take over the dialogue initiative (but not the task initiative) by saying *'We can't go by Dansville because we've got engine E1 going on that track.'* Note that although these utterances contribute indirectly to the formulation of the final plan (by suggesting that the current plan *not* be adopted), since they do not directly propose actions to be added to the plan, they affect initiative only at the dialogue level. The relationship between task and dialogue initiatives is such that when an agent takes over the task initiative, he also takes over the dialogue initiative, since a proposal of actions can be viewed as an attempt to establish the mutual belief that a set of actions be adopted. On the other hand, an agent may take over the dialogue initiative without taking over the task initiative, as in response (3b) in the sample dialogue. This agrees with Cohen et al.'s theory of initiative in which they argued that when an initiative shift occurs, the agent who took the initiative also has taken control of the conversation, but not vice versa (Cohen et al., 1998).

Our distinction between task and dialogue initiatives agrees with Jordan and Di Eugenio's view of initiative, which distinguishes between initiative, applicable to the agents' problem-solving goals, and control, pertaining to the dialogue level (Jordan and Di Eugenio, 1997). This distinction is further supported by Cohen et al.'s theory of initiative where they again separate control from initiative (Cohen et al., 1998). Novick and Sutton proposed a multi-factor model for modeling initiative based on choice of task, choice of speaker, and choice of outcome (Novick and Sutton, 1997). Our task initiative corresponds to their choice of outcome, while our dialogue initiative corresponds to their choice of task.[3] On the other hand, in Guinn's model, an agent has *task initiative* over a goal if he dictates how the agents will go about achieving the goal, while an agent has the *dialogue initiative* when both agents expect the agent to communicate next (Guinn, 1998). However, although Guinn provides distinct definitions for task initiative and dialogue initiative, he also equates task and dialogue initiatives, argues that an agent who holds the task initiative over the current mutual goal must also hold the dialogue initiative, and models only one type of initiative in his system. We contend that Guinn's framework is insufficient for modeling the type of phenomenon we attempt to model in collaborative planning dialogues by distinguishing between task and dialogue initiatives. More specifically, by equating task and dialogue initiatives, Guinn's model equates being expected to communicate next (having the dialogue initiative in his model) to having control over the current goal (having the task initiative in his model). However, our earlier sample dialogue illustrated a counterexample to this view in that although T was expected to communicate next after C's question in utterance (2), she did not have control over the current goal in her response in utterance (3a).

---

[3] Their choice of speaker models initiative at the turn-taking level, which is not represented in our view of initiative.

Table I. Distribution of task/dialogue initiatives

	TIH: System	TIH: User
DIH: System	37 (3.5%)	274 (26.3%)
DIH: User	4 (0.4%)	727 (69.8%)

3.2. CORPUS ANALYSIS

To analyze the distribution of task and dialogue initiatives in collaborative dialogues, we analyzed the TRAINS91 dialogues in which two agents are collaborating on planning a route for cargo shipping along a hypothetical railway system (Gross et al., 1993). The TRAINS91 corpus contains 16 dialogues based on 8 speaker pairs, and contains roughly 1000 dialogue turns. We manually labeled each dialogue turn in the corpus with two labels, *task initiative holder* (TIH) and *dialogue initiative holder* (DIH). Each label can be assigned one of two values, *system* or *user*, depending on which agent holds the task/dialogue initiative during that turn.[4] Table I shows the distribution of task and dialogue initiatives in the TRAINS91 dialogues. The results of our analysis shows that although in the majority of turns the task and dialogue initiatives are held by the same agent, in approximately 27 percent of the turns the agents' behavior can be better accounted for by tracking the two types of initiatives separately.

To further justify the need to distinguish between task and dialogue initiatives, and to assess the reliability of our annotation, approximately 10 percent of the dialogues were annotated by two additional coders. In this subset of the dialogues, the original coder found that in 37 percent of the dialogue turns, the task and dialogue initiatives were held by different agents, while the two additional coders found that the two types of initiatives are held by different participants in 21 percent and 14 percent of the dialogue turns, respectively. Although there is a discrepancy in the percentages presented above, on average, the coders found that in 24 percent of the dialogue turns, the agents' behavior can be better accounted for by tracking the two types of initiatives separately, thus providing further support for the need to distinguish between task and dialogue initiatives.

Next, we used the kappa statistic (Siegel and Castellan, 1988; Carletta, 1996) to assess the level of agreement among the three coders on this subset of the dialogues. In this experiment, K is 0.57 for the task initiative holder agreement and K is 0.69 for the dialogue initiative holder agreement. Carletta reports that content analysis researchers consider $K > 0.8$ to be good reliability, with $0.67 < K < 0.8$ allowing

---

[4] The task/dialogue initiative holder is determined on a turn by turn basis. For instance, an agent holds the task initiative during a turn as long as *some* utterance during that turn directly proposes how the agents should accomplish their goal, as in utterance (3c).

tentative conclusions to be drawn (Carletta, 1996).[5] Strictly based on this metric, our results indicate that the three coders have a reasonable level of agreement with respect to the dialogue initiative holders, but do not have reliable agreement with respect to the task initiative holders. We attribute this low level of agreement to two possible causes. First, the kappa statistic is known to be highly problematic in measuring inter-coder reliability when the likelihood of one category being chosen overwhelms that of the other (Grove et al., 1981), which is the case for the task initiative distribution in the TRAINS91 corpus, as shown in Table I. Second, the low level of agreement may be due to the fact that a small number of dialogues were used in the coding reliability test, and that these dialogues may not be representative of the corpus. Furthermore, as will be shown in Table VI, Section 6, the task and dialogue initiative distributions in TRAINS91 are not representative of collaborative dialogues. We expect that by taking a sample of dialogues whose task/dialogue initiative distributions are more representative of collaborative dialogues, we will lower the value of P(E), the probability of chance agreement in the kappa statistic, and thus obtain a higher kappa coefficient of agreement. However, we leave selecting and annotating such a subset of representative dialogues for future work.

4. Cues for Shifts in Initiative

Given that initiative shifts between dialogue participants during their interaction, we are interested in finding out the reasons that result in such shifts. Whittaker, Stenton, and Walker (Whittaker and Stenton, 1988; Walker and Whittaker, 1990) have previously identified a set of utterance intentions that serve as cues to indicate shift or lack of shift in initiative, such as prompts and questions. We examined our annotated TRAINS91 corpus and identified additional cues that may have contributed to the shift or lack of shift in task and dialogue initiatives. This resulted in eight cue types, which are grouped into three classes, based on the type of knowledge needed to recognize each cue. Table II shows the three classes, the eight cue types, their subtypes if any, whether a cue may affect merely the dialogue initiative (DI) or both the task and dialogue initiatives, and the agent expected to hold the initiative in the next turn.

A cue may affect both the task and dialogue initiatives if the cue may reasonably suggest that the hearer direct how the agents' task will be accomplished in the next dialogue turn. Examples of such cues include cases in which the speaker explicitly asks the hearer to direct the task, and those where the speaker proposes an invalid action, thereby potentially leading the hearer to correct the invalid action and proposing an alternative valid action. On the other hand, a cue only affects the dialogue initiative if the cue suggests that the hearer take the conversational

---

[5] It is an open question as to whether or not this metric (and the kappa statistic in general) is appropriate for measuring reliability in annotating dialogue features. However, short of a better alternative, we adopt this metric in our current discussion.

Table II. Cues for modeling initiative shifts

Class	Cue type	Subtype	Effect	Initiative
Explicit	Explicit requests	give up task	both	hearer
		give up dialogue	DI	hearer
		take over task	both	speaker
		take over dialogue	DI	speaker
Discourse	End silence		both	hearer
	No new info	repetitions	both	hearer
		prompts	both	hearer
	Questions	domain	DI	speaker
		evaluation	DI	hearer
	Obligation fulfilled	task	both	hearer
		discourse	DI	hearer
Analytical	Invalidity	action	both	hearer
		belief	DI	hearer
	Suboptimality		both	hearer
	Ambiguity	action	both	hearer
		belief	DI	hearer

lead in order to establish mutual beliefs between the agents, e.g., when the speaker attempts to verify a piece of domain knowledge.

4.1. EXPLICIT CUES

The first cue class, *explicit cues*, includes explicit requests by the speaker to give up or take over the initiative. Explicit cues may result in shifts in both types of initiatives. For instance, consider the following dialogue segment (where the cue is highlighted in boldface):

(4) *U: Yeah, so go to Bath and pick up the boxcar, bring it back to Corning and then bring it back to Elmira.*

(5) *S: Okay, well that's 8 hours, so you're not gaining anything by doing that.*

(6) *U: Okay [2sec] [sigh] [3sec]* **Any suggestions***?*

(7) *S: Well, there's a boxcar at Dansville and you can use that.*

In utterance (4), *U* has both the task and dialogue initiatives, since *U* is explicitly proposing actions for accomplishing the agents' goal. *S* takes over the dialogue initiative in utterance (5) to point out the invalidity of the proposal. The explicit cue to give up task initiative, *any suggestions*, in utterance (6) suggests that

S should have both the task and dialogue initiatives in the next dialogue turn, as in (7) where S proposes a (partial) solution to U's problem.

Instead of affecting both the task and dialogue initiatives, an explicit cue may be intended to affect merely the dialogue initiative, as in the following example:

(8) *U: So you can start making OJ and then when the OJ is ready you load it up into the tanker car and bring it back to Avon.*

(9)   *Okay,* **summarize the plan at this point** *system.*

(10) *S: Okay, lemme make sure I got all this. You wanna link the boxcar at Elmira to E2 ...*

In utterance (8), U has both the task and dialogue initiatives, and in (9), U employs the give-up-dialogue cue to explicitly hand the dialogue initiative over to S by asking S to summarize the current plan, as realized in (10). Note that these cues merely indicate the speaker's intention regarding task/dialogue initiative shifts for the next dialogue turn, and it is up to the hearer to determine whether or not such shifts actually occur. For instance, instead of utterance (7), S may respond to U's cue *'any suggestions'* by saying *'it's your responsibility to make a proposal'*, i.e., responding to U's question *without* taking over the task initiative.

4.2. DISCOURSE CUES

The second cue class, *discourse cues*, includes cues that can be recognized using linguistic information, such as the surface form of an utterance, and the recognized intentions of the utterances, such as the how the current utterance relates to prior discourse.

We have identified four types of discourse cues. The first type is perceptible silence, or pauses, observed at the end of an utterance, which has been found to correlate with discourse boundaries (Grosz and Hirschberg, 1992; Passonneau and Litman, 1993; Swerts, 1997). We believe that in the context of initiative modeling, silence at the end of an utterance may suggest that the speaker has nothing more to say in the current turn and intends to give up his task/dialogue initiative. For instance, in the following dialogue segment, the silence at the end of U's utterance led S to take over the dialogue initiative and provide what she believed to be the most relevant information at that time, even though it was not explicitly requested.

(11) *U: Can we please send engine E1 over to Dansville to pick up a boxcar and then send it right back to Avon.* **[3 sec]**

(12) *S: Okay, it'll get back to Avon at 6.*

The second type of discourse cues includes situations in which the speaker's utterances do not contribute new information that has not been conveyed earlier in the dialogue. These utterances are further classified into two groups: *repetitions,* a subset of the *informationally redundant utterances* (Walker, 1992), in which the speaker paraphrases an utterance by the hearer or repeats the utterance verbatim, and *prompts*, such as *'yeah'* and *'okay'*, where the speaker merely acknowledges the hearer's previous utterances. Repetitions and prompts also suggest that the speaker has nothing more to say and are indications that the hearer should take over the task/dialogue initiative (Whittaker and Stenton, 1988). In the following dialogue segment, utterance (14) is an informationally redundant utterance since it merely paraphrases part of utterance (13):

(13) *U: Grab the tanker, pick up oranges, go to Elmira, make em into orange juice.*

(14) *S: Okay, then* **we go to Elmira, we make orange juice,** *okay.*

(15) *U: And then send the orange juice back to Avon.*

The third type of discourse cues includes questions which, based on anticipated responses, are divided into *domain* questions and *evaluation* questions. Domain questions are questions in which the speaker intends to obtain or verify a piece of domain knowledge. They usually merely require a direct response and thus typically do not result in a shift in dialogue initiative. Evaluation questions, on the other hand, are questions in which the speaker intends to assess the quality of a proposed plan. They often require an analysis of the proposal, and thus frequently result in a shift in dialogue initiative. In the following dialogue segment, *U* asks *S* to evaluate the feasibility of a proposed plan in utterance (16), resulting in *S* taking over the dialogue initiative in (17).[6] On the other hand, the domain question in utterance (18) required only a direct response, and thus did not result in an initiative shift in (19).

(16) *U:* **Could it take the other boxcar back to Avon to fill up with bananas?**

(17) *S: Okay, we could get back to Avon by noon and that wouldn't leave enough time to get to Corning by 3.*

(18) *U: Right. Okay, so* **how long again between Avon and Bath?**

(19) *S: That's 4 hours.*

The final type of discourse cue includes utterances that satisfy an outstanding task or discourse obligation. Such obligations may have resulted from a prior request by the hearer, or from an interruption initiated by the speaker himself. In either case, when the task/dialogue obligation is fulfilled, the initiative may be reverted back to the hearer who held the initiative prior to the request or interruption. As discussed in the previous section, utterance (20) suggests that *S* take over both the task and dialogue initiatives in the next turn. This also creates a task (and

---

[6] In addition to being an evaluation question, utterance (16) also triggers the analytical cue *invalidity-action*, which will be discussed in Section 4.3.

thus discourse) obligation for S to satisfy the request for suggestions by U. The utterance in boldface in (21) satisfies this outstanding obligation, thus signals that the task and dialogue initiatives should return to U, who initiated the request, as in utterance (22). Utterance (22) is an evaluation question suggesting that S take over the dialogue initiative, and at the same time creating a discourse obligation for S to provide an evaluation of the proposal. Utterance (23) satisfies this outstanding discourse obligation, signaling that the dialogue initiative be returned to U. Thus in (24), U has both the task and dialogue initiatives, and continues the planning process.

(20)   *U: Any suggestions?*

(21)   *S:* **Well, there's a boxcar at Dansville and you could use that,** *but you'd have to change your banana plan.*

(22)   *U: Will the banana plan work if we get the boxcar at Bath instead of Dansville?*

(23)   *S: If you do that, the bananas will get to Corning at 3PM exactly, so* **that will work.**

(24)   *U: Now about the oranges ...*

4.3. ANALYTICAL CUES

The third class of cues, *analytical cues,* includes cues that cannot be recognized without the hearer performing an evaluation of the speaker's proposal using the hearer's private knowledge (Chu-Carroll and Carberry, 1994; Chu-Carroll and Carberry, 1995). After the evaluation, the hearer may find the proposal *invalid, suboptimal,* or *ambiguous.* When such a problem is detected with respect to the speaker's proposal, the hearer may initiate a subdialogue to resolve the problem, resulting in a shift in task/dialogue initiatives.[7] In the following dialogue segment, U evaluates S's proposal in (25) and believes the action to be invalid. Utterances (26a) and (26b) illustrate two alternative ways that S may correct this invalid action. In (26a), S does so by taking over both the task and dialogue initiatives to propose an action that will cause the original proposal to be valid, while in (26b), S takes over only the dialogue initiative to point out the invalidity of the proposal.

(25)   *U:* **Let's get the tanker car to Elmira and fill it with OJ.**

(26a)   *S: You need to get oranges to the OJ factory.*

(26b)   *S: You don't have OJ in Elmira.*

---

[7] Whittaker, Stenton, and Walker (Whittaker and Stenton, 1988; Walker and Whittaker, 1990) treat subdialogues initiated as a result of these cues as interruptions, motivated by their collaborative planning principle.

When the evaluation of a proposal results in the hearer believing that a proposed belief is invalid, the potential effect of the detected cue *invalidity-belief* is for the hearer to take over the dialogue initiative (but not the task initiative). For example, in the following dialogue segment, S responds to U's proposed invalid belief in utterance (27) by taking over the dialogue initiative to correct the belief in (28).

(27)   *U:* **It's shorter to Bath from Avon**

(28)   *S: It's shorter to Dansville. The map is slightly misleading.*

The cues *ambiguity-action* and *ambiguity-belief* are triggered when the hearer cannot unambiguously interpret the speaker's utterances based on her knowledge about the domain and about the world. Their effects are similar to those of *invalidity-action* and *invalidity-belief* described above. Finally, a proposal is considered *suboptimal* if the hearer believes that there exists a better way to achieve their goal than that proposed by the speaker. This would naturally lead the hearer to take over both the task and dialogue initiatives to suggest the alternative to the speaker. For instance, in the following dialogue segment, S takes over the task and dialogue initiatives in utterance (32) to suggest an alternative to U's proposal in utterance (31):

(29)   *U: I'm looking for Saudi Arabian Airlines on the night of the eleventh.*

(30)   *S: Right, it's sold out.*

(31)   *U: Is Friday open?*

(32)   *S: Let me check here.* **I'm showing economy on Pan Am is open on the eleventh.**

5. An Evidential Model for Tracking Initiative

As illustrated by our corpus analysis in Section 3.2, during the course of a dialogue, the task and dialogue initiatives switch back and forth between the dialogue participants. Our goal is to develop a model for tracking such shifts in initiative, using cues identified in the previous section, in order to allow a dialogue system to better manage its interaction with the user. Although having the task initiative means that an agent has the lead in developing the agents' plan, it does not give this agent sole control over determining the content of this plan. Instead, it merely indicates that the agent has a higher level of involvement in directing the task planning process than the other agent at the current point in the dialogue. Thus, in our model for tracking initiative, we associate with each agent a *task initiative index* and a *dialogue initiative index*, which measure the agent's levels of involvement in directing the planning process and in determining the discourse focus (and thus the likelihood that the agent holds the task initiative and dialogue initiative), respectively. In addition, we represent the effect of each cue identified

[62]

in Section 4 in terms of how it affects the existing task/dialogue initiative indices. Then at the end of each dialogue turn, new initiative indices are computed based on the effects that the cues observed during that turn have on changing the current initiative indices. These new initiative indices are then used to determine the task and dialogue initiative holders for the next dialogue turn (Chu-Carroll and Brown, 1997b).

Evidently, some cues provide stronger evidence for a shift in initiative than others. For instance, an explicit request to give up initiative is a stronger cue for initiative shift than, say, silence at the end of an utterance. Thus, in developing a framework for tracking initiative, we need an underlying model that allows us to represent the amount of evidence a cue provides for a shift or lack of shift in initiative. Furthermore, since multiple cues may be observed during a dialogue turn, this model must also provide a mechanism for combining the effects of multiple cues to determine their overall effect on initiative shift. We adopt the Dempster-Shafer theory of evidence (Shafer, 1976; Gordon and Shortliffe, 1984) as such an underlying model. The reasons for this are threefold. First, the Dempster-Shafer theory allows us to use basic probability assignments to represent the effect of each cue on initiative shift, and the Dempster's combination rule allows us to easily compute a new basic probability assignments from two existing ones, i.e., to determine the combined effect of two observed cues. Second, the Dempster-Shafer theory, unlike the Bayesian model, does not require a complete set of *a priori* and conditional probabilities, which is difficult to obtain for sparse pieces of evidence. Third, the Dempster-Shafer theory distinguishes between situations in which no evidence is available to support any conclusion and those in which equal evidence is available to support each conclusion. Thus the outcome of the Dempster-Shafer model more accurately represents the *amount* of evidence available to support a particular conclusion, i.e., the *provability* of a particular conclusion (Pearl, 1990).

In the next section, we give a brief introduction to the Dempster-Shafer theory of evidence. In Section 5.2, we show how the problem of tracking initiative can be framed to utilize the Dempster-Shafer theory, discuss our training algorithm for determining the basic probability assignment used to represent the effect of a cue, and discuss the performance of this model in predicting task/dialogue initiative holders. Finally, in Section 5.3, we perform an analysis of the erroneous predictions resulting from our experiments in Section 5.2.

5.1. THE DEMPSTER-SHAFER THEORY OF EVIDENCE

The Dempster-Shafer Theory is a mathematical theory for reasoning under uncertainty (Shafer, 1976; Gordon and Shortliffe, 1984). It operates over a set of possible outcomes, called the *frame of discernment*, Θ. The elements in Θ are assumed to be mutually exclusive and exhaustive. Associated with each piece of evidence that may provide support for the possible outcomes is a *basic probability assignment* (*bpa*). A bpa is a function that represents the impact of a piece of

Table III. Intersection tableau for computing $m_{t1} \oplus m_{t2}$

	{hearer} (0.5)	{speaker} (0.3)	Θ (0.2)
{hearer} (0.2)	{hearer} (0.1)	$\emptyset$ (0.06)	{hearer} (0.04)
Θ (0.8)	{hearer} (0.4)	{speaker} (0.24)	Θ (0.16)

evidence on the subsets of Θ. It assigns a number in the range [0,1] to each subset of Θ such that the numbers sum to 1. The number assigned to the subset Θ_1 then denotes the amount of support the piece of evidence *directly* provides for the set of conclusions represented by Θ_1. For instance, suppose two bpa's, m_{t1} and m_{t2}, representing the amount of evidence that two hypothetical cues, c_1 and c_2, provide for determining whether or not a task initiative shift should occur are as follows, where $\Theta = \{speaker, hearer\}$:

$$m_{t1}(\{hearer\}) = 0.2, \quad m_{t1}(\Theta) = 0.8;$$

$$m_{t2}(\{hearer\}) = 0.5, \quad m_{t2}(\{speaker\}) = 0.3, \quad m_{t2}(\Theta) = 0.2.$$

m_{t1} indicates that observation of the cue c_1 supports an initiative shift to the hearer to the degree 0.2. The remaining belief, 0.8, is assigned to Θ, indicating that to the degree 0.8, observation of this cue does not commit to identifying whether the speaker or the hearer should have the next task initiative.

When multiple pieces of evidence are present, the theory utilizes Dempster's combination rule to compute a new bpa from the individual bpa's to represent the impact of the combined evidence. Dempster's combination rule uses a combination function, $\oplus$, to combine two bpa's, m_1 and m_2. This process involves two steps. First, $m_1 \oplus m_2(Z)$ is computed by summing all products of the form $m_1(X)m_2(Y)$, where X and Y run over all subsets of Θ whose intersection is Z. Second, if $m_1 \oplus m_2(\emptyset) \neq 0$, then $m_1 \oplus m_2(\emptyset)$ is assigned a value of 0 and the other values are normalized accordingly so that they sum to 1. For instance, given m_{t1} and m_{t2} above, to obtain $m_{t1} \oplus m_{t2}$, we first compute an intersection tableau whose first column and first row are the values assigned to m_{t1} and m_{t2}, respectively. Suppose that $m_{t1}(s_i) = v_i$ is in row i and that $m_{t2}(s_j) = v_j$ is in column j. The element in entry i, j in the tableau is then $s_i \cap s_j$, and its value $v_i * v_j$. Table III shows the intersection tableau for $m_{t1} \oplus m_{t2}$.

Since $m_{t1} \oplus m_{t2}(\emptyset) \neq 0$, the resulting bpa needs to be normalized. This normalization procedure is carried out by assigning 0 to $m_{t1} \oplus m_{t2}(\emptyset)$ and dividing all other values of $m_{t1} \oplus m_{t2}$ by $1 - \kappa$, where κ is the sum of all values assigned to $\emptyset$. In this example, $1 - \kappa$ is 0.94; thus the final results of applying Dempster's combination rule are as follows:

$$m_{t1} \oplus m_{t2}(\{hearer\}) = (0.1 + 0.04 + 0.4)/0.94 = 0.57,$$

$$m_{t1} \oplus m_{t2}(\{speaker\}) = 0.24/0.94 = 0.26,$$

$$m_{t1} \oplus m_{t2}(\Theta) = 0.16/0.94 = 0.17.$$

The final result of computing $m_{t1} \oplus m_{t2}$ represents the combined effect of observing both cues c_1 and c_2. It indicates that when both cues occur at the same time, they provide stronger support for the hearer taking over the initiative in the next dialogue turn than either cue alone.

5.2. UTILIZING THE DEMPSTER-SHAFER THEORY IN TRACKING INITIATIVE

As discussed earlier, our model for tracking initiative can be outlined as follows. We maintain, for each agent, a current task initiative index and a current dialogue initiative index to represent the levels of involvement that the agent has in leading the planning process and in determining the discourse focus in the current dialogue turn. At the end of each dialogue turn, new initiative indices are computed based on the current indices and the effects that the observed cues have on changing these values. These new initiative indices then become the current initiative indices for the next dialogue turn and the process repeats.

In order to utilize the Dempster-Shafer theory in this process, we represent the current initiative indices as two bpa's, m_{t-cur} and m_{d-cur}. More specifically, the bpa for representing the current task initiative indices take the form of m_{t-cur} ($\{speaker\}$) $= x$ and $m_{t-cur}(\{hearer\}) = 1 - x$. At the beginning of a dialogue, default bpa's are used based on the collaborative setting of the application domain. For example, in the TRAINS domain, a reasonable default setting for the initial bpa's may be $m_{t-cur}(\{user\}) = 0.7; m_{t-cur}(\{system\}) = 0.3$, and $m_{d-cur}(\{user\}) = 0.6; m_{d-cur}(\{system\}) = 0.4$. This is because the system's role is to assist the user in devising a plan to achieve his goal; thus the system should have lower task and dialogue initiative indices than the user. On the other hand, in the maptask domain (Canadian Map Task Dialogues, 1996), a reasonable default setting may be $m_{t-cur}(\{giver\}) = 1; m_{t-cur}(\{follower\}) = 0$, and $m_{d-cur}(\{giver\}) = 0.6; m_{d-cur}(\{follower\}) = 0.4$. This is because the instruction giver has sole control over the agents' domain actions (to follow the route on his map), but will allow the follower to ask, for instance, clarification questions when necessary.

In addition to representing the current initiative indices as bpa's, we also associate with each cue two bpa's to represent its effect on changing the values of the current task and dialogue initiative indices, respectively. For instance, the bpa that represents the effect of cue_i on changing the current task initiative bpa is $m_{t-i}(\{speaker\}) = x; m_{t-i}(\{hearer\}) = y; m_{t-i}(\Theta) = 1 - x - y$. Recall this indicates that if cue_i is observed during the current turn, then this observation provides evidence for the speaker taking over the next task initiative to the degree x, for the hearer taking over the next task initiative to the degree y, and to the degree $1 - x - y$, the observation of this cue does not commit to identifying whether the speaker or the hearer should hold the next task initiative. Once we have represented the initiative indices and the effects of cues as bpa's, then at the end of each dialogue turn, we can simply invoke Dempster's combination rule to compute two new bpa's, m_{t-new} and m_{d-new}, to represent the initiative indices for the next dialogue turn based on m_{t-cur} and m_{d-cur}, as well as m_{t-i} and m_{d-i} for each cue_i observed during the turn. However, to employ this model in initiative tracking, we need to first determine the appropriate bpa's to represent the effect of each cue. The next section describes a training algorithm for this purpose.

5.2.1. *Determining the Effect of Cues*

In order to identify the effect that each cue has on determining the next task/dialogue initiative holder, we extended our annotation of the TRAINS91 dialogues to include, in addition to the agent(s) holding the task and dialogue initiatives for each turn, a list of cues observed during that turn. We initialize the task and dialogue bpa's for each cue_i to be $m_{t-i}(\Theta) = 1$ and $m_{d-i}(\Theta) = 1$. In other words, we first assume that a cue will have no effect on determining the new task and dialogue initiative indices. The annotated data are then used to adjust these default bpa's based on whether or not they allow the system to correctly predict the next task and dialogue initiative holders. Figure 1 shows our training algorithm for this adjustment process.

For each turn, the task and dialogue initiative bpa's for each observed cue are used, along with the bpa's representing the current initiative indices (m_{t-cur} and m_{d-cur}), to determine the new initiative indices (step 2). The **combine** function utilizes Dempster's combination rule to combine pairs of bpa's in the given set until a final bpa is obtained to represent the cumulative effect of all given bpa's. The resulting bpa's then represent the new initiative indices, and are used to predict the task/dialogue initiative holders for the next dialogue turn (step 3). If this prediction is confirmed by the actual values in the annotated data, it indicates that the bpa's for the observed cues are appropriate in this instance. On the other hand, if the two values disagree, **Adjust-bpa** is invoked to alter the bpa's for the observed cues, and **Reset-current-bpa** is invoked to adjust the new bpa's to reflect the actual initiative holder (step 4). In our implementation of this algorithm, **Reset-current-bpa** sums the values assigned to *speaker* and *hearer* in each of m_{t-new} and m_{d-new}, and assigns 0.525 of the sum to the actual initiative holder and 0.475 of the sum to the other agent.[8]

---

[8] We ran a series of experiments to determine the optimal distribution of this sum by varying the share assigned to the actual initiative holder from 0.525 to 0.975 (at 0.025 intervals). Our experiment

Train-bpa(annotated-data):

1. m_{t-cur} ← default task initiative indices
   m_{d-cur} ← default dialogue initiative indices
   cur-data ← **read**(annotated-data)
   cue-set ← cues in cur-data
2. /* compute new initiative indices */
   task-bpas ← task initiative bpa's for cues in cue-set ∪ $\{m_{t-cur}\}$
   dialogue-bpas ← dialogue initiative bpa's for cues in cue-set ∪ $\{m_{d-cur}\}$
   m_{t-new} ← **combine**(task-bpas)
   m_{d-new} ← **combine**(dialogue-bpas)
3. /* determine predicted next initiative holders */
   If $m_{t-new}(\{speaker\}) \geq m_{t-new}(\{hearer\})$, t-predicted ← speaker
   Else, t-predicted ← hearer
   If $m_{d-new}(\{speaker\}) \geq m_{d-new}(\{hearer\})$, d-predicted ← speaker
   Else, d-predicted ← hearer
4. /* find actual initiative holders and compare */
   new-data ← **read**(annotated-data)
   t-actual ← actual task initiative holder in new-data
   d-actual ← actual dialogue initiative holder in new-data
   If t-predicted ≠ t-actual,
      Adjust-bpa(cue-set,task)
      Reset-current-bpa(m_{t-cur})
   If d-predicted ≠ d-actual,
      Adjust-bpa(cue-set,dialogue)
      Reset-current-bpa(m_{d-cur})
5. If end-of-dialogue, return
   Else,   /* swap roles of speaker and hearer */
   $m_{t-cur}(\{speaker\})$ ← $m_{t-new}(\{hearer\})$
   $m_{d-cur}(\{speaker\})$ ← $m_{d-new}(\{hearer\})$
   $m_{t-cur}(\{hearer\})$ ← $m_{t-new}(\{speaker\})$
   $m_{d-cur}(\{hearer\})$ ← $m_{d-new}(\{speaker\})$
   cue-set ← cues in new-data
   Goto step 2.

Figure 1. Training Algorithm for Determining BPA's.

Adjust-bpa, which is invoked when the system's predicted task or dialogue initiative holder disagrees with the actual initiative holder, adjusts the bpa's for the observed cues in favor of the actual initiative holder. We developed three adjustment methods by varying the effect that a disagreement between the actual and predicted initiative holders will have on changing the relevant bpa's (bpa's for the observed cues). The first is the *constant-increment* method, where each time a disagreement occurs, the value assigned to the actual initiative holder in each relevant bpa is incremented by a constant (Δ), while that for Θ is decremented by Δ. The second method is the *constant-increment-with-counter* method, which associates with each bpa for each cue a counter which is incremented when the use of the bpa resulted in a correct prediction, and decremented when it resulted in an incorrect prediction. If

showed that values ranging between 0.525 and 0.6 yielded optimal results on tracking the distribution of task and dialogue initiatives on an 8-fold cross-validated test on the TRAINS91 corpus.

the counter is negative, the *constant-increment* method is invoked and the counter is reset to 0. This method ensures that a bpa will only be adjusted if it has no 'credit' for correct prediction in the past. The third method, *variable-increment-with-counter*, is a variation of *constant-increment-with-counter*. However, instead of using the counter to determine whether or not an adjustment is needed, the counter is used to determine the amount to be adjusted. In our implementation of the system, each time a bpa results in the system making an erroneous prediction, the value for the actual initiative holder is incremented by $\Delta/2^{count+1}$, and that for Θ decremented by the same amount. This function is selected to reflect our intention that the adjustment be inversely exponentially related to the value of the counter, i.e., the higher 'credit' the bpa has for correct prediction in the past, the less it should be modified for occasional errors.

5.2.2. *Experiments and Results*

In addition to experimenting with different adjustment methods, we also varied the increment constant, Δ. For each adjustment method, we ran 19 training sessions with Δ ranging from 0.025 to 0.475, incrementing by 0.025 between each session. We then evaluated the system's performance based on its accuracy in predicting the task and dialogue initiative holders for each dialogue turn. We divided the TRAINS91 corpus into eight sets based on speaker/hearer pairs. For each Δ, we evaluated the system's performance in predicting the task and dialogue initiative holders using an 8-fold cross-validation. Figure 2(a, b) shows our system's performance in predicting the task and dialogue initiative holders, respectively, using the three adjustment methods. These results are compared against the prediction results using a baseline method of predicting initiative holders without the use of cues, i.e., always predict that the current initiative holder will have the initiative in the next dialogue turn.

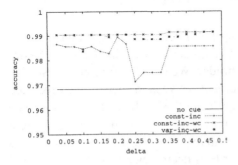

Figure 2a. Task Initiative Prediction Results.

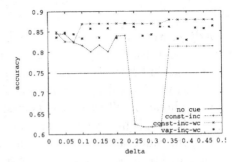

Figure 2b. Dialogue Initiative Prediction Results.

The results in Figure 2(a, b) show that in the vast majority of cases, our prediction methods yield better results than making predictions without cues (baseline

Table IVa. Trained BPA's for Task Initiative Shift

Cue Type	Subtype	Trained BPA
Explicit request	give up task	$m_{t-gut}(\{hearer\}) = 0.35; m_{t-gut}(\Theta) = 0.65$
End silence		$m_{t-es}(\Theta) = 1$
No new info	repetitions	$m_{t-rep}(\Theta) = 1$
	prompts	$m_{t-pro}(\Theta) = 1$
Obligation fulfilled	task	$m_{t-tof}(\{hearer\}) = 0.35; m_{t-tof}(\Theta) = 0.65$
Invalidity	action	$m_{t-ia}(\Theta) = 1$
Suboptimality		$m_{t-sub}(\{hearer\}) = 0.35; m_{t-sub}(\Theta) = 0.65$
Ambiguity	action	$m_{t-aa}(\{hearer\}) = 0.35; m_{t-aa}(\Theta) = 0.65$

strategy labeled 'no cue'). Furthermore, substantial improvement is gained by the use of counters in *constant-increment-with-counter* and *variable-increment-with-counter*. This outcome agrees with our expectation that without counters, the effect of the 'exceptions of the rules' may accumulate and result in erroneous predictions, hence the erratic behavior of the *constant-increment* method. With the aid of counters, the *variable-increment-with-counter* method is able to obtain substantially better and more consistent results than the *constant-increment* method. However, even by restricting the increment to be inversely exponentially related to the 'credit' the bpa had in making correct predictions, the exceptions of the rules still resulted in undesirable effects, hence the further improved performance by *constant-increment-with-counter*.

As Figure 2(a, b) show, the best prediction results occur using the *constant-increment-with-counter* adjustment method with Δ between 0.35 and 0.475. Tables IVa and IVb show the bpa's that result from our training procedure using $\Delta = 0.35$.[9] These bpa's represent the amount of evidence each cue gives to changing the current task and dialogue initiative indices. For instance, the cue *suboptimality* provides support to the degree 0.35 that both the task and dialogue initiatives will shift to the hearer in the next turn.

The trained bpa's in Tables IVa and IVb show that explicit requests to give up task or dialogue initiative provide a moderate amount of evidence for an actual task/dialogue initiative shift to the hearer in the next dialogue turn. The degree of support, however, is not as strong as one may expect for an explicit cue. We believe that this may be the result of the the sparse data problem,[10] since our training algorithm only adjusts the existing bpa for a cue if

---

[9] The cues *Request-take over task* and *Request-take over dialogue* were not used in our experiments since they do not occur in our corpus.

[10] There were only 2 explicit requests to give up task initiative and 4 explicit requests to give up dialogue initiative in the entire corpus.

Table IVb. Trained BPA's for Dialogue Initiative Shift

Cue Type	Subtype	Trained BPA
Explicit request	give up task	$m_{d-gut}(\{hearer\}) = 0.35; m_{d-gut}(\Theta) = 0.65$
	give up dialogue	$m_{d-gud}(\{hearer\}) = 0.35; m_{d-gud}(\Theta) = 0.65$
End silence		$m_{d-es}(\Theta) = 1$
No new info	repetitions	$m_{d-rep}(\Theta) = 1$
	prompts	$m_{d-pro}(\Theta) = 1$
Questions	domain	$m_{d-dq}(\{speaker\}) = 0.35; m_{d-dq}(\{hearer\}) = 0.35;$ $m_{d-dq}(\Theta) = 0.3$
	evaluation	$m_{d-eq}(\{hearer\}) = 0.35; m_{d-eq}(\Theta) = 0.65$
Obligation fulfilled	task	$m_{d-tof}(\{hearer\}) = 0.35; m_{d-tof}(\Theta) = 0.65$
	discourse	$m_{d-dof}(\{hearer\}) = 0.35; m_{d-dof}(\Theta) = 0.65$
Invalidity	action	$m_{d-ia}(\{hearer\}) = 0.7; m_{d-ia}(\Theta) = .3$
	belief	$m_{d-ib}(\{hearer\}) = 0.35; m_{d-ib}(\Theta) = 0.65$
Suboptimality		$m_{d-sub}(\{hearer\}) = 0.35; m_{d-sub}(\Theta) = 0.65$
Ambiguity	action	$m_{d-aa}(\{hearer\}) = 0.7; m_{d-aa}(\Theta) = 0.3$
	belief	$m_{d-ab}(\{hearer\}) = 0.35; m_{d-ab}(\Theta) = 0.65$

(1) the cue is actually observed, and

(2) the existing bpa incorrectly predicts the next initiative holder.

The trained bpa's for discourse cues indicate that the cues *end silence, repetitions,* and *prompts* have no effect on changing either the task or dialogue initiative index. An analysis of these cues in our corpus shows that they often occur in the user's turn and that the system often responds to them with an acknowledgment, such as *yeah* or *uh-huh.* We believe this behavior may be partially due to the role that each agent plays in the TRAINS domain, where the user is expected to make a plan and the system is expected to provide assistance in the process. As a result, the system may be more reluctant to take over the initiative when subtle hints are given, such as the discourse cues under discussion. Our results further show that *domain questions* provide an equal degree of support for a dialogue initiative shift to the hearer and for the dialogue initiative to remain with the speaker, while the remaining discourse cues provide a moderate degree of support for a task/dialogue initiative shift to the hearer.

Finally, Table IVa shows that when the speaker proposes an *ambiguous* or *suboptimal* action, the cue provides a moderate degree of support for the hearer to take over the task initiative. However, the speaker's proposal of an *invalid action* has no effect on task initiative shift. We again believe that this may be due to the agents' roles in the TRAINS domain, causing the system to leave it up to the user to

Table Va. Task Initiative Prediction Errors

Cue Type	Subtype	Shift		No-Shift	
		error	total	error	total
Invalidity	action	2	2	0	13
Suboptimality		1	1	0	0
Ambiguity	action	3	7	1	5

Table Vb. Dialogue Initiative Prediction Errors

Cue Type	Subtype	Shift		No-Shift	
		error	total	error	total
End silence		13	41	0	53
No new info	prompts	1	6	7	193
Questions	domain	13	31	0	98
	evaluation	8	28	5	7
Obligation fulfilled	discourse	12	198	1	5
Invalidity	action	5	15	0	0
	belief	6	19	0	0
Suboptimality		1	1	0	0
Ambiguity	action	6	12	0	0
	belief	3	12	0	0

propose a valid alternative to an invalid action. On the other hand, Table IVb shows that *invalidity-action* and *ambiguity-action* strongly support the hearer taking over the dialogue initiative, while the remaining analytical cues provide a moderate degree of support for the hearer to take over the dialogue initiative.

5.3. ERROR ANALYSIS AND DISCUSSION

We analyzed the cases in which the system, using the *constant-increment-with-counter* method with $\Delta = 0.35$, made erroneous predictions. Tables Va and Vb, which summarize the results of our analysis, show the task and dialogue initiative prediction errors grouped according to the cue classification in Table II. For each cue type, we grouped the errors based on whether or not a shift occurred in the actual dialogue. For instance, the first row in Table Va shows that when the cue *invalidity-action* is detected, the system failed to predict both cases where a task initiative shift occurred. On the other hand, in all thirteen cases where the cue did not result in a shift in task initiative, the system made correct predictions. Table Va also shows that when an analytical cue is detected, the system correctly predicted all but one case in which there was no shift in task initiative. However, 60 percent of the time when an analytical cue is detected, the system failed to predict a shift in task initiative.[11] Similarly, Table Vb shows that 43 percent of the time when an analytical cue at the task level is observed (*invalidity-action*, *suboptimality*, and *ambiguity-action*), the system fails to predict a shift in dialogue initiative, while 29 percent of the time when an analytical cue at the dialogue level is observed (*invalidity-belief* and *ambiguity-belief*), the system fails to predict a shift in dialogue initiative. This suggests that while including these analytical cues improves the system's performance in tracking both task and dialogue initiatives, perhaps other cues need to be identified in order to more accurately model initiative shifts under these circumstances. We leave identifying and incorporating these additional cues for future work.

Table Vb shows that when a perceptible silence is detected at the end of an utterance, when the speaker utters a prompt, or when the speaker fulfills an outstanding discourse obligation, the system is able to correctly predict the next dialogue initiative holder in the vast majority of cases.[12] However, for the cue class *questions*, when the actual initiative shift differs from the norm, i.e., speaker retaining initiative for evaluation questions and hearer taking over initiative for domain questions, the system's performance worsens. Our analysis shows that in the case of domain questions, the erroneous predictions can be grouped into two classes. The first class involves situations in which the response to the question requires more reasoning than that typically expected of a domain question, causing the hearer to take over the dialogue initiative. For instance, in the following dialogue segment, the utterance in boldface answers the question in (33). However, since this answer was not readily available to S, S takes over the dialogue initiative in (34) in order to figure out the answer to U's question.

(33)   U: *We're picking up the tanker, it needs to then go back to Elmira and have those oranges immediately processed into OJ, filling the tanker and zip that off to Avon. How long will that take?*

(34)   S: *Okay, so we get back to Corning, then we have to take the long route to Avon since the other engine is on the track going the other way, and* **that'll get us to Avon at 2pm**.

The second class involves situations in which the hearer, in addition to providing a response to the speaker's question, offers information that she believes is relevant or helpful to accomplishing the agents' task. In the following dialogue segment,

---

[11] In the case of suboptimal actions, we encounter the sparse data problem. Since there is only one instance of the cue in the set of dialogues, when the cue is present in the testing set, it is absent from the training set.

[12] The reason that the system may predict a shift when *end silence* and *prompts* are observed, even though their bpa's (Table IVb) indicate that such cues have no effect on dialogue initiative shifts, is because these cues often co-occur with other cues which affect dialogue initiative indices.

simply *'no'*, or *'no, there aren't'* is sufficient to answer U's question in (35). However, instead of merely answering the question, S provided extra information that he believes to be helpful to U in his response.

(35) *U: Do you know if there are oranges at the orange juice factory?*
(36) *S: Uh* **no**, *the only oranges are in the warehouse.*

In the case of evaluation questions, the erroneous predictions can again be grouped into two classes. The first class involves situations in which the result of the evaluation is readily available to the hearer; thus there is no need for the hearer to take over the dialogue initiative in answering the question. For instance, in utterance (39) of the following dialogue segment, U asks S to evaluate a plan for shipping the bananas. However, since the agents have just reviewed the plan in (37) and (38) and utterances prior to them, the answer to U's question is readily available; thus U does not take over the dialogue initiative to review the proposed plan as in most other evaluation questions.

(37) *U: So that would be 9am, and then if we take it by the top route that would be another 4 hours.*
(38) *S: So it gets there at 1pm.*
(39) *U: Okay, so that's a good enough plan for the bananas, right?*
(40) *S: Right.*

The second class of errors again includes situations in which extra information is provided by the hearer, similar to the case in utterances (35) and (36) where the hearer provided extra information in response to a domain question. Based on this analysis, we believe that although it is difficult to predict when an agent may decide to provide extra information in responding to a question, taking into account the cognitive load that a question places on the hearer may allow us to more accurately predict dialogue initiative shifts. Furthermore, our observation suggests that it may be desirable for the system to take into account, in addition to the existing cues, the possibility of providing additional helpful information to user questions when determining the next task/dialogue initiative holders, if such information exists.

6. Generality of the Model

In the previous section, we discussed the performance of our system cross-validated using an annotated corpus of TRAINS91 dialogues. One interesting question to ask now is: is dialogue participants' behavior in initiative shifts particular to each domain, or is it a higher-level phenomenon that describes how conversants interact with each other in general, regardless of the application domain? To answer this question, we investigated the generality of our system by training it on the TRAINS91 dialogues, and testing it on dialogues from four other corpora.

Using the set of bpa's in Tables IVa and IVb, we evaluated the system on subsets of dialogues taken from the following four corpora: the TRAINS93 dialogues (Heeman and Allen, 1995), airline reservation dialogues (SRI Transcripts, 1992), instruction-giving dialogues (Canadian Map Task Dialogues, 1996), and non-task-oriented dialogues (Switchboard Credit Card Corpus, 1992). In addition, we applied our baseline strategy which makes predictions without the use of cues to each corpus.

Table VI shows comparisons of the features of each of the five dialogue corpora and of the system's performance on these dialogues. The first row in Table 6 shows the number of turns where the *expert*[13] holds the task/dialogue initiative in each corpus, with percentages shown in parentheses in row 2. This analysis shows that the distribution of task and dialogue initiatives varies quite significantly across different corpora, with the distribution biased toward one agent in the TRAINS and maptask corpora, and split relatively evenly in the airline and switchboard dialogues. The third row in the table shows the results of applying our baseline prediction method to each corpus. The numbers shown are correct predictions in each instance, with the corresponding percentages shown in parentheses in row 4. These results indicate the difficulty of the prediction problem in each corpus that the task/dialogue initiative distribution (rows 1 and 2) fails to convey. For instance, although the dialogue initiative is distributed approximately 30/70 percent between the two agents in the TRAINS91 dialogues and 40/60 percent in the airline reservation dialogues, row 4 in the table shows that when predicting dialogue initiative holders without the use of cues, the system achieves approximately a 75 percent correct prediction rate in both domains. This indicates that although the dialogue initiative distribution ratio is different for the TRAINS91 and airline reservation domains, the frequency of dialogue initiative shifts is about the same in these two domains, namely, 25 percent of all dialogue turns. Row 5 in the table shows the prediction results using the bpa's shown in Tables IVa and IVb. The second to the last row shows the improvement in absolute percentage points between our prediction method and the baseline prediction method, while the last row shows such improvement in terms of error reduction rate. To test the statistical significance between the results obtained by the two prediction methods, for each corpus, we applied Cochran's Q test (Cochran, 1950) to the results in rows 4 and 6. The tests show that for all corpora, the differences between the two algorithms when predicting the task and dialogue initiative holders are statistically significant ($p < 0.05$ and $p < 10^{-5}$, respectively).

Based on the results of our evaluation, we make the following observations. First, Table VI illustrates the generality of our prediction mechanism. Although the system's performance varies across domains, the use of cues improves the system's accuracies in predicting the task and dialogue initiative holders in all

---

[13] The *expert* is determined as follows: in the TRAINS domain, the system; in the airline reservation domain, the travel agent; in the maptask domain, the instruction giver; and in the switchboard dialogues, the agent who holds the dialogue initiative the majority of the time.

Table VI. System Performance Across Different Application Domains

Corpus (# turns)	TRAINS91 (1042)		TRAINS93 (256)		Airline (332)		Maptask (320)		Switchboard (282)	
	task	dialogue	task	dialogue	task	dialogue	task	dialogue	task	dialogue
Expert control	41	311	37	101	194	193	320	277	N/A	166
	(3.9%)	(29.8%)	(14.4%)	(39.5%)	(58.4%)	(58.1%)	(100%)	(86.6%)		(59.9%)
No cue	1009	780	239	189	308	247	320	270	N/A	193
	(96.8%)	(74.9%)	(93.3%)	(73.8%)	(92.8%)	(74.4%)	(100%)	(84.4%)		(68.4%)
const-inc-w-count	1033	915	250	217	316	281	320	297	N/A	216
	(99.1%)	(87.8%)	(97.7%)	(84.8%)	(95.2%)	(84.6%)	(100%)	(92.8%)		(76.6%)
Absolute Improvement	2.3%	12.9%	4.4%	11.0%	2.4%	10.2%	0.0%	8.4%	N/A	8.2%
Error Reduction	71.9%	51.4%	65.7%	42.0%	33.3%	39.8%	N/A	53.8%	N/A	25.9%

cases. [14] Second, Table VI shows the specificity of the trained bpa's with respect
to application domains. When trained on the TRAINS91 dialogues, the system
performs similarly well on both the TRAINS91 and TRAINS93 corpora. [15] In terms
of improvement in percentage points (second to the last row in table), the system's
performances on the collaborative planning dialogues (TRAINS91, TRAINS93,
and airline reservation) most closely resemble one another. This suggests that the
bpa's may be somewhat sensitive to application environments since they may affect
how agents interpret cues. Third, our prediction mechanism yields better results
on task-oriented dialogues (all but the switchboard dialogues). We believe this is
because such dialogues are constrained by the goals; therefore, there are fewer
digressions and offers of unsolicited opinion, and thus fewer unsignaled initiative
shifts, as compared to the switchboard corpus.

7. Effects of Initiative Tracking on Response Generation

We argued at the beginning of this paper that in order for a dialogue system to
interact with its user in a coherent and cooperative fashion, it is necessary for
the system to be able to model initiative shifts between the participants during
the dialogues. Furthermore, we have discussed an initiative tracking model that
determines new initiative indices based on the current initiative indices and the
effects that cues observed during the current dialogue turn have on changing the
current indices. Since the current initiative indices in turn depend on the initiative
indices of the previous dialogue turn and the effects of the cues observed during
that turn, this dependency chain backtracks until we reach the default initiative
indices used at the beginning at the dialogue. Thus, the initiative indices of the
next dialogue turn are affected by three factors:

(1) *default initiative indices,*
(2) *dialogue history* (cues observed during the course of the dialogue), and
(3) *effects of observed cues.*

When incorporated into a response generation system, the initiative tracking
model can be used to determine the initiative indices for system turns, thus allowing the system to tailor its responses based on the distribution of task and
dialogue initiatives. This will then allow a generic response generation system to
alter its behavior in different application domains, such as being more active in
correcting invalid proposals and suggesting better alternatives in a collaborative
planning domain, while being passive when playing the role of the follower in an

---

[14] With the exception of task initiative holder prediction in the maptask dialogues where there is
no room for improvement. This is because in the maptask domain, the task specifies that the task
initiative remain with one agent, the instruction giver, throughout the dialogue.

[15] Both of the TRAINS corpora contain dialogues on the planning of cargo shipping, with the participants in the TRAINS93 dialogues solving more complicated problems than those in the TRAINS91
dialogues.

instruction-giving domain. In the rest of this section, we show how varying the three factors that determine the initiative indices may affect the system responses to user utterances.

7.1. DEFAULT INITIATIVE INDICES

To illustrate the effect of the default initiative indices on response generation, consider two domains: the TRAINS domain and the airline reservation domain. In the TRAINS domain, the system's task is to assist the user in devising a plan to achieve his goal. A reasonable default initiative distribution for such a task may be $m_{t-cur}(\{U\}) = 0.7$; $m_{t-cur}(\{S\}) = 0.3$, and $m_{d-cur}(\{U\}) = 0.6$; $m_{d-cur}(\{S\}) = 0.4$. On the other hand, in the airline reservation domain, the system plays a more active role in helping the user make her plan; thus a reasonable default initiative distribution for this task may be $m_{t-cur}(\{U\}) = 0.6$; $m_{t-cur}(\{S\}) = 0.4$, and $m_{d-cur}(\{U\}) = 0.6$; $m_{d-cur}(\{S\}) = 0.4$.

Given these default initial initiative indices, now consider the following dialogue segment in the TRAINS domain, where utterance (41) is the first utterance in the dialogue:

(41) U: *I need to get oranges to Avon.*

(42) S: *Okay.*

(43) U: *Move engine E2 and the boxcar from Elmira to Corning, pick up oranges and send them to Avon.*

The initiative indices for utterance (41) are those of the default initiative setting; thus we have

$$m_{t-(41)}(\{U\}) = 0.7, \quad m_{t-(41)}(\{S\}) = 0.3;$$

$$m_{d-(41)}(\{U\}) = 0.6, \quad m_{d-(41)}(\{S\}) = 0.4.$$

Since no cue is observed during utterance (41), the initiative indices for utterance (42) remain the same as that for (41). The initiative indices indicate that the system should have neither the task or the dialogue initiative in response to the user's utterance. Thus, under this particular dialogue context, it is reasonable for the system to generate an acknowledgment to the user's proposal, as in (42). Utterance (42) triggers the discourse cue *prompt*. However, our trained bpa's (Tables IVa and IVb) show that *prompts* have no effect on shifts in task or dialogue initiative; thus the initiative indices for utterance (43) remain unchanged. The user's utterance in (43) triggers the cue *ambiguity-action*, since there are two possible routes from Corning to Avon. We have the task initiative indices for utterance (43) and the bpa representing the effect of the observed cue, *ambiguity-action*, on task initiative shift (taken from Table IVa, with *hearer* instantiated as the system) as follows

$$m_{t-(43)}(\{U\}) = 0.7, \quad m_{t-(43)}(\{S\}) = 0.3;$$

$$m_{t-aa}(\{S\}) = 0.35, \quad m_{t-aa}(\Theta) = 0.65.$$

Table VIIa. Intersection Tableau for $m_{t-(43)} \oplus m_{t-aa}$

	{U} (0.7)	{S} (0.3)
{S} (0.35)	Ø (0.245)	{S} (0.105)
Θ (0.65)	{U} (0.455)	{S} (0.195)

Table VIIb. Intersection Tableau for $m_{d-(43)} \oplus m_{d-aa}$

	{U} (0.6)	{S} (0.4)
{S} (0.7)	Ø (0.42)	{S} (0.28)
Θ (0.3)	{U} (0.18)	{S} (0.12)

Furthermore, we have the dialogue initiative indices for utterance (43) and the bpa representing the effect of the observed cue on dialogue initiative shift as follows

$$m_{d-(43)}(\{U\}) = 0.6, \quad m_{d-(43)}(\{S\}) = 0.4;$$
$$m_{d-aa}(\{S\}) = 0.7, \quad m_{d-aa}(\Theta) = 0.3.$$

Tables VIIa and VIIb show the intersection tableaus for computing the new task and dialogue bpa's, respectively. Based on the intersection tableaus, the initiative indices for the next dialogue turn can be computed as follows (see Section 5.1)

$$m_{t-(44)}(\{S\}) = (0.105 + 0.195)/(1 - 0.245) = 0.4,$$
$$m_{t-(44)}(\{U\}) = 0.455/(1 - 0.245) = 0.6;$$

$$m_{d-(44)}(\{S\}) = (0.28 + 0.12)/(1 - 0.42) = 0.69,$$
$$m_{d-(44)}(\{U\}) = 0.18/(1 - 0.42) = 0.31.$$

The new initiative indices indicate that the user should have the task initiative while the system should take over the dialogue initiative in the next turn. In the case of an ambiguous proposal, such an initiative distribution may lead the system to point out the ambiguity in the proposal (thus taking over the dialogue initiative), but not actually resolve the ambiguity (thus leaving the task initiative with the user), as follows

(44) *S: Would you like to go from Corning to Avon through Dansville or Bath?*

Now consider a similar dialogue segment in the airline reservation domain, where utterance (45) is again the first utterance in the dialogue:

(45) *U: I need to go to San Antonio on Friday.*

(46) *S: Okay.*

(47) *U: I'd like to leave Newark at around 8am.*

The analysis of initiative indices for this dialogue is similar to that for the previous dialogue, where the initiative indices for utterance (47) are the same as the initial default indices

$$m_{t-(47)}(\{U\}) = 0.6, \quad m_{t-(47)}(\{S\}) = 0.4;$$

$$m_{d-(47)}(\{U\}) = 0.6, \quad m_{d-(47)}(\{S\}) = 0.4.$$

The user's utterance in (47) again triggers the cue *ambiguity-action*, since there are no direct flights from Newark to San Antonio. Thus, computing the new initiative indices based on the initiative indices for utterance (47) and the effect of the observed cue, *ambiguity-action*, we have[16]

$$m_{t-(48)}(\{S\}) = 0.51, \quad m_{t-(48)}(\{U\}) = 0.49;$$

$$m_{d-(48)}(\{S\}) = 0.69, \quad m_{d-(48)}(\{U\}) = 0.31.$$

The new initiative indices indicate that the system should take over both the task and dialogue initiatives in the next turn. Thus, instead of merely pointing out the ambiguity in the proposal and querying the user for disambiguation, as in utterance (44) in the previous example, the system may take a more active role in the planning process as follows

(48) *S: You can either connect through Houston or Dallas. The connection through Houston has a 45-minute layover and through Dallas there's a 75-minute layover. Would you like to connect through Houston?*

These two dialogue segments illustrate how the system's response generation behavior can be affected by the default initiative indices. Thus, one can select the default initiative indices to reflect the degree of task/dialogue initiative the system is expected to have for the particular application domain. As an extreme example, an appropriate bpa representing the default task initiative indices in the maptask domain is $m_{t-cur}(giver) = 1$. In this case, regardless of the observed cues, the instruction giver always has the task initiative when planning her utterances.

---

[16] The intersection tableaus are similar to those in Tables VIIa and VIIb, and will not be shown in subsequent examples.

7.2. EFFECTS OF CUES

As discussed in Section 6, although the trained bpa's performed very well across different domains, they performed better in the domain in which the bpa's were trained. This suggests that perhaps different bpa's are needed to capture the different effects that a cue may have on initiative shifts in different application domains. For example, our trained bpa's in Tables IVa and IVb show that observation of the cue *invalidity-action* in the TRAINS domain has no effect on task initiative shift ($m_{t-ia-trains}(\Theta) = 1$), but strongly suggests a shift in dialogue initiative ($m_{d-ia-trains}(\{hearer\}) = 0.7; m_{d-ia-trains}(\Theta) = 0.3$). However, in a domain where the dialogue participants play more equal roles in the planning process, such as in the airline reservation domain, more appropriate bpa's for this cue may be as follows, where observation of the cue provides a moderate amount of evidence for a shift in task initiative as well:

$$m_{t-ia-airline}(\{hearer\}) = 0.35, \quad m_{t-ia-airline}(\Theta) = 0.65;$$

$$m_{d-ia-airline}(\{hearer\}) = 0.7, \quad m_{d-ia-airline}(\Theta) = 0.3.$$

To illustrate how varying the effects of cues may affect a system's response to user utterances, consider the scenario in which the current initiative indices are as follows

$$m_{t-cur}(\{U\}) = 0.55, \quad m_{t-cur}(\{S\}) = 0.45;$$

$$m_{d-cur}(\{U\}) = 0.6, \quad m_{d-cur}(\{S\}) = 0.4,$$

and the user says

(49) *S: We'll make OJ at Elmira, and ship it to Avon through Corning and Dansville.*

Utterance (49) triggers the cue *invalidity-action* since the track through Dansville is unavailable. Based on the current initiative indices and the effect of *invalidity-action* in the TRAINS domain (where *hearer* is instantiated as the system) shown above, the initiative indices for the next dialogue turn is as follows

$$m_{t-(50)}(\{S\}) = 0.45, \quad m_{t-(50)}(\{U\}) = 0.55;$$

$$m_{d-(50)}(\{S\}) = 0.69, \quad m_{d-(50)}(\{U\}) = 0.31,$$

leading the system to take over the dialogue initiative but not the task initiative in its response to the user's proposal. In the case of an invalid proposal, this may lead to a response that points out the invalidity of the proposal but does not suggest a valid alternative, as follows:

(50) *S: We can't go by Dansville because we've got Engine 1 going on that track.*

[80]

Now consider a similar dialogue in the airline reservation domain where the user proposes:

(51) U: *I want to book a ticket from Newark to Tokyo through San Francisco on March 1.*

Again, this utterance triggers the cue *invalidity-action*, since the system believes that all flights from San Francisco to Tokyo are sold out for that date. Using the same initiative distribution for the current utterance as that for utterance (49), and the bpa's representing the effect of *invalidity-action* in the airline reservation domain ($m_{t-ia-airline}$ and $m_{d-ia-airline}$), we have the following initiative distribution for the next dialogue turn:

$$m_{t-(52)}(\{S\}) = 0.56, \quad m_{t-(52)}(\{U\}) = 0.44,$$
$$m_{d-(52)}(\{S\}) = 0.69, \quad m_{d-(52)}(\{U\}) = 0.31.$$

This will lead the system to take over both the task and dialogue initiatives when responding to the user's utterance as follows:

(52) S: *All flights from San Francisco to Tokyo are full, but I do show availability from L.A. Would you like to do that instead?*

Undoubtedly, the system could have used the bpa's trained for the TRAINS domain and provided a response similar to that in utterance (50), such as '*You can't go by San Francisco because all flights from San Francisco to Tokyo are sold out.*' It is then up to the user to suggest an alternative city for making a connection. Although these two alternative system responses may eventually lead to the same plan for the user, we believe that the response in utterance (52) is more helpful and perhaps more efficient (if the user in fact accepts the system's proposal) in the airline reservation domain. This effect is achieved in our model by using opa's designed specifically for the application domain.[17] As another example, in the maptask domain, the effect of the cue *request-take over task* can be reduced to nil to reflect the fact that the instruction follower cannot ever take over the task initiative.

7.3. DIALOGUE HISTORY

The effect of dialogue history on initiative shift, and hence response generation, can best be illustrated with examples of dialogue segments from the airline reservation

---

[17] In this example, we hypothesized what we believe to be appropriate bpa's for the airline reservation domain. In the actual development of a system, in order to tailor effects of bpa's to specific domains, we need to annotate a corpus in the new domain and perform the training process described earlier in this paper to obtain the new bpa's.

domain where we hypothesize the cue *invalidity-action* to provide a moderate degree of support for a shift in task initiative, as in the previous section. Suppose that in the preceding dialogue the user has stated her goal to travel from Newark to San Francisco then to Seattle, that the current initiative indices are as follows,

$$m_{t-cur}(\{U\}) = 0.7, \quad m_{t-cur}(\{S\}) = 0.3,$$
$$m_{d-cur}(\{U\}) = 0.7, \quad m_{d-cur}(\{S\}) = 0.3,$$

and the user says

(53) *U: For the Newark to San Francisco leg, I would like United 805 leaving Thursday morning at 9am.*

This utterance triggers the cue *invalidity-action* since the system believes that United 805 is sold out. The new initiative indices are

$$m_{t-(54)}(\{S\}) = 0.4, \quad m_{t-(54)}(\{U\}) = 0.6.$$
$$m_{d-(54)}(\{S\}) = 0.59, \quad m_{d-(54)}(\{U\}) = 0.41.$$

suggesting a response in which the system will take over the dialogue initiative but not the task initiative, such as the following:

(54) *S: I'm showing that United 805 is sold out.*

Now suppose that the user continues with:

(55) *U: In that case, I'll go with Continental flight 51, leaving at 9:20am.*

Since utterance (54) triggers the cue *obligation fulfilled-dialogue* and utterance (55) again triggers the cue *invalidity-action*, the initiative indices for the next dialogue turn will be

$$m_{t-(56)}(\{S\}) = 0.51, \quad m_{t-(56)}(\{U\}) = 0.49;$$
$$m_{d-(56)}(\{S\}) = 0.75, \quad m_{d-(56)}(\{U\}) = 0.25.$$

Thus, instead of merely pointing out the invalidity of the proposal, as in utterance (54), the system will take over both the task and dialogue initiatives and suggest a valid alternative, such as in the following:

(56) *S: That flight is full as well. I'm showing that American Airlines flight 104 is open, and it leaves Newark at 9:30am. Will that be ok?*

The extended dialogue in this section illustrates the effect of dialogue history on response generation, i.e., how the cumulative effect of previous cues affects system behavior. Notice that although in both utterances (53) and (55), the cue *invalidity-action* is observed, the system responded to them in different manners, namely, by taking over merely the dialogue initiative in response to the former, while taking over both the task and dialogue initiatives in the latter. This behavior reflects our expectation that in a collaborative planning process, the system may not jump in and take over the planning process at the user's first mistake, but if the system senses that the user is at a lost, e.g., making several mistakes in a row, a cooperative system will offer help by proposing a valid plan.

7.4. DISCUSSION

In the previous sections, we showed how initiative shifts, and hence the system's response generation behavior, may be affected by the default initiative indices, the effects of observed cues, and the dialogue history. We have discussed how the default initiative indices and the effects of observed cues can be affected by the application domain and the role the system plays in the domain. Furthermore, it is possible that, during its interactions with users, the system may modify its default initiative indices to more specific indices tailored to specific users, as well as adapt the bpa's that represent the effects of observed cues based on user behavior. Such adaptation will then allow the system to tailor its model of initiative tracking to individual users in future interactions. Thus, our model of initiative tracking allows the system to tailor its responses to user utterances based on the application domain, the system's role in the domain, user characteristics, as well as prior system-user interaction in the dialogue history.

8. Future Work

We are currently investigating other potential cues that may provide additional information for signaling initiative shifts. To this end, we analyzed the coverage of our existing cues. Our analysis shows that the cues shown in Table II covered 92 percent of the shifts in dialogue initiative in our experiment, leaving 47 unsignaled shifts which can be grouped as follows. First, there are 22 cases in which the hearer, at the end of a dialogue turn, takes over the initiative to provide unsolicited but helpful information. Second, there are 11 cases of interruptions, 7 in which the hearer completes the speaker's utterance and 4 in which the hearer interrupts the speaker and initiates a new topic. Finally, there are 14 cases in which a shift in initiative occurred as a result of a return from a previously unsignaled shift in initiative. We are currently investigating potential cues that may shed some light on the cause of such unsignaled shifts. In particular, we are looking into how prosodic information, such as intonational patterns and final syllable lengthening, may provide information on initiative shifts that our current cues, based solely on linguistic and domain knowledge, fail to convey.

At present, the only evaluation that we have performed on our initiative tracking model is an assessment of how well it can predict the task/dialogue initiative holders in naturally-occurring collaborative dialogues. However, we have not been able to evaluate the effect of this initiative model on the response generation process and the quality of the resultant dialogues. In the longer term, we plan to incorporate this initiative tracking model into the speech-to-speech transaction-based dialogue system we are currently developing. The understanding component of this dialogue system will attempt to automatically identify cues from the user's utterances in order for the system to determine the initiative indices for the next dialogue turn. The initiative indices will then be used by the response generation component to determine an appropriate response to the user's utterance. This dialogue system will then serve as a testbed for varying the system's mixed-initiative behavior in dialogue interaction and for evaluating the cooperativeness and coherence of the dialogues that ensue.

9. Conclusions

In this paper, we presented a model for tracking shifts in initiative between dialogue participants in mixed-initiative dialogue interactions. We showed why it is necessary to distinguish between task and dialogue initiatives, and discussed how this distinction allows us to model phenomena in collaborative dialogues that existing frameworks are unable to explain. We identified eight types of cues that affect shifts in initiative in dialogues, and showed how our evidential model for tracking initiative is able to predict task/dialogue initiative shifts based on the distribution of the current task/dialogue initiative, as well as the effects that observed cues have on changing the current distribution. Our experiments show that by utilizing the *constant-increment-with-counter* adjustment method in determining the basic probability assignments for each cue, the system can correctly predict the task and dialogue initiative holders in 99.1 percent and 87.8 percent of the dialogue turns, respectively, in the TRAINS91 corpus, compared to 96.8 percent and 74.9 percent without the use of cues. The differences between these results are shown to be statistically significant using Cochran's Q test. In addition, we demonstrated the generality of our model by applying it to dialogues in other collaborative dialogue corpora. The results indicate that although the basic probability assignments may be sensitive to application environments, the use of cues in the prediction process consistently provides substantial improvement in the system's performance. Finally, we showed how the use of an initiative tracking model in a dialogue system will allow the system to tailor its responses to user utterances under different circumstances, based on the application domain, system's role in the domain, dialogue history, and particular user characteristics.

Acknowledgments

We would like to thank Lyn Walker, Diane Litman, Susan Haller, Bob Carpenter, Christer Samuelsson, and the three anonymous reviewers for their comments on earlier drafts of this paper, Bob Carpenter and Christer Samuelsson for participating in the coding reliability test, Jan van Santan and Lyn Walker for discussions on statistical testing methods, as well as Jim Hieronymus and Chilin Shih for discussions on prosody.

References

Allen, J.: 1991, 'Discourse Structure in the TRAINS Project'. In: *Darpa Speech and Natural Language Workshop*. pp. 325–330.

Canadian Map Task Dialogues: 1996, 'Transcripts of DCIEM Sleep Deprivation Study, conducted by Defense and Civil Institute of Environmental Medicine, Canada, and Human Communication Research Centre, University of Edinburgh and University of Glasgow, UK'. Distributed by HCRC and LDC.

Carletta, J.: 1996, 'Assessing Agreement on Classification Tasks: The Kappa Statistic'. *Computational Linguistics* **22**, 249–254.

Chu-Carroll, J. and M. K. Brown: 1997a, 'Initiative in Collaborative Interactions — Its Cues and Effects'. In: *Working Notes of the AAAI-97 Spring Symposium on Computational Models for Mixed Initiative Interaction*. pp. 16–22. Also available as AAAI TR SS-97-04.

Chu-Carroll, J. and M. K. Brown: 1997b, 'Tracking Initiative in Collaborative Dialogue Interactions'. In: *Proceedings of the 35th Annual Meeting of the Association for Computational Linguistics*. pp. 262–270.

Chu-Carroll, J. and S. Carberry: 1994, 'A Plan-Based Model for Response Generation in Collaborative Task-Oriented Dialogues'. In: *Proceedings of the Twelfth National Conference on Artificial Intelligence*. pp. 799–805.

Chu-Carroll, J. and S. Carberry: 1995, 'Response Generation in Collaborative Negotiation'. In: *Proceedings of the 33rd Annual Meeting of the Association for Computational Linguistics*. pp. 136–143.

Cochran, W. G.: 1950, 'The Comparison of Percentages in Matched Samples'. *Biometrika* **37**, 256–266.

Cohen, R., C. Allaby, C. Cumbaa, M. Fitzgerald, K. Ho, B. Hui, C. Latulipe, F. Lu, N. Moussa, D. Pooley, A. Qian, and S. Siddiqi: 1998, 'What is Initiative?'. *In this issue*, pp. 171–214.

Gordon, J. and E. H. Shortliffe: 1984, 'The Dempster-Shafer Theory of Evidence'. In: B. Buchanan and E. Shortliffe (eds.): *Rule-Based Expert Systems: The MYCIN Experiments of the Stanford Heuristic Programming Project*. Addison-Wesley, Chapt. 13, pp. 272–292.

Gross, D., J. F. Allen, and D. R. Traum: 1993, 'The TRAINS 91 Dialogues'. Technical Report TN92-1, Department of Computer Science, University of Rochester.

Grosz, B. and J. Hirschberg: 1992, 'Some Intonational Characteristics of Discourse Structure'. In: *Proceedings of the International Conference on Spoken Language Processing*. pp. 429–432.

Grove, W. M., N. C. Andreasen, P. McDonald-Scott, M. B. Keller, and R. W. Shapiro: 1981, 'Reliability Studies of Psychiatric Diagnosis'. *Archives of General Psychiatry* **38**, 408–413.

Guinn, C. I.: 1996, 'An Analysis of Initiative Selection in Collaborative Task-Oriented Discourse'. In: *Proceedings of the 34th Annual Meeting of the Association for Computational Linguistics*. pp. 278–285.

Guinn, C. I.: 1998, 'Principles of Mixed-Initiative Human-Computer Collaborative Discourse'. *In this issue*, pp. 255–314.

Heeman, P. A. and J. F. Allen: 1995, 'The TRAINS 93 Dialogues'. Technical Report TN94-2, Department of Computer Science, University of Rochester.

Jordan, P. W. and B. Di Eugenio: 1997, 'Control and Initiative in Collaborative Problem Solving Dialogues'. In: *Working Notes of the AAAI-97 Spring Symposium on Computational Models for Mixed Initiative Interaction*. pp. 81–84. Also available as AAAI TR SS-97-04.

Kitano, H. and C. Van Ess-Dykema: 1991, 'Toward a Plan-Based Understanding Model for Mixed-Initiative Dialogues'. In: *Proceedings of the 29th Annual Meeting of the Association for Computational Linguistics*. pp. 25–32.

Lambert, L. and S. Carberry: 1991, 'A Tripartite Plan-based Model of Dialogue'. In: *Proceedings of the 29th Annual Meeting of the Association for Computational Linguistics*. pp. 47–54.

Lester, J. C., B. A. Stone, and G. D. Stelling: 1999, 'Lifelike Pedagogical Agents for Mixed-Initiative Problem Solving in Constructivist Learning Environments'. *User Modeling and User-Adapted Interaction* 9(1–2).

Litman, D. and J. Allen: 1987, 'A Plan Recognition Model for Subdialogues in Conversation'. *Cognitive Science* 11, 163–200.

Novick, D. G.: 1988, 'Control of Mixed-Initiative Discourse Through Meta-Locutionary Acts: A Computational Model'. Ph.D. thesis, University of Oregon.

Novick, D. G. and S. Sutton: 1997, 'What is Mixed-Initiative Interaction?'. In: *Working Notes of the AAAI-97 Spring Symposium on Computational Models for Mixed Initiative Interaction*. pp. 114–116. Also available as AAAI TR SS-97-04.

Passonneau, R. J. and D. J. Litman: 1993, 'Intention-Based Segmentation: Human Reliability and Correlation with Linguistic Cues'. In: *Proceedings of the 31st Annual Meeting of the Association for Computational Linguistics*. pp. 148–155.

Pearl, J.: 1990, 'Bayesian and Belief-Fuctions Formalisms for Evidential Reasoning: A Conceptual Analysis'. In: G. Shafer and J. Pearl (eds.): *Readings in Uncertain Reasoning*. Morgan Kaufmann, pp. 540–574.

Pollack, M. E.: 1990, 'Plans as Complex Mental Attitudes'. In: P. R. Cohen, J. Morgan, and M. E. Pollack (eds.): *Intentions in Communication*. MIT Press, pp. 77–104.

Ramshaw, L. A.: 1991, 'A Three-Level Model for Plan Exploration'. In: *Proceedings of the 29th Annual Meeting of the Association for Computational Linguistics*. pp. 36–46.

Rich, C. and C. L. Sidner: 1998, 'COLLAGEN: A Collaboration Manager for Software Interface Agents'. *In this issue*.

Shafer, G.: 1976, *A Mathematical Theory of Evidence*. Princeton University Press.

Siegel, S. and N. J. Castellan, Jr.: 1988, *Nonparametric Statistics for the Behavioral Sciences*. McGraw Hill.

Smith, R. W. and D. R. Hipp: 1994, *Spoken Natural Language Dialog Systems — A Practical Approach*. Oxford University Press.

SRI Transcripts: 1992, 'Transcripts derived from audiotape conversations made at SRI International, Menlo Park, CA'. Prepared by Jacqueline Kowtko under the direction of Patti Price.

Swerts, M.: 1997, 'Prosodic Features at Discourse Boundaries of Different Strength'. *Journal of the Acoustic Society of America* 101(1), 514–521.

Switchboard Credit Card Corpus: 1992, 'Transcripts of telephone conversations on the topic of credit card use, collected at Texas Instruments'. Produced by NIST, available through LDC.

van Beek, P. G.: 1987, 'A model for generating better explanations'. In: *Proceedings of the 25th Annual Meeting of the Association for Computational Linguistics*. Stanford, CA, pp. 215–220.

Walker, M. and S. Whittaker: 1990, 'Mixed Initiative in Dialogue: An Investigation into Discourse Segmentation'. In: *Proceedings of the 28th Annual Meeting of the Association for Computational Linguistics*. pp. 70–78.

Walker, M. A.: 1992, 'Redundancy in Collaborative Dialogue'. In: *Proceedings of the 15th International Conference on Computational Linguistics.* pp. 345–351.

Whittaker, S. and P. Stenton: 1988, 'Cues and Control in Expert-Client Dialogues'. In: *Proceedings of the 26th Annual Meeting of the Association for Computational Linguistics.* pp. 123–130.

Vitae

Jennifer Chu-Carroll

Dr. Jennifer Chu-Carroll is a Member of Technical Staff in the Dialogue Systems Research Department at Bell Laboratories, Lucent Technologies. She received her M. Math degree in Computer Science from the University of Waterloo and her Ph.D. degree in Computer and Information Sciences from the University of Delaware. Her research interests lie in the areas of natural language processing, spoken language dialogue systems, and user modeling.

Michael K. Brown

Dr. Brown is a Member of Technical Staff at Bell Labs and Senior Member of the IEEE. He received his MSEE from the University of Michigan, producing the University's first Master's Thesis, working on control systems for ink jet printing. His PhD degree also came from the University of Michigan, Ann Arbor, working on Handwriting Recognition. Dr. Brown has worked extensively in speech understanding, robotics, and machine intelligence. He has over 50 publications and more than a dozen patents.

User Modeling and User-Adapted Interaction **8**: 255–314, 1998.
© 1998 *Kluwer Academic Publishers.*   255

An Analysis of Initiative Selection in Collaborative Task-Oriented Discourse

CURRY I. GUINN
Research Triangle Institute

(Received 5 November 1997; accepted in revised form 13 April 1998)

Abstract. In this paper we propose a number of principles and conjectures for mixed-initiative collaborative dialogs. We explore some methodologies for managing initiative between conversational participants. We mathematically analyze specific initiative-changing mechanisms based on a probabilistic knowledge base and user model. We look at the role of negotiation in managing initiative and quantify how the negotiation process is useful toward modifying user models. Some experimental results using computer–computer simulations are presented along with some discussion of how such studies are useful toward building human–computer systems.

Key words: Dialog, mixed-initiative, collaboration, dialog initiative, task initiative, negotiation, computer–computer dialogs.

1. Introduction

In Section 1 we propose a number of principles and conjectures for mixed-initiative collaborative dialogs. In Section 2 we explore some methodologies for managing initiative between conversational participants. In Section 3 we examine the role of negotiation in managing initiative and quantify how the negotiation process is useful toward modifying user models. Some experimental results using computer–computer simulations are presented in Section 4 along with some discussion of how such studies are useful toward building human–computer systems.

2. Principles of Mixed-Initiative Dialog

Below we list some principles (and one conjecture) concerning mixed-initiative collaborative dialogs:

Principle 1.1 (Collaboration). Collaboration is an extension of single agent problem-solving.

Principle 1.2 (Impenetrability). Agents' minds are impenetrable. Other agents can only have indirect knowledge of an agent's knowledge and goals.

Principle 1.3 (Dialog as by-product). Dialog behaviors are by-products of collaborative problem-solving.

Principle 1.4 (Inherent Conflict). Conflict is inherent in collaboration.

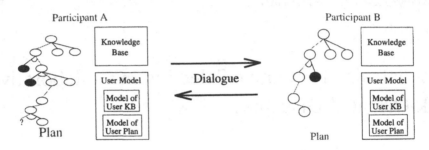

Figure 1. A Model of Collaboration.

Principle 1.5 (Mutual Goals). The establishment of mutual goals is a primary initiator of dialog.

Principle 1.6 (Task Initiative). For each mutual goal, the dialog participants must determine which participant will have task initiative over that goal.

Principle 1.7 (Locality of Initiative). Task initiative is not global. Task initiative is assigned to each mutual goal and, during a dialog, is locally determined by the current active mutual goal.

Principle 1.8 (Negotiation). Negotiation (argumentation) is a battle for task initiative.

Conjecture 1.1 (Initiative Equivalence). Whoever has task initiative over the current mutual goal also has the dialog initiative.

2.1. COLLABORATION IS AN EXTENSION OF SINGLE-AGENT PROBLEM-SOLVING

The agents in human–human collaboration are individuals. Each participant is a separate entity. The mental structures and mechanisms of one participant are not directly accessible to the other. During collaboration the two participants satisfy goals and share this information by some mean of communication. We say effective collaboration takes places when each participant depends on the other in solving a common goal or in solving a goal more efficiently. It is the *synergistic* effect of the two problem-solvers working together that makes the collaboration beneficial for both parties (Calistri-Yeh, 1993). An overview of our collaborative model is presented in Figure 1. Notice that each participant has a private plan, knowledge base (KB), and user model. To collaborate there also must be some dialog between the two participants. We discuss each of these components below.

2.1.1. *Planning and Problem-Solving*

The problem-solvers in our model use top-down planning. Each participant solves a goal by (1) seeing whether the goal is trivially true, i.e. it is already known to be true or (2) decomposing the goal into subgoals and solving these subgoals. This strategy is similar to many problem-solvers, automated theorem proving, planning

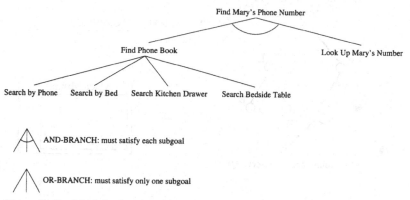

Figure 2. Goal Satisfaction through Decomposition: An Example.

systems and logic programming languages (Bledsoe, 1977; Clocksin & Mellish, 1987; Fikes & Nilsson, 1971; Korf, 1987; Newell & Simon, 1972; Nilsson, 1971; Sacerdoti, 1977; Wilensky, 1983; Wos et al., 1984). Each participant searches for the solution of a goal in its own private data structure. We call this data structure a plan tree or problem-solving tree.

2.1.2. *Knowledge Base*

Knowing which goals are trivially true and how to decompose goals into subgoals requires knowledge. We will call the collection of trivially true goals and the rules that tell how to decompose goals into subgoals the *knowledge base*. Each participant has a private knowledge base.

2.2. IMPENETRABILITY

The only knowledge one participant has of the other is indirect. A participant may have a set of beliefs about the other. We will call the set of beliefs about what knowledge and abilities the other participant has a *user model*. The information in the user model may be acquired in many ways: stereotypes, previous contact with the other participant, or the problem-solver may be given a set of facts about the other participant. Furthermore, we expect the user model to be dynamic. During a problem-solving session, information can be learned about the knowledge or capabilities of the other participant.

In addition to modeling the knowledge its collaborator has, each participant also must model the current plan of the other participant. Without knowing the current intentions of the other participant, a problem-solver will not be able to respond appropriately to goal requests, announcements and other dialog behaviors of the other participant.

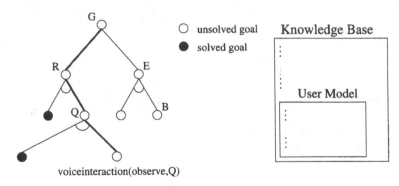

C: Is Q true?

U: Yes.

Figure 3. How Dialog Results from an Application of the Missing Axiom Theory.

2.3. DIALOG AS BY-PRODUCT

In a non-collaborative environment, a problem-solver has several options in trying to satisfy a goal. Perhaps the goal is already achieved. The problem-solver can check the state of the world by looking at its internal representation of the world. If the goal is already believed to be true, then the problem-solver is done. But what if the goal is not known to be true? In this case, a common approach is to break the goal down into subgoals and satisfy those subgoals. For instance, suppose John wants to know the phone number of Mary. He may already know it (off the top of his head) in which case he is done. If he doesn't know it, he may have a rule that says 'To find someone's number, get the phone book and look it up.' John breaks down (or *decomposes*) the goal of knowing Mary's telephone number into finding the phone book and looking up her number. John may have to break down the goal of finding the phone book into 'look by the phone or look by the bed or look in the kitchen drawer or look on the nightstand.' Potentially, these subgoals may break down into further subgoals. An illustration of the problem-solving tree for this task is given in Figure 2.

2.3.1. *The Missing Axiom Theory*

The basic operations of this top-down manner of problem-solving are (1) check to see whether the goal is already satisfied and (2) decompose the goal into subgoals and solve those subgoals. Biermann et al. point out that in a collaborative environment the problem-solvers have another option: ask the other collaborators (Biermann et al., 1993). Smith proposes that the role of language in a problem-solving environment is to supply 'missing axioms' (Smith, 1992). Smith's view is that problem-solving involves the satisfaction of axioms. When a problem-solver cannot satisfy an axiom trivially by looking it up in its knowledge base and the problem-solver cannot decompose the goal into subgoals, it has the option of requesting that the other participant satisfy that axiom. However, the problem-solver will only exercise that option if it believes the other participant is capable of satisfying that axiom. The problem-solver maintains a model of the other participant to determine what is appropriate to request. How this process works is illustrated in Figure 3. A participant **C** is trying to solve goal G. G can be solved by solving either goal R or E. The participant **C** tries to prove goal R. The subgoal R can be satisfied if both P and Q are satisfied. Participant **C** solves goal P (by looking in its knowledge base) and then tries to solve Q. Participant **C** cannot solve Q trivially or by decomposition. Therefore, **C** invokes the Missing Axiom Theory that states that if Q is something that can be asked, then ask the other participant to satisfy Q. Thus **C** looks in its user model to determine whether Q is appropriate to ask. It is appropriate, therefore **C** asks for Q to be satisfied.

The Missing Axiom Theory helps address some of the features and drawbacks of natural language communication mentioned earlier. Similar approaches to dialog have been used in other AI systems. For example, expert systems have similar rule sets and similar mechanisms to invoke user interactions (Shortliffe, 1976).

- Dialogs generated from the Missing Axiom Theory will naturally reflect the underlying task structure. This satisfies the observation made by Grosz that the structure of task-oriented dialogs mirror the structure of the task plan (Grosz, 1978). Thus these dialogs will maintain coherence.
- The focus of the utterances will always be limited to what goal needs to be satisfied next in order to solve the overall goal.
- The structure of the task structure helps provide expectations for the listener. Thus some of the computational difficulty of voice natural language processing will be reduced by restricting the space of possible utterances. Expectations also can help to do error correction if some data has been lost in the voice channel (Erman et al., 1980; Fink & Biermann, 1986; Hipp, 1992; Mudler & Paulus, 1988; Smith, 1991; Smith & Hipp, 1995; Young et al., 1989).
- Utterances are only issued 'as needed.' An utterance is issued only after other problem-solving methods have failed. Thus the Missing Axiom Theory makes use of the fact that *internal* problem-solving mechanisms tend to be much faster than using the communication channel to solve goals.

2.3.2. *Augmentation of Traditional Top-down Problem-Solving*

Traditional top-down problem-solving has the following steps:

1. Is goal trivially true? If so, done.
2. Otherwise, decompose goal into subgoals. Solve subgoals.

3. Backtrack, if necessary. Backtracking involves choosing different decompositions if available or choosing different trivial solutions if available.

The model of collaboration presented here uses the Missing Axiom Theory as a
building block. Each problem-solver will be using a modification of the traditional
top-down problem-solver. This augmented algorithm will have the following steps:

1. Is goal trivially true? If so, done.
2. Else if decomposable, decompose goal into subgoals. Solve subgoals.
3. Else potentially ask collaborators to solve goal.
4. Else backtrack.
5. In addition, provide mechanisms for answering other's queries.

2.4. CONFLICT IS INHERENT IN COLLABORATION

The terms *collaboration* and *conflict* do not seem to go together. Collaboration
involves agents working together, being cooperative. However, even when agents
want to work together, there can be conflict. Even in a cooperative environment,
participants may need to share resources. Two carpenters working together may
both require a drill for the tasks they are doing. Or one carpenter may need help carrying a board. If the other carpenter is concurrently erecting a wall, that carpenter
must interrupt his or her work to help. Thus there is a conflict of task processing
effort.

DEFINITION 1.1 (Conflict over Computational Effort).[1] A conflict over computational effort occurs when

1. Participant A and Participant B have a common goal G.
2. Participant A is exploring a decomposition of G, b_A.
3. Participant B is exploring a different decomposition of G, b_B.
4. Participant A requires Participant B's assistance in solving some goal SG
   which is a subgoal of branch b_A and not a subgoal of branch b_B.

Agents using the Missing Axiom Theory to generate requests can easily generate
conflicts over computational effort as illustrated in Figure 4. In this figure, Participant 1 has chosen to solve subgoal R to solve goal G. Meanwhile, Participant 2
has chosen to solve subgoal E to solve goal G. When Participant 1 ask Participant 2
to solve goal Q, Participant 2 is concurrently trying to solve goal B. This introduces
a dilemma for Participant 2. Participant 2 could abandon its current plan and help
Participant 1. However, if Participant 2 is successful in proving goal B, then it will
have proven goal E and thus the top goal G. Thus it may be inefficient to abandon

---

[1] The terminology *conflict over computational effort* is borrowed from Conry and Meyer who
categorize three kinds of conflict in distributed problem-solving systems: conflict over resource
control, conflict over computational effort, and conflict over locus of problem-solving responsibility
(Conry & Meyer, 1993).

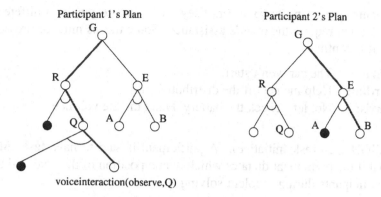

Participant 1: Is Q true?

What should Participant 2 do?

Figure 4. The Missing Axiom Theory Generates Conflicts over Processing Resources.

its current plan to help Participant 1. However, if Participant 1 is close to proving *G*, then it would be efficient for Participant 2 to help. In this example, we see a conflict over processing resources. Each participant has limited resources. For efficiency a participant should only devote its resources to the plan most likely to succeed. Because each participant may have different knowledge about the world, they may differ on which plan to take. Conflict is inevitable when collaborators have limited resources.

2.5. ESTABLISHMENT OF MUTUAL GOALS

Since conflicts are inevitable in collaboration, effective methods for resolving conflict must be explored. There are two goals of conflict resolution: avoidance of deadlock and efficient allocation of resources. Fundamentally, *conflict resolution must resolve conflicts*. If there is more than one concurrent demand on a resource, one demand must succeed in obtaining that resource. Otherwise, neither participant will be able to continue. Furthermore, resources should be allocated so that the collaborative problem-solving is more efficient. In this paper we will explore the usage of **dialog initiative** and **negotiation** in conflict management.

2.6. TASK INITIATIVE

Conflicts can arise in a collaborative environment when each participant believes it should control the decomposition of a goal. Even though both participants may be trying to solve the same goal, they may choose different ways of solving that goal. If there is a conflict because the participants have chosen different branches or decompositions of a goal, then one participant must be given control of that goal's decomposition in order to resolve the conflict. In the following example, the two mechanics are trying to fix a car. They each want to pursue a different path to fix the car, but require the other's assistance. Some means must be provided for resolving this conflict.

Chris: The car won't start.
Jordan: Help me get off the distributor cap.
Chris: No, let's check the battery. Hand me the voltmeter.

DEFINITION 1.2 (Task Initiative). A participant is said to have **task initiative** over a goal if the participant dictates which decomposition of the goal will be used by both participants during problem-solving.

DEFINITION 1.3 (Dialog Mode). **Dialog mode** is the mechanism by which a participant determines the extent of task initiative each participant will have in the solving of a goal.

Ideally, dialog mode mechanisms try to improve efficiency and decrease conflicts before they occur by *varying initiative* between participants. Ideally, the participant best able to guide a goal's solution should be given the task initiative. In the immediately preceding example, both participants appear to have decided to take task initiative in determining the origin of the car's problems. If Chris had instead decided that Jordan should have task initiative, then the following dialog might have resulted:

Chris: The car won't start.
Jordan: Help me get off the distributor cap.
Chris: Ok. We're going to need a screwdriver.

2.7. LOCALITY OF INITIATIVE

Notice that initiative is attached to each goal. During problem-solving, initiative may change back and forth between participants depending on which goals the two participants are working on. This switching of initiative between participants has been called **mixed initiative** by Brown et al. (Brown et al., 1973) and Clancey (Clancey, 1979). Smith introduces the notion that there are levels or degrees of initiative (Smith, 1991). Smith's level of initiative is a measure of how assertive a participant is in defining the conversational direction. In Directive Mode, the participant does not allow its collaborator to change the current task. In Suggestive Mode, the participant may suggest an alternative path does not force its collaborator to take this path. In Passive Mode, the participant allows its collaborator to define which path to take. Smith calls this **variable initiative**. Cohen et al also propose that initiative is not binary but has levels or *strengths* (Cohen et al., 1998). We provide a further dimension to the concept of *variable initiative*:

DEFINITION 1.4 (Variable Initiative). *Variable initiative is the ability of parti-*

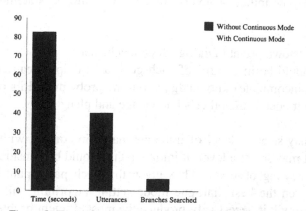

Figure 5. Experimental Evidence of the Benefits of Continuous Mode Changing.

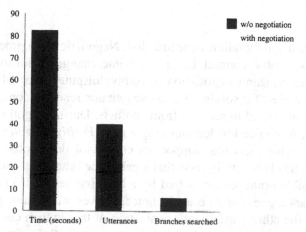

Figure 6. Experimental Evidence of the Benefits of Negotiation.

Mechanisms for determining who should have task initiative for each goal can be simple or complicated. In Section 3 we will explore various mode setting strategies for two participants. An optimal mode setting strategy (Continuous Mode) will be proposed and evaluated. In Section 5 the results of computer-computer problem-solving sessions will be presented. An empirical comparison will be made between a sophisticated mode setting strategy and a naive mode setting strategy. A summary of these empirical studies is presented in Figures 5 and 6. The benefits of good mode setting strategies in improving efficiency can be dramatic as illustrated in Figure 5. These empirical studies rely on computer simulations of dialog and look at the effect on various strategies on efficiency measures of number of utterances, time of dialogue, and number of paths searched in the problem-solving.

However, regardless of how initiative levels are set, the following statements will be true:

- Each participant has its own private Dialog Mode mechanism.
- In evaluating who should be in control of each goal, a participant can only use its own (perhaps incomplete) knowledge about the problem and its own (perhaps incomplete) model of the other's knowledge and plan.[2]

Therefore, a participant may select a level of initiative that is in conflict with its collaborator. A participant may select a level of initiative that would be considered in appropriate to an all-knowing observer. Thus given that each participant has incomplete information, even the best dialogue mode setting algorithm will not resolve all conflicts and nor will it necessarily produce the most efficient problem-solving. Alternative methods of conflict resolution will be necessary to overcome the insufficiencies of Dialog Mode.

2.8. NEGOTIATION

A common feature of human collaboration is negotiation. Negotiation is a process by which problem-solvers resolve conflict through the interchange of information.[3] Our research focuses on using negotiation to resolve disputes over which decomposition or branch to select for solving a goal. Negotiation resolves conflicts after they occur. Negotiation is used to recover from conflicts. During negotiation each participant argues for its choice for decomposing a goal. *Positive negotiation* involves each participant giving facts that support its choice for decomposing a goal. *Negative negotiation* involves giving facts that weaken the branch its collaborator wants to take. Possible branches are sorted by a best-first search heuristic function. When a participant argues for its branch choice, it gives information that will (optimistically) raise the other participant's evaluation of that branch choice. During negative negotiation, a participant gives information that will devalue the evaluation of the other participant's chosen branch. The winner of the negotiation is the participant whose chosen branch is ranked highest after the negotiations. If the heuristic evaluations are effective, the branch of the winner of the negotiation should be more likely to succeed than the loser's branch. Therefore, negotiation should result in more efficient problem-solving. In the following example, the

---

[2] Explicit in this statement in the problem of plan recognition. In the model presented in this paper, faulty plan recognition will cause participants to believe there exist conflicts when there are none and (perhaps more detrimentally) to believe that a participant is following the same line of reasoning when in fact it is not. Within this framework there are several mechanisms that might be proposed to resolve these plan recognition problems (Guinn, 1994).

[3] This paper focuses on negotiation that is used to resolve conflicts. However, there is also a more *benign negotiation* where participants believe their collaborators have valuable information which they wish to elicit. This type of negotiation occurs during 'brain-storming' sessions. When an agent might elicit such negotiation in the absence of conflict is not explored in this paper.

two mechanics disagree on how to proceed in repairing a car. Chris gives a fact that lends evidence to the battery being the problem (positive negotiation). Jordan then gives a fact that reduces the likelihood of the battery's failure (negative negotiation).

[Two people trying to find out why a car won't start]
Jordan: Help me get the distributor cap off so we can check the spark plugs.
Chris: The lights were probably left on last night. It's the battery.
Jordan: The voltage on the battery is fine.

In Section 3 two strategies for negotiation will be explored and evaluated. An empirical evaluation of the effects of positive evaluation will be also presented. The benefits of negotiation are summarized below in Figure 6.

2.9. TASK INITIATIVE = DIALOG INITIATIVE

In the literature, one finds references to both the terms *task initiative* and *dialog initiative*. The term *dialog initiative* usually refers to whose turn it is to speak while *task initiative* refers to who is currently in control of the problem-solving (as has been used in this paper).

DEFINITION 1.5 (Dialog Initiative). A participant, A, is said to have **dialog initiative** during a discourse when it is the expectation of both participants that Participant A will communicate[4] next.

However, we make the strong conjecture that whoever has task initiative over the current mutual goal also has dialog initiative. *A participant who holds the task initiative over the current mutual goal also holds the dialog initiative.*

The distinction between task and dialog initiative taken here differs from the approach taken by a number of researchers. Chu-Carroll and Brown (Chu-Carroll and Brown, 1998) attribute task initiative to a participant if that participant dictates how the agents' task should be accomplished (similar to our definition). However, they attribute dialog initiative to a participant if that participant *takes the conversational lead in order to establish mutual beliefs.* The reason such a distinction seems to make sense is that there appear to be task goals and dialog goals. In a similar vein, Hagen distinguishes between dialog control and dialog initiative (Hagen, 1998). However, the framework given in this paper does not distinguish between task and dialog goals. *Dialog goals* (clarifications, for instance) are subgoals of the overall task. The task tree for a particular collaborative goal does not need to distinguish between communicative goals like *inform A of Y* and other goals like *put tab C*

---

[4] Communication does not necessarily involve language. Gesture, for instance, is an important part of face-to-face communication.

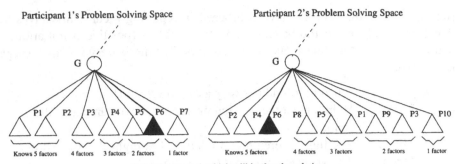

Figure 7. The problem-solving space for two participants for goal *G*.

into slot D. However, there may be pragmatic reasons for distinguishing between task-specific goals and communicative goals as the mechanisms for generating and selecting these goals might be different.

Cohen *et al* present an approach to initiative that also does not distinguish between task and dialog inititiave: *Initiative is control over the flow of conversation* (Cohen et al., 1998).

3. Automating Dialog Initiative

During a collaborative problem-solving session, the two participants may be jointly trying to solve some goal, *G*, as illustrated in Figure 7. Each participant has its lists of possible branches ordered (from left to right) by how by some best-first search ordering (more detail into this ordering will be given in Section 2.1.2). The two participants do not know where the correct branch (the branch that will actually lead to the solution) is in either list; however, they would like the participant with the correct branch ordered highest in its list to be in control. In the absence of a direct request, a decision must be made by each participant as to who will have initiative over a goal if there is a conflict.

Efficient human–computer dialog requires immediate utterance-by-utterance accommodation to the needs of the interaction. The participants must continuously focus all concerns on the goals of the task and avoid extraneous paths. This means that the **dialog initiative** should always pass immediately to the participant who is best able to handle the current task. An agent is said to have *dialog initiative* over a mutual goal when that agent controls how that goal will be solved by the collaborators. In the implemented voice dialog system 'The Circuit Fix-it Shop' (Smith et al., 1992; Smith & Hipp, 1995) the dialog fragment given in Figure 2 occurs between a human user and a computer collaborator. Utterances 2 and 4 indicate that the computer is directing the search for the missing wire in the faulty circuit. However, in Utterance 5 the user takes the initiative and suggests a different wire than has been proposed by the computer. In this paper we will present a the-

Table I. A Dialog Fragment in the Circuit Fix-it Shoppe Domain.

1	U	The LED is displaying an alternately flashing one and the top corner of a seven.
2	C	There is supposed to be a wire between connector nine nine and connector one zero zero.
3	U	It is there.
4	C	There is supposed to be a wire between connector nine eight and connector one zero two.
5	U	There is no wire on connector **one zero four**. [*emphasis mine*]
6	C	There is supposed to be a wire between connector one zero four and connector one zero two.

ory explaining how initiative changes between participants and how computational agents can evaluate who should be in control of solving a goal.

Many implemented dialog systems are question-answer systems with fixed initiative where one agent is in control and the other agent is passive (the master-slave assumption). For instance, in the LADDER system (Hendrix et al., 1978) the user has the initiative while the computer is passive. In contrast, the VODIS system (Young and Proctor, 1989) has the computer taking the initiative while the user is passive. Some dialog systems (like GUS (Bobrow et al., 1977)) allow for a more mixed-initiative interaction; however, the places where the user can take the initiative are limited and defined *a priori*. The dialog model of Smith (Smith and Hipp, 1995) allows for either the computer or the user to assume degrees of initiative; however, Smith presents no algorithm for the computer to change initiative during a dialog. Our model of mixed-initiative dialog allows either participant to be in control of the dialog at any point in time.

Like Smith (Smith & Hipp, 1995) we believe that *the level of initiative in the dialog should mirror the level of initiative in the task* (which is a corollary to Grosz's (Grosz, 1978) *the structure of a dialog mirrors the structure of the underlying task*). Unlike previous research in dialog initiative, however, we attach an initiative level to **each goal** in the task tree. Thus an agent may have initiative over one goal but not another. As goals get pushed and popped from the problem-solving stack, initiative changes accordingly. Thus many initiative changes are done implicitly based on which goal is being solved.

3.1. THE SETTING OF INITIATIVE LEVELS

In our model of dialog, initiative levels for each goal are defined during the interaction based on (1) explicit and implicit initiative-changing utterances and (2) competency evaluation.

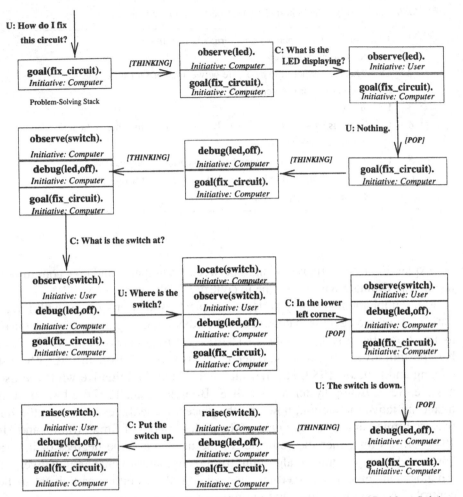

Figure 8. Tracking Initiative via Explicit Initiative-Changing Utterances and Problem-Solving Stack Manipulation.

3.1.1. *Explicit and Implicit Initiative-Changing Utterances*

Several researchers (Whittaker & Stenton, 1988; Walker & Whittaker, 1990) have noted that dialog control can be exchanged through overt cues in the discourse. Our model concentrates on two specific dialog cues: questions and answers. When an agent A_1 asks another agent A_2 to satisfy a goal G, agent A_2 gains initiative over goal G *and all subgoals of G until agent A_2 passes control of one of those subgoals back to agent A_1.* A similar initiative-setting mechanism is fired if agent A_1 announces that it cannot satisfy goal G. When a goal has been answered (satisfied) the problem-solving stack is popped. The initiative will now belong to whomever the initiative is for the goal on top of the stack.[5] In the following human-computer dialog gathered by Smith and Hipp (Smith & Hipp, 1995),

> U: How do I fix this circuit?
> C: What is the LED displaying?
> U: Nothing.
> C: What is the switch at?
> U: Where is the switch?
> C: In the lower left corner.
> U: The switch is down.
> C: Put the switch up.

all initiative changes can be accounted for by explicit initiative-changing utterances or by popping of the problem-solving stack due to goal resolution as illustrated in Figure 8.

3.1.2. *Competency Evaluation for Initiative Setting*

How does an agent decide whether to ask its collaborator for help? An obvious approach is to ask for help when the agent is unable to satisfy a goal on its own. This approach is the basic mechanism for several dialog systems (Young et al., 1989; Smith & Hipp, 1995; Guinn, 1994). An additional approach is to ask the collaborator for help if it is believed that the collaborator has a better chance of solving the goal (or solving it more efficiently). Such an evaluation requires knowledge of the collaborating agent's capabilities as well as an understanding of the agent's own capabilities.

Our methodology for evaluating competency involves a probabilistic examination of the search space of the problem domain. In the process of solving a goal, there may be many branches that can be taken in an attempt to prove a goal. Rather than selecting a branch at random, intelligent behavior involves evaluating (by some criteria) each possible branch that may lead toward the solution of a goal to determine which branch is more likely to lead to a solution. In this evaluation, certain important **factors** are examined to weight various branches. For example, during a medical exam, a patient may complain of dizziness, nausea, fever, headache, and itchy feet. The doctor may know of thousands of possible diseases, conditions, allergies, etc. To narrow the search, the doctor will try to find a pathology that accounts for these symptoms. There may be some diseases that account for all 5 symptoms, others that might account for 4 out of the 5 symptoms, and so on. In this manner, the practitioner sorts and prunes his list of possible pathologies. Competency evaluation will be based on how likely an agent's branch

---

[5] Since each participant is carrying out initiative evaluation independently, there may be conflicts on who should be in control. Numerous researchers have studied how negotiation may be used to resolve these conflicts (Guinn, 1994; Guinn, 1993; Lambert & Carberry, 1992; McRoy, 1993; Sidner, 1993).

will be successful (based on a weighted factor analysis) and how likely the collaborator's branch will be successful (based on a weighted factor analysis and a probabilistic model of the collaborator's knowledge).

In Section 2.2 we will sketch out how this calculation is made, present several mode selection schemes based on this factor analysis, and show the results of analytical evaluation of these schemes. In Section 4 we will present the methodology and results of using these schemes in a simulated dialog environment.

3.2. MATHEMATICAL ANALYSIS OF EFFICIENCY

Our model of best-first search assumes that for each goal there exists a set of n factors, $f_1, \ldots, f_n$, which are used to guide the search through the problem-solving space. For example, f_1 in a medical diagnosis may be the presense of a headache. Associated with each factor are two weights, w_i, which is the percentage of times a successful branch will have that factor and x_i which is the percentage of all branches that satisfy f_i. Again in the medical domain, w_1 for the factor, headache, would represent the probability that having a headache is symptomatic to the solution (the underlying disease). The weight x_1 would represent the percentage of diseases that have headaches as a symptom.

We define that an agent a knows a percentage q_i^a concerning factor f_i to mean that the agent is aware q_i^a percent of branches that satisfy factor f_i. For $f_1 =$ headache we would say q_1^a is the likelihood that agent a knows that some arbitrary disease causes a headache. Specifically, however, an agent may know that particular branch satisfies a certain factor. Thus the probability that the agent knows that branch satisfies that factor is 1. The probability that a branch satisfies factor f_1 but the agent a does not know it is $x_i(1 - q_i^a)$. Thus we define the probability that an agent knows that a particular branch satisfies factor i is

$$
\begin{aligned}
F^b(i) &= 1 && \text{if agent knows branch } b \text{ satisfies factor } f_i \\
F^b(i) &= x_i(1 - q_i^a) && \text{otherwise.}
\end{aligned}
\tag{1}
$$

For a particular branch b the probability that b is the correct branch is dependent on whether b (1) **satisfies** each factor, (2) the **weight** of each factor that it does satisfy, and (3) the **significance** of each factor that it satisfies. Whether b satisfies factor f_i is given by $F^b(i)$. The weight of f_i is given by w_i. The significance of factor f_i can be computed by looking at how many branches there are versus the likelihood that an arbitrary branch will satisfy f_i. This is given by $\frac{(1/k)}{x_i}$. For instance, if there are 200 diseases and half of those diseases can cause a headache, the significance of a particular disease having a headache is $(1/200)/.5 = 1/100$. On the other hand, suppose a particular disease (out of 200) causes black spots to appear on the body and the only 1/100 diseases have such a symptom. The significance of this factor becomes $(1/200)/(1/100) = 0.5$.

If an agent a knows $q_1^a, \ldots, q_n^a$ percentage of the knowledge concerning factors $f_1, \ldots, f_n$, respectively, and assuming independence of factors, using Bayes' rule an agent can calculate the success likelihood of each possible branch of a goal G that it knows:

$$p(b) = 1 - \prod_{i=1}^{n} 1 - F^b(i) w_i \frac{(1/k)}{x_i}, \tag{2}$$

where b is a branch out of a list of k branches.

We define the sorted list of branches for a goal G that an agent knows, $[b_1^a, \ldots, b_k^a]$, where for each b_i^a, $p(b_i^a)$ is the likelihood that branch b_i^a will result in success where $p(b_i^a) >= p(b_j^a)$, $\forall i < j$.

3.3. EFFICIENCY ANALYSIS OF DIALOG INITIATIVE

For efficient initiative-setting, it is also necessary to establish the likelihood of success for one's collaborator's 1st-ranked branch, 2nd-ranked branch, and so on. This calculation is difficult because the agent does not have direct access to its collaborator's knowledge. Again, we will rely on a probabilistic analysis. Assume that the agent does not know exactly what is in the collaborator's knowledge but does know the *degree* to which the collaborator knows about the factors related to a goal. Thus, in the medical domain, the agent may know that the collaborator knows more about diseases that account for dizziness and nausea, less about diseases that cause fever and headache, and nothing about diseases that cause itchy feet. For computational purposes these degrees of knowledge for each factor can be quantified: the agent a may know percentage q^a of the knowledge about diseases that cause dizziness while the collaborator, c, knows percentage q^c of the knowledge about these diseases. Suppose the agent has (1) a user model that states that the collaborator knows percentages $q_1^c, q_2^c, \ldots, q_n^c$ about factors $f_1, f_2, \ldots, f_n$, respectively and (2) a model of the domain which states the approximate number of branches, $\mathcal{N}$. Assuming independence, the expected number of branches which satisfy all n factors is ExpAllN = $\mathcal{N} \prod_{i=1}^{n} x_i$. Given that a branch satisfies all n factors, the likelihood that the collaborator will know that branch is $\prod_{i=1}^{n} q_i^c$. Therefore, the expected number of branches for which the collaborator knows all n factors is ExpAllN $\prod_{i=1}^{n} q_i^c$. The probability that one of these branches is a success-producing branch is $1 - \prod_{i=1}^{n} 1 - w_i \frac{(1/k)}{x_i}$ (from Equation 2). By computing similar probabilities for each combination of factors, the agent can compute the likelihood that the collaborator's first branch will be a successful branch, and so on. A more detailed account of this evaluation is given in Appendix A.

We have investigated four initiative-setting schemes using this analysis. These schemes do not necessarily correspond to any observable human-human or human-computer dialog behavior. Rather, they provide a means for exploring proposed dialog initiative schemes.

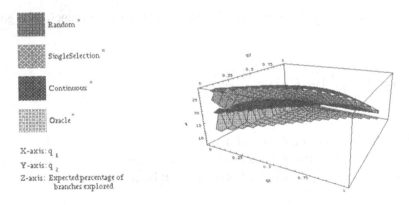

Figure 9. An Analytical Comparison of Dialog Initiative-Setting Schemes.

Random In Random mode, one agent is given initiative at random in the event of a conflict. This scheme provides a baseline for initiative setting algorithms. Hopefully, a proposed algorithm will do better than Random.

SingleSelection In SingleSelection mode, the more knowledgeable agent (defined by which agent has the greater total percentage of knowledge) is given initiative. The initiative is set throughout the dialog. Once a leader is chosen, the participants act in a master-slave fashion.

Continuous In Continuous mode, the more knowledgeable agent (defined by which agent's first-ranked branch is more likely to succeed) is initially given initiative. If that branch fails, this agent's second-ranked branch is compared to the other agent's first-ranked branch with the winner gaining initiative. In general if Agent 1 is working on its ith-ranked branch and Agent 2 is working on its jth-ranked branch, we compare $p^{A_1}(b_i^{A_1})$ to $p^{A_2}(b_j^{A_2})$.

Oracle In Oracle mode, an all-knowing mediator selects the agent that has the correct branch ranked highest in its list of branches. This scheme is an upper bound on the effectiveness of initiative setting schemes. No initiative setting algorithm can do better.

As knowledge is varied between participants we see some significant differences between the various strategies. Figure 9 summarizes this analysis. The x and y-axis represent the amount of knowledge that each agent is given[6], and the z-axis represents the percentage of branches explored from a single goal. Single-Selection and Continuous modes perform significantly better than Random mode. On average Continuous mode results in 40% less branches searched per goal than Random. Continuous mode performs between 15–20% better than SingleSelection.

---

[6] This distribution is normalized to insure that all the knowledge is distributed between each agent. Agent 1 will have $q_1 + (1 - q_1)(1 - q_2)\frac{q_1}{q_1+q_2}$ percent of the knowledge while Agent 2 will have $q_2 + (1 - q_1)(1 - q_2)\frac{q_2}{q_1+q_2}$ percent of the knowledge. If $q_1 + q_2 = 0$, then set $q_1 = q_2 = 0.5$.

The large gap between Oracle and Continuous is due to the fact that Continuous initiative selection is only using limited probabilistic information about the knowledge of each agent.

4. An Algebraic Analysis of Negotiation

In our model of best-first search, each possible branch is weighted by several factors. In car repair, knowing that the lights were left on all night is one factor that would weight that the battery's being dead is the cause of the car's inability to start. If two mechanics are examining the car and one does not know the lights were left on all night, that mechanic might be inclined to believe there is a short in the electrical system (maybe because this particular car has been known to have electrical problems). If the other mechanic knows that the lights were left on, in the interest of efficient problem-solving the knowing-mechanic might inform the other of that piece of knowledge. This informing of relevant factors in order to change how another participant weights a certain branch is *simple negotiation*. This section will investigate how such simple negotiation can help produce more efficient problem-solving.

As in the previous section our mode of analysis will depend on developing a model of the search space for each participant. For each goal, there will be a set of *factors* that are used to weight the branches extending from that goal. For simplicity, we will assume these factors are necessary factors – that is, the correct branch must satisfy all of the factors associated with branches under that goal. It is possible for a branch to satisfy all factors without being the correct branch. The factors that are satisfied by each branch define an equivalence relation on the set of all branches.. If there are n factors, there are 2^n equivalence classes. If there are three necessary factors, then these three factors will break the set of all branches into equivalence classes B_δ where δ is a set representing which factors are known for each branch in B_δ.

We will assume that Participant i knows a percentage p_i of all knowledge. The fact that a branch will satisfy a particular *factor* is to be considered one piece of knowledge. Thus if branch b satisfies factor f_1, there is a probability p_i that Participant i knows that fact. The development of formulas for describing the expected partition of branches by each participant is presented in Appendix A.

In Appendix B we look at two different schemes for employing negotiation. In the first scheme, *OneNegotiation*, the participants will only negotiate once at the beginning of the dialog. The winner will be given control for the remainder of the problem-solving until it gives up control. The second scheme, *AllNegotiation*, allows the participants to negotiate every time a branch is being selected for search. The winner of the negotiation will control the problem-solving until either that branch results in successful completion or that branch fails. If that branch fails, a new branch must be chosen and the participants will negotiate to see which branch will be explored.

4.1. ESTIMATING USER MODEL PARAMETERS USING NEGOTIATION

Negotiation tends to favor the more knowledgeable participant We can make use of this fact to use negotiation to predict the relative knowledge levels between the two participants and then use these predictions to guide mode decisions.

The following examples illustrate this principle. Note that these examples use an arbitrary threshold to estimate knowledge distribution parameters. This arbitrary selection reinforces the heuristic nature of the process of inferring knowledge parameters from behavior.

4.1.1.1. *Example 1.* If there are three necessary factors and a participant announces during the first negotiation that it knows a branch with all three factors, this gives some information about its percentage of total knowledge known.

Define p to be the percentage of all knowledge known to a participant. Define $n_{\{1,2,3\}}$ to be the number of branches that satisfy all three factors, $n_{\{1,2\}}$ to be the number of branches that satisfy factors one and two, and in general, $n_{\{i,\dots,j\}}$ to be the number of branches that satisfy factors $i, \dots, j$.

The probability that a participant knows at least one branch with all three factors is

$$ProbKnows1with3Factors(p) = 1 - (1 - p^3)^{n_{\{1,2,3\}}}. \tag{3}$$

Thus

$$p = (1 - (1 - ProbKnows1with3Factors(p))^{1/n_{\{1,2,3\}}})^{1/3}. \tag{4}$$

By setting $ProbKnows1with3Factors(p)$ to some arbitrary threshold (0.60) and $n_{\{1,2,3\}} = 4$, we can conclude that if $p \geqslant 0.589$, then the probability that the participant knows a branch with all three factors is $\geqslant 0.60$. Thus if we know a participant knows a branch with all three factors, there is a good probability that the percentage of knowledge it has concerning the factors associated with the goal is $\geqslant 0.589$.

4.1.2. *Example 2.* We can continue to carry out these sort of equations to the next stage. Suppose through two sets of negotiation dialogs, it is determined that a participant knows at least two branches with all three factors. The probability of this occurring is

$$ProbKnows2with3Factors(p) = \sum_{i=2}^{n_{\{1,2,3\}}} \binom{n}{i}(p^3)^i (1 - p^3)^{(n_{\{1,2,3\}}-i)}. \tag{5}$$

By setting $n_{\{1,2,3\}} = 4$ and $ProbKnows2with3Factors(p) = 0.60$, we can conclude that there is a good probability that $p \geqslant 0.763$.

4.1.1.3. *Example 3.* As a final illustration of this principle, assume negotiation reveals that one participant knows of no branches with all three factors. The probability of this occurring is

$$ProbKnows0with3Factors(p) = (1 - p^3)^{n_{\{1,2,3\}}}. \tag{6}$$

Thus

$$p = (1 - ProbKnows0with3Factors(p)^{1/n_{\{1,2,3\}}})^{1/3}. \tag{7}$$

With $n_{\{1,2,3\}} = 4$ and *ProbKnows0with3Factors* $(p) = 0.60$, we can conclude that there is a high probability that $p \leqslant 0.49$.

In general, negotiation can be used to estimate user model parameters. Using these parameters the collaborators can then use a dialog mode scheme like *Continuous*. If the estimates gained from the first negotiation are inexact, conflicts will occur. Thus negotiation will take place and a possible resetting of user model parameters may occur. Here, negotiation and dialog mode complement one another. Negotiation provides information necessary for accurate dialog mode settings and dialog mode provides mechanisms that prevent too much conflict; and hence, too much negotiation.

5. Computer Simulations

The dialog model outlined in this paper has been implemented, and computer–computer dialogs have been carried out to evaluate the model and judge the effectiveness of various dialog initiative schemes. In a methodology similar to that used by Power (1979), Carletta (1992) and Walker (1993), knowledge is distributed by a random process between agents, and the resulting interaction between these collaborating agents is observed. This methodology allows investigators to test different aspects of a dialog theory. Details of this experimental strategy are given by Guinn (1995).

5.1.1. *The Usage of Computer–Computer Dialogs*

The use of computer–computer simulations to study and build human-computer dialog systems is controversial. Since we are building computational models of dialog, it is perfectly reasonable to explore these computational models through computer–computer simulations. The difficulty lies in what these simulations say about human–computer or computer-computer dialogs. This author argues that computer–computer simulations are one layer in the multi-layer process of building human–computer dialog systems. Computer–computer simulations allow us to evaluate our computational models and explore issues that can not be resolved analytically. These simulations can help us prune out some mechanisms and suggest mechanisms that may work well in a human–computer system. For instance, if the

Table II. Data on 5008 Non-trivial Dialogs from the Murder Mystery Domain

	Random Mode, No Negotiation	Continuous Mode, No Negotiation	Random Mode, With Negotiation	Continuous Mode, With Negotiation
Time (secs.)	82.398	44.528	70.782	43.263
Utterances	39.921	26.650	26.667	25.784
Branches Explored	6.188	3.412	4.394	3.334

dialogs that result in a computer–computer conversation are incoherent to a human observer, this suggests that the dialog mechanisms employed may be inappropriate for a human–computer system. On the other hand, if the resulting dialogs are coherent and exhibit features that are desired in a human–computer system, this suggests that these mechanisms may work well in a human–computer system. The final test, of course, must be in the implementation of a human–computer dialog system. The scarcity of such systems suggests that it is an extremely expensive process to build a functional human–computer dialog system, and computer-computer simulations can assist in reducing these costs.

5.1.2. *Simulation Results*

A murder mystery domain was created with 22 suspects. An annotated example dialog from a computer–computer collaboration in this domain is presented in Figure 10. Agents were given partial information through a random process. By using either Random mode or Continuous mode, we can evaluate the effect of those mechanisms in this experimental environment. Table 2 presents results computed from 5008 collaborations where the agents had to communicate to solve the task.

5.1. EXTENSION TO HUMAN–COMPUTER DIALOGS

Currently, two spoken-dialog human–computer systems are being developed using the underlying algorithms described in this paper. The Duke Programming Tutor instructs introductory computer science students how to write simple Pascal programs by providing multiple modes of input and output (voice/text/graphics) (Biermann et al., 1997). The Advanced Maintenance Assistant and Trainer (AMAT) currently being developed by Research Triangle Institute for the U.S. Army allows a maintenance trainee to converse with a computer assistant in the diagnosis and repair of a *virtual* M1A1 tank (Guinn & Montoya, 1997). While still in prototype development, preliminary results suggest that the algorithms that were successful for efficient computer–computer collaboration are capable of participating in *coherent* human–machine interaction. Extensive testing remains to be done to determine the actual gains in efficiency due to various mechanisms.

Speaker	Utterance
Watson	Who is the murderer of Lord Dunsmore?[a]
Holmes	Is it the case that Suspect16 is the murderer of Lord Dunsmore?
Watson	Is it the case that Suspect16 had a motive to murder Lord Dunsmore?
Holmes	Suspect16 had a motive to murder Lord Dunsmore.
Watson	Is it the case that Suspect16 had access to the poison?
Holmes	I am unable to determine whether Suspect16 had access to the poison.
Watson	I am unable to determine whether Suspect16 is the murderer of Lord Dunsmore.
Holmes	I am unable to determine whether Suspect16 is the murderer of Lord Dunsmore.
Holmes	Who is the murderer of Lord Dunsmore?[b]
Watson	Is it the case that Suspect10 is the murderer of Lord Dunsmore?
Holmes	Is it the case that Suspect10 had a motive to murder Lord Dunsmore?
Watson	Suspect10 had a motive to murder Lord Dunsmore.
Holmes	Is it the case that Suspect10 had access to the poison?
Watson	Suspect10 had access to the poison.
Holmes	Is it the case that Suspect10 had an opportunity to administer the poison?
Watson	I am unable to determine whether Suspect10 had an opportunity to administer the poison.
Holmes	I am unable to determine whether Suspect10 is the murderer of Lord Dunsmore.
Watson	I am unable to determine whether Suspect10 is the murderer of Lord Dunsmore.
Watson	Is it the case that Suspect9 is the murderer of Lord Dunsmore?
Holmes	Is it the case that Suspect7 is the murderer of Lord Dunsmore?[c]
Watson	I have proven that Suspect9 has a motive to murder Lord Dunsmore and Suspect9 had access to the poison.[d]
Holmes	I have proven that Suspect7 had access to the poison, Suspect7 had an opportunity to administer the poison, and Suspect7 has a criminal disposition.[e]
Watson	Suspect7 is the murderer of Lord Dunsmore.[f]

[a] Watson gives control of the investigation over to Holmes. Each participant uses the Continuous Mode algorithm to determine who should be in control.

[b] Holmes is giving up control of directing the investigation here.

[c] Holmes is challenging Watson's investigative choice.

[d] Watson negotiates for his choice.

[e] Holmes negotiates for his choice.

[f] Watson now has enough information to prove that Suspect7 is the murderer.

Figure 10. A Sample Dialog.

One tenet of our theory is that proper initiative setting requires an effective user model. There are several mechanisms we are exploring in acquiring the kind of user model information necessary for the previously described dialog mode algorithms. Stereotypes (Rich, 1979; Chin, 1989) are a valuable tool in domains where user classification is possible and relevant. For instance, in the domain of military equipment maintenance, users can be easily classified by rank, years of experience, equipment familiarity and so on. An additional source of user model information can be dynamically obtained in environments where the user interacts for an extended period of time. A tutoring/training system has the advantage of knowing exactly what lessons a student has taken and how well the student did on individual lessons and questions. Dynamically modifying the user model based on on-going problem solving is difficult. One mechanism that may prove particularly effective is negotiating problem-solving strategies (Guinn, 1994). The quality of a collaborator's negotiation reflects the quality of its underlying knowledge. There is a tradeoff in that negotiation is expensive, both in terms of time and computational complexity. Thus, a synthesis of user modeling techniques will probably be required for effective and efficient collaboration.

Appendix

A. An Analytical Model of Best-First Search

All possible branches are naturally partitioned by which factors are known for each. Thus the factors that are known for the branches define an equivalence relation on the set of all branches. For example, during a medical exam, a patient may complain of dizziness (factor f_1), nausea (f_2), fever (f_3), headache (f_4) and itchy feet (f_5). The doctor may know of thousands of possible diseases, conditions, allergies, etc. To narrow his search, the doctor will try to find a pathology which accounts for these symptoms. There may be some diseases which would account for all 5 symptoms, others that might account for 4 out of the 5 symptoms, and so on. In this manner, the practitioner sorts and prunes his list of possible pathologies.

If there are n factors, there are 2^n equivalence classes. Suppose there are 3 necessary factors. The three factors will break the set of all branches into equivalence classes B_δ where δ is a set representing which factors are known for each branch in B_δ. For example, every branch, $b_{\{1,3\}_i} \in B_{\{1,3\}}$ has factors f_1 and f_3 but does not have factor f_2.

$$B_{\{1,2,3\}} = [b_{\{1,2,3\}_1}, \ldots, b_{\{1,2,3\}_{n_{\{1,2,3\}}}}],$$

$$B_{\{1,2\}} = [b_{\{1,2\}_1}, \ldots, b_{\{1,2\}_{n_{\{1,2\}}}}],$$

$$B_{\{1\}} = [b_{\{1\}_1}, \ldots, b_{\{1\}_{n_{\{1\}}}}],$$

$$B_{\{1,3\}} = [b_{\{1,3\}_1}, \ldots, b_{\{1,3\}_{n_{\{1,3\}}}}], \tag{8}$$

$$B_{\{2,3\}} = [b_{\{2,3\}_1}, \ldots, b_{\{2,3\}_{n_{\{2,3\}}}}],$$

$$B_{\{2\}} = [b_{\{2\}_1}, \ldots, b_{\{2\}_{n_{\{2\}}}}],$$

$$B_{\{3\}} = [b_{\{3\}_1}, \ldots, b_{\{3\}_{n_{\{3\}}}}],$$

$$B_{\{\}} = [b_{\{\}_1}, \ldots, b_{\{\}_{n_{\{\}}}}]$$

where n_{δ} is the size of equivalence class B_{δ}. Note that $\sum^{\delta} n_{\delta} = $ the total number of branches leading out from a goal.

Each participant will have its own partition of branches based on the knowledge available to that participant. Each participant will know all n factors of the correct branch with some probability or it will know $n - 1$ factors of the correct branch with some probability and so on. This partitioning will guide the best-first search as branches in a higher (more likely to have the correct branch) equivalence class are preferred to branches in a lower equivalence class. If these probabilities can be determined, then the average place of the correct branch in each participant's sorted list of possible branches can be determined and a rational decision can be made on which participant should take the initiative in directing the problem-solving for that particular goal.

A.1. ANALYZING A PARTICIPANT'S SEARCH

Suppose a participant knows a percentage p of the total knowledge. Given this parameter, we would like to compute the following:

1. What does this participant's best-first search space look like on the average for some goal, G?
2. What is the probability the correct branch is in the participant's search space? (Since a participant may lack knowledge, it may not even know about the correct branch.)
3. If it is, what is the expected number of branches the participant will search before finding the right branch?

A.1.1. *The Best-First Search Space*

Given that a participant only knows a portion of the total knowledge, the set of factors known for the branches leading to the solution of a goal will be incomplete. Thus the partition of branches based on the number of factors known for each branch will not be the same as the partition based on complete knowledge.

Let's suppose that there are 3 factors for evaluating a branch. With total world knowledge the partition is as described in Equation 8. However, with incomplete knowledge, only some branches in $B_{\{1,2,3\}}$ will be known, only some in $B_{\{1,2\}}$, and so on. In addition, some branches in $B_{\{1,2,3\}}$ may <u>seem</u> to be in $B_{\{1,2\}}$, $B_{\{1\}}$ and so on. Thus, we can talk about the user's partition of branches, $UserB_{\{1,2,3\}}$,

$UserB_{\{1,2\}}$, ... For the proceeding analysis we will make the following two assumptions:

1. *Knowledge is distributed* **uniformly** *so that a participant knows a percentage p of all factor knowledge.* This assumption is clearly a simplification of what will be required in a sophisticated system. A better model would be to prescribe that a participant knows percentage p_1 of knowledge concerning factor f_1, percentage p_2 of knowledge concerning factor f_2, and so on. The equations and derivations that follow can be extended to handle this model. In actual implementation this extended notion of participant knowledge was used. However, for mathematical analysis these extended calculations get unwieldy.

2. *Knowledge of one particular factor is* **independent** *of knowledge of another factor.* This assumption is only a first approximation at what may be necessary in a sophisticated system. Agents may have groups or sets of knowledge that go together. The probability of knowing fact G may affect the probability of knowing fact H. The following equations could (with great added complexity) be adjusted to accommodate groups or sets of knowledge. This issue has not been developed in this research either analytically or in implementation. How such analysis might be done stands as future research.

Given these assumptions, the expected size of each equivalence class can be probabilistically determined.

$$ExpSize(UserB_{\delta}, p) = ExpKnown(B_{\delta}, p)+$$

$$\sum^{\mathcal{SUPER}} ExpMistakenFor(B_{\mathcal{SUPER}}, B_{\delta}, p), \qquad (9)$$

where $\mathcal{SUPER}$ is a proper superset of δ. $ExpKnown(B_{\delta}, p)$ is the expected number of branches in B_{δ} for which the participant knows all the knowledge. For instance, the probability that a participant knows all three factors for a branch in equivalence class $B_{\{1,2,3\}}$ is p^3, thus the expected number of branches in $B_{\{1,2,3\}}$ known by the participant is the number of elements in $B_{\{1,2,3\}}$ times the probability of knowing all three factors or

$$ExpKnown(B_{\{1,2,3\}}, p) = n_{\{1,2,3\}}p^3.$$

Similarly,

$$
\begin{aligned}
ExpKnown(B_{\{i,j,k\}}, p) &= n_{\{i,j,k\}}p^3 \quad \forall i, j, k \\
ExpKnown(B_{\{i,j\}}, p) &= n_{\{i,j\}}p^2 \quad \forall i, j \\
ExpKnown(B_{\{i\}}, p) &= n_{\{i\}}p \quad \forall i \\
ExpKnown(B_{\{\}}, p) &= n_{\{\}},
\end{aligned}
\qquad (10)
$$

[114]

or more generically,

$$ExpKnown(B_\mathcal{S}, p) = n_\mathcal{S} p^{|\mathcal{S}|} \ \forall \mathcal{S}. \tag{11}$$

$ExpMistakenFor(B_\mathcal{S}, B_\mathcal{T}, p)$ is the expected number of branches that are in equivalence class $B_\mathcal{S}$ that are mistaken for being in equivalence class $B_\mathcal{T}$ because the participant lacks some knowledge. For instance, the probability that a participant with knowledge distribution parameter p mistakes a branch in $B_{\{1,2,3\}}$ for a branch in $B_{\{1,2\}}$ is the probability that the participant knows factors 1 and 2 for goal G but does not know factor 3, or $p^2(1-p)$. Thus the expected number of branches in $B_{\{1,2,3\}}$ that are mistaken for being in $B_{\{1,2\}}$ is

$$ExpMistakenFor(B_{\{1,2,3\}}, B_{\{1,2\}}, p) = n_{\{1,2,3\}} p^2 (1-p).$$

Similarly,

$$ExpMistakenFor(B_{\{1,2,3\}}, B_{\{i,j\}}, p) = n_{\{1,2,3\}} p^2 (1-p) \quad \forall i, j$$

$$ExpMistakenFor(B_{\{1,2,3\}}, B_{\{i\}}, p) = n_{\{1,2,3\}} p (1-p)^2 \quad \forall i$$

$$ExpMistakenFor(B_{\{1,2,3\}}, B_{\{\}}, p) = n_{\{1,2,3\}} (1-p)^3$$

$$mbox ExpMistakenFor(B_{\{i,j\}}, B_{\{k\}}, p) = n_{\{i,j\}} p (1-p) \quad \forall i, j \tag{12}$$

$$\text{where } k \in \{i, j\}$$

$$ExpMistakenFor(B_{\{i,j\}}, B_{\{\}}, p) = n_{\{i,j\}} (1-p)^2 \quad \forall i, j$$

$$ExpMistakenFor(B_{\{i\}}, B_{\{\}}, p) = n_{\{i\}} (1-p) \quad \forall i$$

or more generically

$$ExpMistakenFor(B_\mathcal{S}, B_\mathcal{T}, p) = \begin{cases} n_\mathcal{S} p^{|\mathcal{T}|} (1-p)^{(|\mathcal{S}|-|\mathcal{T}|)} & \forall \mathcal{S}, \mathcal{T} \text{ where } \mathcal{T} \subset \mathcal{S} \\ 0 & \text{otherwise.} \end{cases} \tag{13}$$

From these equations, we can derive the size of each equivalence class in a participant's search space.

A.1.2. *Where is the correct branch?*

Note that the correct branch must be in $B_{\{1,2,3\}}$. Given that a participant only knows a percentage p of the total factors, the participant may know all 3 factors, 2 out of 3, 1 out of 3 or even none of the factors for the correct branch. The probability that the participant does not know any factors for the correct branch is $(1 - p)^3$. If $branch_c$ is the correct branch, then

$$Prob(branch_c \in UserB_{\{1,2,3\}}, p) = p^3$$
$$Prob(branch_c \in UserB_{\{i,j\}}, p) = p^2(1 - p) \quad \forall i, j$$
$$Prob(branch_c \in UserB_{\{i\}}, p) = p(1 - p)^2 \quad \forall i$$
$$Prob(branch_c \in UserB_{\{\}}, p) = (1 - p)^3$$

(14)

or more generically

$$Prob(branch_c \in UserB_\delta, p) = \begin{cases} p^{|\delta|}(1 - p)^{(n-|\delta|)} & \text{where } n \text{ is the number} \\ & \text{of factors,} \\ 0 & \text{otherwise.} \end{cases}$$

(15)

A.1.3. Ordering the User's Equivalence Classes

We will assume that if a participant knows 0 factors for a branch, then the user does not know about that branch at all. Also assume that within an equivalence class, branches are sorted randomly and uniformly. Assume that the user's equivalence classes are ordered $UserB^{1st}$, $UserB^{2nd}$, $UserB^{3rd}$, ..., $UserB^{mth}$ where $m = 2^n - 1$ (the equivalence class $UserB_{\{\}}$ is not in the ordered list because of the Non-awareness Assumption[7]). A function, $UserBOrder(i)$ returns the ith equivalence class in the ordered list. For instance, $UserBOrder(3)$ returns $UserB^{3rd}$. The manner in which the equivalence classes are sorted is done as follows: Given that a branch $Branch_x$ is in $UserB_\delta$, what is the probability that $Branch_x = branch_c$? We order the equivalence classes based on this probability. To compute this probability, we first sort the equivalence classes by the weights assigned to each factor. The value assigned to $B_{\{1,2,3\}}$ would be $w_1 w_2 w_3$, the value assigned to $B_{\{1,2\}}$ would be $w_1 w_2(1 - w_3)$, the value assigned to $B_{\{1\}}$ would be $w_1(1 - w_2)(1 - w_3)$, and so on. If there are ties between equivalence class rankings, additional information is needed to break the ties. We will define a probability inc_i that is the probability that an *incorrect* branch satisfies factor f_i. If factors f_1 and f_2 are necessary factors $(w_1 = w_2 = 1.0)$ and an incorrect branch satisfies f_1 40% of the time and an an incorrect branch satisfied f_2 2% of the time, then a branch which is only known (by a participant with incomplete knowledge) to satisfy f_2 is more likely to be the correct branch than a branch which is only known to satisfy f_1. For example, if you need to find a list of orthopedic surgeons over forty, you would not begin by compiling a list of everyone over forty. You would search for a list of orthopedic surgeons and then begin pruning out those younger than forty. The inc_i values help in searching the smallest subset of branches first.

---

[7] Non-awareness Assumption: If the user knows no factors for a particular branch, the branch is unknown to the user.

The average place within a participant's search space of the correct branch will be the sum over all equivalence classes (save $UserB_{\{\}}$) of the probability that $branch_c$ is in each equivalence class times half the expected size of that equivalence class (since the correct branch will on average be in the middle of an equivalence class because of uniform distribution) plus the size of the preceding (higher ranked) equivalence classes, or

$$AvgPlace(p) = \sum_{i=1}^{m} Prob(branch_c \in UserBOrder(i), p)$$

$$(ExpSize(UserBOrder(i), p)/2+ \qquad (16)$$

$$\sum_{j=1}^{i-1} ExpSize(UserBOrder(j), p))$$

with probability $(1-p)^n$ that $branch_c$ is not in any equivalence class and $m = 2^n - 1$ where n is the number of factors being used to partition the set of branches.

Notice that the total number of branches that a participant has in its list is

$$Length(p) = \sum_{i=1}^{m} ExpSize(UserBOrder(i), p)$$

$$(17)$$

$$= \sum^{\delta} ExpSize(UserB_{\delta}, p) - ExpSize(UserB_{\{\}}, p).$$

A.2. ENSURING COMPLETENESS

The collaborative problem solving model developed in this paper does not guarantee that the goal will be successfully solved by the problem solvers. Clearly, if the problem solving participants lack the necessary knowledge or capabilities, the problem will not be solved. How can we guarantee that the participants will be able to solve the problem? One necessary property is that all of the essential knowledge must in at least one of the two participants world knowledge. How can we guarantee that such a condition is met?

Suppose that all knowledge is distributed in the following manner:

1. Base knowledge parameters, q_1 and q_2, are assigned for Participants 1 and 2.
2. For every fact, f, in the total world knowledge, f is placed in Participant 1's world knowledge with probability q_1, and f is placed in Participant 2's world knowledge with probability q_2. Note that there is a probability, $(1-q_1)(1-q_2)$, that neither participant knows f.
3. If a fact, f, has not been placed in either participant's knowledge base, f is placed in Participant 1's knowledge base with probability $\frac{q_1}{q_1+q_2}$; otherwise, f is placed in Participant 2's knowledge base.[8]

---

[8] If q_1 and q_2 are both zero, then we replace this probability with 0.5.

Using this scheme, every fact is ensured to be in one or the other participant's knowledge. Now, however, the probability that a participant has a particular fact is no longer independent of the other participant's having that fact. The probability that a participant knows a particular fact under this scheme is a function of the base knowledge distribution parameters of the two participants:

$$P \bmod(q_1, q_2) = q_1 + (1 - q_1)(1 - q_2)\frac{q_1}{q_1 + q_2}. \tag{18}$$

A.3. MODE SELECTION SCHEMES

This paper will contrast the following four schemes:

Random Selection In random mode selection, one participant is chosen at random to be 'in control' of solving a particular goal. Our model assumes that 50% of the time Participant 1 has control and 50% of the time Participant 2 has control. The randomly selected controller will then begin to initiate the solution of the goal using its ordered lists of possible branches as a guide. It is possible that the chosen participant will not have the correct branch in its list. In which case, after exhausting its list, the controlling participant will pass the initiative to the other participant.

Single Selection In single mode selection, at the onset of solving a new goal the participants decide which one is more likely to have the correct goal higher in their sorted list of possible branches. How this calculation might be made will be discussed below. The chosen participant will then have control and begin to search using its ordered list of branches.

Continuous Selection In continuous mode selection, not only is a decision made as to who is better suited to solving the goal at the onset, but if the controlling participant selects a branch to explore that **fails** to prove the goal, a decision is made again as to who is better suited to control the solution of the current goal. This new decision will reflect the fact that the current controlling participant failed to select the correct branch. Again, how this decision might be made will be explored below.

Best (Oracle) Selection In best mode selection, an oracle looks at the each participant's ordered list of possible branches and grants initiative to the participant that has the correct goal higher in its list.

A.3.1. *Random Mode Selection*

Under Random Mode Selection we assume that one participant will be given control of the decomposition and branch choice of a goal. For two participants, let's assume that half the time one participant gains control, half the other.

Suppose there are w facts (call this set of facts $\mathcal{W}$) that are necessary for solving the goal G. We will assume that if each of these w facts is known by at least one participant (but it is possible that a single participant may not know all w facts), then goal G will be solved once the correct branch is taken from goal G. Therefore, we are guaranteed solution of goal G if all w facts are in the union of Participant 1 and Participant 2's knowledge and $branch_c$ is in at least one participant's list of possible branches.

Suppose Participant 1 knows a percentage p_1 of all knowledge, Participant 2 knows a percentage p_2 of all knowledge. The probability that the w facts are in the union of Participant 1 and Participant 2's knowledge is

$$Prob(i \in \mathcal{K}_1 \cup \mathcal{K}_2 | i \in \mathcal{W}, p_1, p_2) = [1 - (1 - p_1)(1 - p_2)]^w, \qquad (19)$$

where $\mathcal{K}_i$ is Participant i's set of knowledge. If we assume that the set of factors $f_1, \ldots, f_n$ are a subset of $\mathcal{W}$ then the probability that the two participants have the necessary knowledge to solve the problem is

$$ProbCanSolve(p_1, p_2) = Prob(i \in \mathcal{K}_1 \cup \mathcal{K}_2 | i \in \mathcal{W}, p_1, p_2) \qquad (20)$$

because if all the factors are known between the two participants at least one of the participants has factors for the correct branch.

Using Random Mode Selection, the participant *in charge* will proceed through its ordered list of branches stopping when it chooses the correct branch **assuming all w facts are known**. Obviously, even if the correct branch is chosen they will not solve the goal if all the facts are not available. In this case, both participants will exhaust their search space before failing. However, there is the possibility that the correct branch is not even in the participant-in-charge's list. In this case the participant will proceed through its entire list and then give control to the other participant, who then repeats the process. Note that the second participant may not have the correct branch in its list either in which case the second participant will exhaust its known branches and announce failure.

The following formula, *SearchLength*(p_1, p_2), gives the expected number of branches searched if the participant with the percentage of the knowledge, p_1, is initially given control of directing the search. If this participant fails to find the correct branch after exhausting all of the branches in its list, then the participant with the percentage of knowledge, p_2, gains control. If Participant 1 has the correct branch somewhere in its list, then the search length will be the average place in that list or *AvgPlace*(p_1). If Participant 1 does not have the branch in its list, it will search each branch that it knows (expected length: *Length*(p_1)) and then give control to Participant 2. If Participant 2 has the correct branch somewhere in its list, then *AvgPlace*(p_2) is added to the search length accumulated so far. If Participant 2 does not have the correct branch somewhere in its list, then *Length*(p_2) is added to the total search length.

The *SearchLength*(p_1, p_2), the number of branches searched if the participant with p_1 percent of the knowledge is in control, can be expressed as

$$
\begin{aligned}
SearchLength(p_1, p_2) = \\
AvgPlace(p_1) + (1 - p_1)^n [(Length(p_1) - AvgPlace(p_1)) \qquad (21) \\
+ AvgPlace(p_2) + (1 - p_2)^n (Length(p_2) - AvgPlace(p_2))].
\end{aligned}
$$

A.3.2. *Assuming Complete Knowledge Distribution*

If we assume complete knowledge distribution as described above, Equations 19–21 are modified as follows:

$$Prob(i \in \mathcal{K}_1 \cup \mathcal{K}_2 | i \in \mathcal{W}, p_1, p_2) = 1, \tag{22}$$

where $\mathcal{K}_i$ is Participant i's set of knowledge.

$$ProbCanSolve^*(p_1, p_2) = Prob(i \in \mathcal{K}_1 \cup \mathcal{K}_2 | i \in \mathcal{W}, p_1, p_2) = 1 \tag{23}$$

Note: The *Function** notation will be used to denote modification of formulas that assume complete knowledge distribution, i.e. $Function^*(q_1, q_2) = Function(Pmod(q_1, q_2), Pmod(q_2, q_1))$.

Distributing the knowledge as described in Section A.2 with base probabilities q_1 and q_2 for participants 1 and 2 respectively results in the modified *SearchLength** equation:

$$SearchLength^*(q_1, q_2) = SearchLength(Pmod(q_1, q_2), Pmod(q_2, q_1)) \tag{24}$$

If a participant has a greater percentage of knowledge than the other then that participant is more likely to have the correct branch sorted higher in its list of branches. This precipitates the following:

Postulate A.1. If $p_1 > p_2$, then $SearchLength(p_1, p_2) < SearchLength(p_2, p_1)$.

which is graphically illustrated in Figure 11.

The average number of branches searched using Random Mode Selection is

$$Random(p_1, p_2) = 0.5(SearchLength(p_1, p_2)$$
$$+ SearchLength(p_2, p_1)). \tag{25}$$

Assuming full knowledge distribution,

$$Random^*(q_1, q_2) = 0.5(SearchLength^*(q_1, q_2)$$
$$+ SearchLength^*(q_2, q_1))$$
$$= Random(P\,mod(q_1, q_2), P\,mod(q_2, q_1)) \tag{26}$$

A.3.3. *Single Selection*

An improvement of random mode selection can be obtained by wisely choosing which participant gains control at the start. Suppose the knowledge distribution parameters, p_1 and p_2, are known for Participant 1 and Participant 2, respectively. If both participants know these parameters they can jointly decide to allow the

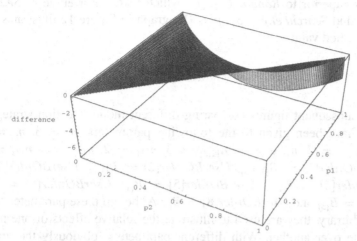

Figure 11. SearchLength(p_1, p_2) - SearchLength(p_2, p_1) with parameter $n = 3$, $w = 3$, $n_{\{1,2,3\}} = 4$, $n_{\{1,2\}} = 3$, $n_{\{1,3\}} = 4$, $n_{\{2,3\}} = 3$, $n_{\{1\}} = 2$, $n_{\{2\}} = 5$, $n_{\{3\}} = 6$, $n_{\{\}} = 3$, UserBOrder[1] = $B_{\{1,2,3\}}$, UserBOrder[2] = $B_{\{1,2\}}$, UserBOrder[3] = $B_{\{1,3\}}$, UserBOrder[4] = $B_{\{2,3\}}$, UserBOrder[5] = $B_{\{1\}}$, UserBOrder[6] = $B_{\{2\}}$, UserBOrder[7] = $B_{\{3\}}$ and UserBOrder[8] = $B_{\{\}}$.

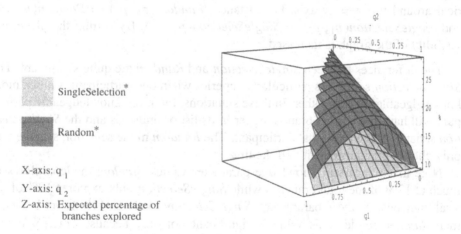

SingleSelection*

Random*

X-axis: q_1
Y-axis: q_2
Z-axis: Expected percentage of
branches explored

Figure 12. Random*(q_1, q_2) and SingleSelection*(q_1, q_2) vs. Percentage of Branches Explored over the range $q_1 \in [q_2, 1]$ and $q_2 \in [0, 1]$.

participant with the higher percentage of knowledge to have control first. Using this selection scheme the two participants will, on average, search the following number of branches:

$$\begin{aligned}SingleSelection(p_1, p_2) = \ &MIN(SearchLength(p_1, p_2),\\ &SearchLength(p_2, p_1))\end{aligned} \tag{27}$$

which is clearly superior to $Random(p_1, p_2)$ which takes an average of *Search-Length* (p_1, p_2) and $SearchLength(p_2, p_1)$. The graph in Figure 12 illustrates this point for the specified values.

Some Notes on Figures

Note 1: In all subsequent figures comparing different mode selection strategies, specific values have been given to the following parameters: $n = 3$, $m = 3$, $n_{\{1,2,3\}} = 4$, $n_{\{1,2\}} = 3$, $n_{\{1,3\}} = 4$, $n_{\{2,3\}} = 3$, $n_{\{1\}} = 2$, $n_{\{2\}} = 5$, $n_{\{3\}} = 6$, $n_{\{\}} = 3$, $UserBOrder[1] = B_{\{1,2,3\}}$, $UserBOrder[2] = B_{\{1,2\}}$, $UserBOrder[3] = B_{\{1,3\}}$, $UserBOrder[4] = B_{\{2,3\}}$, $UserBOrder[5] = B_{\{1\}}$, $UserBOrder[6] = B_{\{2\}}$, $UserBOrder[7] = B_{\{3\}}$ and $UserBOrder[8] = B_{\{\}}$. Although these parameter specifications are arbitrary, they are used to illustrate the relative effects of one mode selection scheme over another. With different parameters, obviously the graphs may differ in some ways, but experimentation with different parameter settings has verified that, generally, the comparative effects of each mode strategy are the same.

Note 2: All subsequent graphs will be cut along the plane $x = y$. This cutting is justified by the fact that all of the functions being graphed are symmetrical around the $x = y$ axis. For instance, $Random(p_1, p_2) = Random(p_2, p_1)$ and $SingleSelection(p_1, p_2) = SingleSelection(p_2, p_1)$. By cutting the plane, the visibility of the graph is increased.

The differences between *SingleSelection* and *Random* are quite significant. The *SingleSelection* scheme is particularly superior when one participant is much more knowledgeable than the other. In these situations, the more knowledgeable participant will have the correct branch higher in its list of branches and the *SingleSelection* scheme will choose that participant. The *Random* mode selection scheme will only choose that participant half the time.

Note that for certain knowledge parameter values *Random* mode explores as much at 17% of the total branches while *SingleSelection* only explores 10% of the total branches. At these parameters, *SingleSelection* explores 41% fewer branches than *Random* mode. This value is significant not only because *SingleSelection* pursues 41% fewer branches at this level, but also because *SingleSelection* will pursue 41% fewer branches at every level in the search tree. The combined total number of branches searched by *Random* mode is of order $O(b^n)$ where b is the branching factor and n is the depth of the search. The combined total number of branches searched by *SingleSelection* will be $O(((1 - .41)b)^n)$ or $0.59^n b^n$. Thus the reduction in branches explored is exponential over the entire search space. If $n = 5$, for instance, the search space of *SingleSelection* will be only 7% of the search space of *Random*.

In general, if the percentage of branches searched by one scheme is x and the percentage of branches searched by another scheme is y, the percentage savings at one level in the search tree is $100\frac{x-y}{x}$. The cost (in terms of number of branches

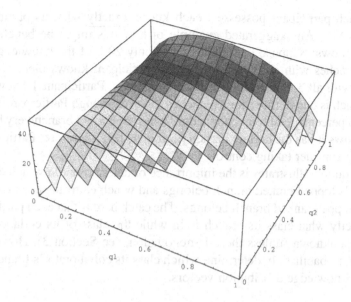

Figure 13. Percentage reduction in branches searched by using $SingleSelection^*(q_1, q_2)$ instead of $Random^*(q_1, q_2)$ or $\dfrac{Random^*(q_1, q_2) - SingleSelection^*(q_1, q_2)}{Random^*(q_1, q_2)}$.

searched) is reduced by a factor $\gamma = 1 - \frac{x-y}{x}$. The percentage savings over the entire search tree will be

$$PercentageReduction(x, y) = (1 - \frac{x-y}{x})^n = \gamma^n \tag{28}$$

where n is the depth of the search tree. In Figure 13, the percentage reduction in branches searched by *SingleSelection* in relation to *Random* is plotted by the formula

$$\frac{Random^*(q_1, q_2) - SingleSelection^*(q_1, q_2)}{Random^*(q_1, q_2)}$$

A.3.4. *Continuous Selection*

A more effective mode selection strategy would change during a collaborative problem solving session to reflect information gathered during the problem solving. Intuitively, if the participant-in-control has repeatedly chosen branches that ended in failure, perhaps, an appropriate strategy would be to allow the other participant to take charge. How might such a strategy be employed in the model presented above?

The reason that *SingleSelection* performs better than *Random* is that, on average, the participant with more knowledge has the correct branch ranked higher in its list of branches. However, there is an important bit of information not being utilized that each participant possesses: each knows exactly what its partition of branches looks like. An exaggerated example of how this might be beneficial is illustrated as follows: Suppose Participant 1 has only 20% of the knowledge, but knows four branches with all 3 factors and the participant knows there are only four branches with all 3 factors. Given those conditions, Participant 1 knows that the correct branch is one of those four branches. So even though Participant 1 has a relatively small percentage of total knowledge, it has the correct branch very high in its lists and **knows** it has the correct branch high in its list. Therefore, Participant 1 should strongly consider taking control.

What this example illustrates is the importance of determining in which equivalence class one's topped ranked branch belongs and which equivalence class one's collaborator's topped ranked branch belongs. The catch here is that each participant will know exactly what class its branch is in while the class of its collaborator's branch will be unknown (unless there is negotiation, see Section 3). However, a participant can probabilisticly determine which class its collaborator's branch is in if it knows the knowledge distribution vectors.

A.3.5. *Continuous Mode Selection Algorithm*

The continuous mode selection algorithm works as follows:

1. If a branch must be chosen in solving a goal, partition the potential branches based on the number of factors known for each.
2. Randomly select a branch from the highest ranked equivalence class. (Ranking: An equivalence class B_δ is ranked according to the probability that it contains the correct branch: $Prob(b_x = branch_c | b_x \in B_\delta)$.) We call the probability that it contains the correct branch *ProbMe*.
3. Compute the probability that the next item of your collaborator's sorted list of branches is the correct branch. Call this value *ProbOther*.
4. If *ProbMe* < *ProbOther*, allow the other participant to take control.
5. Otherwise, try to take control.
6. If both participants try to take control, one is randomly selected.
7. Repeat until solution is reached or both participant's announce failure to prove goal.

A.3.6. *Computing ProbOther*

If the knowledge distribution parameter for a participant and the size of each equivalence class of branches is known, then the probability that the ith branch in the ordered set of equivalence classes is the correct branch can be determined. What follows is one method for determining the probability that the ith branch is the correct branch. By keeping track of the number of branches a participant has proposed (and that have failed to prove fruitful), we can determine at each step the probability that a participant's next suggested branch will be the correct one.

Let *Sizes* be a function with parameter $\mathcal{S}$ that returns the size of the equivalence class $\mathcal{S}$.

$$Sizes(\mathcal{S}) = n_{\mathcal{S}}. \tag{29}$$

For convenience, let's redefine *ExpSize, ExpKnown,* and *ExpMistakenFor* (Equations 9, 11 and 13) so that they take *Sizes* as a parameter.

$$ExpSize(UserB_{\mathcal{S}}, p, Sizes)$$

$$= ExpKnown(B_{\mathcal{S}}, p, Sizes) +$$

$$\sum_{\mathcal{SUPER}} ExpMistakenFor(B_{\mathcal{SUPER}}, B_{\mathcal{S}}, p, Sizes) \tag{30}$$

where $\mathcal{SUPER}$ is a proper superset of $\mathcal{S}$.

$$ExpKnown(B_{\mathcal{S}}, p, Sizes) = Sizes(\mathcal{S}) p^{|\mathcal{S}|} \quad \forall \mathcal{S} \tag{31}$$

$$ExpMistakenFor(B_{\mathcal{S}}, B_{\mathcal{T}}, p, Sizes) =$$
$$\begin{cases} Sizes(\mathcal{S}) p^{|\mathcal{T}|} (1-p)^{(|\mathcal{S}|-|\mathcal{T}|)} \quad \forall \mathcal{S}, \mathcal{T} \text{ where } \mathcal{T} \subset \mathcal{S} \\ 0 \qquad\qquad\qquad\qquad\qquad\qquad \text{otherwise.} \end{cases} \tag{32}$$

The probability that the correct branch is the 1st branch in the sorted list of branches will be denoted by *First*$(p, Sizes)$ where p is the knowledge distribution parameter and *Sizes* is the function described above. The probability that the correct branch is in a particular equivalence class is given in Equation 15. Given that the correct branch is within a particular equivalence class, the probability that the branch is listed first in that class is 1 over the size of that class (given that sorting within a class is uniformly random). The size of a participant's equivalence class **given the correct branch is in that class** will be the expected size of that class plus one. Thus the probability that the correct branch is within a particular *UserBOrder*(x) is

$$\frac{Prob(branch_c \in UserBOrder(x), p)}{(ExpSize(UserBOrder(x), p, NewSizes) + 1)}, \tag{33}$$

where

$$NewSizes(i) = \begin{cases} Sizes(\mathcal{S}) & \text{where } UserBOrder(1) \neq UserB_{\mathcal{S}}, \\ Sizes(\mathcal{S}) - 1 & \text{where } UserBOrder(1) = UserB_{\mathcal{S}}. \end{cases}$$

This modification of the *Sizes* function reflects that the correct branch is 'removed' from computing the expected size of *UserBOrder*(x) since we are assuming that the correct branch is in *UserBOrder*(x).

Now, given that the correct branch is first in a particular $UserBOrder(x)$, what is the probability that this branch is first in the overall list? If all preceding equivalence classes are empty, then this branch will be first overall. Thus the probability that the correct branch is first in $UserBOrder(x)$ and first overall is

$$\frac{Prob(branch_c \in UserBOrder(x), p)}{(ExpSize(UserBOrder(x), p, NewSizes) + 1)} * \prod_{y=1}^{x-1} Empty(y, p, Sizes) \quad (34)$$

where $Empty$ computes the probability that equivalence class $UserBOrder(y)$ contains no elements given the knowledge distribution parameter p and function $Sizes$. The probability that a particular $UserB_\delta$ is empty is the probability that the participant does not have all the factors for any of the branches in B_δ and does not mistake any of the branches in B_T for branches in B_δ. The probability that a participant with knowledge distribution parameter p does not know all the factors for a branch in B_δ is $1 - p^{|\delta|}$. Thus the probability that the participant does not know all the factors for any of the branches in B_δ is $(1 - p^{|\delta|})^{Sizes}(\delta)$. Similarly, the probability that a participant mistakes a particular branch in T for being in δ is $1 - p^\delta (1 - p)^{(|T|-|\delta|)}$ if T is a superset of δ (otherwise the probability is 1), the probability that no branch in T is mistaken for a branch in δ is

$$ProbNotMistaken(T, \delta, p)$$

$$= \begin{cases} (1 - p^\delta(1 - p)^{(|T|-|\delta|)})^{Sizes(T)} & \text{if } \delta \subset T, \\ 1 & \text{otherwise.} \end{cases} \quad (35)$$

Therefore, $Empty$ can be computed

$$Empty(x, p, Sizes) =$$

$$(1 - p^{|\delta|})^{Sizes(x)} *$$

$$\prod_{i=1}^{x-1} ProbNotMistaken(UserBOrder(i), UserBOrder(x), Sizes) \quad (36)$$

where δ is such that $UserBOrder(x) = UserB_\delta$.

Using these results we note that $First$ can be computed by multiplying the probability that the correct branch is in $UserBOrder(1)$ and this branch is the first overall plus the probability that the correct branch is in $UserBOrder(2)$ and this branch is the first overall plus ... or

$$First(p, Sizes) = \sum_{x=1}^{2^n-1} \frac{Prob(branch_c \in UserBOrder(x), p)}{ExpSize(UserBOrder(x), p, Sizes) + 1.0}$$

$$\left(\prod_{y=1}^{x-1} Empty(y, p, Sizes) \right). \quad (37)$$

[126]

The probability that the correct branch is second in the list can be determined by

1. assuming that one branch has been tried and it has failed,
2. removing that branch from the list of all branches,
3. and retrying formula *First* to the new list of branches.

The formula for *Second* can be determined by computing, $\forall \delta$, the probability that a branch was taken from B_δ times $First(p, NewSizes)$ where *NewSizes* is identical with *Sizes* except that the size of δ is reduced by one:

$$Second(p, Sizes) = \sum^{\forall \delta} TakeAway(\delta, p, Sizes)\, First(p, NewSizes), \qquad (38)$$

where

$$NewSizes(j) = \begin{cases} Sizes(j) & \text{If } UserBOrder(j) \neq UserB_\delta \\ Sizes(j) - 1 & \text{If } UserBOrder(j) = UserB_\delta \end{cases}$$

and $TakeAway(\delta, p, Sizes)$ is the probability that a branch in δ is first in the list of branches (but not the correct branch). *TakeAway* is computed using the following set of formulae:

$$TakeAway(\delta, p, Sizes) =$$

$$\begin{cases} Sizes(i) \sum^{\mathcal{T}} FirstIn(\delta, \mathcal{T}, p, NewSizes) & \text{if } Sizes(i) > 0, \\ 0 & \text{otherwise.} \end{cases} \qquad (39)$$

where $UserBOrder(i) = \delta$ and $UserBOrder(j) = \mathcal{T}$.

$$NewSizes(m) = \begin{cases} Sizes(m) & \text{If } m \neq i \\ Sizes(m) - 1 & \text{If } m = i \end{cases}$$

$$FirstIn(\delta, \mathcal{T}, p, Sizes) =$$

$$\begin{cases} \left(\sum_{x=1}^{j-1} Empty(x, p, Sizes) \right) In(\delta, \mathcal{T}, p, Sizes) & \text{If } i <= j, \\ 0 & \text{Otherwise.} \end{cases} \qquad (40)$$

where $UserBOrder(i) = \delta$ and $UserBOrder(j) = \mathcal{T}$.

$$In(\delta, \mathcal{T}, p, Sizes) = \begin{cases} \dfrac{p^{|\delta|}}{n_\delta(ExpSize(\delta, p, Sizes) + 1)} & \text{If } \mathcal{T} = \delta \\[4mm] \dfrac{ExpMistaken(\delta, \mathcal{T}, p, Sizes)}{n_\delta(ExpSize(\mathcal{T}, p, Sizes) + 1)} & \text{Otherwise.} \end{cases} \qquad (41)$$

[127]

In general, the probability that the ith branch is the correct branch can be recursively expressed as

$$Ith(p, i, Sizes) =$$

$$\begin{cases} First(p, Sizes) & \text{If } i = 1 \\ \displaystyle\sum^{\forall \delta} TakeAway(\delta, p, Sizes) Ith(p, i-1, NewSizes) & \text{Otherwise.} \end{cases} \quad (42)$$

where

$$NewSizes(j) = \begin{cases} Sizes(j) & \text{If } UserBOrder(j) \neq \delta \\ Sizes(j) - 1 & \text{If } UserBOrder(j) = \delta. \end{cases}$$

A.3.7. Comparative Analysis of Continuous Mode

On average, how does this mode selection scheme compare with the two previous mode selection schemes presented: *Random* and *SingleSelection*? The expected number of branches explored in computing the solution to a goal can be computed by using the following formulae:

$$Cont(p_1, p_2, i_1, i_2, Sizes) =$$

$$\begin{cases} 0 & \text{If } Ith(p_1, i_1, Sizes) = 0 \\ & \& Ith(p_2, i_2, Sizes) = 0, \\ Ith(p_1, i_1, Sizes) + & \text{If } Ith(p_1, i_1, Sizes) >= \\ (1 - Ith(p_1, i_1, Sizes)) & Ith(p_2, i_2, Sizes), \\ (1 + Cont(p_1, p_2, i_1 + 1, i_2, Sizes)) & \\ Ith(p_2, i_2, Sizes) + & \text{Otherwise.} \\ (1 - Ith(p_2, i_2, Sizes)) & \\ (1 + Cont(p_1, p_2, i_1, i_2 + 1, Sizes)) & \end{cases} \quad (43)$$

which computes the expected number of branches searched given that Participant 1 has already suggested and subsequently failed $i_1 - 1$ branches and Participant 2 has already suggested and failed $i_2 - 1$ branches. Therefore,

$$Continuous(p_1, p_2, Sizes) = Cont(p_1, p_2, 1, 1, Sizes) \quad (44)$$

is the expected number of branches searched. If we assume complete distribution of knowledge,

$$Continuous^*(q_1, q_2, Sizes)$$

$$= Cont(Pmod(q_1, q_2), Pmod(q_2, q_1), 1, 1, Sizes)$$

$$= Continuous(Pmod(q_1, q_2), Pmod(q_2, q_1)). \quad (45)$$

A.4. BEST MODE SELECTION (ORACLE)

What is the best possible mode selection scheme? If an oracle could look at each of the two participants ordered list of branches, the oracle would simply choose the participant that has the correct branch highest in its list. On average, the probability that the first branch selected using oracle mode selection is the probability that either Participant 1 or Participant 2 has the correct branch sorted first in each respective list or

$$FirstOracle(p_1, p_2, Sizes) = First(p_1, Sizes) + First(p_2, Sizes)$$

$$-First(p_1, Sizes)\, First(p_2, Sizes) \qquad (46)$$

In general, the probability that the ith branch selected using oracle selection is

$$IthOracle(p_1, p_2, i, Sizes) = Ith(p_1, i, Sizes) + Ith(p_2, i, Sizes)$$

$$-Ith(p_1, i, Sizes)Ith(p_2, i, Sizes) \qquad (47)$$

Therefore, the average number of branches tried using oracle selection will be

$$Oracle(p_1, p_2, Sizes) = \sum_{i=1}^{2^n-1} i\, IthOracle(p_1, p_2, i, Sizes) \qquad (48)$$

If we assume complete distribution of knowledge,

$$Oracle^*(q_1, q_2, Sizes) =$$

$$\sum_{i=1}^{2^n-1} i IthOracle(Pmod(q_1, q_2), Pmod(q_2, q_1), i, Sizes)$$

$$= Oracle(Pmod(q_1, q_2), Pmod(q_2, q_1)) \qquad (49)$$

A.4.1. Graphical Comparison of mode selection strategies

Random mode selection is presented as a base line for the worse case strategy for mode selection. In this scheme, the controlling participant is selected randomly, without regard for the amount or quality of knowledge the individual participants possess. The *SingleSelection* mode selection scheme chooses the participant that possesses the most knowledge to be in control; on average, this strategy is superior to *Random* selection because the participant with more knowledge is better able to sort rationally the potential branches. *Continuous* selection makes use of the past history of the problem solving in addition to quantity of the knowledge each agent has. Thus *Continuous* selection makes use of the quality of the knowledge an agent

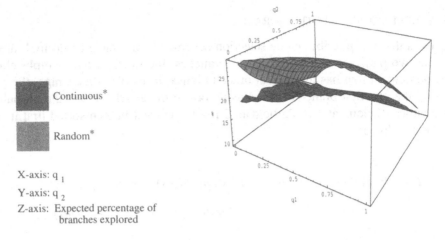

X-axis: q_1
Y-axis: q_2
Z-axis: Expected percentage of
        branches explored

Figure 14. The percentage of branches taken by *Continuous** and *Random**.

possesses. Finally, *Oracle* mode selection is presented as a base line for the best-case for mode selection. This scheme magically picks the agent that has the correct branch closest to the front of its sorted list of branches. No mode selection scheme can do better.

In Figures 14–20 the percentage of possible paths searched using the mode selection schemes, *Random**, *SingleSelection**, and *Oracle**, are plotted in comparison to *Continuous** over all values for the base knowledge distribution vectors, q_1 and q_2. Notice all mode selection schemes converge when one participant has all the knowledge while the other has none.

The difference between *Random** and *Continuous** are dramatic as is illustrated in Figures 14 and 15. The percentage of paths searched by each scheme is plotted in Figure 14. The percentage reduction in paths when *Continuous* mode is used rather than *Random* mode is plotted in Figure 15. The cost reduction factor γ (see Equation 28) may be as high as 0.50 for some knowledge distributions.

The difference between *Continuous** and *SingleSelection** is less dramatic over-all. However, as is illustrated in Figures 16 and 17, the *Continuous* mode scheme greatly outperforms the *SingleSelection** scheme in instances whenever the initial knowledge difference between the two participants is small. In Figure 16 the per-centage of paths searched by each scheme is plotted. In Figure 17, the percentage reduction in paths when *Continuous* mode is used rather than *SingleSelection* mode is plotted.

As a point of comparison, in the Figures 18 and 19, the *Continuous* mode scheme still is quite a ways from what can be obtained by an oracle. To do better than the *Continuous* scheme, however, would require more information than just the knowledge parameters of the two participants and the number of branches tried and failed by each participant.

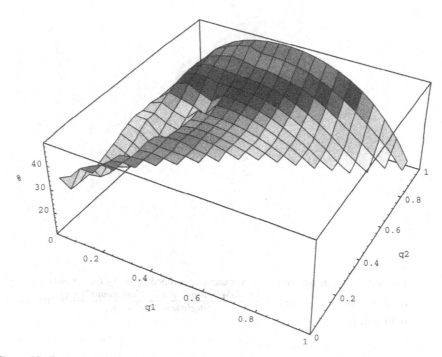

Figure 15. Percentage reduction in branches searched by using $Continuous^*(q_1, q_2)$ instead of $Random^*(q_1, q_2)$ or $\dfrac{Random^*(q_1,q_2) - Continuous^*(q_1,q_2)}{Random^*(q_1,q_2)}$.

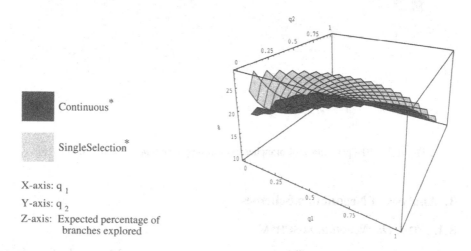

Continuous*

SingleSelection*

X-axis: q_1
Y-axis: q_2
Z-axis: Expected percentage of
       branches explored

Figure 16. The percentage of branches explored by *Continuous** and *SingleSelection**.

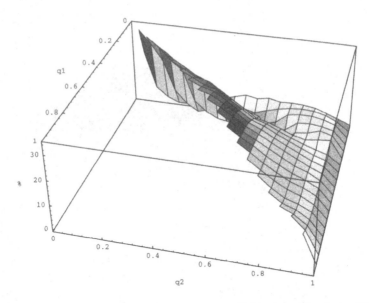

Figure 17. Percentage reduction in branches searched by using *Continuous**(q_1, q_2) instead of *SingleSelection**(q_1, q_2) or $\dfrac{SingleSelection^*(q_1,q_2) - Continuous^*(q_1,q_2)}{SingleSelection^*(q_1,q_2)}$ from a viewpoint of $(3, 0.8, 2)$.

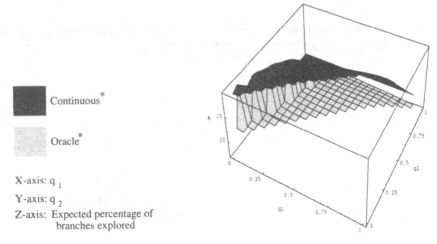

X-axis: q_1
Y-axis: q_2
Z-axis: Expected percentage of
       branches explored

Figure 18. The percentage of branches explored by *Continuous** and *Oracle**.

B. Analysis of Negotiation Schemes

B.1. THE *OneNegotiation* SCHEME

This negotiation scheme will be a counterpoint to Random Mode selection. Instead of randomly choosing at the beginning of a problem-solving session which particpant will be in control of the top goal throughout the dialog, the two participants

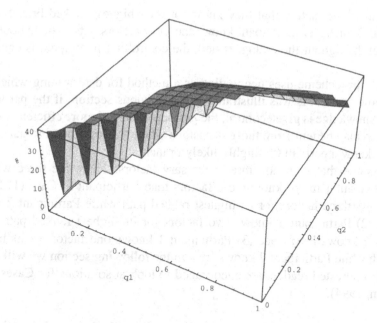

Figure 19. Percentage reduction in branches searched by using $Oracle^*(q_1, q_2)$ instead of $Continuous^*(q_1, q_2)$ or $\frac{Continuous^*(q_1, q_2) - Oracle^*(q_1, q_2)}{Continuous^*(q_1, q_2)}$ from a viewpoint of $(3, 0.8, 2)$.

Random*

SingleSelection*

Continuous*

Oracle*

X-axis: q_1

Y-axis: q_2

Z-axis: Expected percentage of branches explored

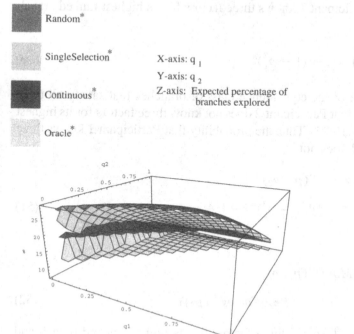

Figure 20. Comparison of Mode Selection Schemes: *Oracle**, *Continuous**, *SingleSelection** and *Random**.

will offer all of the factors that they know for their highest ranked branch under the top goal. Whichever participant knows the most factors gets to be in control of the top goal throughout the dialog. If tied, the controlling participant is chosen at random.

In effect, this scheme uses negotiation as a method for determining which participant knows more. As was illustrated in the previous section, if the participant with more knowledge is given control, the problem is solved more efficiently on average. It also may benefit from those occasions where the less knowing participant happens to know a particularly highly likely branch.

Let's assume that there are three necessary factors. There are three ways in which Participant 1 might know more factors than Participant 2: Case (1) Participant 1 knows three factors for its highest ranked path while Participant 2 knows less; Case (2) Participant 1 knows two factors for its highest ranked path while Participant 2 knows less; Case (3) Participant 1 knows one factor for its highest ranked path while Participant 2 knows less. In the following section we will examine Case 1. Interested readers are encouraged to look at solutions for Cases 2 and 3 in (Guinn, 1994).

B.1.1. *Case 1: Participant 1 knows three factors for its highest ranked path while Participant 2 knows less*

The probability that Participant 1 knows three factors for its highest ranked branch is

$$ProbKnows^{(3)}(p_1) = 1 - (1 - p_1^3)^{n_{\{1,2,3\}}} \tag{50}$$

where $n_{\{1,2,3\}}$ is the size of the equivalence class of branches that satisfy all three factors. The probability that Participant 2 does not know three factors for its highest ranked branch is $(1 - p_2^3)^{n_{\{1,2,3\}}}$. Thus the probability that Participant 1 knows three factors but Participant 2 does not is

$$ParticipantKnowsMore^{(3)}(p_1, p_2)$$

$$= [1 - (1 - p_1^3)^{n_{\{1,2,3\}}}][(1 - p_2^3)^{n_{\{1,2,3\}}}] \tag{51}$$

or

$$ParticipantKnowsMore^{(3)}(p_1, p_2)$$

$$= ProbKnows^{(3)}(p_1)(1 - ProbKnows^{(3)}(p_2)) \tag{52}$$

Suppose that Participant 1 knows three factors for its highest ranked branch and Participant 2 does not. Then the negotiation process will cause Participant 1 to go first. What will be the average length of search? Given that the first branch chosen is in $B_{\{1,2,3\}}$, the probability that the branch is the correct branch is $\frac{1}{n_{\{1,2,3\}}}$. The formula *ProbCorrect*(p, 3) is the probability that the first branch with three factors known for it is the correct branch.

$$ProbCorrect^{(3)}(p_1) = \frac{1}{n_{\{1,2,3\}}} \tag{53}$$

If that branch is not the correct branch, the average search length will be described in a formula very similar to that given in Equation 5.18 except that the size of the set $B_{\{1,2,3\}}$ will be reduced by one in the calculation of that formula.

B.1.1.1. *Computing SearchLength*$^{(3)}$(p_1, p_2)   In the case where Participant 1 has already tried a path in $UserB_{\{1,2,3\}}$, we can note the following: in effect, the search that follows will be identical with the search that would have occurred if $n_{\{1,2,3\}}$ was reduced by one. Thus the necessary transformations are as follows:

$$n_{\{1,2,3\}}^{(3)} = n_{\{1,2,3\}} - 1 \tag{54}$$

We substitute $n_{\{1,2,3\}}^{(3)}$ for every occurrence of $n_{\{1,2,3\}}$ in the equations 5.3, 5.4, 5.5 and 5.6 to compute *SearchLength*$^{(3)}$(p_1, p_2).

So far we have only considered the case where Participant 1 knows three factors for its highest ranked branch and Participant 2 does not. The other ways in which Participant 1 could "win" the negotiation would be if it knows two factors for its highest ranked branch while Participant 2 only knows one or zero, or Participant 1 knows one factor for its highest ranked branch while Participant 2 knows no factors for its highest ranked branch.

B.1.2. *Computing OneNegotiationSearchLength*

We will derive a formula *SearchLength*$^{(i)}$(p_1, p_2) which will be the average search length given that Participant 1 already tried its highest ranked branch (for which i factors were known). Once *SearchLength*$^{(i)}$(p_1, p_2) is derived, the formula for the average search length for the One Negotiation scheme is computed by adding the following components:

1. *ParticipantKnowsMore*$^{(3)}$(p_1, p_2)$*$ [*ProbCorrect*$^{(3)}$(p_1) $* 1+$
   $(1-ProbCorrect^{(3)}(p_1))*(SearchLength^{(3)}(p_1, p_2) + 1)$]
2. *ParticipantKnowsMore*$^{(2)}$(p_1, p_2)$*$ [*ProbCorrect*$^{(2)}$(p_1) $* 1+$
   $(1- ProbCorrect^{(2)}(p_1))*(SearchLength^{(2)}(p_1, p_2) + 1)$]
3. *ParticipantKnowsMore*$^{(1)}$(p_1, p_2)$*$ [*ProbCorrect*$^{(1)}$(p_1) $* 1+$
   $(1- ProbCorrect^{(1)}(p_1))*(SearchLength^{(1)}(p_1, p_2) + 1)$]
4. *ParticipantKnowsMore*$^{(3)}$(p_2, p_1)$*$ [*ProbCorrect*$^{(3)}$(p_2) $* 1+$
   $(1- ProbCorrect^{(3)}(p_2))*(SearchLength^{(3)}(p_2, p_1) + 1)$]
5. *ParticipantKnowsMore*$^{(2)}$(p_2, p_1)$*$ [*ProbCorrect*$^{(2)}$(p_2) $* 1+$
   $(1- ProbCorrect^{(2)}(p_2))*(SearchLength^{(2)}(p_2, p_1) + 1)$]
6. *ParticipantKnowsMore*$^{(1)}$(p_2, p_1)$*$ [*ProbCorrect*$^{(1)}$(p_2) $* 1+$

$$(1 - ProbCorrect^{(1)}(p_2)) * (SearchLength^{(1)}(p_2, p_1) + 1)]$$
7. $NeitherKnowsMore(p_1, p_2) * Random(p_1, p_2)$

or

$$OneNegotiationSearchLength(p_1, p_2) =$$

$$\sum_{i=1}^{3} ParticipantKnowsMore(p_1, p_2, i)[ProbCorrect(p_1, i) +$$

$$(1 - ProbCorrect(p_1, i)) * (SearchLength^{(i)}(p_1, p_2) + 1)] +$$

$$\sum_{i=1}^{3} ParticipantKnowsMore(p_2, p_1, i)[ProbCorrect(p_2, i) +$$

$$(1 - ProbCorrect(p_2, i)) * (SearchLength^{(1)}(p_2, p_1) + 1] +$$

$$NeitherKnowsMore(p_1, p_2) * Random(p_1, p_2). \tag{55}$$

As a recap, note that $ParticipantKnowsMore(p_1, p_2, i)$ can be found in Equations 6.3, 6.6, and 6.14. The formulas for $ProbCorrect(p, i)$ can be found in Equations 6.4, 6.12 and 6.15. The formula for $NeitherKnowsMore(p_1, p_2)$ can be derived from the equations for $ParticipantKnowsMore$:

$$NeitherKnowsMore(p_1, p_2) =$$

$$1 - \left(\sum_{i=1}^{3} ParticipantKnowsMore(p_1, p_2) + \sum_{i=1}^{3} ParticipantKnowsMore(p_2, p_1) \right) \tag{56}$$

B.1.3. *Evaluation of OneNegotiation*

In evaluating the effectiveness of the *OneNegotiation* scheme, we first assume complete knowledge distribution (for reference, see the discussion in Section A.2). Thus we compute

$$OneNegotiation^*(q_1, q_2) =$$

$$OneNegotiationSearchLength(PMOD(q_1, q_2), PMOD(q_2, q_1)). \tag{57}$$

We then compare the average number of branches taken compared to the average taken by *Random**, *SingleSelection** and *Continuous**.

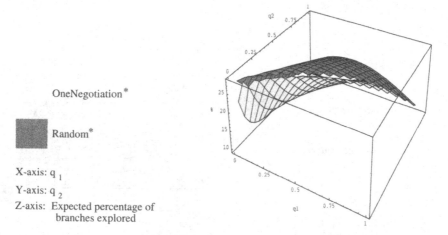

OneNegotiation*

Random*

X-axis: q_1
Y-axis: q_2
Z-axis: Expected percentage of
branches explored

Figure 21. The percentage of branches taken by *OneNegotiation** vs. *Random** from a viewpoint at coordinate (1.3, −2.4, 1.5).

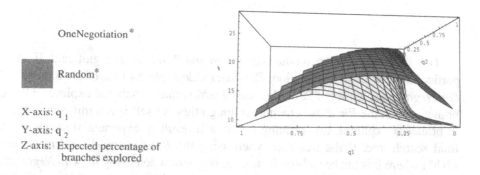

OneNegotiation*

Random*

X-axis: q_1
Y-axis: q_2
Z-axis: Expected percentage of
branches explored

Figure 22. The percentage of branches taken by *OneNegotiation** vs. *Random** from a viewpoint at coordinate (0.15, 2, −0.1).

B.1.3.1. *OneNegotiation vs. Random* In Figures 21 and 22 we compare (from different viewpoints) the percentage of total branches taken by *OneNegotiation** to the percentage taken by *Random**. The percentage of branches taken by *One-Negotiation** is consistently less than *Random**. When the two participants have roughly the same amount of knowledge (along the $x = y$ axis) there does not seem to be any noticeable advantage of one scheme over the other. However, when one participant has substantially more knowledge than the other, the difference is the number of branches searched can be quite large as is indicated by Figure 22. In these instances, the single negotiation act will choose with a high probability the participant with the most knowledge. As was demonstrated by the *SingleSelection* mode scheme in Appendix A, if the most knowledgeable participant is given control, the average number of paths searched will be less than the number searched by the *Random* scheme.

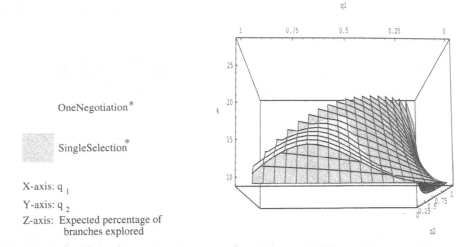

OneNegotiation*

SingleSelection*

X-axis: q_1

Y-axis: q_2

Z-axis: Expected percentage of
branches explored

Figure 23. The percentage of branches taken by *OneNegotiation** vs. *SingleSelection** from a viewpoint at coordinate (0.1, 3, −0.4).

The differences between *OneNegotiation* and *Random* are significant. If under a particular knowledge distribution, *Random* mode explores 18% of the branches and *OneNegotiation* explores 12%, then the *OneNegotiation* scheme explores 33% less branches than the *Random* scheme. Although this in itself is a significant reduction in branches explored, this pruning factor will result in exponential savings in the total search tree. If the tree size when using the *Random* mode scheme is order $O(b^n)$ where b is the branching factor, the tree size when using the *OneNegotiation* scheme is $O(((1 - \frac{1}{3})b)^n)$. The tree size is reduced by a factor of $(1 - \frac{1}{3})^n$. For a tree of depth 5, the tree size is reduced by a factor of $(1 - \frac{1}{3})^5 = 0.132$. The tree explored using the *OneNegotiation* scheme will be 13% of the size of the tree explored by the *Random* mode scheme.

B.1.3.2. *OneNegotiation vs. SingleSelection* In Figure 23 we compare the percentage of total branches taken by *OneNegotiation** to the percentage taken by *SingleSelection**. For a large portion of the possible knowledge distributions, the two schemes are indistinguishable. However, when one participant has a very high percentage (> 75%) of all knowledge and the other has a moderate percentage (> 45% but < 75%) of all knowledge, the *SingleSelection* scheme performs better. An explanation for this phenomenon is that if one participant has a very high percentage of all knowledge, it is preferable for that participant to be in control. If the other participant has substantial knowledge but not as much as the "high percentage" participant, there is a greater likelihood that single act of negotiation will select the "moderate percentage" participant. If the first branch chosen by the "moderate percentage" participant fails, then the advantage of negotiation is lost.

[138]

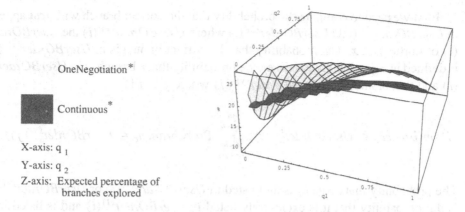

Figure 24. The percentage of branches taken by *OneNegotiation** vs. *Continuous** from a viewpoint at coordinate $(0.8, -2.4, 1.1)$.

That *OneNegotiation* fares favorably with *SingleSelection* overall leads to the observation that the use of negotiation can alleviate one of the problems of the mode schemes described in Appendix A: how do you arrive at an accurate user model? All of the mode setting schemes described depend on having a probabilistic representation of the other participant's knowledge. In practice, this may be extremely difficult to achieve. Negotiation, without depending on a user model, can help achieve some of the same results.

B.1.3.3. *OneNegotiation vs. Continuous* In Figure 24 we compare the percentage of total branches taken by *OneNegotiation** to the percentage taken by *Continuous**. It is clear from this graph that the *Continuous* mode scheme is substantially better. This is not surprising given that if the single act of negotiation picks a less knowledgeable participant to be in control and that participant's highest branch is not the correct branch, there is no mechanism to give control to the more knowledgeable participant.

B.2. THE *AllNegotiation* SCHEME

In this scheme, at each point when a new branch is chosen from a goal, the two participants announce the factors each knows for its highest ranked branch from that goal. This scheme is a counterpoint to the Continuous Mode scheme.

Suppose there are n necessary factors. The result of negotiating each time a branch selection occurs is that all the branches that **either** participant knows n factors for will be done first. Then all the branches that **either** participant knows $n - 1$ factors for will be done next. And so on. The end result of such a negotiation scheme is that the two ordered list of branches that each participant maintains will be merged. It will be a straightforward exercise to compute the average search length using this scheme.

First we need to compute the probability that the correct branch will **first** appear in $UserBOrder^{(1)}(i) \cup UserBOrder^{(2)}(i)$ where $UserBOrder^{(x)}(i)$ the $UserBOrder$ (i) of Participant x. The probability that the correct branch is in $UserBOrder^{(x)}(i)$ is defined in Equation 15. However, the probability that a branch is in $UserBOrder^{(x)}$ (i) <u>and</u> that branch is in $UserBOrder^{(y)}(j)$ where $j > i$ is

$$Prob(branch_c \in UserBOrder^{(x)}(i)) \sum_{j=i+1}^{2^n} Prob(branch_c \in UserBOrder^{(y)}(j)).$$

The probability that $branch_c$ is first listed in $UserBOrder^{(1)}(i)$ or $UserBOrder^{(2)}(i)$ is the probability that it is exclusively listed in $UserBOrder^{(1)}(i)$ and is listed in a later $UserBOrder$ of Participant 2 plus the probability that it is exclusively listed in $UserBOrder^{(2)}(i)$ and is listed in a later $UserBOrder$ of Participant 1 plus the probability that it is listed in both $UserBOrder^{(1)}(i)$ and $UserBOrder^{(2)}(i)$ or

$$Prob(branch_c \in UserBorder^{(1)}(i) \cup UserBOrder^{(2)}(i)) =$$

$$Prob(branch_c \in UserBOrder^{(1)}(i))$$

$$\times \sum_{j=i+1}^{2^n} Prob(branch_c \in UserBOrder^{(2)}(i)) +$$

$$Prob(branch_c \in UserBOrder^{(2)}(i))$$

$$\times \sum_{j=i+1}^{2^n} Prob(branch_c \in UserBOrder^{(1)}(i)) +$$

$$Prob(branch_c \in UserBOrder^{(1)}(i))$$

$$\times Probbranch_c \in UserBOrder^{(2)}(i)). \tag{58}$$

Assume $UserBOrder^{(1)}(i)) = UserBOrder^{(2)}(i)) = UserB_\delta$. The expected size of the union of $UserBOrder^{(2)}(i))$ and $UserBOrder^{(2)}(i))$ can be described

$$NegExpSize(CombinedUserB_\delta, p_1, p_2) = NegExpKnown(\delta, p_1, p_2) +$$

$$\sum_{\mathcal{T}}^{\mathcal{SUPER}} NegExpMistakenFor(B_{\delta\mathcal{SUPER}}, B_\delta, p_1, p_2), \tag{59}$$

where $NegExpKnown$ and $NegExpMistakenFor$ are defined below.

The expected number of branches that are in δ that are known to be in δ by either participant is the size of δ times probability that a branch that is in δ is known to be in δ by at least one of the participants. The probability that at least one participant knows a branch correctly knows a branch is in $\mathcal{S}$ is one minus the probability that neither participant knows the branch is in $\mathcal{S}$.

$$NegExpKnown(B_\mathcal{S}, p_1, p_2) = n_\mathcal{S}[1 - (1 - p_1^{|\mathcal{S}|})(1 - p_2^{|\mathcal{S}|})] \quad \forall \mathcal{S}. \tag{60}$$

The probability that a branch in $\mathcal{S}$ is mistaken for a branch in $\mathcal{T}$ by Participant 1 and not believed to be in a set higher than $\mathcal{T}$ by Participant 2 is

$$p_1^{|\mathcal{T}|}(1 - p_1)^{(|\mathcal{S}|-|\mathcal{T}|)} * \sum_{\mathcal{V}}^{\mathcal{SUPER}} p_2^{|\mathcal{V}|}(1 - p_1)^{(|\mathcal{S}|-|\mathcal{C}|)} \tag{61}$$

where $\mathcal{SUPER}$ is a superset of $\mathcal{T}$.

From this we can deduce that the expected number of branches in $\mathcal{S}$ to be *collectively* mistaken for being in $\mathcal{T}$ is

$$NegExpMistakenFor(B_\mathcal{S}, B_\mathcal{T}, p_1, p_p2) =$$

$$n_\mathcal{S}[p_1^{|\mathcal{T}|}(1 - p_1)^{(|\mathcal{S}|-|\mathcal{T}|)} * \sum_{\mathcal{V}}^{\mathcal{SUPER}} p_2^{|\mathcal{V}|}(1 - p_2)^{(|\mathcal{S}|-|\mathcal{C}|)}+$$

$$p_2^{|\mathcal{T}|}(1 - p_2)^{(|\mathcal{S}|-|\mathcal{T}|)} * \sum_{\mathcal{V}}^{\mathcal{SUPER}} p_1^{|\mathcal{V}|}(1 - p_1)^{(|\mathcal{S}|-|\mathcal{V}|)}+$$

$$p_1^{|\mathcal{T}|}(1 - p_1)^{(|\mathcal{S}|-|\mathcal{T}|)} p_2^{|\mathcal{T}|}(1 - p_2)^{(|\mathcal{S}|-|\mathcal{T}|)} \tag{62}$$

The average place that the correct path will be found can be computed by a simple modification of Equation 5.9. If there are n necessary factors then

$$AllNegAvgPlace(p_1, p_2) =$$

$$\sum Prob(branch_c \in UserBOrder(i, p_1) \cup UserBOrder(i, p_2))$$

$$[NegExpSize(UserBOrder(i), p_1, p2)/2+$$

$$\sum_{j=1}^{i-1}(NegExpSize(UserBOrder(j), p_1, p2))] \tag{63}$$

with a probability of $(1 - p_1)^n(1 - p_2)^n$ that neither participant has the correct path anywhere in their lists (and therefore it will not be in the merged list).

The length of the merged list is also easy to calculate:

$$AllNegLength(p_1, p_2) = \sum_{i=1}^{2^n-1}(NegExpSize(UserBOrder(i), p_1, p_2)) \tag{64}$$

[141]

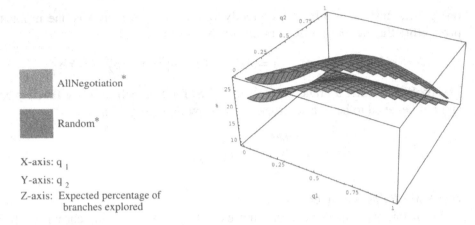

AllNegotiation*

Random*

X-axis: q_1

Y-axis: q_2

Z-axis: Expected percentage of
       branches explored

Figure 25. The percentage of branches taken by *AllNegotiation** vs. *Random** from a viewpoint at coordinate (1.3, −2.4, 1.5).

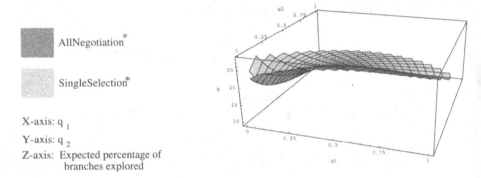

AllNegotiation*

SingleSelection*

X-axis: q_1

Y-axis: q_2

Z-axis: Expected percentage of
       branches explored

Figure 26. The percentage of branches taken by *AllNegotiation** vs. *SingleSelection** from a viewpoint at coordinate (0.8, −2.4, 1.0).

Thus the search length for the AllNegotiation scheme is

$$AllNegSearchLengthAllNeg(p_1, p_2) =$$

$$(1 - (1 - p_1)^n (1 - p_2)^n) \, AllNegAvgPlace(p_1, p_2) +$$

$$(1 - p_1)^n (1 - p_2)^n \, AllNegLength(p_1, p_2) \tag{65}$$

B.2.1. *Evaluation of AllNegotiation*

In evaluating the effectiveness of the *AllNegotiation* scheme, we first assume complete knowledge distribution (for reference, see the discussion in Section A.2). Thus we compute

$$AllNegotiation^*(q_1, q_2)$$

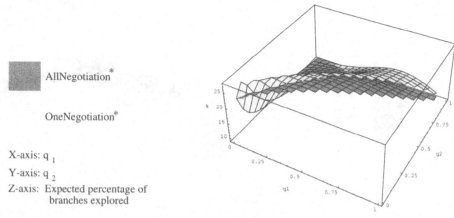

Figure 27. The percentage of branches taken by *AllNegotiation** vs. *OneNegotiation** from a viewpoint at coordinate (1.3, −2.4, 2).

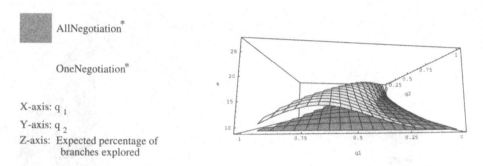

Figure 28. The percentage of branches taken by *AllNegotiation** vs. *OneNegotiation** from a viewpoint at coordinate (0.1, 1.1, −0.1).

$$= AllNegSearchLength(PMOD(q_1, q_2), PMOD(q_2, q_1)) \qquad (66)$$

We then compare the average number of branches taken compared to the average taken by *Random**, *OneNegotiation**, *SingleSelection**, *Continuous**, and *Oracle**.

B.2.1.1. *AllNegotiation vs. Random and SingleSelection* In Figure 25 we compare the percentage of total branches taken by *AllNegotiation** to the percentage taken by *Random**. The *AllNegotiation* scheme is clearly superior over all ranges of knowledge distribution. Similarly *AllNegotiation* is shown to be superior to *SingleSelection* in Figure 26.

B.2.1.2. *AllNegotiation vs. OneNegotiation* When compared to *OneNegotiation*, the *AllNegotiation* scheme performs better in almost all of the possible knowledge distributions as shown in Figures 27 and 28. When one participant has most of the knowledge and the other participant has very little, the two schemes are indistinguishable as can be seen by examining the portion of the graph in the

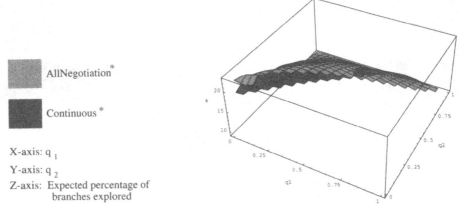

Figure 29. The percentage of branches taken by *AllNegotiation** vs. *Continuous** from a viewpoint at coordinate (1.3, −2.4, 2).

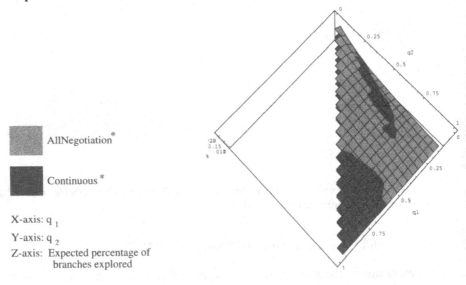

Figure 30. The percentage of branches taken by *AllNegotiation** vs. *Continuous** from a viewpoint at coordinate (0.5, 0.5, 3).

region $0 < q_2 < 1$ and $0 < q_1 < 0.25$. When there is a large difference in the knowledge levels of the two participants, it is unlikely that the unknowledgeable participant will ever win the negotiation. Thus the *AllNegotiation* scheme reverts to the *OneNegotiation* scheme as the knowledgeable participant gains control after the first negotiation and never relinquishes control. In these cases, it can be argued that *AllNegotiation* is less efficient than *OneNegotiation* because of the repeated expensive negotiation subdialogs.

When both participants are knowledgeable, the advantages of *AllNegotiation* begin to manifest themselves. Note in Figure 28 the large gap between the two

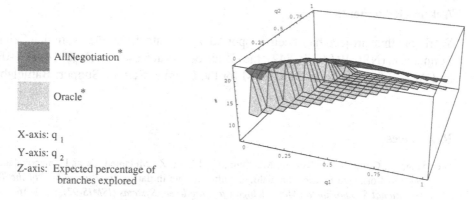

AllNegotiation*

Oracle*

X-axis: q$_1$
Y-axis: q$_2$
Z-axis: Expected percentage of
           branches explored

Figure 31. The percentage of branches taken by *AllNegotiation** vs. it Oracle* from a viewpoint at coordinate (0.8, −2.4, 1.1).

schemes when both participants have substantial knowledge. Unlike *OneNegotiation*, the *AllNegotiation* scheme can adapt to when a controlling participant fails to find quickly the correct path.

B.2.1.3. *AllNegotiation vs. Continuous* In Figures 29 and 30 we compare the percentage of total branches taken by *AllNegotiation** to the percentage taken by *Continuous**. The two schemes are mostly indistinguishable over a broad range of knowledge distribution. Figure 30 indicates, however, that there may be regions in which one scheme performs slightly better than the other. When both participants have a high amount of knowledge, the *AllNegotiation* scheme seems to perform better. This can be accounted for by the observation that negotiation gives more local information about a participant's search space. The *Continuous* mode scheme relies on giving only probabilistic information. This difference shows up more noticeably when more successful negotiation occurs. When both participants have a lot of knowledge, negotiation is likely to result in more switches in control than when there is a disparity between knowledge between the two participants. Despite this disparity, the global difference between the two schemes is rather slight.

Again, the closeness between the *AllNegotiation* scheme and the *Continuous* mode setting scheme suggests that we can dispense with trying to deal with user modeling. However, as negotiation is an expensive process and *AllNegotiation* will require a negotiation subdialog for every decomposable goal, a balance between the two schemes is more desirable.

B.2.1.4. *AllNegotiation vs. Oracle* As a reminder, in Figure 31 we compare the percentage of total branches taken by *AllNegotiation** to the percentage taken by *Oracle**. There is still a large gap between the lower bound of what is possible and what can be reached using *AllNegotiation*.

Acknowledgements

Work on this project has been supported by grants from the National Science Foundation (NSF-IRI-92-21842), the Office of Naval Research (N00014-94-1-0938), and ACT II funding from STRICOM for the Combat Service Support Battlelab.

References

Biermann, A., Guinn, C., Fulkerson, M., Keim, G., Liang, Z., Melamed, D. and Rajagopalan, K.: 1997, Goal-oriented multimedia dialogue with variable initiative. In: *Proceedings of the Tenth International Symposium on Methodologies for Intelligent Systems (ISMIS-97)*, pp. 1–16.

Biermann, A., Guinn, C., Hipp, D. and Smith, R.: 1993, Efficient collaborative discourse: A theory and its implementation. In: *Proceedings of the ARPA Human Language Technology Workshop.*

Bledsoe, W. W.: 1977, Non-resolution theorem proving. *Artificial Intelligence* **9**, 1–35.

Bobrow, D., Kaplan, R., Kay, M., Norman, D., Thompson, H. and Winograd, T.: 1977, GUS, A frame driven dialog system. *Artificial Intelligence* **8**, 155–173.

Brown, J. S., Burton, R. R. and Zydbel, F.: 1973, A model-driven question-answering system for mixed-initiative computer-assisted instruction. *IEEE Transactions on Systems, Man, and Cybernetics* **SMC-3**(3), 248–257.

Calistri-Yeh, R. J.: 1993, Knowledge requirements for human-computer collaboration. *Human-Computer Collaboration: Reconciling Theory, Synthesizing Practice, Papers from the 1993 Fall Symposium Series, AAAI Technical Report FS-93-05.*

Carletta, J.: 1992, Planning to fail, not failing to plan: Risk-taking and recovery in task-oriented dialogue. In: *Proceedings of the 14th International Conference on Computational Linguistics (COLING-92)*. Nantes, France, 896–900.

Chin, D.: 1989, KNOME: Modeling what the user knows in UC. In: A. Kobsa and W. Wahlster (eds.): *User Models in Dialog Systems*. New York: Springer-Verlag, 74–107.

Chu-Carroll, J. and Brown, M. K.: 1998, An Evidential Model for Tracking Initiative in Collaborative Dialogue Interactions. *In this issue.*

Clancey, W.: 1979, Dialogue management for rule-based tutorials. In: *Proceedings of the 6th International Joint Conference on Artificial Intelligence*. 155–161.

Clocksin, W. and Mellish, C.: 1987, *Programming in Prolog*. Berlin: Springer-Verlag, third edition.

Cohen, R., Allaby, C., Combaa, C., Fitzgerald, M., Ho, B., Hui, C., Latulipe, F., Lu, F., Pooley, D., Qian, A. and Siddiqi, S.: 1998, What is initiative? *In this issue.*

Conry, S. E. and Meyer, R. A.: 1993. Conflict management in distributed problem solving. In: Klein, M. (ed.) *Computational Models of Conflict Management in Cooperative Problem Solving, Workshop Proceedings from the 13th International Joint Conference on Artificial Intelligence.* Chambery, France.

Erman, L., Hayes-Roth, F., Lesser, V. and Reddy, D.: 1980, The Hearsay-II speech-understanding system: Integrating knowledge to resolve uncertainty. *ACM Computing Surveys* pp. 213–253.

Fikes, R. and Nilsson, N. J.: 1971, STRIPS: a new approach to the application of theorem proving to problem solving. *Artificial Intelligence* **2**, 189ff.

Fink, P. and Bierman, A.: 1986, The Correction of ill-formed input using history-based expectation with applications to speech understanding. *Computational Linguistics* **12**(1), 13–36.

Grosz, B. J.: 1978, Discourse analysis. In: D. Walker (ed.): *Understanding Spoken Language*. New York, NY: Elsevier, North-Holland, Chapt. IX, 235–268.

Guinn, C.: 1993, Conflict resolution in collaborative discourse. In: *Computational Models of Conflict Management in Cooperative Problem Solving, Workshop Proceedings from the 13th International Joint Conference on Artificial Intelligence*. Chambery, France.

Guinn, C. I.: 1994, *Metal-Dialogue Behaviors: Improving the Efficiency of Human-Machine Dialogue – A Computational Model for Variable Initiative and Negotiation in Collaborative Problem-Solving*. Ph.D. thesis, Duke University.

Guinn, C. I.: 1995, The role of computer-computer dialogues in human-computer dialogue system development. *AAAI Spring Symposium on Empirical Methods in Discourse Interpretation and Generation, Technical Report SS-95-06*, AAAI Press, pp. 47–52.

Guinn, C. I. and Montoya, R. J.: 1997 Natural language processing in virtual reality environments. *19th Interservice/Industry Training Systems and Education Conference (I/ITSEC)*.

Hagen, E.: 1999, An Approach to Mixed Initiative Spoken Information Retrieval Dialogue. *User Modeling and User-Adapted Interaction* **9**(1–2).

Hendrix, G., Sacerdoti, E., Sagalowicz, D. and Slocum, J.: 1978, Developing a natural language interface to complex data. *ACM Transactions on Database Systems* 105–147.

Hipp, D.: 1992, *A New Technique for Parsing Ill-formed Spoken Natural-language Dialog*. Ph.D. thesis, Duke University.

Korf, R.: 1987, Planning as search: A quantitative approach. *Artificial Intelligence* **33**, 65–88.

Lambert, L. and Carberry, S.: 1992, Modeling negotiation subdialogues. *Proceedings of the 30th Annual Meeting of the Association for Computational Linguistics* 193–200.

McRoy, S.: 1993, Misunderstanding and the negotiation of meaning. *Human-Computer Collaboration: Reconciling Theory, Synthesizing Practice, Papers from the 1993 Fall Symposium Series, AAAI Technical Report FS-93-05*, AAAI Press, pp. 57–62.

Mudler, J. and Paulus, E.: 1988, Expectation-based speech recognition. In: H. Niemann, M. Lang, and G. Sagerer (eds.): *Recent Advances in Speech Understanding and Dialog Systems*. New York: Springer-Verlag, 473–477.

Newell, A. and Simon, H.: 1972, *Human Problem-Solving*. Englewood Cliffs, New Jersey: Prentice Hall, Inc.

Nilsson, N. J.: 1971, *Problem-solving Methods in Artificial Intelligence*. New York: McGraw-Hill.

Power, R.: 1979, The Organization of Purposeful Dialogues. *Linguistics* **17**.

Rich, E.: 1979, User Modeling via Stereotypes. *Cognitive Science* **3**, 329–354.

Sacerdoti, E. D.: 1977, *A Structure for Plans and Behavior*. New York: North Holland.

Shortliffe, E. H.: 1976, *Computer-Based Medical Consultations*. New York, NY: Elsevier Press.

Sidner, C.L.: 1993, The Role of Negotiation in Collaborative Activity. *Human-Computer Collaboration: Reconciling Theory, Synthesizing Practice, Papers from the 1993 Fall Symposium Series, AAAI Technical Report FS-93-05*, AAAI Press, pp. 59–92.

Smith, R.: 1991, *A Computational Model of Expectation-Driven Mixed-Initiative Dialog Processing* Ph.D. thesis, Duke University.

Smith, R.: 1992, Integration of domain problem solving with natural language dialog: The missing axiom theory. In: *Proceedings of Applications of AI X: Knowledge-Based Systems*. 270–278.

Smith, R. and Hipp, D.: 1995, *Spoken Natural Language Dialog Systems: A Practical Approach*. New York: Oxford University Press.

Smith, R., Hipp, D. and Biermann, A.: 1992, A dialog control algorithm and its performance. In: *Proceedings of the 3rd Conference on Applied Natural Language Processing*, pp. 9–16.

Walker, M. and Whittaker, S.: 1990, Mixed initiative in dialogue: An investigation into discourse segmentation. In: *Proceedings of the 28th Annual Meeting of the Association for Computational Linguistics* 70–78.

Walker, M. A.: 1993, *Informational Redundancy and Resource Bounds in Dialogue*. Ph.D. thesis, University of Pennsylvania.

Whittaker, S. and Stenton, P.: 1988, Cues and control in expert-client dialogues. In: *Proceedings of the 26th Annual Meeting of the Association for Computational Linguistics* 123–130.

Wilensky, R.: 1983, *Planning and Understanding: A Computational Approach to Human Reasoning*. Addison-Wesley Publishing Company, Reading, Massachusetts.

Wos, L., Overbeek, R., Lusk, E. and Boyle, J.: 1984, *Automated Reasoning: Introduction and Applications*. Englewood Cliffs, NJ: Prentice-Hall.

Young, S., Hauptmann, A., Ward, W., Smith, E. and Werner, P.:1989, High level knowleldge sources in usable speech recognition systems. *Communications of the ACM*, pp. 183–194.

Young, S. and Proctor, C.: 1989, The design and implementation of dialogue control in voice operated database inquiry systems. *Computer Speech and Language* **3**, 329–353.

Author's vita

C. I. Guinn

Research Triangle Institute, Center for Digital Systems Engineering, 3040 Corn-wallis Road, Research Triangle Park, NC, USA, 27709.

Dr. Curry I. Guinn is a Research Engineer at Research Triangle Institute and an Adjunct Assistant Professor at Duke University. Dr. Guinn received his M.S. and Ph.D. degrees in Computer Science from Duke University under the supervision of Dr. Alan Biermann. Since 1995, Dr. Guinn has led the development of spoken natural language dialog within virtual reality-based trainers at Research Triangle Institute. The research described in this volume is based on his Ph.D. work as well as projects conducted at Research Triangle Institute.

User Modeling and User-Adapted Interaction **8**: 315–350, 1998.
© 1998 *Kluwer Academic Publishers.*

COLLAGEN: A Collaboration Manager for Software Interface Agents

CHARLES RICH[1] and CANDACE L. SIDNER[2]
[1]*MERL – A Mitsubishi Electric Research Laboratory, Cambridge, Massachusetts, USA;*
e-mail: rich@merl.com
[2]*Lotus Development Corporation, Cambridge, Massachusetts, USA; e-mail: csidner@lotus.com*

(Received 1 March 1988; accepted in final form 13 May 1998)

Abstract. We have implemented an application-independent collaboration manager, called Collagen, based on the SharedPlan theory of discourse, and used it to build a software interface agent for a simple air travel application. The software agent provides intelligent, mixed initiative assistance without requiring natural language understanding. A key benefit of the collaboration manager is the automatic construction of an interaction history which is hierarchically structured according to the user's and agent's goals and intentions.

Key words: Agent, collaboration, mixed initiative, SharedPlan, discourse, segment, interaction history.

1. Introduction

Current mixed-initiative interactive systems can be difficult to use: the order in which actions must be performed by the user and the system is often inflexible, it's hard to recover from mistakes, and each system has its own interaction conventions. Although many factors contribute to these difficulties, we believe that the essence of the problem is not in the user interface design as viewed over a single or short sequence of interactions, but rather that current systems lack support for the user's problem solving *process* as it unfolds over extended periods of time. The overall goal of this research is to develop a new paradigm for human-computer interaction which explicitly supports the user's problem-solving process based on current theories of collaborative discourse.

Our most fundamental underlying assumption is that a human-computer interface based on familiar human discourse rules and conventions will be easier for people to learn and use than one that is not. Although we cannot yet confirm this assumption by our own empirical studies, we are encouraged by an analogy with the direct-manipulation paradigm for graphical user interfaces, whose success we believe is due in large part to users' familiarity with the rules and conventions of object manipulation in everyday life.

Much is known about the structure of human collaboration and discourse. In this work, we rely specifically on the SharedPlan work of Grosz and Sidner (1986;

1990), Grosz and Kraus (1996), and Lochbaum (1994; 1995; 1998). This work provides us with a well-specified computational theory that has been empirically validated across a range of human tasks. Section 3 describes the basic algorithms we use from SharedPlan theory. Section 7.1 discusses the relationship of this theory to the issue of global initiative in conversation.

A second important methodological choice has been to support the problem-solving level of human-computer interaction via the 'software agent' paradigm. Specifically, we take the approach of adding a collaborative software agent to an existing graphical user interface. Software agents are currently a new research area without precise definition. Roughly speaking, a software agent is an autonomous software process which interacts with humans as well as with elements of its software environment, such as the operating system, application programs, and other agents.

Finally, at the engineering level, our approach has been to develop an application-independent *collaboration manager* for software agents, called Collagen[1] (for *Collaborative agent*). A collaboration manager is a software component that mediates the interaction between a software interface agent and a user. It is similar to what is often called a 'discourse manager,' except that it keeps track of not only the linguistic and attentional state of a discourse, but also the collaborative intentions of the participants. However, it is less than a fully automated planning system, because it does not by itself decide what the agent should do or say next (though it may provide some candidates); it primarily provides a representation for recording the decisions that the agent has made and communicated. Collagen also introduces a new graphical interface device, called the *segmented interaction history*, for displaying and manipulating the state of a collaborative problem-solving session.

To summarize the organization of the remainder of this paper: After further general discussion of our approach, we present a complete example session (Section 2) with an air travel planning application and agent we have built to demonstrate the functionality of Collagen. Following the example session, we review the relevant discourse theory and algorithms (Section 3), in preparation for a discussion of the application-independent architecture of Collagen (Section 4) and, more specifically, the problem-solving state transformations enabled by the segmented interaction history (Section 5). Section 6 focusses on how application-specific task knowledge is represented in Collagen. Section 7 reviews the mechanisms in Collagen and in our example agent which support mixed initiative. Finally, there is a comparison with other work and conclusions.

1.1. COLLABORATIVE INTERFACE AGENTS

Our version of the software agent paradigm (Maes, 1994), which we term a *collaborative interface agent*, is illustrated in Figure 1. This paradigm mimics the

---

[1] Collagen is a fibrous protein that occurs in vertebrates as the chief constituent of connective tissue.

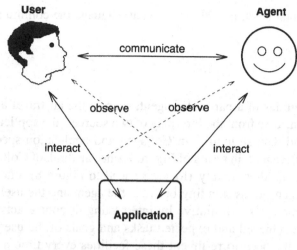

Figure 1. Collaborative interface agent paradigm.

relationships that hold when two humans collaborate on a task involving a shared artifact, such as two mechanics working on a car engine together or two computer users working on a spreadsheet together.

Notice that the software agent is able to both communicate with and observe the actions of the user and vice versa. A crucial part of successful collaboration is knowing when a particular action has been performed. In the collaborative interface agent paradigm, this can occur two ways: either by a reporting communication ('I have done x') or by direct observation. Currently in Collagen, we treat both of these cases equivalently, since we are assuming a kind of close collaboration in which both participants know and intend that all their actions are observed. However, both the underlying theory and architecture of Collagen equally well apply to a situation in which some actions cannot be observed, but only reported, such as if the agent is performing actions at a remote network site.

Another symmetrical aspect of the collaborative interface paradigm in Figure 1 is that both the user and the agent can interact with the application program. There are a number of design alternatives regarding how the agent's interaction with the application program is implemented (see Section 2.2). Typically, the agent queries the application state using the application's programming interface (API). The agent may modify the application state either via the API or via the graphical interface.

Although, in the long run, communication between users and interface agents will very likely be in spoken natural language, we have decided for both practical and methodological reasons *not* to include natural language understanding in our current system. As a practical matter, natural language understanding, even in this limited setting, is a very difficult problem in its own right, which we would like to sidestep for the moment. From a methodological point of view, we want to emphasize that discourse theory addresses the *content* of collaborative communication at a very fundamental level, regardless of what language the communication is in.

1.2. MIXED INITIATIVE

The mixed-initiative capabilities of a particular agent, such as the air travel agent described in the next section, arise from the interplay of two sources: the application-independent algorithms and data structures in Collagen and application-specific code and libraries 'inside' the agent. In terms of Figure 1, one can think of Collagen as a component of the agent. Alternatively (looking ahead to Figure 8), one can think of the collaboration manager as standing between the agent and the user.[2] In either case, Collagen supports mixed-initiative by interpreting discourse acts and maintaining a model of the achieved and expected tasks and goals of the user and agent, thereby eliminating the need to re-invent these facilities every time a new agent is built. As we will see in the next section, given Collagen as a base, an agent with a surprising richness of mixed initiative interaction can be implemented with the addition of very little application-specific programming.

2. An Example Application and Agent

In this section, we first describe the air travel application program we implemented to serve as a test bed for the development of Collagen. We then discuss some of the issues involved in adding an interface agent to this application, culminating with a detailed walkthrough of an implemented example session.

2.1. THE AIR TRAVEL APPLICATION

We wanted our test application program to be more complex than the typical research toy, but less complex than a full commercial program. We also wanted the application interface to be a good example of the current state of the art, i.e., a pure direct-manipulation interface where all of the underlying application state is graphically visible and modifiable.

Figure 2 shows the graphical user interface to the air travel planning system we implemented in Common Lisp using the Garnet graphics package (Meyers et al., 1990). (For the discussion in this subsection, please ignore the overlapping windows in the upper-right and lower-left corners.) The application provides a direct-manipulation interface to an airline schedule data base and a simple constraint checker. By pressing buttons, moving sliders, and so on, the user can specify and modify the geographical, temporal, and other constraints on a planned trip. The user can also retrieve and display possible itineraries satisfying the given

---

[2] This view more obviously generalizes to multiple software agents and users, which is a direction that we may, but have not yet, pursued.

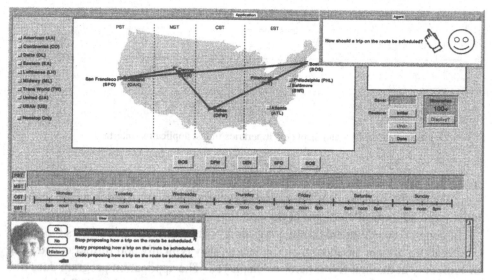

Figure 2. Test application screen.

constraints.

A typical problem to be solved using this application is the following:

> You are a Boston-based sales representative planning a trip to visit customers in Dallas, Denver, and San Francisco next week. You would prefer to leave on Wednesday morning, but can leave on Tuesday night if necessary. Your customer in Denver is only available between 11 a.m. and 3 p.m. on Thursday. You would prefer to fly as much as possible on American Airlines, because you have almost enough frequent-flier miles to qualify for a free trip this summer. You absolutely must be home by 5 p.m. on Friday to attend your son's piano recital.

In order to gain some initial intuitions about the problem-solving process using this application, we asked seven visitors and staff members at MERL to solve this and similar problems using the test application and recorded their behavior via informal notes and the logging facilities we built into the application. A typical problem-solving session lasted about 15 minutes and entailed about 150 user actions (mouse clicks).

In a typical session, the user begins by clicking on the route map to specify the origin, order of layover cities, and final destination for the trip. Next, users typically manipulate some of the small rectangles labelled with city names. These city 'interval' bars can be inserted into the horizontal slider area below the map and moved and stretched to specify latest arrival and earliest departure times at each city (see Figure 3). Users can also restrict the airlines used by setting the buttons to the left of the route map.

Whenever the user enters or changes a constraint, the number of possible itineraries is automatically recomputed from the flight schedule data base and displayed

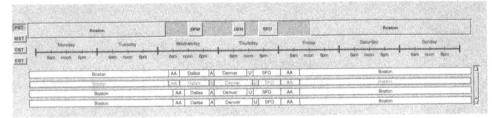

Figure 3. Interval bars and displayed itineraries in test application interface.

in the box labelled Itineraries. By pressing the Display? button in that box, the user can view all the possible itineraries laid out along the same timeline as the interval bars in the large scrollable area at the bottom of the screen (see Figure 3).

In general, users find that displaying more than about ten itineraries is too much information. If there are more than this many, they typically add further constraints or look only at the first few itineraries displayed. The application program does not allow display when there are zero (over-constrained) or more than 100 itineraries (under-constrained).

The main difficulties users experienced using the test application (or at least the ones we paid most attention to) were various forms of getting stuck and getting lost. Users had trouble knowing what to try next when they had over- or under-constrained their trip. They also had trouble keeping track of which combinations of routes and constraints they had already examined. Although the test application does provide a typical Undo button and a 'snapshot' facility (via the Save button and Restore menu), these were not very convenient to use. For example, the snapshot facility requires users to interrupt their work flow to choose a name for and explicitly save the current state in anticipation of possibly needing to return to it later.

One of our general observations from these sessions is that the users can productively be viewed as 'designing' itineraries (sequence of flights). As is typical in design tasks, the strategies used included information seeking (e.g., to see what components–flights are available with various properties), constraint satisfaction (e.g., arrival and departure time preferences), cost reduction (e.g., travel time), searching, backtracking, trade-offs, etc. All of these showed up in simple ways using this application.

Another important property of these scenarios is that the initial problem statement is only partially formalizable within the system.[3] Taking the example problem statement above, notice that the application program does not provide a representation to specify in advance (even if you could) just how much travel inconvenience you would put up with in order to accumulate more frequent-flyer miles on American. This kind of incompleteness is typical of design and many other tasks for which people use interactive systems.

---

[3] A closely related property is that there is usually more than one 'right' answer.

2.2. ASYNCHRONOUS WINDOW SHARING

The first step in adding a collaborative interface agent to the air travel application is to establish the basic communication, observation, and interaction channels required by the paradigm as shown in Figure 1. This was achieved using a window-sharing layer implemented in the *X* Window System and described in detail elsewhere (Rich, 1996).

A key concept in this window-sharing layer is the *home window*. The user and software agent each have a small dedicated window that is used for communication between them. The home windows start out in the corner locations shown in Figure 2; the user may move them to different screen locations in the usual ways provided by the window system.

Each home window contains an identifying face and has an associated *cursor*. The user's cursor is his usual mouse pointer. The agent's cursor is the pointing hand icon shown in its home window. The agent uses this hand to point and click on the shared application window just like the user's mouse pointer. The agent's eyes blink periodically to indicate that its process is still running. The home windows also shrink and expand as they are used. For example, after the user has chosen from her communication menu in Figure 2, both home windows return to their default configurations shown below.

To support asynchronous mixed-initiative interaction, the agent and its home window are serviced by a separate process from the application and user home window. Thus even when the agent has asked a question, the user is free to continue clicking on the application window instead of answering. Furthermore, using a distributed window system like *X*, the agent process may run on a different machine than the user/application process. (Whether or not to run the agent process in the same address space as the application is an engineering tradeoff that depends on the application.)

Returning now to Figure 1, let us account for how each of the arrows was realized with the air travel application:

- Communication from the agent to the user is achieved by printing English text in the agent's home window, as illustrated in Figure 2.
- Communication from the user to the agent is achieved by the user selecting from a menu as illustrated in Figure 2. Internally, a message in the artificial discourse language (see Section 6.1) is transmitted to the input buffer of the agent process.

- The user interacts with the application in the usual way, modifying the application state with her cursor and 'querying' it with her eyes.
- The agent observes the user's actions by virtue of a generic layer in the application that mirrors semantic actions into the input buffer of the agent process.
- The agent modifies the application state with its cursor (see discussion of 'un-GUI' module in Rich, 1996) and queries it using the programming interface (API) provided by the application.
- The user observes the agent's actions by watching the agent's cursor.

The final two points above allow some design alternatives, which may be explored with other target applications. In particular, it may sometimes be difficult to support agent manipulation of the shared graphical interface by generating mouse-level events. A weaker alternative to the complete agent/user symmetry above would be for the agent to modify the application state through the API and just the use its cursor to point to the location where the display changed.

2.3. EXAMPLE SESSION

Figure 4 shows the segmented interaction history of a complete session between a user and our collaborative agent solving the problem posed in Section 2.1 above. This is only one of many possible histories with different structures, depending on what the user chooses to do at each point in time. Also, as we will see in Section 5, this history is an explicit object in the interaction, whose structure can be referred to by both the agent and the user.

The contents of the Figure 4, including indentation, is automatically generated by Collagen (in a separate history window) as a printout of data structures built up during the session by the algorithms described in the next section. Event numbers have been added at the left for exposition.

Indentation in the history indicates the nesting of collaborative goals. The phrase in parentheses at the start of each level of indentation indicates the goal (purpose) being achieved by that segment. A more formal specification of the segmented interaction history representation will be provided in Section 3 after the underlying discourse theory terminology has been formally defined.

Notice that each event in the history is either a communication, represented by an English gloss in quotes '...', or the description of an application-level manipulation (result of a mouse click). Both the user and agent perform both communication and manipulation acts and the initiative moves back and forth between the two.

Whenever a constraint (such as an airline specification) is entered or changed, the application program automatically recomputes the number of possible itineraries and displays this number in the box labelled 'Itineraries.' In the segmented interaction history, the number of possible itineraries after each segment or event is indicated if it is different from the number before.

Given the problem statement in Section 2.1 above, the user could just start working on scheduling this trip herself by pointing and clicking on the applic-

(Jointly scheduling a trip on the route via working backward, allowing 4 itineraries)
1   USER: "Propose scheduling a trip."
2   AGENT: "Ok."
    (Done user identifying route of scheduling a trip as Boston to Dallas to Denver
        to San Francisco to Boston, allowing 100+ itineraries)
3   USER: Add Boston to the route.
4   USER: Add Dallas to the route, allowing 97 itineraries.
5   USER: Add Denver to the route, allowing 100+ itineraries.
6   USER: Add San Francisco to the route, allowing 100+ itineraries.
7   USER: Add Boston to the route, allowing 100+ itineraries.
8   USER: "Ok."
    (Done user proposing a trip on the route be scheduled via working backward)
9   AGENT: "How should a trip on the route be scheduled?"
10   USER: "Propose scheduling a trip on the route via working backward."
    (Done user working on San Francisco to Boston leg, allowing 70 itineraries)
11   AGENT: "Propose you work on San Francisco to Boston leg."
12   USER: Add Boston final interval with arrival Sun 11:30p.
13   USER: Change Boston final interval to arrival Fri noon.
14   USER: Add San Francisco stopover with arrival Wed 1:55a departure Wed 9:55a,
                allowing 70 itineraries.
15   USER: Change San Francisco stopover to arrival Thu 6:00p departure Fri 1:57a.
16   USER: "Ok."
    (Done user working on Denver to San Francisco leg, allowing 61 itineraries)
17   AGENT: "Propose you work on Denver to San Francisco leg."
18   USER: Add Denver stopover with arrival Thu 8:21a departure Thu 3:19p.
         ...
    (Done jointly specifying airlines, allowing 4 itineraries)
36   USER: Add American specification, allowing no itineraries.
    (Done agent adding United specification, allowing 4 itineraries)
37   AGENT: "Propose I add United specification."
38   USER: "Ok."
39   AGENT: Add United specification, allowing 4 itineraries.
    (User displaying and selecting itineraries)
40   USER: Display 4 itineraries.
41   USER: Select itinerary Wed AA/1099 Wed AA/313 Thu UA/343 Fri AA/928.

Figure 4. Segmented interaction history for example session.

ation window. Instead, she chooses to communicate with the agent to initiate a collaboration (event 1). As we will see in the ensuing conversation, the agent not only responds to the user's initiative here, but will also take the initiative itself at appropriate times in the joint activities.

In order to communicate with the agent, the user clicks on the arrow at the bottom of her home window, causing the window to expand to show her the current communication choice(s):

Propose scheduling a trip.   ↖

There is only one possible collaboration to propose here, since this test application was built with only one toplevel goal in mind. A real application would have a range of high-level goals. The agent indicates its acceptance of the user's proposal by displaying 'Ok' in its home window (event 2). This simple utterance by the

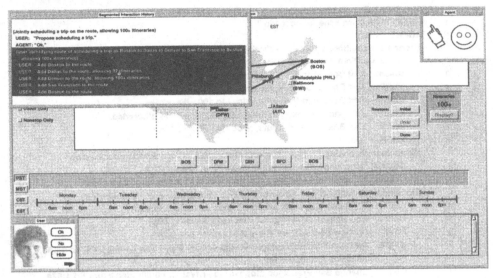

Figure 5. Pop-up window for segmented interaction history.

agent not only communicates acceptance of the proposed action to the user; it also reflects the creation within Collagen of an initial model of the purpose and expected elements of the collaboration.

Note that at this point, however, the agent has only generic knowledge of the typical tasks involved in scheduling a trip and recipes (general methods) for performing them. It does does not know anything about the user's particular problem or preferences.

The user now clicks in order on cities on the map: Boston, Dallas, Denver, San Francisco, Boston. The agent recognizes these actions as forming a segment whose purpose is to identify one of the parameters of the current goal, i.e., the route of the trip.

The segmented interaction history is computed incrementally. Its most basic function is to orient the user. For example, if the user left her computer in the middle of working on this problem and returned after a few hours (or days), the history would help her reestablish where in the problem solving process she was. In particular, if the user requested a display of the history at this point (by pressing the 'History' button in her home window), the pop-up window shown in the upper left corner of Figure 5 would appear with the current segment highlighted.

The user clicks on the 'Ok' button (event 8) in her home window to signal the end of the current segment. The agent now takes the initiative and in its home window asks (event 9):

How should a trip on the route be scheduled?

This question is an example of intelligent assistance in which the agent helps the user focus on what needs to be decided next in order to push the current task forward. Unlike conventional pop-up help windows, however, the user at this point can delay or ignore the agent's question simply by continuing to click on the application window.

Figure 2 shows the moment in the interaction history after the agent's question above when the user is about to answer by choosing a response from the communication menu in her home window. This response is event 10 in the segmented interaction history. Notice that the user's first menu choice has a blank at the end where the name of the recipe is supposed to go. (See Section 5 for an explanation of the other choices.)

Once a communication menu choice is made, the user may be presented with another menu, such as the one below, to choose from the allowable values for any unspecified parameters of the communication action:

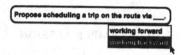

Our agent currently knows only two generic toplevel recipes for scheduling a trip on a given route, gleaned from our informal observations of test application users and study of transcripts of people talking on the phone to real travel agents (Kowtko and Price, 1989). These two recipes are: *working forward* on the legs of the trip starting at the originating city and *working backward* starting at the final destination.

The user chooses working backward (event 10), presumably because of the hard constraint on attending the piano recital after the trip, after which the agent says:

Propose you work on San Francisco to Boston leg.

Here again the agent uses the current context to assist the user, in this case to propose the next subtask. Working on a leg entails manipulating the 'interval bars' in the horizontal slider area below the map to specify latest arrival and earliest departure times at a city (see Figure 3).

Note that the agent's response here results from a simple application-independent strategy, namely to propose the next (in this case, the first) executable step in the current recipe. The same strategy underlies the agent's proposal in event 17 after the user finishes working on the San Francisco to Boston leg. As we will see in the architecture discussion in Section 4, this application-independent strategy is embedded in the collaboration manager, even though the recipes themselves are application-specific.

We skip ahead now to event 36. As mentioned earlier, we observed that one of the main ways that users of the test application get stuck is by over-constraining their itinerary, causing the itinerary count to become zero. Here the user has required all flights to use American airlines, which resulted in no possible itineraries.

The agent's response (event 37) is to suggest reducing constraints by adding United to the set of allowable airlines. The agent did not propose this particular constraint change at random – it used its ability to access the test application's full API to search the flight data base for an airline that would in fact increase the number of itineraries. This is a good example of where the capabilities of one participant in collaboration are usefully different from those of another. With the user's permission (event 38), the agent uses its hand cursor to click on the United airlines button (event 39).

The interaction ends with the user displaying the four possible itineraries in the scrolling window (see Figure 3) and selecting one, which causes detailed information, such as flight numbers, to be printed in the message window above the Itineraries count in the application interface.

2.4. MIXED INITIATIVE IN THE EXAMPLE SESSION

The mixed-initiative behavior in the example session above arises from the interplay of two sources: the application-independent discourse model embodied in Collagen, and application-specific knowledge 'inside' the air travel agent. Application-specific knowledge can be further decomposed into two forms:

(i) a library of recipes that specify the typical steps and constraints for achieving certain goals and
(ii) arbitrary pattern-action rules.

For example, the agent's contributions in events 9, 11, 17 and 39 arise from the application of the following simple and generic discourse principles to the collaborative discourse state at each step (these principles and others used in Collagen are described in more detail in the next section):

- A recipe needs to be identified for the current goal.
- Identification of a recipe may be achieved by asking the other participant.
- A goal or action may be performed when all of its parameters are known and all of its predecessors (in the current recipe) have been achieved.
- A goal or action may be performed by any participant who is capable, unless a specific participant has been specified.

In particular, the agent's question in event 9 arises from the application of the first and second principles above to the state in which no recipe has yet been identified for the goal of scheduling a trip. The agent's proposals in events 11 and 17 arise from the application of the third and fourth principles above to the steps of the working-backward recipe. (Only the user is capable of working on these goals, because only the user knows her travel preferences). The agent's manipulation action in event 39 also arises from the application of the third and fourth principles above, together with an additional collaboration-specific rule which requires the from the application of the third and fourth principles above to the steps of the working-backward recipe. (Only the user is capable of working on these goals, because only the user knows her travel preferences). The agent's manipulation action in event 39 also arises from the application of the third and fourth principles above, together with an additional collaboration-specific rule which requires the agent to seek explicit agreement from the user (event 37) before performing any manipulation actions.

The content of the agent's proposal in event 37 (i.e., the choice of United airlines) arises from an application-specific pattern-action rule for overconstrained situations, as discussed in the preceding section. Collagen plays an important role even in the case of these arbitrary pattern-action rules, since the pattern (situation description) part of such rules typically depends not only on the application state, but also on the current discourse state.

3. Collaborative Discourse Theory and Algorithms

Collaboration is a process in which two or more participants coordinate their actions toward achieving shared goals. Most collaboration between humans involves communication. *Discourse* is a technical term for an extended communication between two or more participants in a shared context, such as a collaboration.

This section provides a brief overview of the collaborative discourse theory and algorithms on which Collagen is based. Since the goal of this work is to use well-established human discourse principles, readers are referred to the referenced literature for more details.

Collaborative discourse in Grosz and Sidner's framework (Grosz and Sidner, 1986; Grosz and Sidner, 1990) is understood in terms of three interrelated kinds of discourse structure:

- intentional structure, which is formalized as partial *SharedPlans*.
- linguistic structure, which includes the hierarchical grouping of actions into *segments*.
- attentional structure, which is captured by a *focus stack* of segments.

We summarize the key features of each of these structures below, followed by a concrete example of Collagen's discourse state representation. Finally, we describe the discourse interpretation and generation algorithms, which are the heart of Collagen's discourse processing.

3.1. SHARED PLANS

Grosz and Sidner's theory predicts that, for successful collaboration, the participants need to have mutual beliefs[4] about the goals and actions to be performed and the capabilities, intentions, and commitments of the participants. The formal representation (Grosz and Kraus, 1996) of these aspects of the mental states of the collaborators is called a SharedPlan.

As an example of a SharedPlan in the air travel domain, consider the collaborative scheduling of a trip wherein participant A (e.g., the user) knows the constraints on travel and participant B (e.g., the software agent) has access to a data base of all possible flights. To successfully complete the collaboration, A and B must mutually believe that they:

- have a common goal (to find an itinerary that satisfies the constraints);
- have agreed on a sequence of actions (a *recipe*) to accomplish the common goal (e.g., choose a route, specify some constraints on each leg, search for itineraries satisfying the constraints);
- are each capable of performing their assigned actions (e.g., A can specify constraints, B can search the data base);
- intend to do their assigned actions; and
- are committed to the overall success of the collaboration (not just the successful completion of their own parts).

Several important features of collaboration should be noted here.

First, due to partial knowledge of the shared environment and each other, participants do not usually begin a collaboration with all of the conditions above 'in place.' They typically start with only a *partial* SharedPlan. An important purpose of the communication between participants is to determine (possibly with the help of individual information gathering) the appropriate recipe to use, who should do what, and so on.

Second, notice that SharedPlans are recursive. For example, the first step in the recipe mentioned above, choosing a route, is itself a goal upon which A and B might collaborate.

Finally, planning (coming to hold the beliefs and intentions required for the collaboration) and execution (acting upon the current intentions) are usually interleaved for each participant and among participants. Unfortunately, there is currently no generally accepted domain-independent theory of how people manage this interleaving. (The current best candidates for a generic theory are the so-called belief/desire/intention frameworks, such as Bratman et al., 1988.) Collagen therefore does not currently provide a generic framework for execution. Another way of saying this is that we provide a generic framework only for *recording* the order in which planning and execution occur, not for *deciding* how to interleave them.

---

[4] A and B mutually believe p iff A believes p, B believes p, A believes that B believes p, B believes that A believes p, A believes that B believes that A believes p, and so on. This is a standard philosphical concept whose infinite formal definition is not a practical problem.

A: 'Replace the pump and belt please.'

  B: 'OK, I found a belt in the back.'

    B: 'Is that where it should be?'
    A: 'Yes.'

  B: Removes belt.
  B: 'It's done.'

  A: 'Now remove the pump.'
    ...
  A: 'First you have to remove the flywheel.'
    ...
  A: 'Now take off the base plate.'
  B: 'Already did.'

Figure 6. Segments in a task-oriented human discourse.

3.2. DISCOURSE SEGMENTS AND FOCUS STACK

The concept of discourse segments is at the very foundation of discourse theory. Analysis of discourses from a range of human interactions has resulted in general agreement that discourse has a natural hierarchical structure. The elements of this hierarchy are called *segments*. A segment is a contiguous sequence of communicative actions that serve some purpose. For example, a question and answer sequence constitutes a discourse segment whose purpose is (usually) to achieved shared knowledge of some fact.

The existence of segments can be seen in everything from pitch patterns in spoken discourse to the way that pronouns are interpreted. Automatic segmentation (i.e., the segmented interaction history) has therefore been our first milestone in applying discourse principles to human-computer interaction.

A simple example of segments in a task-oriented human discourse is shown in Figure 6, which is adapted from (Grosz [Deutsch], 1974). In this discourse, participant *A* is instructing participant *B* how to repair an air compressor. Notice that this analysis of discourse structure includes not only the participants' utterances, but also their actions (e.g., *B* removes belt). This is appropriate in a context, such as collaborative interface agents, where all actions on the shared artifact are known and intended to be mutually observable.

The toplevel segment and three embedded segments in Figure 6 are indicated by the brackets and indentation shown (further subsegments are elided). In Grosz and Sidner's theory, the segment structure of such a discourse is accounted for by assigning a *purpose* to each segment, such that each segment's purpose contributes to successful collaboration on the parent segment's purpose via the SharedPlan conditions described above.

For example, the purpose of the toplevel segment in Figure 6 is to replace the pump and belt, which is the common goal of the collaboration. The purpose of the first subsegment is to remove the belt, which is one of the steps in the recipe for replacing the belt. The purpose of the first subsubsegment is to identify a parameter of the removal action, i.e., the belt to be removed. The purpose of the second subsegment is to remove the pump, which is also one of the steps in the recipe for the toplevel purpose.

The shifting focus of attention in a discourse is captured by a *focus stack* of discourse segments. In the natural flow of a a collaborative discourse, new segments and subsegments are created, pushed onto the focus stack, completed, and then popped off the stack as the SharedPlan unfolds in the conversation. Sometimes participants also interrupt each other, abandon the current SharedPlan even though it is not complete, or return to earlier segments.

Thus, as we will see more concretely in the discussion of Figure 7 below, the attentional (focus stack) and intentional (SharedPlan) aspects of discourse structure theory are connected through the discourse segment purpose: each segment on the stack is associated with a SharedPlan for its purpose (Lochbaum, 1994; 1998).

3.3. DISCOURSE STATE REPRESENTATION IN COLLAGEN

The *discourse state* in Collagen is a concrete representation of the three kinds of discourse structure described above. Figure 7 shows an example discourse state.

The lower part of Figure 7 shows a *plan tree*, which is an approximate representation of a partial SharedPlan. Plan trees are composed of alternating act and recipe nodes as shown. Both acts and recipes have *bindings*, shown as labelled stubs in the figure, with constraints between them specified in their recipe library definitions. An act node has a binding for each of its parameters, who performs it and, if it is non-primitive, a recipe node. A recipe node has a binding for each step in the recipe. To support the nonmonotonic changes in discourse state required for negotiation and history-based transformations (Section 5), bindings and the propagation of logical information in the plan tree are implemented using a truth-maintenance system.

For example, in Figure 7, act6's sole parameter has been bound to value1 and act6's recipe has been bound to recipe6. If a history-based transformation 'undoes' act7 and act8, then act6's recipe binding will be retracted. Similarly, act6's parameter binding will be retracted if the first communication act in its segment is undone.

The upper part of Figure 7 shows the *focus stack* (illustrated as growing downward) and the *history list*, which contains toplevel segments that have been popped off the focus stack. When a segment is popped off the focus stack, it is added to the history list if and only if it has no parent segment. In the figure, there are two segments on the focus stack and two segments in the history list. The elements of

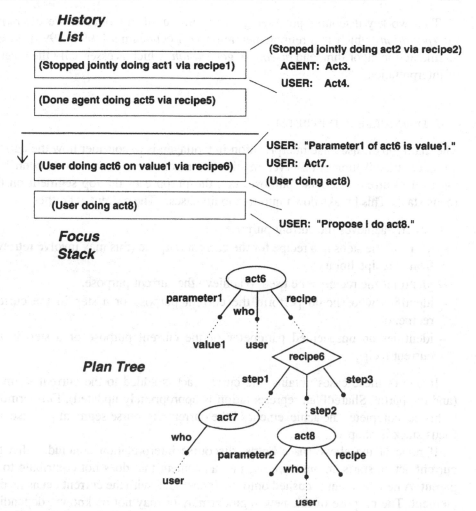

Figure 7. Internal discourse state representation.

one of the segments on the stack and one of the segments in the history list are shown expanded to the right.

Segments on the stack are called *open*, because they may still have acts added to them. Segments that have been popped off the stack are called *closed*. All the segments in the history list and their subsegments are closed. Segments on the stack may have closed subsegments.

Usually, the root of the plan tree (e.g., act6 in Figure 7) is the purpose of the base segment of the focus stack, and each subsegment (e.g., act8) corresponds to a subtree, recursively. The exception is when there is an interruption, i.e., a segment which does not contribute to its parent, in which case we have a disconnected plan tree for that segment. Plan trees remain associated with segments even after they are popped off the stack.

The two key discourse processing algorithms used in Collagen are *discourse interpretation*, which is a reimplementation of Lochbaum's (1994; 1998) rgraph augmentation algorithm, and *discourse generation*, which is essentially the inverse of interpretation.

3.4. DISCOURSE INTERPRETATION

The main job of discourse interpretation in Collagen is to consider how the current direct communication or observed manipulation action can be viewed as contributing to the current discourse purpose, i.e., the purpose of the top segment on the focus stack. This breaks down into five main cases.[5] The current act either:

- directly achieves the current purpose,
- is one of the steps in a recipe for the current purpose (this may involve retrieval from a recipe library),
- identifies the recipe to be used to achieve the current purpose,
- identifies who should perform the current purpose or a step in the current recipe, or
- identifies an unspecified parameter of the current purpose or a step in the current recipe.

If one of these cases obtains, the current act is added to the current segment (and the partial SharedPlan representation is appropriately updated). Furthermore, if this act completes the achievement of the current discourse segment purpose, the focus stack is popped.

If none of the above cases holds, discourse interpretation concludes that the current action starts an *interruption*, i.e., a segment that does not contribute to its parent. A new segment is pushed onto the focus stack with the current act as its first element. The purpose of this new segment may or may not be known, depending on the specific content of the initiating action.

The occurence of interruptions may be due to actual interruptive material in the ongoing discourse or due to an incomplete recipe which does not include the current act even though it ought to. We take the view that, in general, the agent's knowledge will never be complete and it therefore must deal gracefully with unexpected events.

Another phenomenon which manifests itself as interruptions in the current discourse interpretation algorithm is when the user and/or agent are pursuing two (or more) goals in parallel, e.g., arbitrarily interleaving steps from both recipes. In this situation, some higher level representation of the parallel goals would be preferable to the alternating structure of pushes (interruptions) and pops (stop transformations, see Section 5.1) currently required. This is an area for future work.

---

[5] The last three cases are instances of a larger class of explanations that Lochbaum (1995) calls 'knowledge preconditions.'

It is tempting to think of discourse interpretation as the plan recognition problem, which is known to be exponential in the worst case (Kautz, 1990). However,
this misses a key property of normal human discourse, namely that speakers work
hard to make sure that their conversational partners can understand their intentions without a large cognitive search. Notice that only search performed by the
discourse interpretation algorithm above is through the steps of the current recipe
or all known recipes for the current segment's purpose (and this is *not* done recursively). We think it will be reasonable to expect users to communicate enough
so that the agent can follow what is going on without having to do general plan
recognition.

3.5. DISCOURSE GENERATION

The discourse generation algorithm is, as mentioned above, essentially the inverse
of interpretation. It looks at the current focus stack and associated SharedPlan and
produces a prioritized *agenda* of (possibly partially specified) actions which would
contribute (according to the five cases above) to the current discourse segment
purpose. For example, if the current purpose is to jointly schedule a trip, the agenda
includes an action in which the agent asks the user to propose a route. In Collagen,
the agenda contains communication and manipulation actions by either the user or
agent, which would advance the current problem-solving process.

The main reason we believe that the menu approach to user communication
demonstrated in Section 2 is workable is because the discourse generation algorithm typically produces only a relatively small number of communication choices,
all of which are relevant in the current discourse context.

4. The Collagen Architecture

This section focuses on the main technical contribution of this work, which is to
embed the theory-grounded algorithms and data structures described inSection 3
into a practical architecture (Figure 8) for building collaborative interface agents,
such as our air travel example. Figure 8 is essentially an expansion of Figure 1
in which the Collagen discourse manager is made explicit as the mediator of all
communication between the agent and the user.

All of the internal data flow in Figure 8 takes place using Collagen's artificial
discourse language (see Section 6.1). Whenever there is a need for the user to see
information, such as in display of the user communication menu or the segmented
interaction history, these internal representations are given an English gloss by
simple string substitution in templates defined in the recipe library.

We refer to Collagen as a *collaboration manager*, because it provides a standard
mechanism for maintaining the flow and coherence of agent-user collaboration. In
addition to saving implementation effort, using a collaboration manager provides

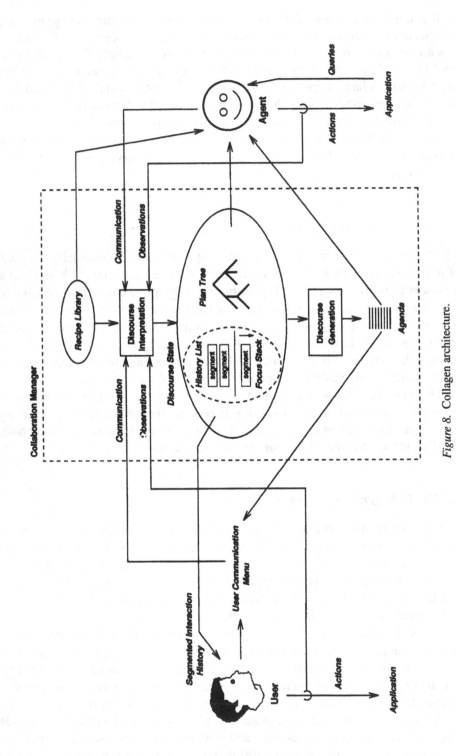

Figure 8. Collagen architecture.

consistency across applications, and to the extent it is based on good principles, leads to applications that are easier to learn and use.

Even when using Collagen, however, a developer still must provide considerable application-specific information. After discussing the generic architecture of Collagen below, we will focus in Section 6 on how this application-specific information is provided via the recipe library and the artificial discourse language.

4.1. THE AGENT

Note that the agent itself is a 'black box' in Figure 8. We are not trying to provide tools for building a complete agent. At the heart of the agent there may be a rule-based expert system, a neural net, or a completely ad hoc collection of code – whatever is appropriate for the application. What Collagen does provides is a generic framework for recording the decisions made and communicated by the agent (and the user), but not for *making* them. We believe this is a good software engineering modularity.

As can be seen in Figure 8, Collagen also provides some important new resources (inputs) for a developer to use in implementing the decision-making part of an interface agent: the discourse state, the agenda, and the recipe library.

The default agent implementation that 'comes with' Collagen always simply chooses to perform the highest priority action in the current agenda for which the actor is either unspecified or itself. Our example agent was constructed by extending this default implementation only a page of application-specific logic, which sometimes proposed other actions based on querying the discourse and application states. For example, this application-specific code was triggered at event 37 in Figure 4, where the agent proposes adding United airlines. All of the agent's other communications in the example session were the result of the default application-independent agent implementation.

4.2. THE BASIC EXECUTION CYCLE

The best way to understand the basic execution cycle of the architecture in Figure 8 is to start with the arrival of a communication or observation event (from either the agent or the user) at the discourse interpretation module at the top center of the diagram. The interpretation module updates the discourse state as described in Section 3.4 above, which then causes a new agenda of expected communication and manipulation acts (by either the user or agent) to be computed by the discourse generation module. As mentioned above, the agent may decide to select an entry in this new agenda for execution.

A subset of the agenda is also presented to the user whenever the user opens the communication menu in his home window. Specifically, the user communication menu is constructed by selecting all the communication actions in the agenda for which the actor is either unspecified or itself. What we are doing here is using

```
(Stopped jointly doing act1 via recipe1)
(Done agent doing act5 via recipe5)
(User doing act6 on value1 via recipe6)
    USER:  "Parameter1 of act6 is value1."
    USER:  Act7.
    ┌─────────────────────────────────────────────┐
    │(User doing act8)                             │
    │    USER:  "Propose I do act8."               │
    └─────────────────────────────────────────────┘
    (Expect step3)
```

Figure 9. Segmented interaction history generated from discourse state in Figure 7.

expectations generated by discourse context to replace natural language understanding. The user is not allowed to make arbitrary communications, but only to select from communications expected by the discourse interpretation algorithm. Thus, unlike usual ad hoc menu-driven interaction, the user menu in Collagen is systematically generated from an underlying model of orderly discourse.

If the user selects one of the communication menu entries, it becomes input to the discourse interpretation module, thus closing an execution cycle.

4.3. SEGMENTED INTERACTION HISTORY

In addition to the user communication menu, the second form of human-readable output produced by the Collagen discourse manager is the *segmented interaction history*, which appears in a pop-up window (see Figure 5) whenever the user presses the 'History' button in her home window. The most basic function of the segmented interaction history is to provide the user with a structured guide to her problem solving process. It also serves as a menu for history-based transformations, which are discussed in the next section.

The segmented interaction history is produced from the current discourse state by the following three steps:

(1) List the purpose of each toplevel segment on the history list started with the oldest.
(2) Recursively, starting with the toplevel open segment (the base segment of the focus stack), list the purpose of each closed subsegment followed by the purpose and elements of each open subsegment, indenting at each recursion.
(3) For each open subsegment, starting with the most deeply nested, list the unexecuted recipe steps, if any, in the plan tree for that segment's purpose, outdenting at each level.[6]

An example of the result of applying these steps to the discourse state in Figure 7 is shown in Figure 9 with the current segment selected.

---

[6] Because it contains both historical and future information, this display might more accurately be called the interaction 'context.' However, we have kept the name 'history' because it is more suggestive.

Notice above and in Figure 4 that the purpose of an open segment is glossed with a present participle, such as 'doing.' Closed segments are glossed starting with 'done' or 'stopped.' Remaining unexecuted steps of a recipe are glossed starting with 'expect.'

Other interactive systems also maintain histories. However, most such histories are flat or, if they do have structure, it is a reflection of the nesting of dialog boxes, rather than, as is the case here, the user's problem solving process.

Users can also exploit the structure of the interaction history to control the level of detail that is presented. The presentation of a segment can alternate between just its purpose or all of its elements by single and double clicking similar to the way that hierarchical file structures are expanded and contracted in graphical file inspectors. For example, Figure 10(a) shows the same discourse state as above in which the oldest toplevel segment has been expanded to two levels of detail, while all the other segments have been contracted to just their purpose.

5. History-Based Transformations

Making the interaction history an explicit, manipulable object, and the fact that it is structured according to the user's intentions, opens the possibility for powerful transformations on the state of the problem solving process. In this section, we describe three basic categories of such transformations, which we call *stopping*, *returning*, and *replay*. The framework in which to understand these transformations is in terms of their different effects on the application state and the discourse state.

The details of the application state representation depend, of course, on the application. For the purpose of this discussion, we assume that the application provides some method for reestablishing any earlier state, neglecting the important engineering tradeoffs between copying the entire state of an application at various 'checkpoints' versus keeping enough information to reconstruct intermediate states by undoing or replaying actions. (If checkpointing is expensive, segment boundaries suggest good places at which to do so.)

In all of the transformations below, the elements of closed segments are never modified. A copy of the focus stack and the plan tree are stored at the start and end of each segment. (Because the elements of a segment are acts and subsegments, the start of a segment does not always correspond to the end of another segment.)

The basic unit to which history-based transformations are applied is the segment. Requests to apply transformations applicable to the current segment (the top of the stack) always appear at the end of the user's communication menu, after the entries derived from the current discourse manager agenda. For example, at the moment in the opening scenario shown in Figure 2, the purpose of the current segment is to propose (the recipe for) how the trip will be scheduled. Therefore, as seen in the figure, the following three lines appear at the bottom of the user communication menu:

Stop proposing how a trip on the route be scheduled.
Retry proposing how a trip on the route be scheduled.
Undo proposing how a trip on the route be scheduled.

To apply transformations to other segments, the user pops up the interaction history window and then selects the desired segment by clicking on it. Applicable transformation requests for the selected segment are then automatically added to the communication menu.

5.1. STOPPING

The simplest history-based transformation is to pop the current segment off the focus stack without changing the application state. Furthermore, if the purpose of the popped segment contributes to its parent, the appropriate unbindings are also performed in the plan tree. The stop transformation is applicable only to open segments.

The user may employ this transformation to let the agent know that, even though the current goal has not been achieved, she is no longer working towards it. It may also be useful when the agent has misunderstood what the current goal is. Stopping is a component of some of the more complicated transformations described below.

5.2. RETURNING

Returns are a category of transformation in which both the application and discourse states are reset to an earlier point in the problem solving process. There are three forms of return, which we call *retry*, *revisit*, and *undo*. In all three forms, the application state is reset to the state at the start (retry and undo) or end (revisit) of the target segment.

5.2.1. *Retry and Revisit*

Intuitively, retry is the transformation to use when you want to return to working on an earlier goal – achieved or not – and try achieving it a different way. Retry is applicable to any segment.

Revisit is the transformation to use when you want to pick up where you left off working on an earlier goal, especially one that was stopped. Revisit is applicable only to closed segments, since all open segments are currently being worked on.

To illustrate retry and revisit, Figure 10(a) shows the history corresponding to the abstract discourse in Figure 7, with the segment to be returned to selected. Figures 10(b) and 10(c) show the interaction histories after a retry or revisit transformation has been applied. Notice that in both cases, there are two segments on

(a) Before return:

```
(Stopped jointly doing act1 via recipe1)
┌─────────────────────────────────────────────┐
│   (Stopped jointly doing act2 via recipe2)   │
│      AGENT: Act3.                            │
│      USER:  Act4.                            │
└─────────────────────────────────────────────┘
(Done agent doing act5 via recipe5)
(User doing act6 on value1 via recipe6)
```

(b) Retry (return to start of) segment:

```
(Stopped jointly doing act1 via recipe1)
(Done agent doing act5 via recipe5)
(Stopped user doing act6 on value1 via recipe6)
(Returning to jointly doing act1 via recipe1)
   (Retrying jointly doing act2)
      USER:   "Retry jointly doing act2."
```

(c) Revisit (return to end of) segment:

```
(Stopped jointly doing act1 via recipe1)
(Done agent doing act5 via recipe5)
(Stopped user doing act6 on value1 via recipe6)
(Returning to jointly doing act1 via recipe1)
   (Revisiting jointly doing act2 via recipe2)
      USER:   "Revisit jointly doing act2 via recipe2."
      AGENT: Act3.
      USER:  Act4.
```

Figure 10. Examples of returning.

the stack after the return.[7] Notice also that in a revisit transformation the recipe is preserved, whereas in a retry the recipe becomes unbound.

In general, resetting the discourse state for a retry or revisit involves an appropriate stop followed by resetting the stack and plan tree to their states at either the start (retry) or end (revisit) of the selected segment. If the segment being returned to (e.g., act2 in Figure 10) is, or its parent is, on the history list, then the appropriate segment to stop is the segment at the base of the stack (e.g., act6), thereby emptying the stack. Otherwise, the appropriate segment to stop is the open sibling segment of the segment being returned to, if any.

5.2.2. *Undo*

Undo is the familiar transformation in which you want to pretend that you never even started working on a goal. Undo is applicable only to open segments, or if the stack is empty, the most recent segment in the history list or any of its terminating subsegments. For example, undoing act6 in the initial state of Figures 7 and 10(a) would yield an empty stack and the following history:

```
(Stopped jointly doing act1 via recipe1)
(Done agent doing act5 via recipe5)
(Undone user doing act6 on value1 via recipe6)
```

---

[7] Act1, the purpose of the parent of the segment being returned to, is glossed as 'returning to' rather than 'retrying' or 'revisiting,' because, in general, we could be returning to the middle of it.

(Jointly scheduling a trip on the route via working forward, allowing 26 itineraries)
   (Done user identifying route of scheduling a trip as San Francisco to Dallas to Boston,
      allowing 100+ itineraries)
   (Done user proposing a trip on the route be scheduled via working forward)
   (Done user working on San Francisco to Dallas leg, allowing 70 itineraries)

   (Done user working on Dallas to Boston leg, allowing 55 itineraries)
     USER: Add Dallas stopover with arrival ... departure ...
     USER: Change Dallas stopover to arrival ... departure ...
     USER: Add Boston arrival ...
     USER: Change Boston to arrival ...

   (Done jointly specifying airlines, allowing 10 itineraries)
   (Done user displaying itineraries)

   (Retried user identifying route of scheduling a trip as Oakland to Dallas to Boston,
      allowing 100+ itineraries)
     USER: "Retry user identifying route of scheduling a trip."
     USER: Add Oakland to the route.
     USER: Add Dallas to the route, allowing 87 itineraries.
     USER: Add Boston to the route, allowing 100+ itineraries.
   (Done user working on Oakland to Dallas leg, allowing 93 itineraries)
   (Replayed working on Dallas to Boston leg, allowing 8 itineraries)
     USER: "Replay user working on Dallas to Boston leg."
     AGENT: Add Dallas stopover with arrival ... departure ...
     AGENT: Change Dallas stopover to arrival ... departure ...
     AGENT: Add Boston arrival ...
     AGENT: Change Boston to arrival ...
   (Done user displaying itineraries)
   (Revisiting jointly specifying airlines, allowing 26 itineraries)
     USER: "Revisit jointly specifying airlines."
     USER: Add American specification, allowing no itineraries.
     (Done agent adding United specification, allowing 10 itineraries)
       AGENT: "Propose I add United specification."
       USER: "Ok."
       AGENT: Add United specification, allowing 10 itineraries.
     USER: Add USAir specification, allowing 26 itineraries.

Figure 11. Transformations in test application.

Resetting the discourse state to undo an open segment involves the same steps as stopping that segment. The only difference is that with undo the application state is also reset. Undoing the last (or terminating) segment on the history list (when the stack is empty) requires only unbinding that segment's purpose from its parent in the plan tree.

5.3. REPLAY

Replay is a transformation which allows the user to reuse earlier work in a slightly different, i.e., the current, context. The basic idea is that all of the application acts in the selected segment are put together into one (possibly hierarchical) 'recipe', which is then executed by the agent in the current context.

When executing such a replay recipe, it is important for the agent to be prepared for the possibility that some of the acts, e.g., adding an airline that has already been specified, may not be valid in the current context. Depending on the specific details of the agent's interface to the application, such errors may need to be handled by application-specific code in the agent, or may be taken care of by the application's existing API or graphical interface.

Figure 11 is example of how replay can be used, together with returns, in the test application. Notice that the scenario in this figure is a shorter trip (only two legs) than the scenario in Section 2. The levels of expansion of the history have been set to show only the details of interest. The segment that is going to be replayed is shown selected and underlining has been added to highlight the three transformation segments.

To motivate this example, suppose that after displaying itineraries (see the blank line in the middle of Figure 11, the user got the idea of trying to leave from the nearby Oakland airport instead of San Francisco. In order to pursue this alternative, she returned to (retried) the first subsegment in the history, this time entering the route Oakland-Dallas-Boston on the map in the application window. Notice that the application state at the end of this retried segment did not include any city arrival/departure constraints.

Next, the user constrained her departure time from Oakland ('Done user working on Oakland to Dallas leg' in the history). Then, instead of manually (re-)entering the arrival/departure constraints for Dallas and Boston, she requested replay of the selected segment.

After displaying and reviewing the possible itineraries starting in Oakland, however, the user decided to return to working on the San Francisco route after all. In particular, at the end of Figure 11, she is revisiting the earlier airline specification segment (fifth subsegment down from the top) in order to see what happens if she adds USAir to the specified airlines.

6. Task Modelling

In order to use Collagen, an agent developer must provide a formal model of the collaborative task(s) being performed by the agent and user. Defining this model is very similar to what is called 'data modelling' in data base or 'domain modelling' in artificial intelligence (Brodie et al., 1982). It also overlaps with modern specification practices in software engineering, although the goals and recipes in a collaborative discourse model include more abstract concepts than are usually formalized in current software practice, except for in expert or knowledge-based systems.

On the one hand, task modelling can be thought of as an unfortunate hidden cost of applying our methodology. On the other hand, the need for an explicit task model should be no surprise. From an artificial intelligence point of view, what the task model does is add a measure of reflection – 'self-awareness,' so to speak – to a system. Reflection is a well-known technique for improving the performance of a problem-solving system. From a software engineering point of view, the task model can be thought of as part of the general trend towards capturing more of the programmer's design rationale in the software itself. Also, since the agent need not rely on the task model alone for its decision making, the model only needs to be complete enough to support communication and collaboration with the user.

In the remainder of this section, we discuss and illustrate some of the issues in building task models, starting with the artificial discourse language and then moving on to the recipe library.

6.1. ARTIFICIAL DISCOURSE LANGUAGE

As the internal representation for user and agent communication acts, we use Sidner's (1994) artificial discourse language. Sidner defines a collection of constructors for basic act types, such as proposing, retracting, accepting, and rejecting proposals. Our current implementation includes only two of these act types: PFA (propose for accept) and AP (accept proposal).

$$\text{PFA}(t, \mathit{participant}_1, \mathit{belief}, \mathit{participant}_2)$$

The semantics of PFA are roughly: at time t, $\mathit{participant}_1$ believes belief, communicates his belief to $\mathit{participant}_2$, and intends for $\mathit{participant}_2$ to believe it also. If $\mathit{participant}_2$ responds with an AP act, e.g., 'Ok', then belief is mutually believed.

Sidner's language at this level is very general – the proposed belief may be anything. For communicating about collaborative activities, we introduce two application-independent operators for forming beliefs about actions: SHOULD(act) and RECIPE($\mathit{act}, \mathit{recipe}$).

The rest of the belief sublanguage is application-specific. For example, to model our air travel application, we defined appropriate object types (e.g., cities, flights, and airlines), relations (e.g., the origin and destination of a flight), and goal/action constructors (e.g., scheduling a trip, adding an airline specification).

Below are examples of how some of the communications in our example scenario are represented in the artificial discourse language. In each example, we show the internal representation of the communication followed by the English gloss that is produced by a straightforward recursive substitution process using string templates associated with each operator. Italicized variables below denote parameters that remain to be bound, e.g., by further communication.

> PFA(37,agent,SHOULD(add-airline(t,agent,ua)),user))
> AGENT: 'Propose I add United specification.'

Notice below that a present participle template is used when the participant performing an act is unspecified.

> PFA(1,user,SHOULD(schedule(t,who,$route$)),agent)
> USER: 'Propose scheduling a trip.'

Questions arise out of the embedding of PFA acts as shown below (ROUTE is a constructor for route expressions).

```
PFA(9,agent,
    SHOULD(PFA(t₁,user,
                RECIPE(schedule(t₂,who,route(bos,dfw,den,sfo,bos)),
                        recipe),
                agent)),
    user)
    AGENT: 'How should a trip on the route be scheduled?'
```

Notice that the glossing algorithm has some limited ability to introduce definite references, such as 'the route' above, based on the focus stack and some application-specific heuristics.

6.2. RECIPE LIBRARY

At its most abstract, a *recipe* is a resource used to derive a sequence of steps to achieve a given goal (the objective of the recipe). Although very general, application-independent recipes exist, such as divide and conquer, we are primarily concerned here with application-specific recipes.

In our implementation, a recipe is concretely represented as a partially ordered sequence of act types (steps) with constraints between them. The recipe library contains recipes indexed by their objective. There may be more than one recipe for each type of objective.

The recipe library for the test application contains 8 recipes defined in terms of 15 different goal or action types. It is probably about half the size it needs to be to reasonably cover the application domain.

Recipes with a fixed number of steps are easily represented in our simple recipe formalism. However, in working on our test application, we quickly discovered the need for more complicated recipes whose step structure depends on some parameters of the objective. For example, two common toplevel recipes for scheduling a trip are working forward and working backward. The working-forward recipe works on the legs of a trip in order starting with the first leg; the working-backward recipe starts with the last leg. In both cases, the number of steps depends on the length of the route.

Rather than 'hairing up' our recipe representation as each difficult case arose, we decided instead to provide a general-purpose procedural alternative, called *recipe generators*. Recipes such as working forward/backward are represented in Collagen as procedures which, given an objective, return a recipe. A predicate can also be associated with a recipe to test whether it is still applicable as it is being executed.

A related category of application-specific procedures in the recipe library are *recipe recognizers*. These are primarily used for the bottom-up grouping of a sequence of similar actions on the same object into a single abstract action. For example, such a recognizer is invoked in our test application when the user moves the same interval bar back and forth several times in a row.

7. Local and Global Initiative in Conversation

Most work on initiative in conversation, e.g., (Clark and Schaeffer, 1989; Walker and Whittaker, 1990; Traum and Hinkelman, 1992), has focused on problems that are *local* to a discourse segment. Phenomena in this realm include:

- turn taking and conversational control (who gets to speak next),
- interruptions, and
- grounding (how the current speaker indicates that she has heard and understood the content of the previous speaker's turn).

Other work, e.g., (Traum and Hinkelman, 1992; Green, 1994; Guinn, 1996; Allen et al., 1996), has looked at initiative more globally in terms of 'having something to say'. This work tends to focus on the conversants' problem-solving level and on choosing appropriate speech acts or discourse plan operators.

In our view, an approach to the so-called 'mixed initiative' issue in interactive systems must address both levels of phenomena: the global level of having something to say that is relevant to what has recently been said or done, and the local level, concerning when and how a participant gets the opportunity to speak.

7.1. GLOBAL INITIATIVE

The collaborative discourse theory upon which Collagen is based provides strong support for dealing with the global constraints on initiative. The maintenance of a discourse state representation and the agenda which is computed from it by the discourse manager provides a Collagen-based agent with an explicit choice of relevant things to say at most points in a conversation. Given this architecture, there is no need for a separate collection of discourse plan operators about 'conversational moves' that compel the agent to answer questions or perform actions requested of it (Chu-Carroll and Brown, 1998). The agent's cooperative behavior results directly from the overall model of collaboration.

As discussed in Section 4.1, the Collagen architecture leaves it up to the agent to decide between answering a question, performing an interface action or choosing some other behavior because that is appropriately a function of application-specific planning rather then discourse processing.

Recent research, e.g., (Guinn, 1994; Chu-Carroll and Carberry, 1994; Chu-Carroll and Carberry, 1995), has also begun to consider negotiation as part of global initiative. By negotiation, we mean the ability to resolve differences in beliefs that are relevant to some shared goal. Negotiation is fundamental to collaboration because collaborators often have differing points of view about the goals and recipes they undertake as well as the state of the world at any point in time. Collagen's artificial language, in particular the full version described in (Sidner, 1994), is a start toward pursuing this idea. However there is much more work to be done before Collagen can incorporate a general negotiation facility.

7.2. LOCAL INITIATIVE

Because current theories of local initiative in conversation do not yet provide general-enough algorithms for turn taking, control and grounding, Collagen does not provide any support in these areas. We have, however, experimented in our test agent for air travel planning with several ad hoc mechanisms for local initiative, which we describe below.

One of the most basic local initiative concerns we needed to address in our agent implementation was how the user relinquishes control to the agent. For example, this needs to happen when the user decides she does not want to contribute any further to the current SharedPlan and instead would like to see what the agent can contribute. To support this specific behavior, we designed the agent to interpret an 'ok' said by the user (other than in answer to a direct yes–no question) as an signal of relinquishing control.[8]

A second local initiative mechanism we built into the agent was a way to get the user's attention when the agent does not have control. Since it was difficult and awkward to physically grab the user's cursor in the middle of use, we gave the agent the ability to wave its cursor 'hand' when it has something important to contribute to the conversation.[9] The resulting behavior is very humanlike and affecting. However, some observers of our interface have urged us to just have the agent 'barge into' the user's interaction with the application interface.

Finally, we agree with Walker and Whittaker's (1990) observation that many discourse initiative phenomena that appear to be local are in fact dependent upon global constraints. More careful attention to global models may result in theories that better explain both levels of mixed initiative.

8. Comparison with Other Work

This work lies at the intersection of many threads of related research in user interface, linguistics, and artificial intelligence. It is unique, however, in its combination of goals and techniques.

Most conventional work on user interface concentrates on optimizing the appearance and functionality of a single interaction or a short sequence of interactions. In contrast, our work is about supporting a user's problem solving process by relating current actions to the global context and history of the interaction.

Our concept of a collaborative interface agent is closest to the work of Maes (1994), although she uses the term 'collaborative' to refer to the sharing of information between multiple software agents, rather than collaboration between the agent and the user. Cohen et al. (1994) has also developed interface agents without

---

[8] We also experimented with an alternate signal of having the user return her cursor to the user home window for a period of two or three seconds, but found this was awkward.

[9] We chose not to use computer keyboards sounds, such as bells, because they introduced new medium for which we had no general framework.

collaborative discourse modelling. Terveen (1991) has explored providing intelligent assistance through collaborative graphical manipulation without explicitly invoking the agent paradigm.

At a more abstract level, recent work on mixed-initiative systems by Guinn (1998) and Cohen et al. (1998) treat collaboration as an extension of single agent problem solving in which some designated participant has the 'task initiative' for each mutual goal. Cohen et al., for example, conclude that task initiative depends on who is proposing a goal. In contrast, our work is based on an underlying formalization (Grosz and Kraus, 1996) in which collaboration is fundamentally a property of groups. Although this distinction is not highlighted in our current scenarios, it will become important in future extensions.

Cohen (1992) and Jacob (1995), among others, have explored discourse-related extensions to direct manipulation that incorporate anaphora and make previous context directly available. However, most work on applying human discourse principles to human-computer interaction, e.g., (Lambert and Carberry, 1991; Yanklovich, 1994), have assumed that natural language understanding will be applied to the user's utterances

In Moore et al.'s work (Lemaire and Moore, 1994; Moore and Swartout, 1990), which focuses on explanation dialogues, users are presented with a full textual history of their interaction with the system, from which they may select any phrase as the context for a further query. Unlike our approach, Moore's history display has no explicit structure other than the alternation of user and system utterances. Internally, however, Moore's work does use a deep representation of the user's and system's goals.

The basic idea underlying Collagen's user communication menu, namely replacing natural language understanding by natural language generation based on the expectations of context, has also been used by Fischer (1994) for cooperative information retrieval and by Mittal and Moore (1995) for clarification subdialogues.

The three systems we know of that are overall closest in spirit to our own are Stein and Maier's MERIT (1995), subsequent work on MIRACLE by Stein et al. (1999), and Ahn et al.'s (1995) DenK. MERIT and MIRACLE use a different discourse theory, which is compiled into a less flexible and less extensible finite-state machine representation. Neither of these systems deal with actions that directly manipulate a graphical interface. DenK has the goal of providing a discourse-based agent, but has not yet modelled collaboration.

9. Conclusions

In summary, applying the software agent paradigm and collaborative discourse theory to human-computer interaction in graphical user interfaces has posed a number of challenges, including:

- applying discourse theory without requiring natural language understanding by the agent,

- embodying the application-independent aspects of the discourse algorithms and data structures in a collaboration manager,
- and providing a modular description for application-specific information.

We believe the current work has made a strong start toward these goals and provides a new conceptual platform upon which we and others can now build higher.

Our future plans include:

- improving the flexibility and robustness of the discourse processing algorithms, especially as related to incompleteness of the agent's recipe library and handling parallel interleaved goals,
- supporting negotiation between the user and agent,
- a pilot user study to compare using the example application with and without the interface agent, and
- using Collagen to build agents that operate remotely in space and time (e.g., on the Internet), which will require more discussion between the agent and user about past and future actions.

A major effort which has occupied much of the past year has been to reimplement the Collagen in Java. This effort is not yet complete at the time of this writing. The Java implementation should greatly facilitate experimentation by other interested researchers, which we invite. Please visit our project home page at http://www.merl.com/projects/collagen for up-to-date information.

References

Ahn, R. M. C., R. J. Beun, T. Borghuis, H. C. Bunt and C. W. A. M. van Overveld: 1995, 'The DenK-architecture: A Fundamental Approach to User-Interfaces'. *Artificial Intelligence Review* **8**, pp. 431–445.

Allen, J. F., B. Miller, E. Ringger and T. Sikorski: 1996, 'A Robust System for Natural Spoken Dialogue'. In: *Proc. 34th Annual Meeting of the ACL*, Santa Cruz, CA, pp. 62–70.

Bratman, M. E., D. J. Israel, and M. E. Pollack: 1988, 'Plans and Resource-Bounded Practical Reasoning'. *Computational Intelligence* **4**(4), 349–355.

Brodie, M., J. Mylopoulos, and J. Schmidt (eds.): 1982, *On Conceptual Modelling*. New York, NY: Springer-Verlag.

Chu-Carroll, J. and M. Brown: 1998, 'An Evidential Model for Tracking Initiative in Collaborative Dialogue Interactions'. In this issue, pp. 215–253.

Chu-Carroll, J. and S. Carberry: 1994, 'A Plan-Based Model for Response Generation in Collaborative Task-Oriented Dialogues'. In: *Proc. 12th National Conf. on Artificial Intelligence*. Seattle, WA, pp. 799–805.

Chu-Carroll, J. and S. Carberry: 1995, 'Response Generation in Collaborative Negotiation'. In: *Proc. 33rd Annual Meeting of the ACL*. Cambridge, MA, pp. 136–143.

Clark, H. H. and E. F. Schaeffer: 1989, 'Contributing to Discourse'. *Cognitive Science* **13**(2), 259–294.

Cohen, P.: 1992, 'The Role of Natural Language in a Multimodal Interface'. In: *Proc. 5th ACM Symp. on User Interface Software and Technology*. Monterey, CA, pp. 143–149.

Cohen et al., P.: 1994, 'An Open Agent Architecture'. In: O. Etzioni (ed.): *Software Agents, Papers from the 1994 Spring Symposium, SS-94-03*. Menlo Park, CA: AAAI Press, pp. 1–8.

Cohen et al., R.: 1998, 'What is Initiative?'. In this issue, pp. 171–214.

Fischer, M., E. Maier, and A. Stein: 1994, 'Generating Cooperative System Responses in Information Retrieval Dialogues'. In: *Proc. 7th Int. Workshop Natural Language Generation*. Kennebunkport, ME, pp. 207–216.

Green, N. L.: 1994, 'A Computational Model for Generating and Interpeting Indirect Answers'. Ph.D. thesis, Univ. of Delaware, Dept. of Computer and Info. Sci.

Grosz, B. J. and S. Kraus: 1996, 'Collaborative Plans for Complex Group Action'. *Artificial Intelligence* **86**(2), 269–357.

Grosz, B. J. and C. L. Sidner: 1986, 'Attention, Intentions, and the Structure of Discourse'. *Computational Linguistics* **12**(3), 175–204.

Grosz, B. J. and C. L. Sidner: 1990, 'Plans for Discourse'. In: P. R. Cohen, J. L. Morgan, and M. E. Pollack (eds.): *Intentions and Communication*. Cambridge, MA: MIT Press, pp. 417–444.

Grosz [Deutsch], B. J.: 1974, 'The Structure of Task-Oriented Dialogs'. In: *IEEE Symp. on Speech Recognition: Contributed Papers*. Pittsburgh, PA, pp. 250–253.

Guinn, C. I.: 1994, 'Meta-Dialogue Behaviors: Improving the Efficiency of Human-Machine Dialogue – A Computational Model of Variable Initiative and Negotiation in Collaborative Problem-Solving, Communication and Miscommunication'. Ph.D. thesis, Duke University.

Guinn, C. I.: 1996, 'Mechanisms for Mixed-Initiative Human-Computer Collaborative Discourse'. In: *Proc. 34th Annual Meeting of the ACL*, Santa Cruz, CA, pp. 278–285.

Guinn, C. I.: 1998, 'Principles of Mixed-Initiative Human-Computer Collaborative Discourse'. In this issue, pp. 255–314.

Jacob, R. J. K.: 1995, 'Natural Dialogue in Modes other than Natural Language'. In: R.-J. Beun, M. Baker, and M. Reiner (eds.): *Dialogue and Instruction*. Berlin: Springer-Verlag, pp. 289–301.

Kautz, H.: 1990, 'A Circumscriptive Theory of Plan Recognition'. In: P. R. Cohen, J. L. Morgan, and M. E. Pollack (eds.): *Intentions and Communication*. Cambridge, MA: MIT Press, pp. 105–133.

Kowtko, J. C. and P. Price: 1989, 'Data Collection and Analysis in the Air Travel Planning Domain'. In: Proceedings of the DARPA Speech and Natural Language Workshop, Cape Cod, MA, pp. 119–125.

Lambert, L. and S. Carberry: 1991, 'A Tripartite Plan-Based Model of Dialogue'. In: *Proc. 29th Annual Meeting of the ACL*, Berkeley, CA, pp. 47–54.

Lemaire, B. and J. Moore: 1994, 'An Improved Interface for Tutorial Dialogues: Browsing a Visual Dialogue History'. In: *Proc. ACM SIGCHI Conference on Human Factors in Computing Systems*. Boston, MA, pp. 16–22.

Lochbaum, K. E.: 1994, 'Using Collaborative Plans to Model the Intentional Structure of Discourse'. Technical Report TR-25-94, Harvard Univ., Ctr. for Res. in Computing Tech. PhD thesis.

Lochbaum, K. E.: 1995, 'The Use of Knowledge Preconditions in Language Processing'. In: *Proc. 14th Int. Joint Conf. Artificial Intelligence*. Montreal, Canada, pp. 1260–1266.

Lochbaum, K. E.: 1998, 'A Collaborative Planning Model of Intentional Structure'. *Computational Linguistics*. Forthcoming.

Maes, P.: 1994, 'Agents that Reduce Work and Information Overload'. *Comm. ACM* **37**(17), 30–40. Special Issue on Intelligent Agents.

Meyers et al., B.: 1990, 'Garnet: Comprehensive Support for Graphical, Highly-Interactive User Interfaces'. *IEEE Computer* **23**(11), 71–85.

Mittal, V. and J. Moore: 1995, 'Dynamic Generation of Follow-up Question Menus: Facilitating Interactive Natural Language Dialogues'. In: *Proc. ACM SIGCHI Conference on Human Factors in Computing Systems*. Denver, CO, pp. 90–97.

Moore, J. and W. Swartout: 1990, 'Pointing: A Way Toward Explanation Dialogue'. In: *Proc. 8th National Conf. on Artificial Intelligence*. Menlo Park, CA, pp. 457–464.

Rich, C.: 1996, 'Window Sharing with Collaborative Interface Agents'. *ACM SIGCHI Bulletin* **28**(1), pp. 70–78.

Rich, C. and C. Sidner: 1996, 'Adding a Collaborative Agent to Graphical User Interfaces'. In: *Proc. 9th ACM Symp. on User Interface Software and Technology*. Seattle, WA, pp. 21–30.

Rich, C. and C. Sidner: 1997a, 'Collagen: When Agents Collaborate with People'. In: *Proc. 1st Int. Conf. on Autonomous Agents*. Marina del Rey, CA, pp. 284–291.

Rich, C. and C. Sidner: 1997b, 'Segmented Interaction History in a Collaborative Interface Agent'. In: *Proc. Int. Conf. on Intelligent User Interfaces*. Orlando, FL, pp. 23–30.

Sidner, C. L.: 1994, 'An Artificial Discourse Language for Collaborative Negotiation'. In: *Proc. 12th National Conf. on Artificial Intelligence*. Seattle, WA, pp. 814–819.

Stein, A. and E. Maier: 1995, 'Structuring Collaborative Information-Seeking Dialogues'. *Knowledge-Based Systems* **8**(2-3), 82–93.

Stein, A., J. A. Gulla and U. Thiel: 1999, 'User-Tailored Planning of Mixed Initiative Information Seeking Dialogues'. *User Modeling and User-Adapted Interaction*.

Terveen, G., D. Wroblewski, and S. Tighe: 1991, 'Intelligent Assistance through Collaborative Manipulation'. In: *Proc. 12th Int. Joint Conf. Artificial Intelligence*. Sydney, Australia, pp. 9–14.

Traum, D. R. and E. A. Hinkelman: 1992, 'Conversation Acts in Task-Oriented Spoken Dialogue'. *Computational Intelligence* **8**(3), 575–599.

Walker, M. A. and S. Whittaker: 1990, 'Mixed Initiative in Dialogue: An Investigation into Discourse Segmentation'. In: *Proc. 28th Annual Meeting of the ACL*, Pittsburgh, PA, pp. 70–79.

Yanklovich, N.: 1994, 'Talking vs. Taking: Speech Access to Remote Computers'. In: *Proc. ACM SIGCHI Conference on Human Factors in Computing Systems*. Boston, MA, pp. 275–276.

Authors' Vitae

Dr. Charles Rich

Senior Research Scientist, MERL – A Mitsubishi Electric Research Laboratory, 201 Broadway, Cambridge, MA 02139, USA. (*rich@merl.com*)

Dr. Rich has had a continuing interest in making interaction with computers more collaborative. As a founder and co-director of the Programmer's Apprentice project at the MIT Artificial Intelligence Laboratory from 1980 to 1991, he pioneered research on intelligent assistants for software engineers. As a founding member of MERL, Dr. Rich led the implementation of the laboratory's first multi-user interactive multimedia environment. Dr. Rich is a Fellow and past Councillor of the American Association for Artificial Intelligence and was Program Co-Chair of the AAAI'98 conference. Dr. Rich received a Ph.D. in Artificial Intelligence from MIT in 1980.

Dr. Candace L. Sidner

Research Scientist, Lotus Development Corporation, 55 Cambridge Parkway, Cambridge, MA 02139, USA. (*csidner@lotus.com*)

Dr. Sidner has been a research scientist at Lotus Development Corporation since 1993. She is a past President of the Association of Computational Linguistics

(1989), and is a Fellow and past Councillor of the American Association of Artificial Intelligence. She has served on numerous program committees and journal boards for societies in artificial intelligence and natural language processing. Dr. Sidner received a Ph.D. in Computer Science from MIT in 1979.

User Modeling and User-Adapted Interaction **9**: 1–44, 1999.
© 1999 *Kluwer Academic Publishers.*

1

Lifelike Pedagogical Agents for Mixed-Initiative Problem Solving in Constructivist Learning Environments

JAMES C. LESTER[1], BRIAN A. STONE[2] and GARY D. STELLING[1]

[1]*Department of Computer Science, Engineering Graduate Research Center, North Carolina State University, Raleigh, NC 27695-7534, USA; e-mail: {lester,gdstelli}@csc.ncsu.edu*
[2]*Department of Computer Science, North Carolina State University, Raleigh, NC 27695-8206, USA; e-mail: bastone@eos.ncsu.edu*

(Received 27 November 1997; accepted in revised form 12 May 1998)

Abstract. Mixed-initiative problem solving lies at the heart of knowledge-based learning environments. While learners are actively engaged in problem-solving activities, learning environments should monitor their progress and provide them with feedback in a manner that contributes to achieving the twin goals of learning effectiveness and learning efficiency. Mixed-initiative interactions are particularly critical for *constructivist* learning environments in which learners participate in active problem solving. We have recently begun to see the emergence of believable agents with lifelike qualities. Featured prominently in constructivist learning environments, *lifelike pedagogical agents* could couple key feedback functionalities with a strong visual presence by observing learners' progress and providing them with visually contextualized advice during mixed-initiative problem solving. For the past three years, we have been engaged in a large-scale research program on lifelike pedagogical agents and their role in constructivist learning environments. In the resulting computational framework, lifelike pedagogical agents are specified by

(1) a *behavior space* containing animated and vocal behaviors,
(2) a *design-centered context model* that maintains constructivist problem representations, multimodal advisory contexts, and evolving problem-solving tasks, and
(3) a *behavior sequencing engine* that in realtime dynamically selects and assembles agents' actions to create pedagogically effective, lifelike behaviors.

To empirically investigate this framework, it has been instantiated in a full-scale implementation of a lifelike pedagogical agent for DESIGN-A-PLANT, a learning environment developed for the domain of botanical anatomy and physiology for middle school students. Experience with focus group studies conducted with middle school students interacting with the implemented agent suggests that lifelike pedagogical agents hold much promise for mixed-initiative learning.

Key words: lifelike agents, pedagogical agents, animated agents, knowledge-based learning environments, mixed-initiative interaction, intelligent tutoring systems, intelligent multimedia presentation, intelligent interfaces, task models.

1. Introduction

Mixed-initiative problem solving lies at the heart of knowledge-based learning environments. Since the birth of the field more than twenty-five years ago (Carbonell, 1970), it has become apparent that developing computational models of mixed-initiativity is critical to the learning environment enterprise. While learners are actively engaged in problem solving activities, learning environments should monitor their progress and provide them with feedback in a manner that contributes to achieving the twin goals of learning effectiveness and learning efficiency. By carefully monitoring a learner's progress, learning environments should control the course of the interaction in such a way that they maximize the quality of the learning experience.

We have recently begun to see the emergence of believable agents with lifelike qualities (Bates, 1994; Blumberg & Galyean, 1995; Kurlander & Ling, 1995; Maes et al., 1995; André & Rist, 1996). By building on developments in these intriguing interactive characters, we can create a new generation of knowledge-based learning environments that are inhabited by animated *lifelike pedagogical agents*. Featured prominently in learning environments, they could couple key feedback functionalities with a strong visual presence by observing learners' progress and providing them with visually contextualized problem-solving advice.

Lifelike pedagogical agents offer particularly significant potential for *constructivist* learning environments. Constructivist learning (Piaget, 1954) has received increasing attention in the education community in recent years because of its emphasis on the active role played by the learner as he or she acquires new concepts and procedures. A particularly intriguing form of the constructivist's learning-by-doing techniques is 'learning-by-designing.' In the process of designing an artifact, learners – by necessity – come to understand the rich interconnections between the artifacts they devise and the environmental constraints that determine whether a given design will meet with success. Because design tasks are inherently complex, design-centered problem solving provides an excellent testbed for studying mixed-initiative interactions that are contextualized in a learners' problem-solving activities.

To investigate these issues, we have been engaged in a large-scale research program on lifelike pedagogical agents and constructivist learning environments (Lester et al., 1996; Stone & Lester, 1996; Lester & Stone, 1997; Lester et al., 1997a,b,c). The long-term goal of the project is to create pedagogically effective computational mechanisms that contribute to fundamental improvements in learning environments. To date, we have focused on developing a *pedagogical agent behavior sequencing engine* that dynamically controls the behaviors of lifelike pedagogical agents in response to the rapidly changing problem-solving contexts in constructivist learning environments. Applying this framework to create an agent entails constructing a behavior space, a design-centered context model, and a behavior sequencing engine that dynamically selects and assembles behaviors:

(1) *Agent Behavior Space*: A behavior space contains

    (a) animated behaviors of an agent performing a variety of pedagogical behaviors including explanatory and advisory actions,

    (b) animated behaviors of the agent engaged in a variety of 'believability-enhancing' actions, and

    (c) narrative utterances spoken by the agent, including verbal reminders and interjections.

(2) *Design-Centered Context Model*: A model of a design-centered context consists of

    (a) an *environmental context* representing the critical features of the problem,

    (b) a *multimodal advisory history* representing the explanations and advice that have been presented by the agent, and

    (c) an *artifact-based task model* representing the features of the artifact being designed by the learner. These are dynamically updated as problem-solving episodes unfold.

(3) *Behavior Sequencing Engine*: At runtime, a behavior sequencing engine orchestrates an agent's behaviors in response to the changing problem-solving context by exploiting the design-centered context model. A sequencing engine selects an agent's actions by navigating coherent paths through the behavior space and assembling them dynamically to create global behaviors in which the agent provides visually contextualized problem-solving advice.

To empirically investigate this framework, it has been instantiated in an implemented lifelike pedagogical agent, Herman the Bug (Figure 1), who inhabits a constructivist learning environment for the domain of botanical anatomy and physiology for middle school students, DESIGN-A-PLANT.[1] The agent interactively provides contextualized advice to learners as they graphically assemble plants from a library of plant structures such as roots and stems.

    In DESIGN-A-PLANT, a learner's goal in each problem-solving episode is to design a plant that will thrive in a given natural environment with specified conditions such as the amount of available sunlight. As learners solve problems by constructing plants, the agent provides them with advice about botanical anatomy and physiology. Together, Herman and the DESIGN-A-PLANT learning environment constitute a proof-of-concept embodiment of the lifelike pedagogical agent behavior sequencing framework and provide a 'laboratory' for studying mixed-initiative problem-solving interactions in constructivist learning environments.

    Based on the experience of the first three years of the DESIGN-A-PLANT project, this article provides an account of the representations and computational

---

[1] The DESIGN-A-PLANT learning environment project is a large-scale multidisciplinary project involving computer scientists, animators, graphic designers, voice actors, curriculum and instruction specialists, and cognitive scientists. For example, all of the 3D graphics and animations were designed, modeled, and rendered by a twelve-person graphic design and animation team.

Figure 1. The DESIGN-A-PLANT lifelike pedagogical agent.

mechanisms underlying the design and construction of lifelike pedagogical agents for mixed-initiative problem solving in constructivist learning environments. It is structured as follows. Section 2 sets forth design criteria for mixed-initiativity in lifelike pedagogical agents, describes the DESIGN-A-PLANT learning environment testbed, and presents an extended mixed-initiative session to illustrate the desired phenomena. Section 3 presents the design-centered context model used to represent problem-solving and advisory contexts. Section 4 describes dynamic behavior sequencing engines for lifelike agents, including the mechanisms for controlling the initiative, for making intervention decisions, and for interjecting advice and explanations. Section 5 illustrates these computational mechanisms with an extended example interaction. Section 6 puts the work in perspective by describing the principal 'lessons learned' from the experiences of iterative design, implementation, and evaluation via focus group studies with middle school students. Section 7 concludes with a summary and a discussion of future directions.

2. Mixed-initiativity in Lifelike Pedagogical Agents

Since their conception more than a quarter of a century ago, knowledge-based learning environments (Hollan et al., 1987; Wenger, 1987; Lesgold et al., 1992; Anderson et al., 1995) have offered significant potential for fundamentally changing the educational process. It has long been believed – and recently rigorously demonstrated (Mark & Greer, 1995) – that presenting knowledgeable feedback to students increases learning effectiveness. Despite this promise, few learning environments have made the difficult transition from the laboratory to the classroom, and the challenge of developing learning environments that are both pedagogically sound and visually appealing has played no small part in this situation.

Lifelike animated agents could play a central communicative role in learning environments by providing visually contextualized problem-solving advice. Although knowledge-based graphical simulations (Hollan et al., 1987) are virtually *de rigueur* in contemporary learning environments, and the problem of planning multimedia presentations has been the subject of much study (André et al., 1993; Feiner & McKeown, 1990; Maybury, 1991; Roth et al., 1991; Mittal et al., 1995), work on lifelike agents has begun in earnest but is still in its infancy (Bates, 1994; Blumberg & Galyean, 1995; Kurlander & Ling, 1995; Maes et al., 1995; André & Rist, 1996). Despite the promise of lifelike pedagogical agents, with the exception of work on the DESIGN-A-PLANT project (Lester et al., 1996; Stone & Lester, 1996; Lester & Stone, 1997; Lester et al., 1997b,c) (described in this article) and the Soar Training Expert for Virtual Environments (STEVE) project (Rickel & Johnson, 1997), which focuses on agents that provide instruction about procedural tasks, lifelike agents for pedagogy have received little attention.

In the same manner that human-human tutorial dialogues are characterized by changes in initiative (Smith & Hipp, 1994; Hale & Barsalou, 1995; Freedman, 1996), learner-agent interactions between a lifelike agent and a learner should be characterized by problem-solving episodes where control of the initiative frequently changes. Mixed-initiativity is such an extraordinarily complex phenomenon (Cohen et al., 1998), that developing a computational model of mixed-initiative tutorial interactions is especially challenging. Below we characterize the kinds of initiative changes we target for tutorial interactions.

At the beginning of each episode, learners are unfamiliar with the problem, so the agent should take control and introduce the problem. For example, in the DESIGN-A-PLANT learning environment, the agent should open by describing the environmental conditions that hold on the particular environment for which a plant will be designed. Once learners begin solving problems, the initiative may change frequently. Learners should be able to take control while they are performing problem-solving actions, agents should regain control when it appears that learners are experiencing difficulty or when learners request assistance, and control should then be relinquished to learners so they may continue their problem solving. For example, in the DESIGN-A-PLANT learning environment, the agent should monitor students as they assemble plants and intervene to provide explanations about botanical anatomy and physiology when they reach an impasse. In the same manner that human interlocutors engaged in mixed-initiative interactions frequently generate responses that include highly relevant information that was not specifically requested (Green & Carberry, 1999), the agent should be prepared to provide learners with assistance even though it may not be explicitly requested.

Once problem solving is successfully completed by the learner, the agent should again regain control to complete the problem solving transaction. This might involve a simple statement that a correct solution has been constructed or perhaps a more elaborate congratulatory utterance accompanied by a visually compelling behavior. For example, at the end of each successful problem-solving episode in DESIGN-A-PLANT, the agent might congratulate learners and cartwheel across the screen.

Well designed intervention strategies are especially critical in constructivist learning environments. The frequency and content of intervention should be appropriate for the particular aspects of the design task on which the learner is focusing, and advice should be relevant to the problem-solving goals currently being pursued. In the same manner that coherence plays a critical role in assisting readers' comprehension of text (Grimes, 1975), the behaviors of an animated pedagogical agent should be molded by considerations of pedagogical coherence.

Perhaps most central among these requirements is that an agent's advisory and explanatory interjections be *situated* (Brown et al., 1989): all of its explanatory behaviors – not merely its advisory actions but also its communication of fundamental conceptual knowledge – should take place in concrete problem-solving contexts. For example, learners interacting with the DESIGN-A-PLANT environment should learn about leaf morphology in the context of selecting a particular type of leaf as they design a plant that will thrive in particular environmental conditions. Moreover, agents' behaviors should obey prerequisite relationships and include transitions (both verbal and visual) that are the hallmark of spoken discourse.

Creating agents that intervene appropriately requires inferring the learner's intentions. However, diagnosis should be conducted as non-invasively as possible because continually interrupting learners to determine their current intent and to ferret out their misconceptions would interrupt constructivist learning. For example, it would go against the spirit of constructivist learning to prevent the learner from pursuing his or her design activities in order to issue a number of probes to detect precisely which misconceptions were active at a given time.

To achieve mixed-initiative interaction with lifelike agents, believability (Bates, 1994) is a key feature of these agents. We define the *believability* of lifelike agents as the extent to which users interacting with them come to believe that they are observing a sentient being with its own beliefs, desires, intentions, and personality. Although it is possible that increasing believability may yield substantial rewards in learners' motivation, when learners have the initiative, agents must exhibit believability-enhancing behaviors such as standing up and sitting down in such a manner that they do not distract from problem solving. Some behaviors such as moving from one location to another have high visual impact, while others, such as small head movements, have low visual impact. In general, the higher the visual impact, the more interesting a behavior will be, but agents must control the visual impact of their behaviors in such a manner that they do not divert a learner's attention at critical junctures.

In short, agents' behaviors should be sequenced in such a way that, in the normal course of a learner's problem-solving activities, the transfer of initiative between the learner and the agent plays out as smoothly as possible, interventions are provided in a timely and topical manner, diagnosis is non-invasive, and believability-enhancing behaviors do not interfere with but rather enhance the learning experience.

2.1. A TESTBED LEARNING ENVIRONMENT FOR MIXED-INITIATIVITY

To empirically investigate mixed-initiative interaction with lifelike pedagogical agents, we have implemented an animated agent, Herman the Bug (Figure 1), who interacts with learners solving problems in the DESIGN-A-PLANT learning environment. Herman and DESIGN-A-PLANT are the central computational artifacts of a long-term project.[2] The implemented behavior sequencing engine operates in realtime to dynamically monitor and update the environmental context, advisory history, and task model and to select and compose the agent's behaviors approximately once every 200 milliseconds.[3]

The agent is a talkative, quirky insect with a propensity to fly about the screen and dive into the plant's structures as he provides problem-solving advice. In the process of explaining concepts, he performs a broad range of activities including walking, flying, shrinking, expanding, swimming, fishing, bungee jumping, teleporting, and acrobatics. His *behavior space* was designed to 'stress-test' the behavior sequencing algorithms and representations. Containing more than 50 animated behaviors and approximately 100 verbal behaviors, the behavior space houses a variety of pedagogical and believability-enhancing behaviors. The pedagogical behavior space includes a variety of advisory and explanatory behaviors pertaining to botanical anatomy, physiology, environmental constraints, and their interactions. The believability-enhancing behavior space includes re-orientation behaviors (e.g., standing up, lying down), restrictive body behaviors (e.g., back scratching, head scratching, toe tapping, body shifting), prop-based behaviors (e.g., glasses cleaning), and full-screen celebratory behaviors (e.g., bungee jumping, cartwheeling).

Learners interact with the agent as they graphically assemble customized 3D plants (pre-rendered on an SGI) from a library of plant anatomical structures.[4]

---

[2] The first three years of the project have been devoted to iteratively designing and building the animated agent and its 'laboratory' (the DESIGN-A-PLANT ENVIRONMENT for studying mixed-initiative human-agent interactions). The second three years will be devoted to empirical investigations of the cognitive processes and the results of constructivist human-agent learning.

[3] The behavior sequencing engine runs on a Power Macintosh 9500/132.

[4] A general goal of the DESIGN-A-PLANT project is creating learning episodes that revolve around learners' active design-centered problem solving. Although constructivism has come to dominate contemporary theories of learning, arriving at a clear definition of it has proved challenging indeed. Two closely related approaches to learning are that of constructionism and constructive learning. *Constructionist* theories emphasize that learning 'happens especially felicitously in a context where the learner is consciously engaged in constructing a public entity, whether it's a sand castle on the beach or a theory of the universe' (Papert, 1991). *Constructive* learning, unlike the

Their goal in each design episode is to create a plant that will survive under a specific set of environmental conditions. Each environment (visualized as a different imaginary planet) is rendered as an intriguing landscape. Specific environmental factors are depicted iconically, and the roots, stems, and leaves in the artifact component library are 3D objects. 'Rollover' definitions are provided for all environmental factors and components. The DESIGN-A-PLANT testbed is a fully functional learning environment containing the following elements:

- *Environments*: 16 environments (4 types of environments, each with 4 complexity levels)
- *Artifact Component Library*: 8 types of roots, 8 types of stems, and 8 types of leaves.
- *Domain Model*: 31 constraint packets that relate 6 environmental factors to the anatomical structures and physiological functions.

All interactions between learners and the agent take place in DESIGN-A-PLANT's *design studio*. To make progress on issues of mixed-initiativity without awaiting solutions to the natural language understanding problem, the DESIGN-A-PLANT learning environment operates without an NLU component, just as the collaborative interface agent in the COLLAGEN system does (Rich & Sidner, 1998). The design studio is an interactive workbench (Figure 1) that was crafted to enable learners to attack design problems flexibly: they have the freedom to begin working on a sub-task, effortlessly move to new sub-tasks, revise design decisions in light of the agent's advice, and return to previously considered sub-tasks with ease. To simultaneously achieve this flexibility and to enable the system to monitor their tasks non-invasively, the interface state and its functionalities are tightly coupled to the task model.

Learners design plants in the design studio's 'plant bubble'. They graphically assemble their designs by first positioning the component task bar vertically on the screen. This requires only a single mouse click. When the component task bar is in the bottom-most position, the root library is displayed; when it is mid-level, stems are displayed; and when it is at the top, leaves are displayed. Learners then indicate design decisions by choosing a component of the selected type. This also is accomplished by a single mouse click. Because all workbench actions are directly mapped to their corresponding sub-tasks, learners (perhaps unknowingly) signal their intent to the behavior sequencing engine during the natural course of the design process. When they believe their design is complete and correct, they click on the *Done* button at the bottom of the screen, and the system evaluates their plant with respect to the given environment by searching for violations of constraints in the underlying domain model.

---

above, places no emphasis on authenticity or the social environment in which learning plays out. Hence, though we refer to learning in DESIGN-A-PLANT as 'constructionist', we acknowledge the important differences between constructivism, constructionism, and constructive learning and intend no philosophical claims.

Figure 2. The learner visits a new environment and undertakes root design.

2.2. SAMPLE MIXED-INITIATIVE TUTORIAL INTERACTION

To illustrate the nature of the desired mixed-initiative interactions we seek, consider the following series of exchanges in a DESIGN-A-PLANT learning session. A learner has watched Herman's overview of elementary plant anatomy and has visited two planets. The first had a simple, high rainfall, environment which required her to choose thin leaves, for flexibility. In the second environment, a planet with dim sunlight and a low watertable, she needed assistance twice. She has now been escorted to a planet with low rainfall and high temperature (Figure 2).[5] In this environment, roots and leaves are both in the environmental focus.

The agent first takes the initiative to introduce the learner to the problem.

---

[5] To emphasize artifacts and environmental variables that exercise concepts with which the learner is experiencing difficulty, some versions of DESIGN-A-PLANT dynamically select environments. By inspecting the task model, they not only present types of problems that have proved difficult for the learner in the past, but they also control the level of complexity (as measured by the number of constraints) that the environment will exhibit. To do so, they exploit an *environment matrix*, where each element of the matrix is an environment (Lester et al., 1997c). Each column represents a particular environmental 'intent,' i.e., a particular sub-task to be exercised, and each row represents additional complexity. By navigating the environment matrix, these versions of DESIGN-A-PLANT select environments that produce customized, challenging design experiences.

Animated agent: Whoa! I'm feeling hot, hot, hot! Too bad there's no raindrops to fall upon my head. Well, the roots better be well chosen to soak up all the water they can. The stem and leaves still need to store as much water as possible, but at these high temperatures, they also need to be able to use some of that water to stay cool, by transpiration.

Initiative is then transferred from agent to the learner who begins her problem solving. In general, learners can begin with any sub-task they wish.

Learner: Opts to begin plant construction with roots.

To avoid distracting the learner while she addresses difficult problems, the agent stands quietly, attentively looking at the transparent chamber in which the learner is designing her plant.

Learner: Spends a while considering the rollover descriptions of the environment elements and roots settings icons, but cannot make a decision.

Because the learner has made limited progress, the agent takes the initiative and provides verbal advice about the relevant features of the component on which the learner currently focuses.

Animated agent: Because of the light rain in this environment, one of the choices you have to make is between branching and non-branching roots. Which type would increase the roots' contact with the scarce moisture?

Animated agent: After a slight pause, raises a similar question about deep and shallow roots.

After offering the advice, the agent returns the initiative to the learner.

Learner: Speculating that branching roots are more efficient and, deciding that shallow will, in Herman's words, 'gather up the moisture as it soaks into the ground', chooses roots that are branching and shallow.

Because the learner's design decision will yield an artifact that will flourish in the given environment (assuming all of the remaining design decisions are reasonable), the agent takes the initiative to issue a verbal congratulation for the intermediate success.

Animated agent: Congratulates the learner.

Learner: Raises the task bar to choose a stem.

Learner: Mindful of Herman's comment about storing water in the stem and leaves, chooses a thick stem that is also short and covered with bark.

Although some aspects of the learner's design decision are reasonable, others are not. The agent intervenes to offer verbal advice about the particular aspects on which she requires assistance.

Animated agent: Whoo-eee! If the plant's in a hot area, there's a danger it could overheat. Like me, I'm so hot! To avoid this, the plant transpires, losing water through the stomata. Which will allow the plant to transpire more freely, a stem with bark on it or a stem with no bark?

Because the learner has demonstrated that she has understood some of the critical features of the current sub-task, the agent can now be more visually active. Even so, he waits a respectable amount of time before performing an interesting behavior, such as polishing his glasses or deploying a yo-yo, to remind the learner of his presence. The learner retains the initiative.

Learner: Correctly concludes that a stem with no bark will 'transpire more freely'.

The agent takes the initiative to issue congratulations on this successfully completed sub-task and then returns the initiative to the learner.

Animated Agent: Expresses his congratulations.

Learner: Shifts the focus to the leaves sub-task.

When the learner was working on the preceding two tasks, Herman remained standing on the task bar. However, because the task bar is now high on the screen as the learner shifts to the leaves sub-task, Herman sits down as the taskbar rises so as not to bump his head on the top of the screen.

Learner: Knows to choose thick leaves for their ability to store the scarce moisture, but has not yet generalized her understanding of maximizing cooling by transpiration to choosing thin-skinned' leaves; selects thick, large, thick-skinned leaves.

Because one of the features of the component currently under consideration will result in an artifact that cannot satisfy the current environmental constraints (the learner has made a design decision that is valid with respect to the leaves' overall thickness feature but not with respect to their skin thickness), the agent will intervene to provide advice about the specific problematic features.

Animated agent: In a hot climate, a plant needs to release excess water as vapor to cool itself off. Huh-huh. Basically it's sweating, just as we do, to prevent itself from overheating. Choose between those leaves which have a thick skin and those with a thin skin; which is better to keep the plant from overheating?

The agent returns the initiative to the learner.

Learner: Makes a second incorrect design decision of thick, small leaves with thick skin.

The learner has again demonstrated that she may have a misconception about the relationship between skin thickness and the active environmental attributes. The agent therefore intervenes. He first takes advantage of the opportunity to provide an animated explanation about external leaf anatomy. Then, because it appears that the learner was unable to operationalize the abstract verbal advice provided above, he visually advises the learner about the anatomical requirements imposed by this particular environment. The intervention begins with a verbal meta-comment about the upcoming interjection, after which the agent lies down on the task bar prior to presenting the explanations and advice. At their conclusion he returns to his original orientation.

Animated agent: OK, OK, so we're having some difficulty. But, that's OK, we're here to learn. I tell you what, see if this helps.

Animated agent: Stretches out on the task bar to watch the animations ('home movies' of himself interacting with the plant) along with the learner.

Animated agent: Provides the learner with her first task-specific background information about plant anatomy, flying in with his jetpack to point out major parts of the leaf.

Animated agent: Watches grimly as a leaf bursts open in the intense heat, while he explains, 'Well, thick-skinned leaves just won't be able to give off enough water vapor to cool the plant in this hot climate. In order for the plant to transpire freely, the leaves should be thin-skinned.' He then sits up and returns the initiative to the learner.

Learner: Considers the agent's advice but again proposes thick, thick-skinned leaves.

Because the learner has now repeatedly experienced difficulties with the abstract, conceptual advice, the agent determines that more direct advice is warranted and intervenes.

Animated agent: Thin, thin, thin! Choose thin-skinned leaves.

Learner: Follows this direct advice then clicks on the *Done* button.

If the learner instead had made another inappropriate leaf design decision, the agent would have taken the problem-solving initiative. After first exclaiming empathetically, 'I know, sometimes this plant construction stuff can be really frustrating. But, that's when I help! Why don't you let me get this choice so we can move on to the next task. We may see hazards like this later on, on some other planet', he would then have performed an appropriate problem-solving action himself, and the leaves he created would have then been displayed in the design chamber. A final check is made to determine whether all tasks have been accomplished correctly, since the learner always has the option of shifting her attention from an incomplete task to work on one of the others. If there had been unresolved suboptimal design decisions on other sub-tasks, Herman would have offered advice at the appropriate level as described above, just as he would have done had the sub-task not been interrupted. Because all is well, the behavior sequencing engine directs the agent to exhibit an episode-completing congratulatory behavior.

Animated Agent: Cartwheels across the screen, teleports to the edge of the cliffs for a spectacular bungee jump, and then returns to introduce the next environment.

This article presents the computational mechanisms required to achieve precisely this style of mixed-initiative problem-solving interaction between lifelike pedagogical agents and learners.

3. Context Modeling for Mixed-initiative interaction

To facilitate mixed-initiative problem-solving, lifelike pedagogical agents must have access to a well-represented model of the problem-solving context. Specifically, to make decisions about which behaviors a pedagogical agent should perform, when they should be exhibited, and how they should be sequenced, the agent behavior sequencing engine maintains a dynamically updated design-centered contextual representation of mixed-initiative design episodes (Figure 3). In the figure, each V_i is an environmental variable, e.g., the amount of sunlight; each C_i is a component type of the artifact being designed, e.g., the roots; and each $SubTask_i$ is that of determining particular features for a given component type, e.g., selecting large, thin, and thick-skinned leaves. The arrows within the learning environment module represent the links between each component type and its related sub-task in the learner's current design episode. As the learner makes her design decisions, the behavior sequencing engine monitors the activity, updates the task model, selects behaviors from the behavior space, and assembles them into a multimodal behavior stream (as described in a section below). The design-centered context representation consists of an *environmental context*, a *multimodal advisory history*, and a *task model*:

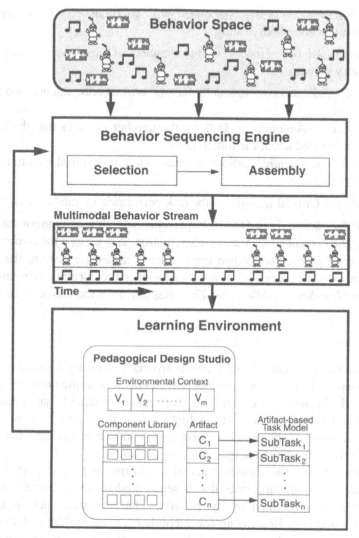

Figure 3. The behavior sequencing engine, design studio and artifact-based task model

- *Environmental Context*: Critical features of the environment which have been presented to the learner:

  - *Current Environment*: Environmental factors (and their values) in the current design episode.

  - *Environmental Intent*: Set of component types from the artifact library which that environment is intended to exercise.

  - *Environmental Complexity*: Associated with every environment is an environmental complexity that indicates the expected difficulty that learners will experience with problems in that environment.

- *Sub-Task Complexity*: Associated with each sub-task for every environment is a complexity rating.

– *Multimodal Advisory History:* Critical features of the advisory dialogue, where each entry consists of:

- *Topic*: Indicates environmental factors, artifact components, and constraint packets.
- *Frequency Annotations*: Indicate the number of times that the learner has been advised about the topic(s).
- *Media Annotations*: Indicate the media that were employed to communicate the advice.

– *Task Model*: Critical features of the task performed by the learner:

- *Artifact-based Task Model*: Represents selection of component instances for the current artifact under construction, as well as a *focused component*.
- *Design Evaluation*: When the learner completes a design, the artifact is evaluated as successful or not successful in the current environment.
- *Problem-Solving Idle Time*: Time elapsed since the learner's last action.

3.1. ENVIRONMENTAL CONTEXT

Design-centered problem solving revolves around a carefully orchestrated series of design episodes. To illustrate, consider design episodes in the domain of botanical anatomy and physiology. Learners are given an environment that specifies biologically critical factors in terms of qualitative variables. Environmental specifications, for example, might include the average incidence of sunlight, the amount of nutrients in the soil, and the height of the water table.

Learners consider these environmental conditions as they inspect components from a library of plant structures that is segmented into roots, stems, and leaves. Each component is defined by its structural characteristics such as length and amount of branching. Employing these components as building blocks, learners work in a 'design studio' to graphically construct a customized plant that will flourish in the environment. Each iteration of the design process consists of the learners inspecting the library, selecting plant components to design a complete plant, and determining how the plant would then fare in the given environment. If they find that the plant would not survive, learners modify their plant's components to improve its suitability and the process continues until they have developed a robust plant that prospers in the environment.

The environmental context guides the behavior sequencing engine's problem-solving advice by providing it with knowledge about the current environment and the pedagogical import of this environment. The *current environment* is encoded as a feature vector of active environmental features and their qualitative values. To illustrate, Table I depicts four representative environments from DESIGN-A-PLANT. The *environmental intent* represents the types of components the current

Table I. Sample environments from DESIGN-A-PLANT.

Environment	Feature	Value
Desert canyon	sunlight	low
	rain	low
	wind	high
	water table	low
Alpine meadow	water table	high
	temperature	low
	rain	low
	wind	high
Tropical cliffs	rain	low
	temperature	high
	nutrients	low
	water table	low
Southern marsh	rain	high
	sunlight	low
	water table	high
	temperature	high

environment is intended to exercise. For example, several of the environments in DESIGN-A-PLANT are intended to exercise learners' knowledge of leaves and the relation of leaf attributes to the features of the current environment, e.g., the amount of available light. The *environmental complexity* represents an estimate of the expected relative difficulty that curriculum designers expect learners will experience in solving problems of that environment. Finally, each environment also includes *sub-task complexity* ratings which indicate expected difficulty levels for each sub-task; computationally, this is the number of component features for that sub-task which must be correctly selected to design a component for the environment. For example, in low rainfall environments, designing successful roots requires the learner to grapple with both depth and branchiness issues. All aspects of the environmental context are used in determining topics of advisory interventions.

To relate features of the environmental context to problem-solving actions, a constraint-based domain model can furnish the essential representational structures to support mixed-initiative pedagogical dialogue. For example, DESIGN-A-PLANT's domain model was developed for middle school students learning about botanical anatomy and physiology. It consists of constraint packets that relate environmental factors to plant components and the roles they play in plant physiology. In particular, these constraint packets encode the relationships between binary-valued environmental factors (e.g., incidence of sunlight, temperature, amount of nutrients in the soil), binary-valued features of the plant structures (roots, stems, and leaves), and the primary physiological processes (respiration, photosynthesis, osmosis, nutrient transport, water transport, and transpiration).

3.2. MULTIMODAL ADVISORY HISTORY

To enable agents to provide learners with advice that is timely, that is delivered at appropriate levels of abstraction, and that employs appropriate media, the behavior sequencing engine requires a multimodal advisory history. Accordingly, the advisory history consists of a temporally ordered set of advice entries, which is updated the moment the agent provides advice. Each entry in the advisory context encodes three aspects of the advice. First, the *topic* of the advice represents the environmental factors, artifact components, and constraint packets about which the agent communicates. Second, agents need to take into account difficulties that the learner may be experiencing with a particular topic. Hence, *frequency annotations* indicate the number of times that the agent has advised the learner about the given topic(s) of the entry. Annotations on particular topics are suggestive of marks on an *overlay user model* (Carr & Goldstein, 1977); overlay marks indicate which subskills a learner has mastered, while frequency annotations indicate the topics about which the agent has advised the student. [6] Frequency annotations are used by the behavior sequencing engine to assess the level of abstraction at which advice should be provided, as discussed below. Third, because some advice is communicated with large-scale animated behaviors while others (e.g., reminders) are communicated primarily with verbal behaviors, the agent needs to be able to reason about the media that were employed to communicate the particular advice. *Media annotations* on each entry enable the behavior sequencing engine to reason about appropriate modes of expression. Together, the components of the multimodal advisory history are used to determine which topics of explanation and advice have been covered previously by the agent.

3.3. TASK MODEL

Finally, of the three components of the design-centered context representation, the task model is the most critical to agents' pedagogical effectiveness. To make appropriate decisions about initiative control and behavior sequencing, the behavior sequencing engine requires an up-to-date representation of the task performed by the

---

[6] Higher frequency annotations are produced for topics with which the learner has experienced the most difficulty.

Table II. Instance of the artifact-based task model for
DESIGN-A-PLANT.

Subtask	Design history	Current subtask?
Leaf Subtask		
Stem Subtask	Large, thick, woody Small, thick Small, thin Small, thin, green	✓
Root Subtask	Deep, thick Deep, thin Shallow, thick	

learner. The task model provides this knowledge by tracking the learner's problem-solving activities with an artifact-based task model, continuous evaluations of the viability of design decisions, and a problem-solving clock.

Dynamically providing goal-specific interventions requires the system to recognize learners' intent, but plan recognition is a notoriously difficult problem (Carberry, 1989; Chu-Carroll & Carberry, 1994; Hill & Johnson, 1995). To address the problem, artifact-based task models exploit (1) a well designed interface, e.g., learners interacting with the DESIGN-A-PLANT design interface (described below) signal their intentions through the normal course of problem solving, and (2) the 'nearly decomposable' property of problems (Simon, 1981) to segment design tasks into sub-tasks $SubTask_1 \ldots SubTask_n$, where each $SubTask_i$ represents the sub-task of making a decision about components of a particular type, e.g., choosing between different types of leaves. Artifact-based task models encode three features:

– Each $SubTask_i$ records a history of design decisions made by the learner for that aspect of the design.
– Each completed $SubTask_i$ records the most recent design decision with the selected component (from C_i).
– Some sub-task $SubTask_f$ on which the learner is currently focused (the *focused component*) is marked.

To illustrate, suppose a learner interacting with DESIGN-A-PLANT has begun to solve the problems of which types of roots and stems to incorporate in her design for a particular environment. Furthermore, suppose she is currently considering issues bearing on stems, but has not yet begun to make decisions about leaves.

The task model will be configured as shown in Table II, with the design history for each sub-task recorded in temporal order (most recent first).[7] Here, the learner has completed the `root` sub-task and the `stem` sub-task is currently in focus. The task model indicates that in considering this sub-task, her most recent decision was large, thick, woody stems.

The artifact-based task model serves the critical function of providing a dynamically maintained design history, which informs the behavior sequencing engine's initiative control decisions. However, these decisions must take into account the quality of the learner's proposed designs and some measure of the learner's rate of progress and her engagement with the process. This supporting information is provided by

(1) the *design evaluation*, which is supplied by a simple constraint system underlying the learning environment that determines whether a proposed design is appropriate for the given environmental conditions, and

(2) the *problem-solving idle time*, which is computed by a running clock that tracks the amount of time that has elapsed since the learner's last design decision.

4. Dynamic Agent Behavior Sequencing for Mixed-initiativity

Given a rich behavior space, the behavior sequencing engine (Figure 3) exploits the representations of the environmental context, the multimodal advisory history, and the task model to dynamically navigate through the behavior space, select agent behaviors, and assemble them in realtime, thereby enabling agents to engage in pedagogically effective mixed-initiative problem-solving episodes. Behavior sequencing for pedagogical agents is analogous to the topic sequencing that must be performed by pedagogical planners (Woolf & McDonald, 1984; Peachey & McCalla, 1986; Murray, 1990; Brusilovsky, 1992). Just as, for example, a discourse management network makes decisions about when to introduce a new problem, which topic to pursue next, and when to intervene, the behavior sequencing engine must also track learners' progress. Hence, behavior sequencing engines can exploit solutions to classic problems studied in the ITS community such as curriculum sequencing (Wescourt et al., 1981), simulation-based learning (Hollan et al., 1987; White & Frederiksen, 1987) and student modeling (Brown & Burton, 1978; Burton, 1982; Carr & Goldstein, 1977). However, behavior sequencing engines must also address new problems in orchestrating the agents' visual behaviors, coordinating visual behaviors with verbal behaviors, keeping the agent 'alive' onscreen, and determining when visual, verbal, or both types of modes of intervention are appropriate. Below we describe the initiative control and intervention methods that address both the verbal and the visual modes of mixed-initiativity.

---

[7] The top-to-bottom order of Leaf, Stem, and Root in Table II mirrors the spatial relation of tasks in the interface; in fact, the actual order in which the sub-tasks are performed is under the learner's control.

As learners solve problems, the behavior sequencing engine inspects the environmental context to identify the design criteria that the learner is attempting to satisfy and to determine which aspects of the design are most critical from a pedagogical perspective. It inspects the advisory history to track previously presented advice, and it inspects the task model to monitor the learner's progress and to note possible impasses. By extracting key features from these context models, using them together with ontological, intentional, and rhetorical indices to index into the behavior space, and dynamically sequencing the resulting behaviors, the behavior sequencing engine weaves together 'local' behaviors from the behavior space to create 'global' behaviors. These resulting behaviors enable the agent to share the initiative with the learner, to achieve pedagogical and visual coherence, and to appear lifelike.

At all times, the behavior sequencing engine maintains the agent's visual presence by keeping him[8] onscreen, visually immersed in the learning environment, and on or near the artifact which the learner is designing. In response to the learner's problem-solving activities, it directs the agent to provide problem-solving advice and to communicate fundamental knowledge of the domain to learners as they interactively design artifacts. After describing the types of behaviors critical for mixed-initiative interaction, the strategies and algorithms for controlling initiative, handling interventions, and selecting and assembling advisory, explanatory, and transition behaviors are presented below. [9]

4.1. PEDAGOGICAL AGENT BEHAVIOR CATEGORIES

To provide an agent with the flexibility required to respond to a broad range of mixed-initiative problem-solving contexts, its behavior space must be populated with a large, diverse set of animated and narrative pedagogical behaviors. In contrast to the linear storyboarding approach employed in traditional animation (Noake, 1988), the pedagogical and visual connectivity of behavior spaces requires a *networked storyboarding* approach. Posing significant pedagogical and aesthetic challenges, the design of a networked storyboard is a complex, labor-intensive task requiring a multidisciplinary team of computer scientists, graphic artists, animators, and voice actors. Networked storyboarding consists of designing specifications for several animated and audio-primary behaviors and imposing a coherence structure on them.

Pedagogical agents must be able to engage in a variety of explanatory, advisory, and believability-enhancing behaviors. Constructing a networked behavior space

---

[8] Because the agent inhabiting the DESIGN-A-PLANT learning environment appears more masculine than feminine, we employ the masculine pronoun. Agents of course may be masculine, feminine, or indeterminate.

[9] Each of the algorithms described below has been employed in one or more versions of the implemented agent.

for an animated pedagogical agent capable of facilitating mixed-initiative problem solving entails specifying the following categories of behaviors:

- *Conceptual Explanatory Animated Behaviors*: The agent explicates the structures and functions of the artifact which is the subject of learning episodes. For example, the DESIGN-A-PLANT agent's behavior space contains an animated behavior of the agent explaining how root hairs absorb water through osmosis.
- *Problem-solving Advisory Animated Behaviors*: The agent provides abstract, principle-based advice. Students must then operationalize this advice in their problem solving activities. For example, one animated behavior of the DESIGN-A-PLANT agent depicts him pointing out the relation between leaf size and low sunlight. (Plants in limited sunlight often have larger leaves.)
- *Problem-Solving Advisory Verbal Behaviors*: The agent provides abstract, principle-based advice as above, but in a verbal form.
- *Animated Transition Behaviors*: These portray the agent moving from one keyframe[10] to another keyframe, or performing an action that will set the stage for several upcoming behaviors.
- *Audio-primary Problem Overviews*: The agent introduces a learner to a new problem. For example, the DESIGN-A-PLANT agent's behavior space contains audio clips of the agent describing environmental conditions. These utterances are played at the beginning of problem-solving episodes.
- *Audio-primary Advisory Reminders*: The agent briefly reminds a learner about principle-based advice that was presented earlier. For example, an audio clip in the DESIGN-A-PLANT agent's behavior space is a voiceover of the agent stating, 'Remember that small leaves are struck by less sunlight'.
- *Audio-primary Direct Suggestions*: The advice presented by the agent is immediately operationalizable. For example, the DESIGN-A-PLANT agent's behavior space contains a voiceover of the agent stating, 'Choose a long stem so the leaves can get plenty of sunlight in this dim environment'. The agent makes this type of suggestion when a learner is experiencing serious difficulties.
- *Audio-primary Interjections*: The agent remarks about the learner's progress and makes off-the-cuff comments. For example, the DESIGN-A-PLANT agent's behavior space includes Audio-primary Interjections in which the agent congratulates the learner about the successful completion of a plant design. Because a large repertoire of interjections contributes significantly to an agent's believability, a behavior space should include a variety of Audio-primary Interjections.
- *Audio-primary Transitions*: The agent makes meta-comments that signal an upcoming behavior. For example, the DESIGN-A-PLANT agent's Audio-Primary Transitions include his stating, 'It seems we're having some difficulty. Let's see if this helps ...'

---

[10] A keyframe is a frame of an animation that represents a 'still' of a character that serves as a reference position.

– *Believability-enhancing Behaviors*: To enhance believability, the agent should perform a variety of physical actions. For example, the DESIGN-A-PLANT agent's Believability-enhancing Behaviors include full motions such as re-orientation (e.g., standing up, lying down) and smaller motions such as micro-body movements (e.g., toe tapping, slight body shifts) and prop-based movements (e.g., glasses cleaning).

Informal empirical evidence from interactions of students with a variety of versions of the implemented agent suggests that each of the above behavior categories is necessary. For example, in the absence of Audio-primary Advisory Reminders, the agent is forced to repeat (perhaps lengthy) advice again and again, rather than being in a position to issue a less verbose reminder. While no claims are made about the sufficiency of these categories, it appears that each is necessary.

4.2. MIXED-INITIATIVE PEDAGOGICAL AGENT BEHAVIOR SEQUENCING

4.2.1. *Initiative Control*

To foster effective learning, we believe a key desirable feature of interaction of learners with pedagogical agents is that learners should be able to take control while they are performing problem-solving actions, and the agent should be able to take control when it appears that learners are experiencing difficulty or when they ask a question. After providing assistance, the agent should then relinquish control to learners so they may continue their problem solving.

To enact initiative transfers, the behavior sequencing engine operates in the following manner to transfer control back and forth from the agent A to the student S:

(1) *Session Introduction*: At the beginning of a problem-solving session, the behavior sequencing engine directs A to introduce the learning environment. A *problem-solving session* consists of a series of *problem-solving episodes*. For example, in DESIGN-A-PLANT, learners travel from planet to planet, each with different environmental conditions for which they will design a plant.

(2) *Episode Introduction*: At the beginning of each problem-solving episode, the behavior sequencing engine directs A to introduce the current problem.

(3) *Relinquishing Control for Problem Solving*: Control is then transferred from A to S who undertakes problem-solving actions. Although S retains the initiative here, A may, nonetheless, perform Believability-enhancing behaviors unless S is grappling with problems with high complexity.

(4) *Yielding and Taking Advisory Initiative*: At any time, S may either request assistance or perform a problem-solving action. If (a) S requests assistance or (b) the intervention monitor determines that an intervention is warranted (see below), initiative is transferred to A, which becomes more alert visually, e.g., by sitting up or standing up, and then provides assistance according to the pedagogical behavior sequencing algorithms (described in detail below).

(5) *Yielding and Taking Problem-solving Initiative*: If after repeated attempts *S* demonstrates that she cannot solve the problem, *A* takes the initiative and performs the problem-solving action itself.

(6) *Learner Problem-solving Control Transfer*: After *A* has delivered relevant advice and explanations (or performed the problem-solving action), initiative control is returned immediately to *S* for continued problem solving.

(7) *Episode Completion*: When *S* completes a problem-solving episode, the behavior sequencing engine directs *A* to exhibit a high-visual-impact congratulatory behavior. For example, in the DESIGN-A-PLANT environment, the agent cartwheels across the screen when learners successfully design a plant for an environment.

The pedagogical motivation underlying this initiative control scheme is straightforward. We wish to empower the learner to the greatest extent possible while at the same time providing a dialogue/problem-solving structure in which she may be the most successful. Hence, in contrast to a more didactic approach, we cede control to the learner immediately after the initial problem-solving introductions have been made and we intervene (see below) only when the problem-solving has reached an impasse.

4.2.2. *Task-oriented Intervention*

A critical feature of controlling mixed-initiative interactions – particularly those that are to support learning – is *intervention*, where one of the interlocutors proactively takes control from another. Intervention decisions consist of determining the conditions under which an intervention should be performed and, if needed, determining the content of the intervention. The behavior sequencing engine monitors the state of the task model to assess when the learner requires assistance. If the learner makes an incorrect design decision (as indicated by her partial solutions), or if the problem-solving idle time exceeds a threshold, then the agent is directed to intervene. Empirical evidence with middle school students interacting with the DESIGN-A-PLANT learning environment indicates that the maximum period of 'impasse' time without intervention for this age group should be approximately forty-five seconds.

In the general case for mixed-initiative design-centered problem-solving, the behavior sequencing engine must determine which component in artifact design its advice should address. This component selection strategy is especially significant for the 'least invasive' learning environments. For example, in versions of the DESIGN-A-PLANT system in which the learner is free to make a number of design decisions before committing, the agent must determine which design decision to focus on. Hence, when the behavior sequencing engine determines that the agent should take the initiative, it determines the component *C* about which an interjection of advice (and possibly of explanations) should be provided according to the following prioritized strategy:

(1) If the artifact-based task model's problem-solving idle time has exceeded its threshold, indicating the learner may be experiencing difficulty with the focused component C_f, the behavior sequencing engine directs the agent to provide advice about C_f.

(2) If the task model indicates that the learner has just made an incorrect decision about a single component C, the behavior sequencing engine directs the agent to provide advice about C.

(3) If the task model indicates that the learner has made incorrect decisions about multiple components $C_1 \ldots C_n$ of the artifact, the behavior sequencing engine inspects the focused component C_f (the component to which the learner is currently attending). If C_f is incorrect, the behavior sequencing engine directs the agent to provide advice about it. (This clause comes into play in versions of DESIGN-A-PLANT when the learner is free to begin addressing other components before the component to which she was previously attending has been completed correctly.)

(4) Otherwise, the behavior sequencing engine inspects the environmental intent[11] of the current environment and determines if one of the inappropriate components $C_1 \ldots C_n$ is the subject of the environmental intent. If so, it will provide advice about that C_i.

(5) If no component satisfies any of these criteria, then the behavior sequencing engine randomly selects one of the inappropriate components C_i.

The design of the initiative control scheme and the prioritized intervention strategy were motivated by the desire to ensure that problem-solving episodes remain as coherent and 'on-task' as possible. Hence, although there are numerous situations in which a more aggressive intervention strategy could seize the initiative, the alternate approach taken here seeks to strike a balance between the benefits of clearly (though perhaps verbosely) explaining fundamental domain knowledge on the one hand, and providing the learner the opportunity to absorb this knowledge in appropriate problem-solving contexts on the other hand. Therefore, with the exception of introductions to problems, the initiative control scheme strongly favors initiative being held for the most part by the learner.

4.2.3. Advice Interjection

Once the decision to intervene has been made and the component C on which the intervention will focus has been determined, the behavior sequencing engine must then determine how to provide the learner with appropriate advice: it must carefully orchestrate the agent's behaviors to ensure that the advice is properly constructed for the current problem-solving context. To do so, it inspects the current environment and the artifact-based task model to determine the active environmental features and the relevant artifact components. It then uses an *intentional*

---

[11] Recall that the environmental intent is the set of component types from the artifact library which that environment is intended to exercise, such as stems.

index structure to identify advisory topics that are germane to the current problem-solving situation. To do this, it employs the intentional indices to map the following problem-solving context variables onto relevant advisory topics $T_1 \ldots T_n$:

- *C*: The component selected above, e.g., leaves.
- *EnvtComplexity*: Associated with every environment is an environmental complexity that indicates the expected difficulty that learners will experience with problems in that environment. The *EnvtComplexity* for a particular environment is determined by curriculum designers by determining the number of active constraints in that environment. For example, one level 2 environment requires plant designs to work under the conditions imposed by both a high watertable and a low ambient temperature.
- *EnvtType*: Also associated with every environment is an *EnvtType* indicating the type of the environment, e.g., alpine.

Each of these problem-solving context variables is critical for identifying appropriate topics of advice. *C* and *EnvtType* guide the selection of advice that is relevant to the current design component. Using *EnvtComplexity* assists the behavior sequencing engine in finding advice whose degree of sophistication (or simplicity) is appropriate. Indexing on these yields the relevant advisory topics $T_1 \ldots T_n$.

Finally, the value of *DesignEval*, which is the learning environment's evaluation of the particular componential solution proposed in the current sub-task, is used to select all of the relevant T_i that are helpful. *DesignEval* indicates not merely a binary correctness vs. incorrectness evaluation, but also the correctness of individual features of the proposed solution. For example, leaves in the alpine environment in DESIGN-A-PLANT must have three correct features: (size small), (thickness thick), and (skin-thickness thick). *DesignEval* for a learner's proposed leaf structure in the alpine environment indicates correctness for each of these features. By employing this 'feature-specific' variable *DesignEval*, we enable the agent to provide advice that is as specific as possible for the particular features of the learners' design decisions that may be problematic and, therefore, deserving of the agent's (and the learners') further attention.

4.2.4. *Selecting Stratified Problem-solving Advice Levels*

A particularly critical decision to be made is to determine the *level* at which the advice should be delivered. Adopting the *knowledge compilation* view of learning, e.g., (Anderson, 1983; Newell, 1990), the pedagogical behavior sequencing algorithm is designed to provide learners with advice at a level appropriate for their mastery of the domain. An agent's high-level (indirect) advice provides assistance couched in terms of the knowledge contained in constraint packets, i.e., the functional relation between environmental factors and artifact components. An agent's low-level (direct) advice provides assistance couched in terms of very specific design decisions. While direct advice is easily operationalized, the opportunity for learning is reduced, so the algorithm gives preference to indirect advice.

This adaptive advisory strategy is captured in a stratification of advisory behaviors into four levels that represent varying degrees of directness. After the behavior sequencing engine has determined that the agent should provide advice about a particular topic T, it uses the following stratification of advisory behaviors relevant to T to interject advice that is cast at the appropriate level L. When it has been determined that advice about T should be delivered, it consults the multimodal advisory history to determine the previous L at which advice on T was delivered and then selects advisory behavior(s) A at $L - 1$:[12]

1. *Direct Action*

   – *Role*: After commenting about the difficulty of the problem, the agent performs the optimal problem-solving action himself.
   – *Features*: Selected as a last resort only after all problem-solving advice has failed.
   – *Example*: Herman intervenes by first explaining, 'Wait, I know this one! Let me make this choice so we can get on to the next task. And, you may get a chance at this hazard again in some other environment'. He then performs the problem-solving action himself.

2. *Direct Verbal*

   – *Role*: The agent provides verbal advice that is direct and immediately operationalizable.
   – *Features*: Terse and does not require deduction; only provided after both forms of abstract advice have failed.
   – *Example*: In a low sunlight environment, Herman might say, 'Make those leaves large'.

3. *Abstract Animated*

   – *Role*: The agent provides advice that is abstract and requires operationalization by the learner.
   – *Features*: Animated but indirect; provided only after abstract verbal advice proved ineffective. More visually distracting but clearer.
   – *Example*: In a low sunlight environment, Herman can appear suspended by his jetpack next to a small leaf. He can explain, 'A plant with small leaves in dim sunlight cannot conduct enough photosynthesis and will have, ugh, no food!' With a wide smile, he demonstrates stretching the leaf out to a much larger surface area and tells the learner, 'We can help this plant by giving it larger leaves; then it can do more photosynthesis and have plenty of food to eat'.

---

[12] Note that at runtime, the behavior sequencing engine first attempts the most abstract advice (level 4) and, if the learner continues to experience difficulty, gradually proceeds downwards through these stratification levels toward more direct advice and, eventually, action (level 1).

4. *Abstract Verbal*

- *Role*: The agent provides the most abstract advice possible so the learner is required (if possible) to operationalize it.
- *Features*: Terse and verbal, thereby requiring the greatest deduction and having a minimal visual distraction.
- *Example*: In environments with low sunlight, which require learners to provide for increased photosynthesis, Herman might say, 'In this environment, there's not much sunlight. Remember that photosynthesis, the plant's way of making food, occurs mostly in the leaves. Think about what types of leaves are gonna allow the plant to still make plenty of food even though there's not much sunlight; large leaves or small leaves?'

4.2.5. *Explanation Interjection*

In addition to providing problem-solving advice, pedagogical agents can also facilitate learning by providing explanations of fundamental knowledge about the domain. By opportunistically interjecting explanations of domain phenomena that are relevant to (but not absolutely critical for) problem solving activities, pedagogical agents can broaden learners' knowledge in a situated manner. However, it is critical to interject this knowledge in a way that (a) is topical, (b) temporally distributes fundamental knowledge explanations in an even manner across the entire problem-solving session, and (c) obeys prerequisite requirements. If the behavior sequencing engine opted for abstract animated advice above, unless the current intervention was triggered by a problem-solving idle time violation – if a problem-solving idle time violation occurred, it is inferred that the learner is experiencing great difficulty and, therefore, that her attention should not be diverted by including auxiliary explanations – the behavior sequencing engine determines relevant animated explanatory behaviors E^P by performing the following computations:

(1) *Select explanatory behaviors E that are relevant to the current problem-solving context.* Using an *ontological index structure*, it maps the selected component C to candidate explanatory behaviors E (Conceptual Explanatory Animated Segments) that are currently relevant.

(2) *Compute m, the number of explanatory behaviors to exhibit.* This quantity is computed by $\lfloor b/f \rfloor$. The quantity b is the number of explanatory behaviors that have not yet been exhibited. The function f, which is determined from empirical data, is the predicted number of future problem-solving situations in which explanatory behaviors can be exhibited. [13] The floor is taken for non-integer results to be conservative – representing the number of Conceptual Explanatory Animated Segments that should be exhibited.

---

[13] For example, f in the behavior sequencing engine of the current version of DESIGN-A-PLANT considers the efficiency with which the learner has reached the current level of environmental complexity (*EnvtComplexity*) and, from the number of remaining levels, estimates the number of environments left to be visited.

(3) *Select the subset E^P of not more than m explanatory behaviors E that are pedagogically viable.* We say that an explanatory behavior is *pedagogically viable* if (a) it has not been exhibited previously in this problem-solving session and (b) all of its prerequisite behaviors have already been exhibited. Explanatory behaviors are organized in a prerequisite structure, where prerequisite relations impose a partial order on explanatory behaviors: a behavior can be performed only if all its (immediate and indirect) prerequisite behaviors have been performed. In general, prerequisites should be imposed conservatively; by imposing only those relations that are clearly mandated by the domain, greater flexibility is provided to the sequencing engine because the number of behaviors it may select at any given time will be greater.

(4) *Mark the explanatory behaviors E^P.* Record in the multimedia dialog history that the selected behaviors have been exhibited.

Each of the steps in the explanation interjection algorithm plays an important role in ensuring that the most relevant fundamental knowledge is presented. Step (1) eliminates explanations of fundamental knowledge that are not germane to the current component. Employing m in step (2) has the effect of evenly distributing these explanations over the course of the entire learning session. Because many domains and tasks are highly complex and learning time is limited, step (3) allows agents to take into account temporal resources to provide the greatest coverage of the domain in the given time. Finally, step (4) ensures that the multimedia dialogue history remains up-to-date.

To illustrate, the DESIGN-A-PLANT agent's behavior space currently includes five explanatory behaviors which the agent can exhibit to progressively reveal the rationale of the constraint relationships that drive leaf design. These are organized in a prerequisite ordering from explanations of macro-level leaf anatomy to micro-level leaf anatomy. For example, in one of the macro-level leaf anatomical explanations, he describes the blade of the leaf, the lamina, the petiole, and the midrib. In other leaf anatomy explanations he dives into the leaf, using his laser and a magnifier to show finer details. At deeper levels he takes the learner on a tour of cell anatomy, and at the deepest level, he provides a molecular explanation of photosynthesis chemistry.

Assuming that C was selected to be leaf, the behavior sequencing engine would first determine the relevant E (the Conceptual Explanatory Animated Segments) by identifying the leaf explanatory behaviors. Next, it would compute m by considering pedagogical factors in the following way: if the learner first has problems with leaf design at the pedagogical behavior sequencer's second level of complexity, the calculation of how many explanatory behaviors for the agent to exhibit uses the total number of explanatory behaviors in E (five), the learner's progress (three environments visited to date) and the number of levels remaining (two) to decide to request the agent to exhibit just one of the five. It chooses the subset E^P by identifying a behavior in E whose prerequisite behaviors have already been exhibited, which in this case is the first, most macro-level, explanatory behavior about gross leaf anatomy.

It is important to note that explanatory behaviors are invoked only when animated advice is invoked. Because explanatory behaviors typically involve visually sophisticated animations, they can convey more complex knowledge than purely verbalized advice; they are more powerful, but they are also more visually distracting. Consequently, the behavior sequencing engine is designed to maximize usage of bandwidth while simultaneously minimizing visual interruptions.

4.2.6. *Verbal and Visual Transitions*

In the same manner that coherence plays a critical role in assisting readers' comprehension of text (Grimes, 1975), the behaviors of lifelike pedagogical agents should be molded by considerations of both verbal and visual coherence. To achieve this, the behavior sequencing engine introduces both audio and visual transitions. Verbal transitions T_A are provided in the form of meta-comments about the learning episode and the agent's intention to set the stage for upcoming advice and explanations. Since all verbal behaviors are organized by rhetorical indices – in the current implementation, these are fairly coarse-grained and include Audio-primary Problem Overviews, Audio-primary Direct Suggestions, Audio-primary Interjections, and Audio-primary Transitions – the behavior sequencing engine notes that a verbal transition is called for and selects a verbal transition. For example, if by using the mechanisms above it has been deemed that advice is called for, Herman might first say, 'OK, we're having some trouble here, but we're here to learn. Maybe this will help . . . '

Visual transitions are equally critical, both to help focus the learner's attention on animated explanations and to contribute to believability. Depending on the agent's current physical state within the learning environment (described below), the behavior sequencing engine will optionally select a *prefixing* visual transition $T_{V_{pre}}$ to anticipate animated explanations and a *postfixing* visual transition $T_{V_{post}}$ to conclude an animated explanation and yield the initiative to the learner. To determine whether $T_{V_{pre}}$ and $T_{V_{post}}$ behaviors are warranted and, if so, which ones, the behavior sequencing engine maintains spatial knowledge about the agent and adheres to physical constraints on movement for visual continuity. Spatial knowledge about the agent's current state is represented with a locational pair (P, O), where P symbolically (rather than geometrically via a coordinate-based representation) represents the agent's screen position and O represents its orientation, e.g., (mid-bar-left, reclining), and physical constraints stipulate continuity relationships between behaviors. For example, the DESIGN-A-PLANT agent employs an orientation constraint: if the agent is standing, he cannot perform the lying down behavior; rather, he must first sit down before lying down.

Hence, if the behavior sequencing engine has determined that animated explanatory behaviors will be exhibited, it will also include visual and verbal transition behaviors. While adhering to the physical constraints, the behavior sequencing engine prepares a learner for an animated explanation by selecting a $T_{V_{pre}}$ that re-orients the agent into a more relaxed state (i.e., sitting if it is currently standing, reclining if it is currently sitting). In a similar fashion, it selects a $T_{V_{post}}$ by reversing this state. The net visual effect of these actions is that the agent appears to be relaxing to watch the animated explanations *with* the learner.

4.2.7. *Behavior Assembly and Presentation*

As it assembles the final set of behaviors determined above, the behavior sequencing engine must create a 'global' behavior from each of the 'local' behaviors in a manner that produces visually and pedagogically coherent actions in the learning context. It must transition the agent from a state of observing the learner's problem-solving, to a state of taking the initiative, to a state of holding the initiative during the intervention by exhibiting relevant explanatory and advisory behaviors, to the final state of returning the initiative to the learner. To accomplish these transitions, it imposes the following temporal ordering on the selected behaviors:

(1) Verbal (audio) transition behavior T_A.
(2) Prefixing visual transition behaviors $T_{V_{pre}}$.
(3) Pedagogically viable explanatory behaviors E^P relevant to the selected component C, where $|E^P| \leq m$ and the behaviors are ordered by prerequisite structure.
(4) Advisory behavior A about topics $T_1 \ldots T_n$, each with appropriate levels L_i and, consequently, each with appropriate mode (visual and/or auditory), that is relevant to the selected component C.
(5) Postfixing visual transition behavior $T_{V_{post}}$.

The inclusion and ordering of each type of behavior play a critical role in the overall intervention. Introducing T_A behaviors first paves the way for upcoming explanations and advice; without them, the agent's behavior appeared abrupt. Inserting $T_{V_{pre}}$ behavior plays a similar role, but for the visual mode. Including E^P *before* A is very important. Pilot studies with learners interacting with different versions of the behavior sequencing engine suggested revealed that some arrangements of behaviors are considerably more effective than others. For example, in an earlier version of the system, the agent exhibited the A behaviors before the E^P behaviors: this ordering turned out to be problematic since learners tended to forget the advice offered in A because, we hypothesize, there were intervening conceptual explanations. The sequencing engine's assembly mechanism was therefore modified to present advisory behaviors after the explanatory behaviors. Finally, $T_{V_{post}}$ behaviors play an important role in visually signalling that the initiative has again shifted back to the learner.

The behavior sequencing engine directs the agent to immediately exhibit the resulting behaviors in the learning environment, and the process is repeated – monitoring followed by sequencing and assembly – as the learner continues to interactively solve problems in the environment. In addition, the agent continues to be attentive to the learner's activities through its physical positioning. For example, when learners interacting with the DESIGN-A-PLANT environment move the component task bar on which the agent is standing to the top level, the behavior sequencing engine directs the agent to shift to an orientation in which he does not bump his head on the top of the interface. The net effect of the sequencing engine's activities is rich problem-solving sessions where learners perceive they are interacting with an intriguing lifelike character who is attentively observing their problem-solving activities and actively providing customized multimedia advice.

5. Mixed Initiative Interaction: A Detailed Example

To illustrate the operation of the behavior sequencing algorithms, consider the DESIGN-A-PLANT learning scenario introduced earlier. A learner has watched Herman's Session Introduction, in which he presented explanations of elementary plant anatomy, and she has visited two planets. The first had a simple, high rainfall, environment which required her to choose thin leaves, for flexibility. In the second environment, a planet with dim sunlight and a low watertable, she needed assistance twice. She has now been escorted to a planet with low rainfall and high temperature.

EnvtType is now tropical cliffs, and *EnvtComplexity* is level 2, indicating that the learner must attend to two environmental constraints during her problem solving here, and, because this environment focuses equally on all three tasks, the *environmental intent* includes roots, stems, and leaves. Because we have reached the beginning of a new problem-solving episode, the behavior sequencing engine directs the agent to introduce the current problem. Herman therefore exhibits the Audio-primary Problem Overview associated with the current environment:

Animated agent: Whoa! I'm feeling hot, hot, hot! Too bad there's no raindrops to fall upon my head. Well, the roots better be well chosen to soak up all the water they can. The stem and leaves still need to store as much water as possible, but at these high temperatures, they also need to be able to use some of that water to stay cool, by transpiration.

Initiative is then transferred from agent to the learner who begins her problem solving. In general, learners can begin with any sub-task they wish.

Learner: Opts to begin plant construction with roots.

Since the roots task is fairly complicated, as indicated by the *sub-task complexity* of roots in this environment, Herman is directed to avoid performing any potentially distracting Believability-enhancing behaviors; rather, he stands quietly, attentively looking at the transparent chamber in which the learner is designing her plant.

Learner: Spends a while considering the rollover descriptions of the environment elements and roots settings icons, but cannot make a decision.

Throughout learning sessions, the behavior sequencing engine tracks the *problem-solving idle time*, which has just reached 45 seconds. Because this period of time exceeds the threshold, the behavior sequencing engine directs Herman to take the initiative. To perform a task-oriented intervention, the behavior sequencing engine determines that the focused component (roots) is the component C about which advice should be provided. The behavior sequencing engine now uses the value of C, together with the current values of *EnvtType* and *EnvtComplexity* to index into the behavior space to determine the relevant advisory topics $T_1 \ldots T_n$. In this case, it determines that advice should be provided about two topics: T_1 will be advice about the effects of low rainfall on branchiness; T_2 will be advice about the effects of low rainfall on root depth. Next, it determines the level L at which to provide the advice. Because no advice has been provided before, it gives advice at level 4, which is *Abstract Verbal*. Finally it determines that no explanatory advice should be provided because no explanatory behaviors are exhibited in response to an 'exceeded problem-solving idle time' intervention. Because the advisory mode is verbal, no verbal transitions or visual transitions are needed.

Animated agent: Because of the light rain in this environment, one of the choices you have to make is between branching and non-branching roots. Which type would increase the roots' contact with the scarce moisture?

Animated agent: After a slight pause, raises a similar question about deep and shallow roots.

After completing his exhibition of the advisory behaviors, the agent returns the initiative to the learner.

Learner: Speculating that branching roots are more efficient and, deciding that shallow roots will, in Herman's words, 'gather up the moisture as it soaks into the ground', chooses roots that are branching and shallow.

After the learning environment determines that the learner has made a valid design decision for the roots sub-task, *DesignEval* is updated, and the behavior sequencing engine directs the agent to exhibit a congratulatory Audio-primary Interjection for successful completion of the current sub-task and then returns the initiative to the learner.

Animated Agent: Congratulates the learner.

Learner: Raises the task bar to choose a stem.

The environment remains the same as above, but now the *sub-task complexity* is updated to indicate the difficulty of the stem task.

Learner: Mindful of Herman's comment about storing water in the stem and leaves, chooses a thick stem that is also short and covered with bark.

DesignEval is now updated to reflect the fact that the learner has made a design decision that is valid with respect to the stem's thickness feature but not with respect to the bark decision. Because one of the features of the component currently under consideration will result in an artifact that cannot satisfy the current environmental constraints, the behavior sequencing engine takes the initiative from the learner and gives it to the agent. To perform a task-oriented intervention, it determines that the component C about which advice should be provided is the focused component, stems.

The behavior sequencing engine now uses the value of C, together with the current values of *EnvtType* and *EnvtComplexity* to index into the behavior space to determine the relevant advisory topics $T_1 \ldots T_n$. In this case, it determines that advice should be provided about a single topic T_2, namely, the environmental factors governing the presence or absence of bark on stems. Next, it determines the level L at which to provide the advice.

Because no advice has been provided before, it gives advice at level 4, which is *Abstract Verbal*. Finally it determines that no explanatory advice should be provided (explanatory behaviors are exhibited only when the advice is animated) and therefore that no transitions are required.

Animated agent: Whoo-eee! If the plant's in a hot area, there's a danger it could overheat. Like me, I'm so hot! To avoid this, the plant transpires, losing water through the stomata. Which will allow the plant to transpire more freely, a stem with bark on it or a stem with no bark?

Because the learner has demonstrated that she has understood one of two critical features of the current sub-task, the *sub-task complexity* is reduced. Noting this development, the behavior sequencing engine leaves the initiative with the learner but permits the agent to be more active. Even so, he waits a respectable amount of time before performing a self-absorbed behavior, such as polishing his glasses or deploying a yo-yo, as if to say 'Don't forget I'm here to help, but you can take more time if you need to . . .' Later, he will exhibit a random fidget or a toothy grin, as if to encourage the student to make a choice.

Learner: Correctly concludes that a stem with no bark will 'transpire more freely.'

After the learning environment determines that the learner has made a valid design decision for the stem sub-task, *DesignEval* is updated, and the behavior sequencing engine directs the agent to exhibit a congratulatory Audio-primary Interjection for successful completion of the current sub-task and then returns the initiative to the learner.

Animated agent: Expresses his congratulations.

Learner: Shifts the focus to the leaves task.

When the learner was working on the preceding two tasks, Herman remained standing on the task bar. However, because the task bar is now high on the screen as the learner shifts to the leaves sub-task, the behavior sequencing engine leaves the initiative with the learner but at the same time directs Herman to sit down as the taskbar rises so as not to bump his head on the top of the screen. The environment remains the same as above, but now the *sub-task complexity* is updated to indicate the difficulty of the leaves task.

Learner: Knows to choose thick leaves for their ability to store the scarce moisture, but has not yet generalized her understanding of maximizing cooling by transpiration to choosing 'thin-skinned' leaves; selects thick, large, thick-skinned leaves.

DesignEval is now updated to reflect the fact that the learner has made a design decision that is valid with respect to the leaves' overall thickness feature but not with respect to the leaves' skin thickness decision. Because one of the features of the component currently under consideration will result in an artifact that cannot satisfy the current environmental constraints, the behavior sequencing engine takes the initiative from the learner and gives it to the agent. To perform a task-oriented intervention, it determines that the component C about which advice should be provided is the focused component, leaves.

The behavior sequencing engine now uses the value of C, together with the current values of *EnvtType* and *EnvtComplexity* to index into the behavior space to determine the relevant advisory topics $T_1 \ldots T_n$. In this case, it determines that advice should be provided about a single topic T_3, namely, the environmental factors governing leaf skin thickness. Next, it determines the level L at which to provide the advice. Because no advice has been provided before, it gives advice at level 4, which is *Abstract Verbal*. Finally it determines that no explanatory behaviors should be provided (explanatory behaviors are exhibited only when the advice is animated) and therefore that no transitions are required.

Animated agent: In a hot climate, a plant needs to release excess water as vapor to cool itself off. Huh-huh. Basically it's sweating, just as we do, to prevent itself from overheating. Choose between those leaves which have a thick skin and those with a thin skin; which is better to keep the plant from overheating?

The behavior sequencing engine returns the initiative to the learner.

Learner: Makes a second incorrect design decision of thick, small leaves with thick skin.

DesignEval is now updated to reflect the fact that the learner has made a design decision that is valid with respect to the leaves' overall thickness feature but not with respect to the leaves' skin thickness decision. Because one of the features of the component currently under consideration will result in an artifact that cannot satisfy the current environmental constraints, the behavior sequencing engine takes the initiative from the learner a second time by performing a task-oriented intervention about C, which is still leaves. It uses this value, together with the *EnvtType* and *EnvtComplexity* to index into the behavior space as before to determine the relevant advisory topic, which is again T_3, skin thickness. However, this time the advisory level L is decremented to level 3, which is *Abstract Animated*. As a result, it now has an opportunity to interject animated explanatory behaviors.

Before it is ready to do so, however, it first selects explanatory behaviors E that are relevant to the selected component C (leaves), namely, all of the explanations of leaf anatomy. Next, it computes the m, the number of explanatory behaviors to exhibit. Because the number of environments remaining to be visited is high, the behavior sequencing engine determines that significant opportunities remain for providing explanations of leaf anatomy, so it chooses m to be 1. Pedagogical viability of the candidate behaviors is assessed by examining which explanations have both (a) not yet been exhibited (as indicated in the multimodal dialog history) and (b) have all of their prerequisites met. The explanatory behavior that satisfies these requirements E^P is the one in which the agent provides an introduction to external leaf anatomy, and finally E^P is then marked in the multimodal dialog history as having been exhibited.

Next, because animated advisory behaviors will be exhibited, an Audio-primary Transition T_A is selected by choosing an introductory meta-comment. Finally, a prefixing visual transition $T_{V_{pre}}$ is selected in which the agent will sit down to watch the animations and a postfixing visual transition $T_{V_{post}}$ is selected in which the agent returns to his previous orientation. These behaviors are ordered as follows: T_A, $T_{V_{pre}}$, E^P, T_3, and $T_{V_{post}}$.

Animated agent: OK, OK, so we're having some difficulty. But, that's OK, we're here to learn. I tell you what, see if this helps.

Animated agent: Lies down on the task bar to watch the animations along with the learner.

A somber variation on the musical theme of this environment is playing.[14]

---

[14] Learning sessions in DESIGN-A-PLANT are accompanied by a context-sensitive soundtrack. In several experimental versions of the learning environment, the soundtrack composer provides thematic consistency of voicing and melody within a problem-solving episode and thematic consistency across problem-solving episodes. It exploits the task model to adapt its tempo, mood, and number of instrumental voices to the learner's progress.

Animated agent: Provides the learner with her first task-specific background information about plant anatomy, flying in with his jetpack to point out major parts of the leaf.

Animated agent: Watches grimly as a leaf bursts open in the intense heat, while he explains, 'Well, thick-skinned leaves just won't be able to give off enough water vapor to cool the plant in this hot climate. In order for the plant to transpire freely, the leaves should be thin-skinned'. He then sits up and returns the initiative to the learner.

Learner: Considers the agent's advice but again proposes thick, thick-skinned leaves.

DesignEval is now updated to reflect the fact that the learner has yet again made a design decision that is valid with respect to the leaves' overall thickness feature but not with respect to the leaves' skin thickness decision. It indexes into the advisory behavior space as before. This time, however, having exhausted the high-level, more abstract hints, the agent is forced to give more direct advice. Computationally, this is accomplished by decrementing the advisory level L to level 2, which is *Direct Verbal*. Because this advice is verbal, no auxiliary explanations are provided to accompany it and no transitions are required.

Animated agent: Thin, thin, thin! Choose thin-skinned leaves.

Learner: Follows this direct advice then clicks on the *Done* button.

If the learner instead had made another inappropriate leaf design decision, the behavior sequencing engine would have given control to the agent, who would then take the problem-solving initiative. This would have been accomplished by decrementing L to level 1, which is *Direct Action*. The agent would have been directed to say, 'I know, sometimes this plant construction stuff can be really frustrating. But, that's when I help! Why don't you let me get this choice so we can move on to the next task. We may see hazards like this later on, on some other planet'. The agent would then make the leaf design decision himself, and appropriately chosen leaves would then be displayed in the design chamber. A final check is made to determine whether all tasks have been accomplished correctly, since the learner always has the option of shifting her attention from an incomplete task to work on one of the others. If there had been unresolved suboptimal design decisions on other sub-tasks, Herman would have offered advice at the appropriate level as described above, just as he would have done had the sub-task not been interrupted. Because all is well, the behavior sequencing engine directs the agent to exhibit an episode-completing congratulatory behavior.

Animated agent: Cartwheels across the screen, teleports to the edge of the cliffs for a spectacular bungee jump, and then returns to introduce the next environment.

6. Discussion

Lifelike pedagogical agents hold much promise for constructivist learning environments. Because of agents' potential pedagogical benefits and their lifelike qualities, they can play a critical role in mixed-initiative problem solving. However, assessing agent design decisions in the absence of a large body of empirical evidence is exceptionally difficult. Although we can abstractly formulate hypotheses about how to design behavior spaces, how to create representational structures for constructivist problem-solving contexts, and how to develop computational mechanisms for behavior sequencing engines, such conjecturing is unlikely to yield informative theories.

While work on lifelike pedagogical agents has just begun and our understanding of their design is therefore limited, during the past three years a number of 'lessons learned' have begun to emerge from experiences with the DESIGN-A-PLANT agent. Through a series of iterative refinements consisting of design, implementation, and empirical evaluation, the agent has evolved from a stationary creature capable of providing only rudimentary assistance to a much more intriguing, lifelike character that monitors learners' progress, gives them helpful feedback, and gracefully intervenes in appropriate problem-solving contexts.

The primary impetus for the agent's successful evolution has been the findings of focus group studies. Conducted with more than twenty middle school students from Martin Middle School in Raleigh, North Carolina and with the Raleigh Chapter of the Women in Science Mentoring Program, these informal studies consisted of learners interacting with the agent for forty-five minutes to one hour. As each learner traveled with Herman from planet to planet, he or she solved design problems in DESIGN-A-PLANT environments. Learners were confronted with problems of varying levels of difficulty; some were very simple, involving only a single constraint, while others were complex, requiring learners to address multiple constraints simultaneously. As they designed plants for a variety of environmental conditions, the agent introduced problems, explained concepts in botanical anatomy and physiology, provided problem-solving advice, and interjected congratulatory and off-the-cuff remarks.

In general, Herman was unanimously well received by the students. His pedagogical and visual coherence, together with his immersive property – the fact that he inhabits the scenes of the environments to which learners travel – were perceived as strikingly lifelike behaviors. Herman's visual behaviors seemed to flow so well that no learner commented or displayed surprise during transitions. Because of the use of visual transition behaviors, initiative changes were for the most part visually flawless. His verbal reminders enabled learners to continue with their problem solving uninterrupted, and during the study learners made frequent (and unprompted) positive comments about his physical actions and remarks. The variety of his behaviors maintained their interest throughout the sessions, and most learners commented positively about the continuously updated score. Perhaps not surprisingly considering the middle-school audience, Herman's quirky asides were well received.

These studies suggest that lifelike pedagogical agents whose behaviors are selected and assembled with a well-designed sequencing engine can effectively guide learners through a complex subject in a manner that exhibits both pedagogical and visual coherence. The primary lessons gleaned from the studies are summarized below.

6.1. RICH BEHAVIOR SPACES FOR MIXED-INITIATIVITY

To create mixed-initiative interactions, it is critical to populate an agent's behavior space with *at least* the nine types of behaviors identified earlier. Conceptual Explanatory Animated Behaviors and Problem-Solving Advisory Animated Behaviors constitute the core of an agent's repertoire. They provide the central means for communicating explanations of fundamental conceptual knowledge and for providing advice when interventions are required. Animated Transition Behaviors provide visual continuity, and an agent's verbal behaviors complement the visual behaviors. Audio-primary Problem Overviews are important for introducing problems; without them, learners who have limited experience with a new learning environment may become confused. Audio-primary Advisory Reminders and Audio-primary Direct Suggestions provide multiple levels of advice. Audio-primary Transitions provide rhetorical coherence. Agents' verbal meta-comments such as bridging phrases can also usher in topic transitions, and without them, agents' actions appear 'choppy' and unmotivated. Audio-primary Interjections and Believability-enhancing Behaviors are essential for achieving the illusion of life.

6.2. POPULATION-SPECIFIC INTERVENTION STRATEGIES

With appropriate intervention strategies, lifelike pedagogical agents can engage in effective mixed-initiative problem-solving interactions. By tracking changes in a task model representing the crucial problem-solving activities, the behavior sequencing engine can share the initiative with learners, enable them to interact freely with a learning environment to solve problems, take the initiative when assistance is warranted, and then relinquish the initiative as dictated by learners' progress. Intervention strategies should be motivated by an understanding of target user populations, problem-solving tasks, and domains. For example, observations of the students interacting with Herman during the focus group studies suggest that a relatively aggressive intervention strategy is perhaps most appropriate for design tasks for this user group. Although the agent told learners that they could ask for his help by clicking on him, in practice very few of the students in the focus group studies took advantage of the functionality, almost never requesting assistance. To address this, the intervention monitor was designed to be very sensitive to problem-solving difficulties. When learners make design decisions that violate environmental constraints, the agent immediately intervenes to assist them. In general, creating population-specific intervention strategies is critical to the whole mixed-initiative tutorial enterprise. Some target learner populations may need to be encouraged to explore the domain at their leisure, as in the classic work on microworlds where experimentation is a key component of the learning process (Cauzinille-Marmeche & Mathieu, 1988; Lawler & Lawler, 1987; Thompson, 1987). In contrast, in many training applications, concerns of efficiency prevail, so intervention must be conducted considerably more aggressively. Analogous differences obtain in different age groups as well. For example, adults can frequently help themselves after initially reaching an impasse, but children learning a new task sometimes get stuck in problem-solving 'local minima' and require assistance in extricating themselves. We expect that it is for this reason that Herman's help was warmly received, but whether such an aggressive strategy is generally desirable is a subject for future studies.

6.3. LIGHTWEIGHT TASK MODELS

To enable lifelike pedagogical agents to exhibit the flexibility required to assist learners in constructivist problem-solving, they must be provided with an up-to-date model of the problem-solving context. Perhaps no result from the last three years' experience is stronger than the following: without dynamically maintained task models that accurately reflect learners' problem-solving progress, lifelike pedagogical agents would be unable to engage in meaningful mixed-initiative problem-solving interactions. However, this does not imply that unusually expressive task models are required. In fact, the artifact-based task models employed in DESIGN-A-PLANT are of the 'lightweight' variety. The task models are 'lightweight' in somewhat the same sense that the user models in the PHELPS just-in-time training system (Collins et al., 1997) are lightweight: while they are not particularly expressive, they are in practice highly accurate and can provide essential problem-solving tracking knowledge. Moreover, they permit non-invasive diagnosis. Because learners signal their intentions through interface actions that are observable by the task modeller, learners' problem solving can proceed uninterrupted. However, it is important to note that as the complexity of design tasks increase, the fairly simple non-invasive diagnostic techniques here may very well need to be replaced by those that are more invasive. For example, as we increase the degrees of freedom of the design tasks, the ability to create an interface that so clearly signals learners' intent may be reduced, and this may have the effects of, first, requiring a more 'heavyweight' task model, and, second, forcing the agent to intervene more aggressively to ascertain learners' misconceptions.

6.4. INTERVENING WITH MULTI-LEVEL, MULTIMODAL ADVICE

The problem-solving advice provided by lifelike pedagogical agents should have three interrelated properties:

(1) it should be delivered at multiple levels of abstraction,
(2) it should be delivered with media that are determined in a context-sensitive fashion, and
(3) it should be carefully structured.

The first property, multi-level advice, is a capability that is critical for agents which are intended to support knowledge compilation approaches to learning. High-level advice provides assistance that is couched in terms of more abstract domain concepts, e.g., the DESIGN-A-PLANT agent's high-level advice discusses the contents of constraint packets, while low-level advice is immediately operationalizable. By providing advice at these multiple levels, agents can attempt to foster knowledge compilation but will also have a fallback technique when learners experience difficulty with abstractions. The second property, context-sensitive media allocation, enables agents to effectively use both visual and auditory channels. They can perform more visually oriented behaviors for explaining new (and perhaps complex) concepts and more verbal behaviors for simple reminders. The former permits them to be significantly more expressive when needed, and the latter permits them to interject brief reminders and asides without distracting or disorienting learners. The third and final property, delivering advice that is carefully structured, was revealed by early focus group studies. In one of its early incarnations, the behavior sequencing engine first directed the agent to provide advice (advisory behaviors) and then to provide more conceptual explanations (explanatory behaviors) immediately prior to relinquishing the initiative so learners could return to their tasks. Because it was found that learners were confused by the agent first providing advice in response to a particular problem-solving impasse and then providing more conceptual knowledge, the initial behavior sequencing algorithms were modified to correct this problem by reversing the behavior orderings so that they conclude with advice.

6.5. SCALING UP MIXED-INITIATIVE TUTORIAL INTERACTIONS

An important open issue in lifelike pedagogical agents is scalability. At this early stage in the research program, creating a lifelike pedagogical agent requires a fairly large investment in labor in terms of designing the entire approach to its behaviors, creating the behavior space, and building a behavior sequencing engine. While it is not conceivable that this effort could be reduced to zero in creating lifelike pedagogical agents for new tasks and domains, it has become clear that several techniques will contribute to scalability in the future. First, it has taken considerable effort to investigate, construct, and experiment with different intervention strategies, advice, and explanation. While this has been and will continue to be a critical research question, our understanding of how to create the overall design for lifelike agents has improved to a considerable degree from when the DESIGN-A-PLANT project began (hence, the current article). As we learn more about how mixed-initiative human-human tutorial interactions work in practice, the labor required for this aspect of the enterprise will be reduced substantially. Second, on a related topic, much of the early work on the DESIGN-A-PLANT agent was spent experimenting with different types of behavior spaces. While it seems that other types of behaviors will need to be identified to fill gaps not yet anticipated, much of this early exploratory work is now complete. Third, the behavior sequencing engine itself is a fairly complex system that currently requires an enormous amount of effort to iteratively design, construct, and refine. Although for 'pedagogically sophisticated' lifelike agents, behavior control is likely to be an issue for some time to come, we expect that high-level tools for creating behavior sequencing engines will begin to appear in the not too distant future. In the same manner that a broad range of animation tools have brought multimedia to the general public, it seems likely that analogous authoring tools for lifelike pedagogical agents will enable instructional designers to create agents for mixed-initiative interaction on a cost-effective basis. Precisely what form these tools take and when they arrive remains to be seen.

7. Conclusions and Future Work

Lifelike pedagogical agents offer significant potential for mixed-initiative problem solving. Because they combine context-sensitive advisory behaviors with great visual appeal and they proactively assist learners performing exploratory problem-solving activities, they hold much promise for constructivist learning environments. In addition to their educational benefits, pedagogical agents with a strong lifelike presence may capture learners' imaginations and play a critical motivational role to keep them deeply engaged in problem solving.

We have proposed a computational framework for lifelike pedagogical agents that enables them to control the initiative in problem-solving interactions, achieve pedagogical and visual coherence, and exhibit believability. With a rich behavior space of animated and verbal behaviors, a behavior sequencing engine can exploit an environmental context, a multimodal advisory history, and an artifact-based task model to dynamically select and assemble an agent's behaviors in realtime. Focus group studies with middle school students interacting with an implemented agent in a fully functional constructivist learning environment suggest that lifelike pedagogical agents can contribute in important ways to constructivist learning. By taking advantage of a behavior space with ontological, intentional, and rhetorical indices and of dual pedagogical and believability-enhancing sequencers, a behavior sequencing engine can enable agents to provide context-specific multimedia advice while at the same time appearing lifelike and entertaining.

We believe that this work represents a promising first step toward creating life-like pedagogical agents and that it consequently suggests a number of directions for future research. In particular, three lines of investigation are especially compelling: conducting formal empirical studies of pedagogical agents' effectiveness in learning environments; investigating the full spectrum of mixed-initiative interactions; and endowing pedagogical agents with full-scale realtime natural language generation and speech synthesis capabilities. These possibilities are discussed below.

First, as with all new learning environment technologies, full exploitation of lifelike pedagogical agents calls for a comprehensive research program to formally study their pedagogical and motivational effects. Results from initial studies of learner-agent interactions that were conducted with cognitive scientists have begun to emerge and are encouraging (Lester et al., 1997a; Lester et al., 1997b), but a significant body of work needs to be undertaken to determine precisely which intervention strategies, what types of behavior space representations, what task model representations, and which behavior sequencing algorithms are most effective in real-world classroom conditions. While the space of possible strategies, representations, and algorithms is enormous, we are optimistic that controlled empirical studies with learners interacting with multiple versions of the agent will demonstrate which design decisions are most effective in which situations. The DESIGN-A-PLANT agent and its learning environment will serve as a testbed for these types of studies.

Second, investigating the full spectrum of mixed-initiative interaction will reap important benefits for learner-agent problem solving. With significant advances in computational models of conversation-based, task-oriented dialogue (Walker, 1993; Smith & Hipp, 1994; Traum, 1994; Guinn, 1995; Freedman, 1996), we can expand the types of mixed-initiativity in which learners and agents can participate. For example, while the DESIGN-A-PLANT agent can provide a variety of types of explanations and advice, it cannot participate in complex dialogues requiring turn-taking, back channeling, or even rudimentary discourse segmentation. Extending its discourse functionalities to enable it to engage in 'justification dialogues' in which learners could justify their design decisions would significantly improve its utility. As the discourse community continues to build a firm foundation for these capabilities and the quality of off-the-shelf speech recognition technologies increases, pedagogical agents can be extended to support considerably more sophisticated interactions with commensurate increases in pedagogical effectiveness.

Finally, providing pedagogical agents with full-scale realtime natural language generation and speech synthesis capabilities could significantly improve their flexibility in mixed-initiative interaction. For example, if the DESIGN-A-PLANT agent, which now employs vocal behaviors created by a voice actor, could employ the full arsenal of natural language generation techniques, it could exploit the generativity of natural language to provide advice whose content, discourse structure, phrase structure, lexicalizations, and prosody were carefully tailored to individual learners in much the same manner that human-tutorial dialogues are. Creating these capabilities will entail incorporating state-of-the-art explanation generation techniques (Suthers, 1991; Cawsey, 1992; Hovy, 1993; Mittal, 1993; Moore, 1995; Lester & Porter, 1997) and surface generators (Elhadad, 1991) and then extending them to take into account conversational, gestural, and deictic aspects of discourse (Cassell et al., 1994; Towns et al., 1998).

In summary, it appears that lifelike pedagogical agents have much to offer and that much remains to be done to bring them to fruition.

Acknowledgements

The authors wish to thank all of the members of the North Carolina State University IntelliMedia Initiative for their invaluable contributions to the DESIGN-A-PLANT project. Special thanks are extended to the following individuals and organizations:

Patrick FitzGerald, Director of the School of Design's branch of the IntelliMedia Initiative; the implementation team, particularly Robert Stevenson and Michael O'Leary, for their work on the behavior sequencing engine; the 3D modelers and animators, particularly John Myrick, James Dautremont, and Philip McKay, for their work on the animated agent, plant models, and environments; Chris Tomasson and her seventh grade class at Martin Middle School and the Raleigh Chapter of the Women in Science Mentoring Program for participating in the focus group studies; Stuart Towns and Charles Callaway for comments on earlier drafts of this article; the anonymous reviewers, whose insightful comments significantly improved the article. Support for this work was provided by the following organizations: the National Science Foundation under grants CDA-9720395 (Learning and Intelligent Systems Initiative) and IRI-9701503 (CAREER Award Program); the North Carolina State University IntelliMedia Initiative; Novell, Inc.; and equipment donations from Apple and IBM.

References

Anderson, J., A. Corbett, K. Koedinger, and R. Pelletier: 1995, Cognitive tutors: lessons learned. *Journal of the Learning Sciences* **4**(2), 167–207.

Anderson, J. R.: 1983, *The Architecture of Cognition*. Harvard University Press.

André, E., W. Finkler, W. Graf, T. Rist, A. Schauder, and W. Wahlster: 1993, WIP: The automatic synthesis of multi-modal presentations. In: M. T. Maybury (ed.): *Intelligent Multimedia Interfaces*. Cambridge, MA: MIT Press, pp. 94–116.

André, E. and T. Rist: 1996, Coping with temporal constraints in multimedia presentation planning. In: *Proceedings of the Thirteenth National Conference on Artificial Intelligence*. pp. 142–147.

Bates, J.: 1994, The role of emotion in believable agents. *Communications of the ACM* **37**(7), 122–125.

Blumberg, B. and T. Galyean: 1995, Multi-level direction of autonomous creatures for real-time virtual environments. In: *Computer Graphics Proceedings*. pp. 47–54.

Brown, J., A. Collins, and P. Duguid: 1989, Situated cognition and the culture of learning. *Educational Researcher* **18**(1), 32–42.

Brown, J. S. and R. R. Burton: 1978, Diagnostic models for procedural bugs in basic mathematical skills. *Cognitive Science* **2**, 155–191.

Brusilovsky, P.: 1992, A framework for intelligent knowledge sequencing and task sequencing. In: *Proceedings of the Second International Conference, ITS '92*. pp. 499–506.

Burton, R. R.: 1982, Diagnosing bugs in a simple procedural skill. In: D. Sleeman and J. S. Brown (eds.): *Intelligent Tutoring Systems*. London: Academic Press.

Carberry, S.: 1989, Plan recognition and its use in understanding dialog. In: A. Kobsa and W. Wahlster (eds.): *User Models in Dialog Systems*. Berlin: Springer-Verlag, pp. 133–162.

Carbonell, J. R.: 1970, AI in CAI: An artificial-intelligence approach to computer-assisted instruction. *IEEE Transactions on Man-Machine Systems* **4**, 190–202.

Carr, B. and I. P. Goldstein: 1977, Overlays: A theory of modelling for computer aided instruction. Technical Report AI Memo 406, Massachusetts Institute of Technology, Artificial Intelligence Laboratory.

Cassell, J., C. Pelachaud, N. Badler, M. Steedman, B. Achorn, T. Becket, B. Douville, S. Prevost, and M. Stone: 1994, ANIMATED CONVERSATION: Rule-based generation of facial expression, gesture and spoken intonation for multiple conversational agents. In: *SIGGRAPH '94*.

Cauzinille-Marmeche, E. and J. Mathieu: 1988, Experimental data for the design of a microworld-based system for algebra. In: H. Mandl and A. Lesgold (eds.): *Learning Issues for Intelligent Tutoring Systems*. New York: Springer-Verlag, pp. 278–286.

Cawsey, A.: 1992, *Explanation and Interaction: The Computer Generation of Explanatory Dialogues*. MIT Press.

Chu-Carroll, J. and S. Carberry: 1994, A plan-based model for response generation in collaborative task-oriented dialogues. In: *AAAI-94: Proceedings of the Twelfth National Conference on Artificial Intelligence*, vol. 1. pp. 799–805.

Cohen, R., C. Allaby, C. Cumbaa, M. Fitzgerald, K. Ho, B. Hui, C. Latulipe, F. Lu, N. Moussa, D. Pooley, A. Qian, and S. Siddiqi: 1998, What is initiative? *User Modeling and User-Adapted Interaction*. **8**(3–4), pp. 171–214.

Collins, J., J. Greer, V. Kumar, G. McCalla, P. Meagher, and R. Tkatch: 1997, Inspectable user models for just-in-time workplace training. In: *Proceedings of the Sixth International Conference on User Modeling* Chia Laguna, Italy. pp. 327–337.

Elhadad, M.: 1991, FUF: The universal unifier user manual version 5.0. Technical Report CUCS-038-91, Department of Computer Science, Columbia University.

Feiner, S. K. and K. R. McKeown: 1990, Coordinating text and graphics in explanation generation. In: *Proceedings of the Eighth National Conference on Artificial Intelligence*. Boston, MA, pp. 442–449.

Freedman, R. K.: 1996, Interaction of discourse planning, instructional planning and dialogue management in an interactive tutoring system. Ph.D. thesis, Northwestern University.

Green, N. and S. Carberry: 1999, A computational mechanism for initiative in answer generation. In this issue.

Grimes, J. E.: 1975, *The Thread of Discourse*. The Hague: Mouton.

Guinn, C. I.: 1995, Meta-dialogue behaviors: Improving the efficiency of human-machine dialogue – A computational model of variable initiative and negotiation in collaborative problem-solving. Ph.D. thesis, Duke University.

Hale, C. R. and L. W. Barsalou: 1995, Explanation content and construction during system learning and troubleshooting. *The Journal of the Learning Sciences* **4**(4), 385–436.

Hill, R. W. and W. L. Johnson: 1995, Situated plan attribution. *Journal of Artificial Intelligence in Education* **6**(1), 35–66.

Hollan, J. D., E. L. Hutchins, and L. M. Weitzman: 1987, STEAMER: An interactive, inspectable, simulation-based training system. In: G. Kearsley (ed.): *Artificial Intelligence and Instruction: Applications and Methods*. Reading, MA: Addison-Wesley, pp. 113–134.

Hovy, E. H.: 1993, Automated discourse generation using discourse structure relations. *Artificial Intelligence* **63**, 341–385.

Kurlander, D. and D. T. Ling: 1995, Planning-based control of interface animation. In: *Proceedings of CHI '95*. pp. 472–479.

Lawler, R. W. and G. P. Lawler: 1987, Computer microworlds and reading: An analysis for their systematic application. In: R. W. Lawler and M. Yazdani (eds.): *Artificial Intelligence and Education*, Vol. 1. Norwood, NJ: Ablex, pp. 95–115.

Lesgold, A., S. Lajoie, M. Bunzo, and G. Eggan: 1992, SHERLOCK: A coached practice environment for an electronics trouble-shooting job. In: J. H. Larkin and R. W. Chabay (eds.): *Computer-Assisted Instruction and Intelligent Tutoring Systems: Shared Goals and Complementary Approaches*. Hillsdale, NJ: Lawrence Erlbaum, pp. 201–238.

Lester, J. C., S. A. Converse, S. E. Kahler, S. T. Barlow, B. A. Stone, and R. Bhogal: 1997a, The persona effect: Affective impact of animated pedagogical agents. In: *Proceedings of CHI'97 (Human Factors in Computing Systems)*. pp. 359–366.

Lester, J. C., S. A. Converse, B. A. Stone, S. E. Kahler, and S. T. Barlow: 1997b, Animated pedagogical agents and problem-solving effectiveness: A large-scale empirical evaluation. In: *Proceedings of Eighth World Conference on Artificial Intelligence in Education*. pp. 23–30.

Lester, J. C., P. J. FitzGerald, and B. A. Stone: 1997c, The pedagogical design studio: Exploiting artifact-based task models for constructivist learning. In: *Proceedings of the Third International Conference on Intelligent User Interfaces*. pp. 155–162.

Lester, J. C. and B. W. Porter: 1997, Developing and empirically evaluating robust explanation generators: The KNIGHT experiments. *Computational Linguistics* **23**(1), 65–101.

Lester, J. C. and B. A. Stone: 1997, Increasing believability in animated pedagogical agents. In: *Proceedings of the First International Conference on Autonomous Agents*. pp. 16–21.

Lester, J. C., B. A. Stone, M. A. O'Leary, and R. B. Stevenson: 1996, Focusing problem solving in design-centered learning environments. In: *Proceedings of the Third International Conference on Intelligent Tutoring Systems*. pp. 475–483.

Maes, P., T. Darrell, B. Blumberg, and A. Pentland: 1995, The ALIVE system: Full-body interaction with autonomous agents. In: *Proceedings of the Computer Animation '95 Conference*.

Mark, M. A. and J. E. Greer: 1995, The VCR tutor: Effective instruction for device operation. *Journal of the Learning Sciences* **4**(2), 209–246.

Maybury, M. T.: 1991, Planning multimedia explanations using communicative acts. In: *Proceedings of the Ninth National Conference on Artificial Intelligence*. Anaheim, CA, pp. 61–66.

Mittal, V., S. Roth, J. D. Moore, J. Mattis, and G. Carenini: 1995, Generating explanatory captions for information graphics. In: *Proceedings of the International Joint Conference on Artificial Intelligence*. pp. 1276–1283.

Mittal, V. O.: 1993, Generating natural language descriptions with integrated text and examples. Ph.D. thesis, University of Southern California.

Moore, J. D.: 1995, *Participating in Explanatory Dialogues*. MIT Press.

Murray, W. R.: 1990, A blackboard-based dynamic instructional planner. In: *Proceedings of the Eighth National Conference on Artificial Intelligence*. pp. 434–441.

Newell, A.: 1990, *Unified Theories of Cognition*. Harvard University Press.

Noake, R.: 1988, *Animation Techniques*. London: Chartwell.

Papert, S.: 1991, Situating constructionism. In: I. Harel and S. Papert (eds.): *Constructionism*. Norwood, NJ: Ablex, pp. 1–12.

Peachey, D. R. and G. I. McCalla: 1986, Using planning techniques in intelligent tutoring systems. *International Journal of Man-Machine Studies* **24**, 77–98.

Piaget, J.: 1954, *The Construction of Reality in the Child*. New York: Basic Books.

Rich, C. and C. L. Sidner: 1998, COLLAGEN: A collaboration manager for software interface agents. *User Modeling and User-Adapted Interaction*. **8**(3–4), 317–351.

Rickel, J. and L. Johnson: 1997, Intelligent tutoring in virtual reality: A preliminary report. In: *Proceedings of the Eighth World Conference on AI in Education*. pp. 294–301.

Roth, S. F., J. Mattis, and X. Mesnard: 1991, Graphics and natural language as components of automatic explanation. In: J. W. Sullivan and S. W. Tyler (eds.): *Intelligent User Interfaces*. New York: Addison-Wesley, pp. 207–239.

Simon, H. A.: 1981, *The Sciences of the Artificial*. Cambridge, MA: MIT Press.

Smith, R. W. and D. R. Hipp: 1994, *Spoken Natural Language Dialog Systems*. Cambridge, Massachusetts: Oxford University Press.

Stone, B. A. and J. C. Lester: 1996, Dynamically sequencing an animated pedagogical agent. In: *Proceedings of the Thirteenth National Conference on Artificial Intelligence*. pp. 424–431.

Suthers, D. D.: 1991, A task-appropriate hybrid Architecture for explanation. *Computational Intelligence* **7**(4), 315–333.

Thompson, P. W.: 1987, Mathematical microworlds and intelligent computer-assisted instruction. In: G. Kearsley (ed.): *Artificial Intelligence and Instruction: Applications and Methods*. Reading, MA: Addison-Wesley, pp. 83–109.

Towns, S., C. Callaway, J. Voerman, and J. Lester: 1998, Coherent gestures, locomotion, and speech in life-like pedagogical agents. In: *Proceedings of the Fourth International Conference on Intelligent User Interfaces*. pp. 13–20.

Traum, D.: 1994, A computational theory of grounding in natural language generation. Ph.D. thesis, University of Rochester.

Walker, M.: 1993, Informational redundancy and resource bounds in dialogue. Ph.D. thesis, University of Pennsylvania.

Wenger, E.: 1987, *Artificial Intelligence and Tutoring Systems: Computational and Cognitive Approaches to the Communication of Knowledge.* Los Altos, California: Morgan Kaufmann.

Wescourt, K. T., M. Beard, and A. Barr: 1981, Curriculum information networks for CAI: Research on testing and evaluation by simulation. In: P. Suppes (ed.): *University-Level Computer-Assisted Instruction at Stanford: 1968–1980.* Stanford, California: Stanford University, pp. 817–839.

White, B. Y. and J. R. Frederiksen: 1987, Qualitative models and intelligent learning environments. In: R. W. Lawler and M. Yazdani (eds.): *Artificial Intelligence and Education*, vol. 1. Norwood, New Jersey: Ablex, pp. 281–305.

Woolf, B. and D. D. McDonald: 1984, Building a computer tutor: Design issues. *IEEE Computer* **17**(9), 61–73.

Authors' Vitae

James C. Lester

Dr. James C. Lester is Assistant Professor of Computer Science at North Carolina State University, and founder and director of the IntelliMedia Initiative at NC State's College of Engineering. Dr. Lester received his B.A. degree in History from Baylor University and his B.A. (Phi Beta Kappa), M.S.C.S., and Ph.D. degrees in Computer Sciences from the University of Texas at Austin. Dr. Lester has worked in several areas of artificial intelligence including computational linguistics (discourse planning and realization in natural language generation), knowledge-based learning environments (animated pedagogical agents and 3D learning environments), and intelligent multimedia systems (intelligent virtual camera planning and coordinated 3D animation/speech generation).

Brian A. Stone

Brian A. Stone is a Ph.D. candidate in Computer Science at North Carolina State University. He received his B.S. degree in Mathematics and Computer Science from Carnegie Mellon University in 1992 and his M.S. degree in Computer Science from North Carolina State University in 1995. His primary interests in artificial intelligence lie in the areas of machine learning (neural networks) and knowledge-based learning environments (animated pedagogical agents).

Gary D. Stelling

Dr. Gary D. Stelling is an M.S. student in Computer Science at North Carolina State University. Dr. Stelling received his B.A. in Chemistry from Washington University in 1965, his Ph.D. degree in Organic Chemistry from Stanford University in 1970, and his B.S. degree in Data Processing from Washington University in 1988. His research in chemistry focused on emulsion polymerization, and his current research in artificial intelligence lies in knowledge-based learning environments (animated pedagogical agents).

User Modeling and User-Adapted Interaction **9:** 45–78, 1999.
© 1999 *Kluwer Academic Publishers.*

Mixed-Initiative Issues in an Agent-Based Meeting Scheduler

AMEDEO CESTA[1] and DANIELA D'ALOISI[2]
[1]*IP-CNR, Consiglio Nazionale delle Ricerche, Viale Marx 15, I-00137 Rome (Italy)*
e-mail: amedeo@pscs2.irmkant.rm.cnr.it
[2]*FUB, Fondazione Ugo Bordoni, Via B. Castiglione 59, I-00142 Rome (Italy)*
e-mail: dany@fub.it

(Received: 16 November 1997; accepted in revised form: 13 May 1998)

Abstract. This paper concerns mixed-initiative interaction between users and agents. After classifying agents according to their task and their interactivity with the user, the critical aspects of delegation-based interaction are outlined. Then MASMA, an agent system for distributed meeting scheduling, is described, and the solutions developed to control interaction are explained in detail. The issues addressed concern: the agent capability of adapting its behavior to the user it is supporting; the solution adopted to control the shift of initiative between personal agents, their users and other agents in the environment; the availability of features, e.g. the inspection mechanism, that endow the user with a further level of control to enhance his sense of trust in the agent.

Key words: personal assistants, mixed-initiative interaction, multi-agent systems, human computer interaction.

1. Introduction

The term mixed-initiative usually refers to dialogue systems (Walker & Whittaker, 1990), in which the turns of conversation, along with an analysis of the type of utterances, determine which actor has control of the dialogue. There are several possible definitions for the term and different contexts in which mixed-initiative models can be applied (see for example (Allen et al., 1996; Lochbaum et al., 1990; Lester et al., 1998; Hagen, 1998)). An overview is presented in (Cohen et al., 1998) that shows several case studies where the actors can be either two people or a person and a system. It is interesting to understand how the definition for mixed-initiative changes when the system is an intelligent autonomous agent.

In this paper, mixed-initiative issues are considered in the scenario offered by a specific personal assistant, a meeting scheduler. This context seems particularly suitable to verify the usefulness of an agent-based assistant, although an under-evaluation of issues concerning the user-agent interaction might prevent the user from actually using the system. A possible solution was to consider the agent-user pair as a mixed-initiative system and to test how mixed-initiative models were able to describe the flow of the interaction between the two. The system, named

MASMA (Multi-Agent System for Meeting Automation), is used as a laboratory for studying interaction between agents and users. In this context, the common understanding of mixed-initiative needs to be slightly modified (Section 2). Actually, a clear definition of the term has not been stated yet as emerges from the analysis in (Cohen et al., 1998).

The idea of considering a user and his personal assistant as a mixed-initiative system is strengthened by the need for reconciling two contrasting issues. The first is related to the fact that agent-based systems are regarded as useful tools, that can relieve users from their work overload by completely mechanizing repetitive and time-consuming functions. Most agent systems can be relied upon to autonomously set and achieve these routine goals. On the other hand, their autonomy is often seen as an obstacle to their success (Shneiderman, 1997). As a matter of fact, their independence does not always seem to be necessary or even useful in every application domain.

An intermediate position is to consider the initiative as being shared between the user and the agent. This paper claims that, in interactive applications, agents are more effective when associated with human users to form an integrated mixed-initiative system: indeed the agent-user couple is a multi-agent system that should avoid conflicts in order to work effectively.

The representation of the agent-user pair as a mixed-initiative system allows for the modeling of the different roles the two actors play in the interaction. Moreover, the reasons underlying decisions and actions may be described; the interaction model will be clearer and the control mechanisms will be better identified. The apparatus should allow the user to have the feeling of being continuously in control of the task: as a consequence, he could gradually increase his trust in the agent and vary little by little the number of tasks he comfortably delegates to the agent[1].

In particular, attention is given to the competence exhibited by the agents that directly interact with the user. The claim is that at least three types of 'abilities' are needed in order to make the agents participate in a mixed-initiative interaction with their users:

- Agents should adapt their behavior to the user they are supporting, according to the philosophy of adaptive interfaces.
- Agents should move according to some principles of initiative shift between them, their users and other agents in the environment (when they exist). The agents follow a behavioral protocol that takes different types of constraints into account.
- Agents should leave the user a level of 'super-control' in order to enhance his sense of trust towards them. The user must have the possibility of inspecting

---

[1] The concept of trust is orthogonal to the meaning given to it in other agent systems, for example in (Maes, 1994). In our case, it is the user who must learn to trust the agent, even when the agent is not a learning agent, by testing its reliability in solving problems. We do not measure the agent threshold of confidence in making a choice, since our agents do not necessarily improve their performance in the long run.

the agent[2] and then he will be able to prevent any undesirable operations and failures.

These issues will be discussed in greater depth in the following sections and examples of solutions adopted in MASMA will be presented.

1.1. PLAN OF THE PAPER

The paper is organized as follows. The following section introduces a possible definition of mixed-initiative in the scenario of agent-based systems. Section 3 sets the scenario introduced above by defining the classes of agents that are considered in the paper and the issues in mixed-initiative interaction they are expected to support. Section 4 gives a short description of the meeting scheduling problem and introduces the general features of MASMA. Section 5 presents in detail aspects connected with mixed-initiative issues by introducing three specific problems, their solution in MASMA and examples from the working system. The three aspects considered are:

(1) the personalization of agent behavior according to user preferences (Section 5.1),
(2) the negotiation protocol that controls the shift of initiative (Section 5.2) and
(3) the mechanism that allows the user a dynamic control of agent's behavior (Section 5.3).

Some comments with respect to related literature are contained in Section 6. Finally some conclusions are drawn.

2. A Definition for Mixed Initiative in Agent-Based Systems

A major difference between person-person and agent-person interactions lies in the type of relationship between the pairs of actors involved.

In the first case, the partners can take the conversational lead, answer or ask a question, demand or supply information, etc. The initiative passes back and forth between the two actors (Walker & Whittaker, 1990), and its flow is strongly influenced by the type of utterances (Whittaker & Stenton, 1988) and by the content of the conversation (Grosz & Sidner, 1986). The conversational lead may be held longer by one of the two partners or may be equally shared in accordance with their roles.

The case of task delegation to agents represents an interesting new situation. Our agents are designed to support or even to substitute a user in several daily activities; the hypothesis is that the user is committed to delegating a task to an

---

[2] An effective inspection mechanism must supply tools to allow the user to: (a) understand what the agent is doing; (b) verify the underlying processes; (c) inspect the values of the different constraints on the solution. The inspection mechanism used in MASMA is described in Section 5.3.

agent since that task is boring or complex or time consuming. In this case, the agent-user pair becomes a *system* with common goals in which the initiative shifts from one to another. This scenario requires a suitable definition of *mixed-initiative*. Our aim is to represent the shift of initiative between an agent and a user having as a model the case of human-human dialogue.

In a human-human dialogue, the person who wants to delegate a task explains the problem to the other person, and usually the dialogue finishes when the problem has been described and the deputy ensures the other of his competence in carrying out the task. Other conversations can follow to better focus particular issues or to report the results obtained by the executor.

In agent-human interaction, the objects are the task(s) to be accomplished and the decisions to take to solve it (them).

In using an artificial personal assistant, the user is interested in getting acquainted with the agent and exploiting its competence; the user wants the agent to work on his behalf, and the agent has the implicit goal of satisfying its user. That implies that the agent is autonomous, although the user can delegate it more or less autonomy also according to its reliability. The user evaluates the agent's behavior to decide the amount of autonomy to give it. Even when the agent results particularly reliable, the user may prefer to maintain control of the system. Of course, maintaining control does not necessarily involve a continuous check on what the agent is doing.

Furthermore, the need to solve the user's problem will imply taking decisions according to the current constraints and the model of the *system*, considered as the user-agent pair. This requires accounting for different *system* features, as user preferences, status of the user involved, current state of affairs, etc.

Moreover, the distinctive features of the interaction can change in the long run; the user modifies his preferences and attitudes, and also the environment can undergo changes. In other words, the user's model can evolve and, as a consequence, several consolidated standpoints need to be revised.

In defining what *mixed-initiative* means in a user-agent pair, we need to refer not to conversation turns or to activities only connected with a natural language dialogue. The analysis of the initiative turns has to be related to who decides at a certain moment. Hence, a possible definition is the following.

DEFINITION. In an agent-based system, in which the actors are a user and his personal agent, the flow of initiative and the flow of decisions coincide. At any moment, the initiative is held by the actor able to decide the next step. A mixed-initiative agent-based system is a user-agent pair in which the decision making is shared between the user and the agent.

The modeling of the user-agent pair according to mixed initiative principles can be improved by considering results obtained in task delegation studies in the case of human-human interaction. In (Muir, 1987), the authors show that delegation is rarely total, and an important role is played by factors such as lack of trust, need of control, possibility of inspection, need for privacy. These issues have all been considered in our model (Section 5).

Although our definition of initiative means making a decision on what to do, it does not imply the decision will be acted upon. It is likely that the agent will also execute actions based on the user's choices or decisions. In addition, Walker and Whittaker have demonstrated that in a conversation, the speaker is not always the initiative holder (Walker & Whittaker, 1990).

Another critical issue in modeling the initiative in agent systems is the role of control. For control here we mean the possibility for one actor to supervise and influence an ongoing process.

Arguments in favor of the user's need to control the agent emerge from research in the human-computer interaction area: in (Shneiderman, 1997) for example, the agent autonomy is considered as an obstacle to an effective employment of agent systems. Control has to be wisely managed, since the risk is to spoil the quality of the interaction. In fact, a situation in which continuously the user inspects the underlying processes and the agent asks the user would result in a poor mixed-initiative system. In our model, initiative and control are different, since the user has the possibility to inspect and verify the agent behavior even when it is the agent who is to decide (see the inspection mechanism shown in Figure 7).

The following corollary can be added to the previous definition

COROLLARY. *In a user-agent pair, the control and the initiative are separate, and an actor can hold initiative but not control. Also the execution and the initiative are separate, and an actor can decide even if he does not practically carry out the effects of the decision.*

Given this definition, it is now to establish how it is possible to generate an initiative flow between a user and his agent by satisfying the contrasting needs of the user. On the one hand the user wants to delegate a complex or boring or time-consuming task to the agent; on the other hand, he wishes to control how the agent accomplishes its duties and be sure that the problem is correctly solved.

Our solution consists of defining one or more interaction protocols that drive the initiative flow according to

- the user's profile and general preferences,
- the user's preferences on the methods to solve the task,
- a list of constraints on the degrees of freedom allowed to the agent,
- the criticality of a decision or choice,
- an analysis of the current situation and the past history of the interaction (when possible).

The protocol has to specify –following the directions extracted by the list above– who can take the decision at a certain moment. This implies that the agent will not continuously ask its user: 'Can I take the initiative? I think I can decide on this point.' The protocol will help the agent to determine whether it is able to decide by itself. For example, when an agent is requested to attend a meeting, the protocol may suggest it to verify its knowledge base concerning rules about the organizer and the subject of the event. For certain sets of these values, the agent can be authorized to proceed, otherwise it has to wait for the user's suggestion. For example, let us suppose the user has defined a rule stating he does not want to attend meetings about 'agent-based systems' unless the organizer is 'Red Brown'. Let us also suppose the agent receives two requests for two meetings about 'agent-based systems'. The organizer of the first meeting is 'John Smith', so the agent decides for a negative answer without waiting for the user's suggestion. The organizer of the second meeting is 'Red Brown', then the user is asked by his agent.

The implemented protocols may be quite simple –as the two presented in this paper– or sophisticated –as those we are currently experimenting in a new version of MASMA (D'Aloisi & Cesta, 1997).

In the human-human case, the analysis of a dialogue allows for deciding who takes the initiative (not necessarily the speaker). In the user-agent case, the analysis of a behavior protocol allows for establishing who takes the initiative (not necessarily who is performing the current actions). Such an analysis has to be integrated with an analysis of the current state of affairs and the features of the user involved.

The evaluation of how many times the agent takes the initiative gives a measure of the agent autonomy. A completely autonomous agent will never relinquish the initiative, while a *slave* agent will simply be able to execute the user's directions. Most implemented software agents–along with MASMA–exhibit an intermediate behavior.

3. Agent Systems and Mixed-Initiative

In order to better identify the contribution of MASMA, some distinctions are needed to clarify our position in Agent Systems and Mixed-Initiative research efforts.

3.1. DIFFERENT INTERACTION REQUIREMENTS OF AGENTS

The 'agents' area of research is relatively new and very creative/active at the moment. A lot of different terminologies exist to identify similar things: e.g., some works prefer the distinction between interface agents and problem solving agents (Milewski & Lewis, 1997), some distinguish personal agents from service agents (Brancaleoni et al., 1997). Several attempts exist to summarize different research directions, e.g., (Wooldridge & Jennings, 1995; Nwana, 1996). For our current purpose, we need quite a broad subdivision to better understand our contribution. We focus the attention on the task the agent is designed to do and distinguish four classes of agent:

- *robotic agents*: hardware/software autonomous systems that behave in a physical environment that changes continuously (like an everyday office environment or an unknown outer space). An amount of research exists, an example being (Simmons et al., 1997).
- *softbots*: software systems that are able to perform tasks by synthesizing their behavior in software environments. Examples are autonomous planners for Internet applications (Etzioni & Weld, 1994) or autonomous controllers for spacecraft (Pell et al., 1997). In these classes of systems the main difficulty is in the task to be performed that very often requires quite an amount of computational effort.
- *personal assistants*: different types of software agents that assist humans in tasks like decision making, information gathering, daily activities, etc. These systems are continuously in contact with the users while working: significant examples are interface agents (Maes, 1994) and collaborative systems (Rich & Sidner, 1997).
- *synthetic or believable agents*: agents that operate in artificial environments like interactive games or virtual worlds (Bates, 1994). These types of entities exhibit believable features, e.g., personality traits, and are not focussed on showing problem solving skills. Also the pedagogical agents (Lester et al., 1998; Sticker & Johnson, 1997) can be included in this class.

These four areas are quite comprehensive for all possible kinds of agents[3]. Some may consider arbitrary the distinction between *softbots* and *personal assistants*, but if the classification is placed alongside the dimension of the interactivity with the user, it can be further justified. Let us consider the criticality of the user-agent interaction with respect to the task performed by the agent. The following distinction is possible:

- *low-interactive agents*: both the softbots and the robotic agents fall into this category. In these systems, in fact, the major effort is on the task the agents are aimed at. Tasks are generally quite complex but require very few interactions with human users. In robotics, the aim is building completely autonomous robots that incidentally meet human beings in their environment (Simmons et al., 1997). Also softbots mainly work by themselves and just occasionally they interact to receive new tasks or to give back results or operational reports. In both cases, the human-computer interface is not required to model the interaction but simply to study some form of information format and information presentation.
- *highly-interactive agents*: personal assistants and believable agents can be placed here. Both types of systems have as a goal the interaction with the user both for carrying out an expert task together with him (as in the case of personal

---

[3] A similar classification is proposed in (Hayes–Roth, 1997) but with significant differences in the definition of personal assistants that are called expert assistants with a broader meaning that mostly overlaps with softbots.

assistants) and for playing with him at some level (like in the case of synthetic characters for entertainment in virtual worlds).

Because of their task, highly-interactive agents need 'competence' about how to interact with the user, they need to support forms of dialogue with him and need to relinquish the initiative during a conversation or collaborative decision making.

Indeed differences exist also inside the class of highly-interactive agents. A believable agent has the goal of convincing the user about its being independent, while an assistant is designed around the idea of acting as a system integrated 'with' the user. In the two cases, the topic of how to endow such systems with 'mixed-initiative' will differ [4].

In the case of believable agents, it seems relevant to endow systems with the ability to manage a dialogue with humans and with abilities in natural language generation. Expert assistants may interact in a more structured way, so it is possible to simplify their dialogue skills: for example, the interaction through a graphical interface is not necessarily a limitation. A relevant issue in this application is how the user perceives the system, e.g., the user's feelings towards the agent. In order to accept the system, the user should develop trust in the agent and should always have the perception of being in control over the agent. As a consequence some constraints on the agent's autonomy are worth introducing.

3.2. ASPECTS OF MIXED-INITIATIVE RESEARCH

The definition of MASMA as a mixed-initiative system requires at least a broad classification of the existing approaches to computational models of mixed-initiative interaction. Different communities assign distinct meanings to the term mixed-initiative although common problems exist (Cohen et al., 1988). We are not interested in giving more definitions for mixed-initiative, but in outlining the differences between systems that make sense mainly for their interaction with the user and systems that want to include the user in their problem solving cycle to increase their possibility to actually solve the problem. More precisely, two views of mixed initiative can be identified:

– *Dialogue-oriented approaches to mixed-initiative*: approaches concerned with mixed-initiative interaction between a system and user to talk about (among other things) how to do a task, or make a plan for doing a task. The models are human-to-human conversations. The problem is to have a computational model of the dialogue, its different phases, the transition of phases, etc. Starting from the analysis of sampled conversations (Walker & Whittaker, 1990), general formal models have been derived (Lochbaum et al., 1990) and quite robust dialogue systems have also been developed (Allen et al., 1996).

---

[4] Obviously any classification is arbitrary at some level. It is worth noting that cases exist in which the division is not at all clear cut, for example the pedagogical agent like (Lester & Stone, 1997).

– *Task-oriented approaches to mixed-initiative*: approaches concerned with building systems that can partially plan and eventually execute a task on its own on behalf of a user, but that interacts with the user for guidance at critical decision points in the task. A solution to this problem does not necessarily involve the study of human-to-human behavior because the research topics are rather different. Critical issues are how to make the system understand when to ask the user, how to make understandable to the user the problem solving process, which is the right level of generality that allows the user to answer questions or to take the initiative. Even if the field is still relatively unestablished and a clear theory is missing, a number of mixed-initiative problem solving architectures have been proposed (Hsu et al., 1993; Smith & Lassila, 1994; Ferguson et al., 1996; Tate, 1997).

As usual in a bipartition of this kind, a continuum of cases exists. For the purpose of this paper, we identify a category of systems, that includes also MASMA, with elements from both the previous classes. Such a category has quite a clear characterization, and falls in the middle of the range:

– *Delegation-oriented systems*: the aim of these systems is to automate tasks that are not particularly difficult but rather very tedious. It is not the case of the complex planning of thousands of manufacturing activities but rather the task, very tedious but not impossible, of scheduling a meeting involving a group of people as done in MASMA. Carrying out a task like this does not involve complex conversational ability. The dialogue can take place in a simplified form since only the effectiveness of the communication is relevant. The relative simplicity of the task makes it important to convince the user of the reliability of the system and of the convenience of task delegation.

Furthermore, some authors (Milewski & Lewis, 1997) have observed that when humans can choose whether or not to delegate a task several issues play a role: the costs of delegation, the need for interaction with others, the feeling with respect to interaction, the need of assessing the performance on the delegated action and the trust in the delegated actor. All these aspects become very important and will bias the approach to the various mixed-initiative issues.

In some classes of systems the roles are clear. In a pedagogical system, the agent knows what the user wants to know. In a planner, the agent can plan while the user cannot. In a meeting scheduler, both the agent and the user know how to carry out the task: so the system has to give reasons to the user in order to be used.

Despite the large diffusion of software agent technology, an actual acceptance and use of agents is still restricted to experts and enthusiasts. 'Normal' users do not rely upon agents capabilities and competence as a result of limited trust in decision aids (Muir, 1987). Another reason, closer to a human-computer interaction view of the problem, is the possible loss of control that humans perceive as a negative feeling (Whittaker & Sidner, 1996). A further point is the fact that users may perceive the system as something that limits their usual behavior constraining them from a free choice (Friedman & Nissenbaum, 1997).

A closer investigation assesses different motivations, also common to human aids, strictly connected with task delegation. In (Milewski & Lewis, 1997), the authors examine design issues connected with delegation-based interfaces. Their analysis summarizes the following critical points:

- the tradeoff between benefits and costs of delegation must be positive;
- the effort in communicating and explaining tasks must not be excessive;
- delegation requires that users trust agent reliability;
- users should have the opportunity to control the agent performance;
- user's personality and culture influence delegation.

From this brief analysis, at least three classes of problems emerge that need to be carefully considered when designing an agent:

- the nature of trust and the development of a trustful relationship between agents and users;
- the user's concern about a possible loss of control over the agent decisions;
- task delegation seems to be a good solution in several situations, but it is not always a natural and well accepted form of human behavior.

By its nature, an agent is an autonomous entity, designed to act on behalf of the user. Yet it is advisable to moderate its independence with measures suitable to increase its acceptance and use. The *user-agent* pair is a mixed-initiative system in which the agent can act autonomously but the user can control it (the agent) and decide how, when and why to relinquish the initiative to it.

4. MASMA: A Distributed Agent-Based Meeting Scheduler

As stated in Section 1, this paper describes aspects of 'mixed-initiative' in a personal assistant that supports users in managing their personal agenda and in organizing and scheduling appointments, meetings, conferences and seminars. A multi-agent solution to this problem is presented in a system called MASMA (Multi-Agent System for Meeting Automation). The present section introduces the problem and gives a quick overview of MASMA, while the following section furnishes the details of various mixed-initiative control mechanisms plugged into the system.

4.1. THE MEETING SCHEDULING PROBLEM

In every-day life, scheduling meetings for a set of users involves a high number of actors and requires a massive organizational effort, complex negotiation strategies and a huge number of communication acts, e.g., e-mail messages, phone calls, faxes, etc. Moreover, it usually requires a compromise among the different users' constraints, the availability of the resources and the need to satisfy the highest number of people.

The problem can be seen as a particular example of the distributed task scheduling in which the tasks are the appointments (meetings) to be fixed and the resources are the participants. Given a set $\mathcal{U}$ of n users the distributed scheduling problem consists of organizing a meeting M_x on a particular subject and with particular resource requirements (e.g., dimension of the room, equipment, etc.). The meeting concerns a number of invited users $\mathcal{I} \subseteq \mathcal{U}$ subdivided among necessary invitees $\mathcal{N}\mathcal{I}$, such that the meeting cannot take place if one of them is not available, and optional invitees $\mathcal{O}\mathcal{I}$ whose participation is not strictly necessary. One user $\mathcal{U}_o$ acts as the organizer or *host* of the meeting. The users' availability over intervals of time is defined by using the set of preference values $\{high, medium, low, null\}$. An interval of time has availability *null* when either a previous meeting exists in that interval or the user explicitly sets his unavailability.

The organization of meetings involving a varying number of people requires an overload of repetitive tasks and makes the development of an automated solution particularly desirable. Although the problem has always been challenging for developers of decision support tools, the proposed solutions have never been widely diffused. The problem has been addressed with traditional tools (e.g., Kincaid et al., 1985), has been considered as a reference problem in the CSCW area (e.g., Grudin, 1988; Beard et al., 1990) and has been recently addressed from different perspectives in agent-based research (e.g., Kozierok & Maes, 1993; Hayes et al., 1997).

4.2. A MULTI-AGENT SOLUTION

In developing yet another solution to the meeting scheduling problem, we drew on our experience in designing previous systems (Cesta et al., 1995; Cesta & D'Aloisi, 1996; Amati et al., 1997), and set up several co-existing goals:

(a) to develop a comprehensive solution to the problem;

(b) to use an agent-based architecture;

(c) to obtain a software system that is easy to use, efficient, and extendible;

(d) to study aspects of the interaction between agents and human users.

MASMA proposes a solution in which competence is distributed amongst different types of agents. The system architecture consists of a personal assistant for each user, called *Meeting Agent*, and three *service (middle) agents* that are shared among the community, and execute tasks for other agents requiring that service. In MASMA three service agents are used: the *Server Agent*, the *Resource Agent* and the *Travel Agent*.

Each agent is an instance of a general model that is flexible and adaptable to guarantee an incremental and modular development of the whole framework. The architecture follows a *Body/Head/Mouth* metaphor (Steiner et al., 1990) and it is described in (Cesta & D'Aloisi, 1996). It consists of three components:

- The *body* is in charge of task execution. It carries out the specific tasks of the agent in the application domain. For example, the functionalities of inspecting and updating the user agenda are part of the Meeting Agents' body. The functionality to access a data-base of travel information is part of the Travel Agent's body. Our design guarantees a high level of adaptability, since it allows for incorporating and/or using both newly developed and pre-existing software thus avoiding having to build everything from scratch. It is possible to plug it into pre-existing software, public-domain programs, purpose-built software or hardware components.

- The *head* is devoted to coordinating the different functionalities; to managing the representation of the external world, of the agent and of the current state of affairs; to reasoning, solving problems and taking decisions; to coordinating and negotiating with other agents. Inside, it consists of four components: the controller, the reasoner, the knowledge base and the working memory. The controller guarantees the basic level of functionality, it continuously checks for new information and activates a task for the body to subsequently execute. When a conflict arises about the next step to undertake, the controller gives responsibility to the reasoner who is able to perform higher level functionalities to resolve conflicts and to decide the more appropriate future plan.

- The *interface* is in charge of communication with the user, other agents and the environment. It consists of a *KQML Message Manager* (Finin et al., 1994) to support the interactions between agents; a set of *Sensors* and *Actuators* to exchange data with the software environment; a *User Interface Manager* to communicate with the users.

A *Meeting Agent* is associated with each user. It manages his agenda, maintains the user's profile and negotiates with other agents to determine meetings schedules.

Both the agent and the user can access the user's electronic calendar. The calendar is a separate software module that is also a task in the agent body; the user manipulates the calendar separately through his usual and preferred interface. Due to a mechanism for concurrency control, the common data structure allows both user and meeting agent to independently access and write information about appointments.

In the organizational process, the Meeting Agent represents the user according to his profile. The profile, as explained in Section 5.1, contains information on the user's preference values assigned to the different dates and times. It also maintains data about the user's general interests.

Usually the process of determining a meeting needs a negotiation phase to decide the date and the place of the event, the duration of which depends on the imposed constraints. The Meeting Agent can play the role of organizer or attendee by applying a corresponding negotiation protocol described in Section 5.2. At present, it is possible to include more than one negotiation protocol: each protocol can influence differently the flow of decisions according to the current context and status represented in the agent working memory. It is also possible to envisage more sophisticated protocols that take several issues into account, for instance the role of the users in the community, the weight of previous engagements, the type of event, etc. This solution is currently being experimented (D'Aloisi & Cesta, 1997).

The current meeting agents are designed to fully mechanize the decision-making process and the activities connected to the achievement of an agreement, leaving the user the responsibility of the final decisions. In the decision-making process, the control moves according to the content of the profile and to the role played by the agent. Looking at the whole task of scheduling a certain event, the organizer's Meeting Agent–that starts the process–and the other Meeting Agents involved follow their respective protocols that allow the control to move from one agent to another. Instead, in the case of a 'local' decision, that is a decision concerning the user acceptance of certain meeting proposals, the control shifts from the agent to its user.

A Meeting Agent can also interact with a service agent to obtain information. In this case the control moves temporarily to such a service agent. The three middle agents work as specialized knowledge servers to which some common tasks have been delegated.

The *Server Agent* is in charge of managing the network addresses and of maintaining a knowledge base with the users' addresses by respecting their privacy needs. In case of new users, it is able to get the addresses by querying an external server. It also manages a service of free distribution of announcements about conferences, workshops and seminars. The users can subscribe to the service by transmitting a list of keywords and topics they are interested in. The keywords are inserted in a database managed by the Server Agent so that it can help the organizer agent to spread announcements out in a selective way without disturbing all the connected users.

The *Resource Agent* adopts a centralized administration of the common resources to avoid conflicts in selecting them. The Congress Centers or Universities or other similar sites are crucial resources in a meeting organization. Each site is characterized by ⟨attribute-value⟩ pairs that describe it. The *Resource Agent* maintains the databases and provides the Meeting Agent with a list of structures satisfying the problem constraints, for example the list of rooms containing at least 20 people and having a slide projector. When a decision is taken, the agent carries out the operations necessary to reserve the place.

The *Travel Agent* helps the user to mechanize the last step in organizing a meeting, the lodging and travel decisions. The agent can connect the user to train and flight timetables, decide the best path between two places, inform him about prices, show a list of possible hotels. It could also furnish a reservation service. At present it works on local databases.

4.3. AN INTRODUCTORY EXAMPLE

To make the reader familiar with the basic functionality MASMA provides, we introduce an example that can actually be produced by the system. The example involves three people named Amedeo, Daniela and Marcello each represented by a Meeting Agent, respectively labeled as $\mathcal{MA}_A$, $\mathcal{MA}_D$ and $\mathcal{MA}_M$. The users are able to set the level of autonomy (see details in Section 5.1) they allow to their personal agents. This example assumes that Amedeo has been using $\mathcal{MA}_A$ for a long time so he delegates it a lot of decisions, while Marcello is more careful in his use of $\mathcal{MA}_M$.

Marcello has been hired by the firm 'XYZ' and his boss is Amedeo. He has subsequently been involved in the project 'Masma' which Daniela is also working on as a project leader. This is the scenario Marcello wants his agent $\mathcal{MA}_M$ to be acquainted with and to define his profile on.

Suppose now that Daniela wants to organize a meeting with Marcello about 'Masma' within the firm. Before filling in an announcement, she consults her agenda and notices that on November 16th she just has a short meeting at 11 o'clock. She starts to organize the new meeting filling in the dialogue window 'Organize meeting' in Figure 1. She decides the meeting length of two hours, and sets the meeting as quite important announcing a priority of 8 in the range 0–10. Marcello, being a project scientist, will be a necessary invitee, whereas Amedeo, Marcello's boss, will be also invited but, since the meeting is a technical one, his attendance is not necessary and Daniela declares Amedeo as an optional attendant. At this point, Daniela's agent sends the meeting announcement to Amedeo's and Marcello's agents.

$\mathcal{MA}_A$ evaluates the meeting relevance and decides that Amedeo is not interested in it and, being set on autonomous decision for that step, sends $\mathcal{MA}_D$ its rejection.

$\mathcal{MA}_M$, instead, evaluates the meeting positively and, in accordance with its settings, turns to Marcello for a decision providing him with a suggestion (window 'Announce advise' in Figure 1). Marcello accepts the suggestion and $\mathcal{MA}_M$ sends a confirmation to $\mathcal{MA}_D$.

At this point a negotiation begins between $\mathcal{MA}_D$ and $\mathcal{MA}_M$ (see details in Section 5.2) to actually schedule the meeting. $\mathcal{MA}_D$ asks $\mathcal{MA}_M$ for time intervals with high availability. If no satisfactory interval is found, it will ask $\mathcal{MA}_M$ for medium availability and afterwards for low. In case no agreement is reached, $\mathcal{MA}_D$ asks for relaxation of constraints. $\mathcal{MA}_M$ cannot decide by itself since Marcello requires being explicitly asked at critical points (Figure 2). It is in fact a critical decision which might cause the cancellation of a meeting previously fixed and a consequent costly reorganization, let alone considering the disappointment of the other invitees. $\mathcal{MA}_M$'s first choice is to ask Marcello to cancel a meeting with Amedeo (first window in Figure 2) but Marcello rejects this possibility. Then the agent points out a second possibility in Marcello's schedule: removing his usual

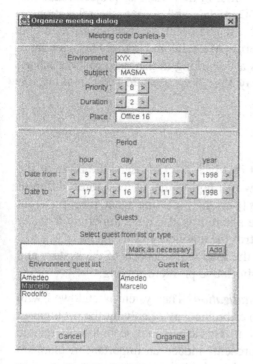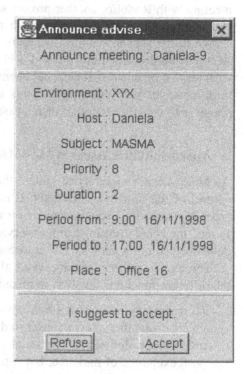

Figure 1. Definition of a meeting and a suggestion from a personal agent

Figure 2. Two different cases of relaxation request

meeting with Rodolfo, another project scientist in the 'Masma' project. Marcello considers this meeting less relevant than Daniela's and accepts the relaxation as shown in the second window in Figure 2. At this point the meeting is fixed and $\mathcal{MA_D}$ sends confirmation and $\mathcal{MA_M}$ informs Marcello and updates his agenda.

It should be noted that personal agents are working in the background exchanging messages with one other; in this way they help users to avoid making the phone calls usually needed in such a case.

5. Mixed-Initiative Issues in MASMA

As MASMA is an interactive system that involves a set of users, the issue of the control of the initiative is relevant. It is worth noting that at least three different types of interaction happen, human user *vs* (personal) meeting agent, meeting agent *vs* meeting agent, meeting agent *vs* service agent. It is also quite important that any developed solution allows the user to control the autonomy of its agent.

Three main mechanisms supervise all the interactive aspects of the system and the different functions involved in mixed-initiative problem solving:

- *User centered control through personalization.* The system is endowed with mechanisms that allow the user to describe his way of solving the problem of meeting scheduling to his personal agent. This aspect may seem loosely related with exchange of initiative, but it represents indeed an important mechanism for developing the trust of the user in mixed-initiative interaction.

  Furthermore, personalization allows the user to contextualize the agent behavior according to situations that are described in the personal database. In this way, a sort of indirect control on different interactions is developed that modifies the shift of initiative when actual problem solving activity goes on.
- *Task driven control of the initiative.* This is the way to define the rules for relinquishing control during standard problem solving activity. This initiative flow can be modified by the specific information in the user's profile and by the direct intervention of the user.

  As often happens in multi-agent systems, the interacting agents execute a protocol according to their role in the interaction. In this way, the agents behavior is framed within a structured flow that avoids interaction conflicts. The protocols regulate the negotiation phase necessary to achieve an agreement on the current meeting. According to specific subtasks, a protocol gives control about the current decision to specific agents or to the user.
- *Mechanisms to allow control by the user.* With this further feature, we allow the user to observe the current negotiation going on and eventually to directly or indirectly influence the negotiation behavior of the agents. This feature has been designed to increase the possibility for the user to control its agent, and consequently gain confidence in the behavior of the agent. The third class of mechanisms is aimed at allowing the user to alter the usual flow of information, according to contingent needs. These requests are independent from the

knowledge in the user's profile and from the current step of the negotiation protocols.

Before entering the specific description of the three aspects, it is worth noting that the kind of solution developed is a compromise between the generality of the approach and the desire to develop a solution which can be handled by a running system. Indeed the problems addressed are common between the class of personal assistants for highly interactive tasks, where personal information of users is manipulated.

5.1. USER CENTERED CONTROL THROUGH PERSONALIZATION

Modeling the agent on the user's behavior makes a system able to decide and solve problems following the same rules and laws of the user. This provides at least two advantages: the user identifies himself with the agent; the user can better understand the agent way of *thinking*.

There are two ways to enable the agent to behave similarly to the user: (a) allowing the user to communicate his typical behavior to the agent; (b) allowing the agent to infer or learn the user's typical behavior. This problem has been addressed in agent literature. For example, Maes (Maes, 1994) argues that the first approach– classified as belonging to the class of the 'knowledge-based' approaches–requires a massive implementation effort. Moreover, it is difficult to assess its effectiveness. On the contrary, the 'learning based' approach is judged more viable because the typical behavior is incrementally and automatically built while the user works.

We choose the first solution trying to take into account the cognitive difficulty in letting the user define his personal knowledge. MASMA allows the user to build a knowledge base concerning his preferences and his rules of behavior. The reasons for this choice are:

(a) the need for users to effectively profit by the tool from the very moment they start to use it. Although appealing, the learning methods like the one proposed in (Maes, 1994) begin with a blank behavior pattern that is incrementally filled by observing the user. Their performance becomes quite reliable only after a reasonable number of instances of user behavior patterns have been submitted to the learning algorithm.

(b) the option of preserving the user autonomy as much as possible. As also pointed out in (Friedman & Nissenbaum, 1997), the rules inferred from a learning algorithm are not always reasonably explainable to users. For example, it is not easy to explain the algorithm applied to obtain a similarity measure. On the contrary, our choice makes the user directly responsible for the rule definition.

(c) the opportunity of storing different memory stages. In learning approaches, it is difficult to account for the memory of the past situations. In fact, it is difficult to distinguish whether a certain behavior has been acquired four years ago or more recently. Moreover, due to the time necessary to get acquainted with a specific behavior, it is not easy to revise knowledge, or to modify a behavior no longer compatible with the user's preferences. On the contrary, it is quite straightforward to introduce a new rule reflecting the user's new inclination. Concerning the recovery of past situations, an inactive database of rules and preferences can be maintained along with the current one.

Of course we are aware of the problem, pointed out by (Maes, 1994), of how to define and maintain symbolic knowledge. We have also paid particular attention to the interface between the user and the rule formal language.

A Partitioned User Profile. In MASMA, the user directly and interactively defines and maintains his profile. This profile contains a formal representation of the user's standard behavior in meeting scheduling. The profile is internally represented in a database of rules, describing behaviors, and in a database of facts, representing preferences. The agent also offers tools to update the profile following the user's evolution and changes of habit.

The user profile is partitioned in knowledge areas that represent different classes of rules. The partition facilitates the definition and the revision of the profile since it offers functional distinctions to the user. At present, the profile contains three classes of rules and/or preferences that characterize the user behavior in organizing meetings and maintaining his personal agenda:

- temporal preferences,

- contextual preferences,

- autonomy preferences.

The *temporal preferences*, expressed by *availability rules*, allow the user to describe his habits on how to manage his time with respect to the calendar. The user can specify a level of availability of the different time intervals, i.e., when, how and why he is engaged. *When* concerns a date or a time interval, *how* specifies the degree of availability (chosen in the set *{high, medium, low, null}*), *why* regards the type of appointment. In MASMA the preferences can be either manually set by the user or deduced by the agent from the defined preference rules. The Meeting Agent takes over the calendar system in the environment (in our case the calendar manager of the UNIX systems), so that it can examine the user's regular agenda. The agent automatically sets the availability to *null* on time intervals in which appointments have already been fixed.

For the free intervals, in which the user has no appointment, the agent figures out the value according to the preference rules. The user can set his availability over time using either the *specific availability specification* or the *generic availability specification* facilities.

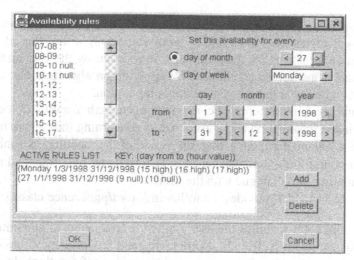

Figure 3. The generic availability specification window

The specific availability specification facility involves the description of particular types of habits with respect to meetings. At present, we have two types of availability rules[5]:

(1) The `Holiday-DB` associates a preference value to holiday time. So if the user likes to work on Sunday morning, he can assign the value 'high' to this interval. Holidays are automatically extracted by the calendar, but the user can also set his own holiday time.

(2) The `Proximity-DB` allows the user to give a preference value to a time interval around a type of meeting. For example, it is possible to specify the term between two different appointments in the same town, e.g., 2 hours, or in different towns, e.g., two days.

The generic availability specification facility is illustrated in Figure 3. The idea is to allow the user to specify any 'regularity' in his schedule. So in this way it is possible, as in the previously defined rule in the figure, to specify that from March to December of the current year, he is fully available for meetings on Monday from 3 to 5 p.m. He also sets to 'null' his availability for any 27th day of any month for the whole year in the first hours of the morning. This is a quite powerful possibility offered to the user because he can easily set very informative rules for his personal agent. For example, he can say that only in the morning of any day he can attend meetings. In this way, the simple use of a dialogue window can strongly influence the behavior of the agent in negotiation phases.

---

[5] We use the suffix '-DB' to indicate a data base of information of the same type. Actually, the distinction in different databases is virtual but useful to offer a conceptual frame to the user. The information is homogeneously managed by the agent.

Starting from the user's preferences, the calendar direct settings and the rules, the agent calculates the final value by applying an algorithm that also accounts for different alternatives for the same term introduced by the user himself. These inconsistencies are solved at run time by applying an algorithm that chooses the strongest conditions at the moment of the computation.

A second group of preferences concerns the 'contextualization of the choice'. It is used to insert information about usual habits concerning the content of a meeting (e.g., who is organizing the meeting, the venue of the meeting, its subject). These rules are used to force automated behavior according to this contextual information without entering into dialogue with the user.

Currently MASMA provides the following rules/preference classes:

(1) The People-DB specifies the user's bias towards personal appointments, e.g., colleagues, relatives, friends, doctors, etc., and sets priority values on a person or classes of people who are potential organizers of meetings. In this way he can express the weight of having a date with his dentist, e.g., 'if needed always cancel', or with his wife, e.g., 'never cancel unless it is my boss calling me'.

(2) The Meeting-Type-DB allows the user to set his predisposition to different types of engagements, e.g., working groups, project meetings, conferences, etc.

(3) The Travel-DB allows the user to specify his options on traveling and accommodation. For example, the user could be afraid of flying: consequently any invitation for conference overseas should be automatically rejected.

The last group of preferences concerns general preferences that influence the level of autonomy of the agent with respect to the user. Currently the following rules are extracted:

(1) The Date-DB specifies what kind of information about the agenda can be passed to other agents. For example, the user could specify that only dates with 'high' or 'medium' values can be passed to other Meeting Agents organizing a meeting. So the agent can autonomously decide about these dates without bothering the user, since the assigned values implies that those dates are not crucial to the user schedule. On the contrary, the dates labeled with 'low' or 'null' are more critical, so the user takes over the initiative.

(2) The Auto-Var is a single variable that when 'true' gives the agent the authority to directly make appointments without asking confirmation to its user, otherwise the agent has to apply the standard protocol and to ask the user for the final decision (examples of both cases are shown in the example in Section 4.3).

Even though it could seem that there is an indirect connection with mixed-initiative aspects, the rules are part of the knowledge concerning the interaction. We will see in the next section how this knowledge interacts with the negotiation protocol thus influencing the dialogue between user and agent.

5.2. TASK DRIVEN CONTROL OF THE INITIATIVE

This section deals with the aspects more immediately related to the shift of initiative during the continuous use of the tool. The basic work of the system consists of deciding dates for appointments after having checked the availability of the needed resources (the invited users). Usually, the phase of reaching an agreement between the needs of different users requires a lot of work. Hence, the choice of a tool whose basic task is to automate the very heavy activity of repetitive commitments, cancellations, etc. that are the usual tasks of secretaries.

In multi-agent systems, including those involving both humans and agents, a major problem is to coordinate efforts and avoid conflicts. To address those problems, we have endowed MASMA with negotiation protocols that are devoted to regulating the behavior of the different actors during the decision making for each meeting. When executed, such protocols follow a standard behavior which is personalized by the interaction with features of the user profile (in particular with *contextual* and *autonomy* information). All these mechanisms make the shift of initiative 'dynamic', since it depends on the current solutions, the current preferences of users, etc.

Since a Meeting Agent can play the role of organizer or attendee, two different basic protocol —one for each role— have been defined. Looking at the whole task of scheduling a certain event, the organizer's Meeting Agent that leads the way and the other Meeting Agents rely on their own protocols to guide their behavior. According to the steps in the protocol, the initiative shifts from one agent to another or from a personal agent to its user and back.

A main goal of meeting agents is to achieve an agreement maximizing the personal utility of the users. In particular, the organizer agent maximizes a common utility function and minimizes the requests for constraints relaxation. Instead, the attendees' agents try to protect their users, and hence they apply a strategy to safeguard their privacy and to avoid the relaxation of important constraints.

The activity of the whole multi-agent system is started by one user who decides to organize a meeting. He calls his meeting agent which starts to execute the organizer protocol sketched in Figure 4. The notation is the same used in Section 4.1 with the addition of $\mathcal{MA}_o$ to denote the meeting agent of the organizing user $\mathcal{U}_o$, $\mathcal{CS}$ to denote a set of variables that dynamically account for the *current status* of the computation during the negotiation behavior, and $\mathcal{IMA}$ to denote the set of $\mathcal{MA}$s of the participants.

Once the organizer user $\mathcal{U}_o$ has defined the features of an event M_x, his Meeting Agent $\mathcal{MA}_o$ sends the announcement to the interested users through the Server Agent (*AnnounceMeeting*). The agent $\mathcal{MA}_o$ collects the answers of the participants. If some of the attendees marked as necessary refuse to participate, the control turns back to $\mathcal{U}_o$ with this information (*PassControl*). In this case, the user can either stop or modify the meeting setting. Then he starts the organizer protocol again.

$\mathcal{MA}_o$ **Protocol**
begin
  $DefineMeeting(\mathcal{U}_o, \mathcal{MA}_o, M_x)$
  $AnnounceMeeting(\mathcal{MA}_o, \forall_i \mathcal{MA}_i \in \mathcal{IMA}, M_x)$
  $CollectAnswer(\mathcal{MA}_o, \mathcal{CS})$
  if $(\exists \mathcal{U}_j \in \mathcal{NI} \mid Reject(\mathcal{U}_j, M_x))$
    then $PassControl(\mathcal{MA}_o, \mathcal{U}_o, \mathcal{CS})$
    else
        while $not(FindSolution(\mathcal{MA}_o, \mathcal{CS}))$ **do**
           if $possible\_dates$ and $more\_values$
             then $AskPossibleDates(\mathcal{MA}_o, \forall_i \mathcal{MA}_i \in \mathcal{IMA},$
                $value \in (high, medium, low))$
              else $AskRelaxDates(\mathcal{MA}_o, \exists_j \mathcal{MA}_J, date_k)$
           fi
        od
        if $solution$
           then $Organize(\mathcal{MA}_o, M_x)$
           else $CancelMeeting?(\mathcal{MA}_o, \mathcal{U}_o, \mathcal{CS}, M_x)$
        fi
  fi
end

Figure 4. The organizer protocol

If at least the necessary attendees have answered positively, the actual negotiation begins. $\mathcal{MA}_o$ applies the procedure *FindSolution* with the goal of balancing the different preferences of the participants. It involves the other agents, since $\mathcal{MA}_o$ requires the different time intervals in which the participants are available for the meeting (*AskPossibleDates*); eventually, it may ask for constraint relaxation when a compromise is not reached (*AskRelaxDates*). $\mathcal{MA}_o$ requests the other Meeting Agents $\mathcal{MA}_i$ about time intervals with decreasing preference values, starting from dates with 'high' values in which the users have the highest availability. The $Ask-$ functions represent calls to the attendees' meeting agents which receive control for the continuation of the organization (it should be noted that, in general, the $Ask-$ functions may give control in parallel to the multiple agents involved in the request). A meeting agent $\mathcal{MA}_i$ of an invited user executes a protocol to answer an invitation. This protocol is personalized according to the user profile.

In Figure 5 an instance of the attendee protocol for a generic agent $\mathcal{MA}_k$ is shown. This instance has been filled in with information from the profile of its user $\mathcal{U}_k$. According to this protocol, $\mathcal{MA}_k$ can furnish the user's available dates only for intervals marked with *high* and *low* (see line C:1 where $\mathcal{MA}_k$ sends the dates by *SendDates*), otherwise the initiative returns to $\mathcal{U}_k$ (see line C:2 where $\mathcal{MA}_k$ queries its user to confirm the chosen dates by *AskConfirm*).

When $\mathcal{MA}_o$ is not able to find a solution within available dates, it starts asking other agents to relax previously unusable dates (*AskRelaxDates*). The steps in $\mathcal{MA}_k$ protocol are synchronized with steps in $\mathcal{MA}_o$ protocol: for example, the line C:3 in Figure 5 corresponds to *AskRelaxDates* in Figure 4. In order to speed up the convergence of the decision process, the agent suggests the interval with the

$\mathcal{MA}_k$ **Protocol**
begin
  $AskUser(\mathcal{MA}_k, \mathcal{U}_k, M_x)$
  if $Accept(\mathcal{U}_k)$
    then
        while $SendRequest(\mathcal{MA}_o, \mathcal{MA}_k)$ **do**
          $\underline{\mathbf{C}}: 1[AskPossibleDates(\mathcal{MA}_o, \mathcal{MA}_k, (\text{``high''} \vee \text{``medium''})]$
          $SendDates(\mathcal{MA}_k, \mathcal{MA}_o, (\text{``high''} \vee \text{``medium''})$
          $\underline{\mathbf{C}}: 2[AskPossibleDates(\mathcal{MA}_o, \mathcal{MA}_k, \text{``low''})]$
          $AskConfirm(\mathcal{MA}_k, \mathcal{U}_k)$
          if $Confirm(\mathcal{U}_k, \mathcal{MA}_k)$
            then $SendDates(\mathcal{MA}_k, \mathcal{MA}_o, \text{``low''})$
              else $RefuseDates(\mathcal{MA}_k, \mathcal{MA}_o)$
          fi
          $\underline{\mathbf{C}}: 3[AskRelaxDates(\mathcal{MA}_o, \mathcal{MA}_k, date_k)]$
          $AskConfirm(\mathcal{MA}_k, \mathcal{U}_k)$
          if $Confirm(\mathcal{U}_k, \mathcal{MA}_k)$
            then $SendDates(\mathcal{MA}_k, \mathcal{MA}_o, date_k)$
                $ReBuiltAgenda(\mathcal{MA}_k, \mathcal{U}_k)$
              else $RefuseDates(\mathcal{MA}_k, \mathcal{MA}_o, date_k)$
          fi
        od
      else $SendRejection(\mathcal{MA}_k, \mathcal{MA}_o)$
  fi
end

Figure 5. A generic protocol for the attendee

highest number of adhesions and with the highest total preference values; it asks to make it free only to the agents having previously rejected that date. If at least one of them rejects the proposal, the step is applied again within the successive intervals until either an agreement is reached or there are no more alternatives. It is to be noted that $\mathcal{MA}_k$ cannot decide whether or not to relax dates since its protocol requires a specific request to its user. In fact, after the line C:3, the step *AskConfirm* is executed.

When the organizer agent finds a solution, the initiative shifts to the service agents that are in charge of local organization and accommodation.

To sum up the kind of approach followed, we show Figure 6 in which all the involved aspects are exemplified. In MASMA, the user communicates to its personal agent his rules of behavior and preferences with respect to the meeting scheduling task; he also directly inserts appointments in his electronic calendar. His Meeting Agent has a representation of the user in the profile that is used to set up time interval preferences over a supporting agenda.

When a user wants to organize a meeting, he prompts a potential scenario as that represented in Figure 6 in which the nodes are labeled with an *actor-action* pair and the edges represent the action of passing control. The boxes indicate the most critical points in which the control might be relinquished to the other actor. The agent organizer (Agent$_o$) broadcasts the announcement, received by the user

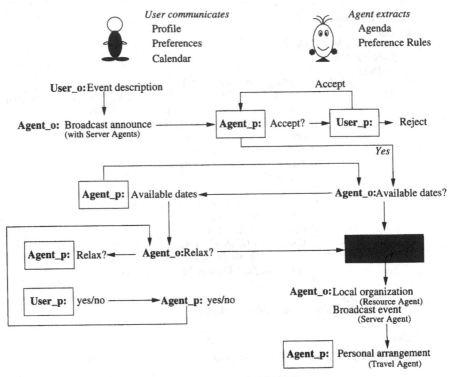

Figure 6. A sketched example of mixed-initiative in MASMA

(User$_o$), to the other agents: in effect the initiative moves to the Server Agent[6]. Also in the final steps, the Resource Agent, the Server Agent and the Travel Agent take the control over using some of the rules defined trough the Meeting Agent.

The agent of a potential participant (Agent$_p$) asks its user (User$_p$) whether it can or cannot start the negotiation. In the affirmative, Agent$_p$ is able to communicate the available dates to Agent$_o$ according to its Date-DB. If an agreement is not reached, Agent$_p$ must query the user to know which dates can be made free.

In this example, Agent$_p$ can autonomously decide for dates labeled with 'high', 'medium' and 'low', but it has to relinquish the initiative for previously fixed appointments. The example is quite simple since only few features have been considered, for instance there is no reference to the type of meeting, to the organizer, the place, etc. A real situation would assume a complex scenario in which at each step the current situation is compared with the databases to decide the entity in charge.

---

[6] The issues concerning the interaction between different types of agents is not within the scope of the current paper.

5.3. MECHANISMS TO ALLOW CONTROL BY THE USER

In MASMA, particular attention has been paid to those issues that are essential to the user so that he may accept the system, i.e., the simplicity of utilization of the whole tool, the respect of data privacy, the possibility of overseeing the agents 'work' (inspection).

To increase the possibility of agent-acceptance, attention has been paid to the decisions about *how* to interact with the user. In particular we have tried to make the user-agent dialogue as simple as possible. The agents communicate with their users by means of effective windows that can be adapted to the current needs and that hide the complexity of the system. We have also taken into account how to treat the user's working activity with consideration, as a consequence the interfaces do not encroach and remain discrete. A further issue influencing the acceptance of the system from the user is the respect of privacy, particularly when the data is sensitive as in the case of personal agendas.

We have therefore paid close attention to detail in restricting the management of personal data. Indeed only that data made available following the priorities set up by the user is handled by the agent.

It is to be noted that in this domain personal agents have to strictly represent the interests of their users, so they cannot communicate aspects of the user's profile to other agents.

The HCI community usually ascribes the user's loss of control on the activities of a software agent as a drawback to agent technology. Indeed some reasons for this complaint exist, because of the limited research dedicated to examining the role of a software agent tool as a mixed-initiative interactive system as opposed to that dedicated to a completely automated system. Although exciting, the possible autonomy of software agents should be held under control in systems that continuously interact with the user, in spite of the requested autonomy for an agent-based active interface. An agent should be endowed with the capability of acting and autonomously proposing solutions according to the current problem, but the user must have the possibility of controlling and inspecting the agent decisions.

Generally speaking, the need for control emerges at different phases in an agent life-cycle[7]. There are different situations in which the user would prefer to directly decide or modify the current configuration. Different scenarios can be hypothesized:

– Training phase: the user observes the agent behavior to decide about its reliability. The user has set up his profile but he prefers to maintain the control and the initiative since he is likely not to trust the agent yet.

---

[7] We distinguish two phases in a personal agent life-cycle: (a) we call 'training phase' the period in which the user is defining and tuning the behavior of his personal agent; (b) we call 'working phase' the subsequent period in which the user is satisfied with the standard behavior of his agent and uses it regularly.

- Working phase: after a while the user achieves a level of trust towards his agent and can leave decisions to it. Two different situations may influence the regular behavior of the agent-user pair:

  (1) usually the level of confidence in the user depends on the importance of the task and on the agent's capabilities. The user would like to take back the control at any time or to relinquish more initiative to the agent according to his experience;

  (2) at run time, the user would like to change his habits and so decide to modify (directly or implicitly) the working parameters.

A first aspect related to the control comes in deciding *when* the meeting agent has to involve its user in ordinary activities. This is a rather important aspect with respect to mixed–initiative. On the one hand, the agent should not intrude; on the other hand it should not independently make decisions that could be too critical for the user. The choice of always involving the user in decisions would result in a system that continuously asks for confirmation; such a system would fail in its main task. Over-intrusion can be a problem in all systems of this type. Our choice has been to ask the user or not according to the relevance –in the user's view– of decisions: this means that it is the user who decides when to relinquish the initiative to the agent. In fact, the relevance of a decision is assessed by the user through his preferences.

As to this point, it is worth making a comparison with (Maes, 1994). In her meeting scheduling, the user's intervention is requested when the agent is not confident enough about the decision that its internal algorithm suggests. In that system two thresholds exist, named 'tell-me' and 'do-it', that create three areas in which the agent is autonomous, the agent has doubts and consults its user, the agent recognizes it cannot take decisions due to lack of knowledge. In any case, it is the agent that decides to give control back to the user.

Our point of view is rather different, because we start from the standpoint that the user's lack of control over his agent seems to negatively influence the acceptance of the system. Hence, we always give the user the possibility to decide when the agent has to involve him in the decision. The level of autonomy of the agent is not decided according to its knowledge of the current decision but on the criticality of the decision for the user. This motivation also further justifies the choice of the strong role given to the definition of the user's profile.

A further feature we have introduced to allow the user to increase his *sense of control* is the *possibility of inspection* of the agent behavior. The agent is endowed with an inspection mode about its activities, that at present is implemented as follows.

In its main dialogue window, MASMA allows for the verification of the status of the agent and then for the inspection of the details of the current activity. When no negotiation is running, the agent is free, and it is busy when involved in an organizational process. In this case, a button is active that displays a window (Figure 7(left))

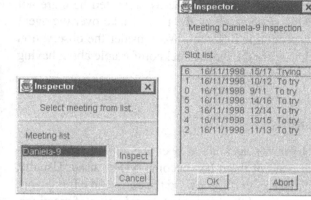

Figure 7. Windows for dynamic inspection of the agent behavior

that shows the user the list of the current running meeting organizations[8]. Selecting one of the meetings, it is possible to have both the specific information about the meeting or display the list of potential time intervals that the agent is going to contribute during negotiation. The Figures 7(center) and 7(right) show this second window in two subsequent instants of the negotiation described in Section 4.3. In these windows a set of intervals are contained that match the requirement of the current meeting. Intervals are ordered by priority, obtained from the user's preferences, and a marker shows the status of the interval. The labels 'Trying', 'To Try' and 'Failed' respectively indicate if the interval is currently object of negotiation, if it is still to be considered and if it has been previously rejected.

The inspection facility can be used either to observe the agent behavior, to analyze the running processes, to verify the information and data at agent disposal or to interfere or take the agent over if necessary.

The user can influence the organization and negotiation processes by dynamically modifying the preferences and rules. This is an implicit way of addressing the running process. For example, the user might remember to be already engaged on November 16th: he accesses his calendar and turns the preference value to 'null'. The agent records the change and consequently modifies its negotiation parameters.

We have been experimenting in some detail with the problem of inspection and we are now trying to understand those issues connected to explaining to the user the priorities and allowing him to directly alter the priority.

The inspection window does not interrupt the agent activity that goes on with the negotiation process. The change of the preferences may happen at any time independently from the achieved results: the job of re-contracting is left to the software agents not to humans.

---

[8] The more recent release of our meeting scheduler allows each meeting agent to take part in the negotiation of more meetings in parallel (Cesta et al., 1998).

As far as we know, the functionalities of inspection as presented here are not contained in similar systems. Other systems allow the user to take over the agent as we do, but our meaning of inspection is different. We consider the observation of the agent behavior be very relevant for the user to feel comfortable about having control over the agent reasoning.

6. Discussion and Comparisons

The mechanized management of a user's agenda has been the goal of several software utilities over the years, but none of them has become widely used. Usually, these kinds of system mainly offered an interface toward the diary and a framework for communications, and rarely concerned the automated organization of meetings. Moreover, several studies (e.g., Kincaid et al., 1985) point out that these tools are considered of limited utility due to their lack of flexibility with respect to usual paper-based diaries.

For these reasons, the agent technologies immediately focused on this particular problem considered somehow challenging for the application of the task delegation metaphor. Apart from some investigations that point to the problem just as a demonstration of agent technology, several works have addressed questions connected to the development of meeting schedulers. In particular, the problem of distributed scheduling heuristics is addressed in (Sen & Durfee, 1996), the distributed negotiation with the game-theory approach in (Ephrati et al., 1994) and the use of machine learning techniques in (Kozierok & Maes, 1993; Mitchell et al., 1994). The role of agents as interface towards the user is particularly emphasized in (Kozierok & Maes, 1993; Maes, 1994).

Sen's work (Sen & Durfee, 1996) is a detailed investigation of the distributed meeting scheduling problem. In particular, the work considers a context in which a contract-net negotiation protocol is used and it analyzes different heuristics for the problem and the role played by different variables that may contribute to the solution (e.g., users' commitments in their choices). These aspects are not deeply analyzed in our work, while we have developed in much greater depth the aspects of agent software architecture, and human-agent interaction. According to our experience, the problem solving heuristics represent only one feature, and not the most relevant, in the development of a complete approach to meeting scheduling. To be fair, this author in a more recent work (Hayes et al., 1997) describes a complete system in which some interest is shown for the issues of the user's involvement. Again this last proposal seems rather preliminary, the user's preferences are considered relevant for the problem solving heuristics and not included in a comprehensive work aimed at increasing the acceptance of the system like done in MASMA.

In (Ephrati et al., 1994), the authors re-use their own work in multi-agent negotiation to investigate issues like security and privacy in the specific context. In particular, the authors formalize some properties that guarantee the correct proposals for the meeting participants, the avoidance of unfair manipulation of the schedule, and so on. All those issues of the meeting scheduling problem are very relevant but they are not yet addressed in our work. We do pay attention to the privacy of information in several parts of MASMA for example when communicating preferences about time intervals or names of participants and so on. Nevertheless, MASMA is a support for negotiating agreements that is not 'manipulation free'. It is indeed to be noted that MASMA is a tool designed to be open with respect, for example, to the addition of new users while the results obtained in (Ephrati et al., 1994) are not of immediate use under such an assumption.

In (Kozierok & Maes, 1993; Mitchell et al., 1994), the idea of a personal assistant is introduced with the attention focused on automated learning of the user's behaviors or preferences. Our choice as motivated in Section 5.1 is rather the opposite; we do not involve learning but focus on a direct personalization of the personal agent from the user.

Indeed more connections with the meeting scheduler of Maes (Kozierok & Maes, 1993; Maes 1994) and our own work exist, as it was also pointed out in previous sections but it is worth underlining them here again. The similarity between the works lies in these claims:

(a) the agent-user couple has to interact a lot in order to realize an effective application;
(b) the personalization of the agent behavior is relevant for the success of the agent system;
(c) the interaction between agent and user needs to be as simple as possible.

The methods for demonstrating these claims are indeed radically different. Maes' system is built around the memory based learning algorithm, while MASMA relies more on a solution that draws from multi-agent system research coupled with ideas from user-adapted interaction. A detailed comparison is not possible, given the description of that system at our disposal, but we would add that: (a) some advantages seem to exist in our approach with respect to memory-based reasoning concerning the compactness of the information, because the second reasoning style is quite memory intensive; (b) (Maes, 1994) presents a modality of personalization based on 'asking to other agents' that we strongly disagree with since in a domain such as personal diary management the respect of users' privacy is a strong requirement.

In Section 3.2 we have introduced some distinctions in the literature on mixed-initiative interaction. We distinguish between dialogue-oriented and task-oriented approaches and we also point out the existence of delegation-based systems where the development of trust from the user towards his personal agent is very relevant. On this last type of application, a relation can be made with the approach to collaboration proposed in COLLAGEN (Rich & Sidner, 1997; Rich & Sidner, 1998). In both MASMA and COLLAGEN the point is raised of developing an interaction style that is somehow similar to the way humans behave in the same situation. Again, the emphasis in the solutions is on different aspects. COLLAGEN represents a relevant example of practical use of discourse theories relying on the fact that users are attracted to a style inspired by human collaboration. In MASMA a more 'traditional' interaction is chosen based on graphical user interfaces but attention is given to the knowledge needed to build a problem solving approach that reminds the user of his own style. We do not claim here that one approach is better than another because the aspects are quite complementary. We argue that this area of research generally requires more attention to develop a generation of systems that are likely to match the requirements of the users.

7. Conclusions

This paper concerns agent systems and mixed-initiative interaction. We started from observing that in applications devoted to assist users in critical assignments, task delegation to agents is not necessarily desirable. In contexts where agents manage personal data and take decisions that might be critical for the user (e.g., anything related to his personal agenda), the user would probably prefer to maintain continuous control over the process since he is not likely to immediately trust how his agent could act on his behalf.

This standpoint generates a set of issues not completely investigated in current agent literature, e.g.: why the user should trust his agent, when responsibility is or is not up to the user, etc.

We have presented a meeting scheduling system, MASMA, that is devoted to directly addressing these problems starting from the multi-agent approach and tradition. MASMA is a completely implemented system with two currently running versions. The first, developed in CommonLisp and with GARNET (Myers et al., 1990) as a tool for interface development, is described in (Brancaleoni et al., 1997). Recently a new release, entirely re-designed in Java, has been implemented elaborating on the same key idea of a user centered system and empowered with new features (Cesta et al., 1998).

MASMA pays particular attention to the agent role with respect to critical issues that could compromise its actual use. Keywords like acceptability, trust, privacy and control are considered as very relevant and lead to studying the agent-user pair as a mixed-initiative system. We are investigating mechanisms to constrain the agent autonomy while preserving the user's own autonomy.

In MASMA the following aspects are particularly taken into account:

- the user can easily explain to MASMA his way of solving the meeting scheduling task and his preferences on how to carry out the task;
- the delegation of tasks between user and agent is controlled via a negotiation protocol that is integrated with the user's profile;
- it is possible to select what decisions (or classes of decisions) can be relinquished to the agent and decide when the initiative can be relinquished to the agent. In both cases the choice is made according to the criticality of decisions;
- the user is able to control and inspect what the agent is doing at any moment.

Acknowledgments

We would like to thank Rodolfo Brancaleoni and Marcello Collia for their contribution in the implementation of MASMA and in their investigation of several aspects of the project. We are also grateful to Susan Haller and the two anonymous reviewers for their precious comments. Amedeo Cesta's work has been partially supported by ASI (Italian Space Agency) and by CNR Committee 12 on Information Technology (Projects SARI, SIAD and SCI*SIA). Daniela D'Aloisi carried out her work in the framework of the agreement between the Italian PT Administration and the FUB.

References

Allen, J., Miller, B., Ringger, E. and Sikorski, T.: 1996, A robust system for natural spoken dialogue. In: *Proceedings of the 34th Annual Meeting of the Association for Computational Linguistics*, Santa Cruz (CA), 62–70.

Amati, G., D'Aloisi, D., Giannini, V. and Ubaldini, F.: 1997, A framework for filtering news and managing distributed data. *Journal of Universal Computer Science* 3(8), 1007–1021.

Bates, J.: 1994, The role of emotion in believable agents. *Communications of the ACM* 37(7), 122–125.

Beard, D., Palaniappan, M., Humm, A., Banks, D., Nair, A. and Shan, Y.: 1990, A visual calendar for scheduling group meetings. In: *Proceedings of the ACM Conference on Computer Supported Cooperative Work*, Los Angeles (CA), 279–290.

Brancaleoni, R., Cesta, A. and D'Aloisi, D.: 1997, MASMA: A multi-agent system for scheduling meetings. In: *Proceeding of the 2nd International Conference on the Practical Application of Intelligent Agents and Multi-Agent Technology*, London (UK). 31–50.

Cesta, A., Collia, M. and D'Aloisi, D.: 1998, Tailorable interactive agents for scheduling meetings. In: F. Giunchiglia (ed.): *Artificial Intelligence: Methodology, Systems and Applications*. Lecture Notes in Artificial Intelligence 1980, Berlin: Springer, 153–166.

Cesta, A. and D'Aloisi, D.: 1996, Active interfaces as personal assistants: a case study. *SIGCHI Bulletin* 28(3), 108–113.

Cesta, A., D'Aloisi, D. and Giannini, V.: 1995, Active interfaces for useful software tools. In: Y.Anzai, K.Ogawa, and H.Mori (eds.): *Symbiosis of Human and Artifacts*. New York: Elsevier Science, 225–230.

Cohen, R., Allaby, C., Cumbaa, C., Fitzgerald, M., Ho, K., Hui, B., Latulipe, C., Lu, F., Moussa, N., Pooley, D., Qian, A. and Siddiqi, S.: 1998, What is initiative? User Modeling and User-Adapted Interaction 8:3–4, 171–214.

D'Aloisi, D. and Cesta, A.: 1997, Controlling Initiative in an Agent-Based System. Technical Report 5T06797, FUB.

Ephrati, E., Zlotkin, G. and Rosenschein, J.: 1994, Meet your destiny: A non-manipulable meeting scheduler. In: *Proceedings of the ACM Conference on Computer Supported Cooperative Work*, Chapel Hill (NC), 359–371.

Etzioni, O. and Weld, D.: 1994, A softbot-based interface to the internet. *Communications of the ACM* 37(7), 72–76.

Ferguson, G., Allen, J. and Miller, B.: 1996, TRAINS-95: Towards a mixed-initiative planning assistant. In: *Proceedings of the Third International Conference on Artificial Intelligence Planning Systems (AIPS-96)*, Edimburgh (Scotland), 70–77.

Finin, T., Weber, J. and et al.: 1994, Specification of the KQML Agent-communication language (Draft). http://www.cs.umbc.edu/kqml/papers/kqmlspec.ps.

Friedman, B. and Nissenbaum, H.: 1997, Software agents and user autonomy. In: *Proceedings of the First International Conference on Autonomous Agents*, Marina del Rey (CA), 466–469.

Grosz, B. and Sidner, C.: 1986, Attention, intentions, and the structure of discourse. *Computational Linguistics* 12(3), 175–204.

Grudin, J.: 1988, Why CSCW applications fail: Problems in the design and evaluation of organizational interfaces. In: *Proceedings of the ACM Conference on Computer Supported Cooperative Work*, Portland (OR). 65–84.

Hagen, E.: 1998, An Approach to Mixed-Initiative Spoken Information Retrieval Dialogue. *In this issue*.

Hayes, T., Sen, S., Arora, N. and Nadella, R.: 1997, An automated meeting scheduling system that utilizes user preferences. In: *Proceedings of the First International Conference on Autonomous Agents*, Marina del Rey (CA), 308–314.

Hayes-Roth, B.: 1997, Introduction. In: *Proceedings of the First International Conference on Autonomous Agents*, Marina del Rey (CA), xi–xii.

Hsu, W.-L., Prietula, M. J., Thompson, G. L. and Ow, P. S.: 1993, A mixed initiative scheduling workbench: Integrating AI, OR and HCI. *Decision Support Systems* 9, 245–257.

Kincaid, C., Dupont, P. and Kaye, A.: 1985, Electronic calendars in the office: An assessment of user needs and current technology. *ACM Transactions on Office Information Systems* 3(1), 89–102.

Kozierok, R. and Maes, P.: 1993, A learning interface agent for scheduling meetings. In: *Proceedings of the 1993 International Workshop on Intelligent User Interfaces*, Orlando (FL), 81–88.

Lester, J., Stone, B. and Stelling, G.: 1998, Lifelike pedagogical agents for mixed-initiative problem solving in constructivist learning environments. *In this issue*.

Lester, J. C. and Stone, B. A.: 1997, Increasing believability in animated pedagogical agents. In: *Proceedings of the First International Conference on Autonomous Agents*, Marina del Rey (CA), 16–21.

Lochbaum, K., Grosz, B. and Sidner, C: 1990, Models of plans to support communication: An initial report. In: *Proceedings of the Eighth National Conference on Artificial Intelligence*, Boston (MA), 485–490.

Maes, P.: 1994, Agents that reduce work and information overload. *Communication of the ACM* 37(7), 30–40.

Milewski, A. E. and Lewis, S. H.: 1997, Delegating to software agents. *International Journal of Human-Computer Studies* 46(4), 485–500.

Mitchell, T., Caruana, R., Freitag, D., McDermott, J. and Zabowski, D.: 1994, Experience with a learning personal assistant. *Communication of the ACM* 37(7), 80–91.

Muir, B. M.: 1987, Trust between humans and machines, and the design of decision aids. *International Journal of Man-Machine Studies* 27(4), 527–539.

Myers, B. A., Giuse, D., Dannenberg, R. B., Zanden, B. V., Kosbie, D., Mickish, A. and Marchal, P.: 1990, GARNET: comprehensive support for graphical, highly-interactive user interfaces. *IEEE Computer* 23(11), 71–85.

Nwana, H. S.: 1996, Software agents: an overview. *The Knowledge Engineering Review* 11(3), 205–244.

Pell, B., Bernard, D. E., Chien, S. A., Gat, E., Muscettola, N., Nayak, P. P., Wagner, M. D. and Williams, B. C.: 1997, An autonomous spacecraft agent prototype. In: *Proceedings of the First International Conference on Autonomous Agents*, Marina del Rey (CA), 253–261.

Rich, C. and Sidner, C. L.: 1997, COLLAGEN: When agents collaborate with people. In: *Proceedings of the First International Conference on Autonomous Agents*, Marina del Rey (CA), 284–291.

Rich, C. and Sidner, C. L.: 1998, COLLAGEN: A collaboration manager for software interface agents. User Modeling and User-Adopted Interaction 8:3–4, 315–349.

Sen, S. and Durfee, E.: 1996, A contracting model for flexible distributed scheduling. *Annals of Operations Research* 65, 195–222.

Shneiderman, B.: 1997, Direct manipulation versus agents: Paths to predictable, controllable, and comprehensible interfaces. In: J. M. Bradshaw (ed.): *Software Agents*. AAAI Press/The MIT Press, 97–106.

Simmons, R., Goodwin, R., Haigh, K.Z., Koenig, S. and O'Sullivan, J.: 1997, A layered architecture for office delivery robots. In: *Proceedings of the First International Conference on Autonomous Agents*, Marina del Rey (CA), 245–252.

Smith, S. F. and Lassila, O.: 1994, Toward the development of mixed-initiative scheduling systems. In: M. H. Burstein (ed.): *Proceedings ARPA-Rome Laboratory Planning Initiative Workshop*, Tucson (AZ), 145–154.

Steiner, D. D., Mahling, D. E. and Haugeneder, H.: 1990, Human-computer cooperative work. In: *Proceedings of the 10th International Conference on Distributed Artificial Intelligence*, Bandera (TX), 22:1–28.

Stickel, J. and Johnson, W.: 1997, Mixed-initiative interaction between pedagogical agent and students in virtual environments. In: S. Haller and S. McRoy (eds.): *Papers from 1997 AAAI Spring Symposium on Computational Models for Mixed Initiative Interaction*, Stanford (CA), 128–134.

Tate, A.: 1997, Mixed-initiative interaction in O-PLAN. In: S. Haller and S. McRoy (eds.): *Papers from 1997 AAAI Spring Symposium on Computational Models for Mixed Initiative Interaction*, Stanford (CA). 163–168.

Walker, M. and Whittaker, S.: 1990, Mixed initiative in dialogue: An investigation into discourse segmentation. In: *Proceeding of the 28th Annual Meeting of the Association for Computational Linguistics*, Pittsburgh (PA), 70–78.

Whittaker, S. and Sidner, C.: 1996, Email overload: Exploring personal information management of email. In: *Proceedings of CHI '96 Human Factors in Computing Systems (ACM)*, Vancouver (Canada), 276–283.

Whittaker, S. and Stenton, P.: 1988, Cues and control in expert-client dialogues. In: *Proceeding of the 26th Annual Meeting of the Association for Computational Linguistics*, Buffalo (NY), 123–130.

Wooldridge, M. J. and Jennings, N. R.: 1995, Intelligent agents: Theory and practice. *The Knowledge Engineering Review* **10**(2), 115–152.

Authors's Vitae

Amedeo Cesta

IP-CNR, Italian National Research Council, Institute of Psychology, Viale Marx 15, I-00137 Rome, Italy.

Dr. Cesta is a research scientist for the Italian National Research Council (CNR). He received a 'Laurea' degree in Electronic Engineering and a 'Dottorato di Ricerca' in Computer Science at the University of Rome in 1983 and 1992 respectively. Since 1991 he works in the Division of Artificial Intelligence, Cognitive Modeling and Interaction at the CNR Institute of Psychology where he conducts research on artificial intelligence architectures for planning and scheduling, multi-agent systems and intelligent man-machine interaction.

Daniela D'Aloisi

FUB, Fondazione Ugo Bordoni, Via B. Castiglione 59, I-00142 Rome, Italy.

Daniela D'Aloisi is a senior research scientist at Fondazione Ugo Bordoni. She obtained a 'Laurea' in Electronic Engineering from the University of Rome in 1985 and then joined the Information Systems Group at FUB. From 1992 to 1996 she has also been a research fellow at IP-CNR of the Italian National Research Council. Her current interests include agent systems, intelligent man-machine interaction and information filtering and retrieval. At present, she is developing distributed and cooperative systems for actively helping users in daily and complex activities.

User Modeling and User-Adapted Interaction **9:** 79–91, 1999.
© 1999 *Kluwer Academic Publishers.*

Exploring Mixed-Initiative Dialogue Using Computer Dialogue Simulation

MASATO ISHIZAKI[1], MATTHEW CROCKER[2] and CHRIS MELLISH[3]
[1]*Japan Advanced Institute of Science and Technology, Tatsunokuchi, Nomi, Ishikawa, 923-1292 Japan*
[2]*Centre for Cognitive Science, Univ. of Edinburgh, 2 Buccleuch Place, Edinburgh EH8 9LW, UK*
[3]*Dept. of Artificial Intelligence, Univ. of Edinburgh, 80 Southbridge, Edinburgh EH1 1HN, UK*

(Received: 1 December 1997; accepted: 10 July 1998)

Abstract. This paper experimentally shows that mixed-initiative dialogue is not always more efficient than non-mixed initiative dialogue in route finding tasks. Based on the dialogue model proposed in Conversation Analysis and Discourse Analysis a lá the Birmingham school and Whittaker and Stenton's definition of initiative, we implement dialogue systems and obtain experimental results by making the systems interact with each other. Across a variety of instantiations of the dialogue model, the results show that with easy problems, the efficiency of mixed-initiative dialogue is a little better than or equal to that of non-mixed-initiative dialogue, while with difficult problems mixed-initiative dialogue is less efficient than non-mixed-initiative dialogue.

Key words: mixed-initiative dialogue, computer dialogue simulation, efficiency of dialogue, discourse analysis, task-oriented dialogue.

1. Introduction

In keyboard human-computer dialogue research, user input has been used to track knowledge states. For example, when a navigation system sometimes give directions using a landmark unfamiliar to the user, the user will interrupt to request information from the system. The necessity of so-called subdialogues has been recognised and some mechanisms have been proposed to handle such interruptions. Systems that allow user interruptions were called mixed initiative dialogue systems. In these systems, the task domains are ones in which the roles of conversational participants are relatively fixed, and the initiative changes in limited situations. Recently, there has been increasing interest in collaboration with computer systems having incomplete knowledge. One reason for this is that humans do not have complete knowledge and they make the best use of interaction with others and the environment. The other reason concerns robustness of systems, which can work not only in a toy world but also in a real world. In this area, autonomous programs called 'agents', which enable users to effectively use computers for solving problems, have been extensively studied. How agents cooperate to solve problems in a distributed environment is one of the most important research topics. The situations where agents with incomplete knowledge should take the initiative are not limited to cases of interruption.

Why does user modelling research concern 'initiative'? One of the aims of user modelling research is to realise more friendly and efficient use of computer systems by taking knowledge states of users into account. In some expert systems, for example, user models can be used to change explanations of their output according to the user's knowledge level (Paris, 1993). If the system can reason that the user does not know some of the terms in the explanation, the system adds some sentences or a paragraph to elucidate the unknown terms to improve the original's understandability (Cawsey, 1993; Moore, 1994). If there is a chance a user might draw the wrong conclusion from the explanation, the system tries to choose expressions that will prevent this. Even if the user does not make a request explicitly, the system can provide useful information by reasoning based on the user model. Allen et al. (1996) proposed and incorporated a mixed initiative planning model into their spoken human-computer dialogue systems. In their model, a system makes a plan based on incomplete information, communicates it with the user, and examines if it can work. If the plan can work, the system proceeds to make the next plan; if not, the system re-plans using new information. When should the system provide information to the user or when should the system patiently wait for the user's input? 'Initiative' can be a key concept to explore this question. Research on 'initiative' is at the early stage, and thus this paper focuses on a basic question of whether mixed initiative dialogue is always more efficient than non-mixed initiative dialogue using computer dialogue simulation.

This paper is organised as follows. Firstly, previous studies on the initiative are reviewed. Secondly, experimental settings and programs are explained. Lastly, example outputs and results of the computer dialogue simulations of initiative are discussed.

2. Related Work

Keyboard human-computer dialogue systems are normally developed in instruction or tutoring and information providing domains. The term mixed-initiative dialogue systems signifies those systems that can handle clarifications or interruptions. Because of the particular task domains they target, the roles of conversational participants are fixed and initiative changes are rather limited.

Whittaker and Stenton (1988) defined initiative using a classification of utterance types, such as assertions, commands, questions and prompts. According to their definition, a conversational participant has the initiative when she makes some utterance other than a response to her partner's utterance. The reasoning here is that a responsive utterance should be thought of as one elicited by the previous speaker rather than one directing a conversation in its own right. A participant does not have the initiative (or a partner has the initiative) when a prompt is used, since this clearly abdicates the opportunity for expressing some propositional content. Whittaker and Stenton (1988) analysed software consulting dialogues between users and consultants. They showed that the initiative changes after utterances with no propositional content like repetition, that cue phrases are not reliable predictors of initiative change, and that in these dialogues, users tend to take the initiative in the first half, while consultants take it in the second half. Walker and Whittaker (1990) analysed the relationship between the initiative and the distribution of anaphoric expressions using problem solving and advisory dialogues. They observed that in problem solving dialogues both conversational participants equally take the initiative, while in advisory dialogues experts, who give advice to novices, take the initiative in most cases. They showed that all anaphoric relations except demonstratives hold within a segment delimited by initiative change.

Smith and Hipp (1994) built a spoken dialogue system for trouble shooting in electric circuits, and implemented a mechanism for gradually changing the initiative from 'directive' to 'passive' between the system and the user by changing goal adoption strategies. They conducted system-evaluation experiments in which subjects actually conversed with computers using speech to fix problems in an electric circuit. With regard to initiative, they compared the 'directive' mode in which the system always tries to achieve its own goal, with the 'declarative' mode, in which the system tries to find and adopt a common (sub)goal with the user, and showed that in the 'declarative' mode the system can achieve a goal with fewer, but more effective, utterances than in the 'directive' mode.

Guinn (1998) conducted computer dialogue simulations of selecting an answer which has some specified characteristics, from a set of candidates. Determining a criminal from suspects or a faulty gate in an electric circuit are examples of this domain. Problems in this domain can be solved by examining candidates one by one if they have some specified characteristics, and the order of the examination affects the efficiency of the problem solving. He characterised this problem domain as collaborative search and conducted experiments in which domain knowledge is distributed over computer agents. He showed that agents can solve their problems when they share information with each other faster than when only one agent provides information, and that giving information on internal states can reduce the search space when agents cannot decide which candidate they will examine.

Chu-Carroll and Brown (1998) pointed out the necessity of making a distinction between task initiative and dialogue initiative. They built a decision tree of predicting initiative change by applying ID4.5 machine learning algorithm to TRAINS corpora (Gross et al., 1995) annotated with dialogue structures and cue phrases. Their study focuses on response generation. Based on the distinction of the types of initiative introduced by Chu-Carroll and Brown (1998), Guinn's study and our study – both use computer dialogue simulation – can be clearly differentiated. That is, Guinn's concerns task initiative and ours does dialogue initiative.

Table I. I-R modelling of non-MID dialogues w/ and w/o clarifications

A:	$U_A^{I_1}$	**A:**	$U_A^{I_1}$
B:	$U_B^{R_1}$	**B:**	$U_B^{CI_1}$
A:	$U_A^{I_2}$	**A:**	$U_A^{CR_1}$
B:	$U_B^{R_2}$	**B:**	$U_B^{R_1}$
A:	$U_A^{I_3}$		...
B:	$U_B^{R_3}$		
	...		

Research on initiative is at its early stage, and thus this paper intends to contribute to this research area by examining a basic question of whether mixed initiative dialogue is always more efficient than non-mixed initiative dialogue using computer dialogue simulation.

3. Computer Dialogue Simulation

3.1. DIALOGUE MODELLING

In Conversation Analysis (Schegloff and Sacks, 1974; Levinson, 1983) and Discourse Analysis a lá the Birmingham school (Stubbs, 1983; Coulthard, 1985; Stenström, 1994), dialogues are modelled by a basic unit consisting of initiating utterances (I) and responding utterances (R) (This is called an adjacency pair in conversation analysis.) The basic unit can include another unit like $I_1 I_2 R_2 R_1$, in which I and R with the same subscript form an adjacency pair. [1] Ahrenberg et al. (1995) used this modelling to build their spoken dialogue system.

Whittaker and Stenton (1988)'s definition can be re-stated based on this modelling. That is, a conversational participant takes the initiative when she initiates an utterance other than one responding to the other participant's initiating utterance. Dialogues in which one participant always takes the initiative with (in the right-hand side) and without embedding (in the left-hand side) are shown in Table I. 'U' represents an utterance, and 'I', 'R' and 'A', 'B' indicate the roles and speakers of an utterance, respectively. The numbers attached shows the correspondence between initiating and responding utterances. Non-mixed initiative dialogue without embedding in the left-hand side of Table I shows that speaker **A**'s first initiating utterance $U_A^{I_1}$ is responded by speaker **B**'s utterance $U_B^{R_1}$, while non-mixed initiative dialogue with embedding in the right-hand side represents that speaker **A**'s first initiating utterance $U_A^{I_1}$ is interrupted by speaker **B**'s clarification

---

[1] This is called insertion sequence in conversation analysis and embedding in discourse analysis.

Table II. I-R modelling of MID dialogues w/ & w/o clarifications

A:	$U_A^{I_1}$		**A:**	$U_A^{I_1}$	
B:	$U_B^{R_1}$	$U_B^{I_2}$	**B:**	$U_B^{R_1}$	$U_B^{I_2}$
A:	$U_A^{R_2}$	$U_A^{I_3}$	**A:**	U_A^{CI2}	
B:	U_B^{CI}		**B:**	$U_B^{CR_2}$	
	...		**A:**	U_A^{R2}	
			B:	$U_B^{I_3}$	
			A:	$U_A^{R_3}$	$U_A^{I_4}$
				...	

$U_B^{CI_1}$ responded by **A**'s clarification answer $U_A^{CR_1}$ and is responded by speaker **B**'s answer $U_B^{R_1}$.

Mixed initiative dialogue can be modelled by allowing conversational agents to respond to each other's initiating utterance and initiate a new utterance. Table II shows I-R modelling of mixed initiative dialogue with and without embedding. Mixed initiative dialogue without embedding in the left-hand side of Table II shows that speaker **A**'s first initiating utterance $U_A^{I_1}$ is responded by speaker **B**'s answer $U_B^{R_1}$ while speaker **B** initiates a new utterance $U_B^{I_2}$ in the same turn. Mixed initiative dialogue with embedding in the right-hand side represents that in the third turn speaker **A** initiates clarification utterance $U_A^{CI_2}$, which is responded by speaker **B**'s answer $U_B^{CR_2}$. In the fifth turn, speaker **A** closes the clarification exchange, which is followed by speaker **B**'s new initiating utterance.

The I-R model abstracts utterances in two respects: the types of utterances, such as a request and a question, and the contents. In the following, we examine the efficiency of mixed- and non-mixed initiative dialogues by instantiating these variations of the I-R modelling.

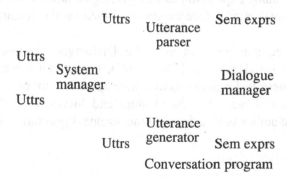

Figure 1. A module diagram of the computer dialogue simulation programs.

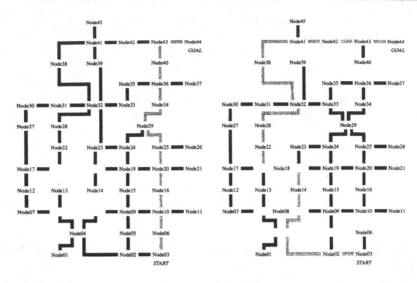

Figure 2. Example maps for both speakers (**A** and **B**).

3.2. Experimental Programs

Figure 1 shows the set-up for the computer dialogue simulation. The simulation programs are a system management program and two conversation handling programs. The conversation programs exchange messages through the system management program. The system management program can activate and de-activate the conversation programs. The conversation programs consist of an utterance parser, a dialogue management program, and an utterance generator. The utterance parser analyses an input string from the system management program and outputs its semantic expression. The dialogue management program updates the system state based on the history of the system and the sematic expression created by the parser, and builds an output semantic expression using a given goal and the system state. The utterance generator makes a surface expression based on the semantic expression.

We used the system management program made for DiaLeague, computer-computer dialogue system contest (Hasida and Den, 1997), the utterance parser and generator made for a Japanese-to-English machine translation system by ATR Interpreting Telecommunications Research Labs (Tashiro and Morimoto, 1995; Akamine et al., 1994). The first author built a dialogue management program using 4000-line LISP code.

Table III. The characteristics of maps used in computer dialogue simulation

	# of nodes	# of links	# of nodes w/o names	Length of shortest route	Length of answer route
Maps 1	45, 45	56, 56	3, 3	12, 15	15
Maps 2	43, 43	54, 55	3, 3	7, 8	17
Maps 3	50, 50	58, 58	3, 3	12, 16	50

4. Experimental Results and Discussions

4.1. EXPERIMENTAL TASK

In the route finding task, both conversational participants have train route maps showing connections among stations or nodes. These maps have the start and goal stations; the map one agent has might be different from that of the other concerning station names and connections between stations: The stations whose positions are the same on the two maps might have their names written on one map, but not on the other; the connection between two stations on one map might not be on the other. Under these circumstances, the conversational participants are asked to find the shortest connected path from the start to goal stations, where the path must be connected on both maps. The route finding task can be thought of as a modified version of the Map Task (Anderson et al., 1991) for computer simulation on mixed initiative dialogues. The route finding can be simulated as graph search and the roles of conversational participants are not fixed, since neither participant has dominant information or social status.

Figure 2 shows example maps, in which nodes are are represented by rectangular boxes with or without node names and links are represented by black and gray lines. Gray lines signify the shortest path for each map. Japanese place names used in the original maps are simplified to 'Node' and sequential node numbers for improving understandability of the maps. In cases where a conversational participant has nodes without names, she is instructed to find them by obtaining information from her partner. In the experiments, three maps created for DiaLeague (Hasida and Den, 1997) were used. The number of nodes, links, nodes whose names are unknown, the lengths of the shortest path, and lengths of the answer (common shortest) route are shown in Table III.

Table III shows that

(1) maps are almost all the same size,

(2) the number of nodes whose names are unknown is the same, and

(3) the difficulty of solving a problem, which is estimated by the ratio of the lengths between a shortest route and answer route, is gradually increased from map 1 to 3.

Table IV. Dialogue simulation example of non-mixed-
initiative dialogue

1	**A**	I would like you to go from Node03 to Node06.
2	**B**	(No.) I am not going from Node03 to Node06.
3	**A**	I would like you to go from Node03 to Node02.
4	**B**	(Ok.) I am going from Node03 to Node02.
5	**A**	I would like you to go from Node02 to Node04.

Table V. Dialogue simulation example of non-mixed-ini- tiative dialogue

1	**A**	I would like you to go from Node03 to Node06.
2	**B**	(No.) I am not going from Node03 to Node03.
3	**A**	I would like you to go from Node03 to Node02.
4	**B**	(Ok.) I am going from Node03 to Node02.
		I would like you to go from Node02 to the stop at the left of Node02.
5	**A**	(Ok.) I am going from Node02 to Node04.
		I would like you to go from Node04 to the stop above Node04.

4.2. SIMULATED DIALOGUE EXAMPLES

The system can make variable dialogues with respect to initiative, utterance types
and the amount of contents in a turn. Here the amount of contents is measured
by the number of a unit path connecting adjacent nodes: a single content and
multiple contents signify one unit path and multiple unit paths, respectively. The
actual system output for the example maps in Figure 2 are explained to contrast
the difference of one parameter while holding the others constant. The original
Japanese output is translated into English.

As a base example, Table IV shows non-mixed initiative, request-based, and
single content dialogues. At the first and the second turns, speaker A proposes a
path from Node03 to Node06, and speaker B rejects A's request, because there
is no outgoing links from Node06 on B's map. At the third and the fourth turns,
A proposes another candidate path from Node03 to Node02, and B accepts the
proposed route, because A's and B's route candidates are the same up to Node08.
At the fifth turn, A proposes a next path from Node02 to Node04.

Table V shows mixed initiative, request-based, and single content dialogues. At
the first two turns are the same as non-mixed initiative, request-based and single
content in a turn dialogue. However, at the third and fourth turns, A proposes a
path from Node03 to Node02, which is accepted by B at the fourth turn. In the
same turn, B takes the initiative by proposing a new path from Node02 to Node04.
In this utterance, B describes Node04 as "the stop at the left of Node02", since
there is no name on Node04 on A's map. At the fifth turn, A accepts B's proposal,

Table VI. Dialogue simulation example of question-based dialogue

---

1	**A**	Is Node03 connected to Node06?
2	**B**	(Yes.) Node03 is connected to Node06.
3	**A**	I would like you to go from Node03 to Node06.
4	**B**	(No.) I am not going from Node03 to Node06.
5	**A**	Is Node03 connected to Node02?

Table VII. Dialogue simulation example with multiple utterances in a turn

---

1	**A**	I would like you to go from Node03 to Node06.
		I would like you to go from Node06 to Node10.
2	**B**	(No.) I am not going from Node03 to Node06.
3	**A**	I would like you to go from Node03 to Node02.
		I would like you to go from Node02 to Node04.
4	**B**	(Ok.) I am going from Node03 to Node02.
		(Ok.) I am going from Node02 to Node04.

---

in which A explicitly mentions Node04 so that B can learn it, and proposes a new path from Node04 to "the stop above Node04".

Table VI shows mixed initiative, question-based, and single content dialogues. At the first turn, speaker A checks the connection between Node03 and Node06, and proposes this path after receiving B's positive answer about the connection. Upon receiving B's rejection of going from Node03 to Node06, A again checks the connection between Node03 to Node02. The difference between request- and question-based is that the former just proposes a path while the latter checks the connection before proposing one.

Table VII shows mixed initiative, request-based and multiple contents dialogues. At the first and the second turns, speaker A consecutively proposes a path from

Table VIII. The experimental results for map 1

			Spkr 2			
		NMID	MID:RS	MID:QS	MID:RM	MID:QM
Spkr1	RS	51, 780	31, 691	51, 1167	27, 889	33, 1327
	QS	90, 1647	54, 1180	89, 1955	36, 1082	48, 1713
	RM	27, 889	26, 890	32, 1015	29, 1023	35, 1469
	QM	40, 1785	35, 1402	51, 1974	29, 1443	30, 1741

Table IX. The experimental results for map 2

		NMID	MID:RS	Spkr 2 MID:QS	MID:RM	MID:QM
	RS	62, 1056	70, 1784	93, 2383	55, 2141	79, 3285
Spkr1	QS	105, 2103	119, 3002	170, 4276	75, 2629	75, 2921
	RM	34, 1203	37, 1518	51, 1847	36, 1543	38, 1825
	QM	47, 2188	55, 2530	65, 2729	63, 3068	66, 3414

Table X. The experimental results for map 3

		NMID	MID:RS	Spkr 2 MID:QS	MID:RM	MID:QM
	RS	136, 2382	164, 4132	213, 5404	90, 3643	154, 6567
Spkr1	QS	252, 5076	215, 5461	258, 6470	115, 4327	136, 5999
	RM	69, 2749	87, 3679	113, 4311	90, 4048	125, 5891
	QM	130, 5565	152, 6882	130, 5911	130, 6708	148, 7389

Node03 to Node10, and speaker B rejects the proposal. At the third turn, A again proposes a path from Node3 to Node04, which is accepted by B.

4.3. EXPERIMENTAL RESULTS AND DISCUSSIONS

Table VIII, IX and X show the experimental results, the number of turns and characters, obtained by running the implemented dialogue system for the three kinds of maps explained above. Variations of initiative are abbreviated as NMID (non-mixed initiated dialogue) and MID (mixed initiated dialogue), utterance types are R (request-based), Q (question-based), and the number of contents is S (single content in a turn) and M (multiple contents in a turn).

4.3.1. *The Characteristics of the Task*

The problem difficulty calculated by the ratio between the length of the shortest common route and that of each shortest route can predict the efficiency of a dialogue. The problem difficulty approximately reflects the search space for solving the problem. Thus, difficult problems, such as those using map 3 require more information exchanges than easy ones, such as those using map 1. The reason the difficulty ratios between the maps are not exactly reflected in the number of characters is that some information might be able to efficiently reduce the number of solution candidates.

4.3.2. Question-based vs. Request-based

Question-based dialogues (route connection or precondition checking) are at the worst case two-times less efficient than request-based ones in terms of the number of turns and characters. In the route finding tasks, proposing a route can function as a check of the route connection, because the second speaker should reject the first speaker's proposal when the route is disconnected. Thus, in question-based dialogues, precondition checking and proposal do the same job. This duplication is the reason dialogues with precondition checking are less efficient than those without it. In spite of this fact, conversational participants tend to ask the other participants about the route connection in actual human-human dialogues in the route finding task (Ishizaki, 1997). This can be explained by the Grice's maxim of quality 'do not say for which you lack adequate evidence'. In our case, when people use expressions of request, they should have some evidence for the truth of the content of the request. If human-computer systems are supposed to be used in the situations where efficiency of interaction is the most important, friendliness (or naturalness) of interaction is not so important and some operation failures due to interactional misunderstanding are not serious, request-based dialogues are better than question-based dialogues.

4.3.3. Single Content vs. Multiple Contents

Dialogues with single content is less efficient than those with multiple contents in most cases in terms of the number of turns, however the former is more efficient than the latter in half of the cases in terms of the number of characters. The reason for this result is that multiple content dialogues need less number of turns, however, their efficiency is degraded by the contents based on the wrong assumptions (of the route connection). Multiple content dialogues can be said to be suitable for the applications in which the communication cost is high, not for the applications in which the cost of utterances are high or there are many uncertain factors in the dialogue tasks.

4.3.4. Non-mixed Initiative vs. Mixed Initiative

With easy problems such as those using map 1, the efficiency of mixed-initiative dialogue is a little better than or equal to that of non-mixed-initiative dialogue. However, with difficult problems mixed-initiative dialogue is less efficient than non-mixed-initiative dialogue. In the case of easy problems, the agents can solve them by alternately proposing solution candidates, and the proposals can reduce fruitless solution candidates. In the case of difficult problems, however, the agents have more opportunities to propose solution candidates that make the partner search useless problem space.

Collaboration is expected to improve task performance, including the efficiency of goal achievement. However, these simulations show that mixed initiative dialogue is not always more efficient than non-mixed initiative dialogue. In this paper, we simulate simple utterances rather than simulating complex utterances, implementing various strategies of recovering from the misunderstanding and considering the communication costs. This is because we want to confirm a basic fact about initiative, in which as many unknown factors are excluded as possible. Which factors needs to be considered depend on the purposes of the applications. Our finding here establishes a starting point for the inquiry on initiative and the dialogue simulation techniques, and dialogue modelling developed here can be used as a means to further examine initiative from empirical and theoretical perspectives.

5. Conclusion

This paper confirmed a basic fact of whether mixed-initiative dialogue is always more efficient than non-mixed initiative dialogue on the basis of computer dialogue simulation for the route finding tasks. We adopted the dialogue modelling proposed in Conversation Analysis (Schegloff and Sacks, 1974; Levinson, 1983) and Discourse Analysis a lá the Birmingham school (Stubbs, 1983; Coulthard, 1985; Stenström, 1994). The definition of initiative is based on Whittaker and Stenton (1988). We implemented a system to simulate the dialogue model for the route finding task, and instantiated variations of this modelling. The results showed that mixed initiative dialogue is not always more efficient than non-mixed initiative dialogue.

Acknowledgements

We would like to thank Dr. Jean Carletta of the Human Communication Research Centre of the University of Edinburgh and Dr. Yasuharu Den of the Graduate School of Information Science of Nara Advanced Institute of Science and Technology for their helpful comments and suggestions.

References

Ahrenberg, L., N. Dahlbäck, and A. Jonssön: 1995, Coding scheme for studies of natural language dialogue. In: *Proceedings of AAAI Spring Symposium on Discourse Interpretation and Generation*. Stanford University, California, USA, pp. 8–13.
Akamine, T., O. Furuse, and H. Iida: 1994, A comprehensive Japanese sentence generation for spoken language translation. *Technical Report of Japan Society of Artificial Intelligence* SIG-J-94-01, 135–142. (in Japanese).
Allen, J., B. Miller, E. Ringger, and T. Sikorski: 1996, A robust system for natural spoken dialogue. In: *Proceedings of the Thirty-fourth Annual Meeting of the Association for Computational Linguistics*. University of California, Santa Cruz, California, USA, pp. 62–70.
Anderson, A. H., M. Bader, E. G. Bard, G. Doherty, S. Garrod, S. Isard, J. Kowtko, J. McAllister, J. Miller, C. Sotillo, H. Thompson, and R. Weinert: 1991, The HCRC maptask corpus. *Language and Speech* 34(4), 351–366.
Cawsey, A.: 1993, *Explanation and Interaction*. The MIT Press.
Chu-Carroll, J. and M. K. Brown: 1998, An evidential model for tracking initiative in collaborative dialogue interaction. *User Modeling and User-Adapted Interaction*. 8(3–4), pp. 215–254.

Coulthard, M.: 1985, *An Introduction to Discourse Analysis*. Longman.

Gross, D., J. Allen, and D. Traum: 1995, The TRAINS 91 dialogues. Technical report, Computer Science Department, The University of Rochester. TRAINS Technical Note 92-1.

Guinn, C. I.: 1998, Principles of mixed-initiative human-computer collaborative discourse. *User Modeling and User-Adapted Interaction*. 8(3–4), pp. 255–314.

Hasida, K. and Y. Den: 1997, A synthetic evaluation of dialogue systems. In: *Proceedings of the First International Workshop on Human-Computer Communication*. Grand Hotel Villa Serbelloni, Bellagio, Italy, pp. 77–82.

Ishizaki, M.: 1997, Mixed-initiative natural language dialogue with variable communicative modes. Ph.D. thesis, The Centre for Cognitive Science and The Department of Artificial Intelligence, The University of Edinburgh.

Levinson, S. C.: 1983, *Pragmatics*. Cambridge University Press.

Moore, J. D.: 1994, *Participating in Explanatory Dialogues*. The MIT Press.

Paris, C.: 1993, *User Modelling in Text Generation*. Frances Pinter.

Schegloff, E. A. and H. Sacks: 1974, Opening up closings. In: *Ethnomethodology: Selected Readings*. Penguin Education, pp. 233–264.

Smith, R. W. and D. R. Hipp: 1994, *Spoken Natural Language Dialogue Sytems*. Oxford University Press.

Stenström, A. B.: 1994, *An Introduction to Spoken Interaction*. Longman.

Stubbs, M.: 1983, *Discourse Analysis*. Blackwell.

Tashiro, T. and T. Morimoto: 1995, A parsing toolkit for spoken language processing. *Technical Report of Information Processing Society of Japan* SIG-NL-95-106, 67–72. (in Japanese).

Walker, M. A. and S. Whittaker: 1990, Mixed initiative in dialogue: An investigation into discourse segment. In: *Proceedings of the Twenty-eighth Annual Meeting of the Association for Computational Linguistics*. University of Pittsburgh, Pennsylvania, USA, pp. 70–78.

Whittaker, S. and P. Stenton: 1988, Cues and control in expert-client dialogues. In: *Proceedings of the Twenty-sixth Annual Meeting of the Association for Computational Linguistics*. State University, New York at Buffalo, Buffalo, New York, USA, pp. 123–130.

User Modeling and User-Adapted Interaction **9**: 93–132, 1999.
© 1999 *Kluwer Academic Publishers.*

93

A Computational Mechanism for Initiative in Answer Generation

NANCY GREEN[1] and SANDRA CARBERRY[2]
[1]*School of Computer Science, Carnegie Mellon University, Pittsburgh, Pennsylvania 15213;*
e-mail: Nancy.Green@cs.cmu.edu
[2]*Dept. of Computer Science, University of Delaware, Newark, Delaware 19716;*
e-mail: carberry@cis.udel.edu

(Received 15 November 1997; accepted in final form 7 March 1998)

Abstract. Initiative in dialogue can be regarded as the speaker taking the opportunity to contribute more information than was his obligation in a particular discourse turn. This paper describes the use of *stimulus conditions* as a computational mechanism for taking the initiative to provide unrequested information in responses to Yes–No questions, as part of a system for generating answers to Yes–No questions. Stimulus conditions represent types of discourse contexts in which a speaker is motivated to add unrequested information to his answer. Stimulus conditions may be triggered not only by the discourse context at the time when the question was asked, but also by the anticipated context resulting from providing part of the response. We define a set of stimulus conditions based upon previous linguistic studies and a corpus analysis, and describe how evaluation of these stimulus conditions makes use of information from a User Model. Also, we show how the stimulus conditions are used by the generation component of the system. An evaluation was conducted of the implemented system. The results indicate that the responses generated by our system containing extra information provided on the basis of this initiative mechanism are viewed more favorably by users than responses without the extra information.

Key words: natural language dialogue, discourse initiative

1. Introduction

We view *initiative* in dialogue as a speaker taking the opportunity to contribute more information than was his obligation in a particular discourse turn. Although research on initiative has generally studied who has control of a conversation and when a speaker should take control of a conversation to solicit information or direct the course of problem-solving (Whittaker & Stenton, 1988; Smith & Gordon, 1997; Guinn, 1998), a speaker also exhibits discourse initiative when he provides extra unsolicited information in his response (Chu-Carroll & Brown, 1998). For example, in (1)[1] the responder (labelled R) has provided an explanation of why R will not have enough time to come although the questioner (labelled Q) has not explicitly asked for that information.

---

[1] Levinson's (1983) example (55).

[277]

(1a)   Q: *What about coming here on the way or doesn't that give you enough*
              time?
(1b)   R: *Well no I'm supervising here.*

We have investigated conditions that motivate a responder to provide unrequested but relevant information in his response. More specifically, we are interested
in types of unrequested information that may be used as an indirect answer to a
Yes–No question, i.e., information which the speaker has decided to provide on his
own initiative but from which the direct answer can still be inferred. By a Yes–No
question we mean one or more utterances used as a request by Q (the questioner)
that R (the responder) convey R's evaluation of the truth of a proposition p. An
indirect answer implicitly conveys via one or more utterances R's evaluation of
the truth of the questioned proposition p, e.g., that p is true, that p is false, that
there is some truth to p, that p may be true, or that p may be false. While the
provision of a direct answer alone does not require the responder to take initiative,
the selection of the *content* of an indirect answer does. Since the motivation for
providing extra information depends heavily on beliefs about the questioner, a
system for generating indirect answers in dialogue must maintain and reason on
a model of the questioner.

According to one study of questions and responses in English (Stenström, 1985)
85 percent of responses to Yes–No questions containing a direct answer were accompanied by unrequested but relevant information. According to the author of
that study, this unrequested information was the same kind of information as that
used as indirect answers. (In other words, the presence or absence of a direct answer determined whether the information was classified as accompanying a direct
answer or as an indirect answer.). Moreover, 13 percent of responses to requests for
a Yes–No decision (realized as subject-auxiliary inverted questions or disjunctive
questions) and 7 percent of responses to requests for confirmation (realized by
tag questions or questions in declarative form) were indirect answers. Thus taking
the initiative to include extra unrequested information – whether manifested as an
indirect answer or in the occurrence of unrequested information accompanying a
direct answer – is common in dialogue.

This paper presents a computational mechanism for taking the initiative to provide
unrequested information in responses to Yes–No questions, as part of a general
model for generating and interpreting indirect answers (Green, 1994). One goal
of our work, and the focus of this paper, is to account for the selection of the
unrequested information. Unrequested information is selected during the first phase
of response generation, *content planning*. In this phase, the system makes use of
discourse plan operators to attempt to construct a full answer to the question, where
by a *full answer* we mean the direct answer and any warranted but unrequested
extra information. This extra information must satisfy an informational coherence
constraint (Moore & Pollack, 1992) and other applicability conditions of an operator. However, satisfaction of operator applicability conditions is not sufficient.

Our model makes uses of *stimulus conditions* associated with each of these discourse plan operators to characterize the speaker's motivation for including the extra information which can be provided by the operator. In short, only unrequested information which both satisfies the operator's applicability conditions and is motivated by one of its stimulus conditions will be included. (Thus, if nothing satisfies these requirements, then only the direct answer will be provided. On the other hand, a response that conveys multiple propositions, each motivated by a different stimulus condition, may be constructed in this model.) During the second phase of generation, *plan pruning*, the system prunes propositions that are inferrable from other parts of the full answer. (If the direct answer is one of the pruned propositions, then the remaining propositions function as an indirect answer.)

This model has been implemented in Common Lisp. To evaluate the model's initiative mechanism, we conducted a study in which human subjects were asked to select their preferred response from among several alternatives. The subjects preferred the responses produced by our system over the alternatives, one of which consisted solely of a direct answer. Moreover, the subjects declined to select responses containing extra information that was not motivated by one of our stimulus conditions. Thus the evaluation (described in Section 7.2) indicates that the responses generated by our system containing extra information provided on the basis of this initiative mechanism are viewed more favorably by users than responses without the extra information.

Section 2 describes motivation for including extra unsolicited information in a response, and provides examples from linguistic studies and a corpus of dialogues that we examined. Section 3 summarizes previous work on user modeling that provides the basis for inferring the kind of belief model that our system assumes is available. Section 4 describes the discourse plan operators used in our model to encode generic knowledge about constructing full answers, how these operators use stimulus conditions to trigger the inclusion of appropriate extra information, and how they use coherence rules to ensure that the intended informational coherence relations between generated propositions will be recognized. Section 5 describes the use of stimulus conditions in our generation algorithm, Section 6 discusses other factors that can affect the generation process, Section 7 describes the implementation and preliminary evaluation of our system, and Section 8 discusses related work.

2. Motivation for Initiative

We use the term *stimulus conditions* to refer to conditions that motivate a speaker to include unrequested information in a response. Stimulus conditions can be thought of as triggers that give rise to new speaker goals. While stimulus conditions may be derivative of deeper principles of cooperativity (Grice, 1975) or politeness (Brown & Levinson, 1978), they provide a level of precompiled knowledge which reduces the amount of reasoning required for content determination. Note that the situation triggering a stimulus condition may be either the actual situation before the system has begun constructing a response, or the *anticipated* situation which would result from providing part of the planned response.

Our methodology for identifying stimulus conditions was to survey previous linguistic studies, as well as to analyze the possible motivation of the speaker in a corpus of naturally occurring dialogues (SRI, 1992). (Our analysis focused just on stimulus conditions relevant to the generation of indirect answers to Yes–No questions.) In the linguistics literature, the motivation for providing unrequested information falls into four categories (following Stenström's list of reasons why speakers provide unrequested information in responses to Yes–No questions (Stenström, 1984)):

(1) to answer an implicit wh-question,
(2) to provide an explanation for an unexpected answer,
(3) to qualify a direct Yes or No answer, and
(4) social reasons.

To give an example of the first category, in (2)[2], Q's response both answers the implicit request for identification as well as indirectly answers the Yes–No question.

(2a)   Q: *Isn't your country seat there somewhere?*
(2b)   R: *Stoke d'Abernon.*

As for the second category, Stenström notes that extra information is often provided to justify a negative answer. Levinson (1983) claims that the presence of an explanation is one of several structural features of dispreferred responses such as refusals or unexpected answers to questions. For example, in (1b), R included extra information to explain his negative response, even though this information was not requested by Q.

To give an example of the third category, Hirschberg (1985) claims that speakers may give indirect answers to block potential unintended scalar implicatures of a *yes* or *no* alone. For example, in (3),[3] R's response is preferable to just *no* since that would license the incorrect scalar implicature that R had not read any of chapter one.

(3a)   Q: *Did you read the first chapter?*
(3b)   R: *I read the first half of it.*

To expand on the category of social reasons, Brown & Levinson (Brown & Levinson, 1978) show how various uses of language are motivated by politeness. According to Brown and Levinson, certain communicative acts are intrinsically *face-threatening acts* (FTAs). That is, doing an FTA is likely to injure some conversational participant's *face*, or public self-image. For example, orders and requests

---

[2] Stenström's (1984) example (65).

[3] Based on Hirschberg's (1985) example (211).

Table I. Stimulus conditions of satellite discourse plan operators

Satellite operator	Stimulus conditions
Use-cause	Explanation-indicated
	Excuse-indicated
Use-condition	Clarify-condition-indicated
Use-contrast	Appeasement-indicated
	Answer-ref-indicated
	Clarify-extent-indicated
	Substitute-indicated
Use-elaboration	Answer-ref-indicated
	Clarify-concept-indicated
Use-obstacle	Explanation-indicated
	Excuse-indicated
Use-otherwise	Explanation-indicated
	Excuse-indicated
Use-possible-cause	Explanation-indicated
Use-possible-obstacle	Explanation-indicated
	Excuse-indicated
Use-result	Explanation-indicated
Use-usually	Explanation-indicated

threaten the recipient's *negative face*, 'the want ... that his actions be unimpeded by others' (p. 67). On the other hand, disagreement or bearing 'bad news' threatens the speaker's *positive face*, the want to be looked upon favorably by others. Brown and Levinson describe a set of strategies, several of which are particularly relevant to the inclusion of extra information in a response:

(1) perform the FTA with *redressive action*, i.e. in a manner which indicates that no face threat is intended, using *positive politeness* strategies (strategies which increase the hearer's positive face). Such strategies include

- Strategy 1: attending to the hearer's interests or needs
- Strategy 6: avoiding disagreement, e.g., by displacing an answer

(2) perform the FTA with redressive action, using *negative politeness* strategies (strategies for increasing negative face). These include

- Strategy 6: giving an excuse or an apology, e.g., as in example (1b).

Stimulus conditions are used by the generation algorithm, described in Section 5, to aid in the selection of extra unrequested information. To give a preview, different *satellite* discourse operators (described in Section 4) are used to generate unrequested information in a response. In these operators, the function of a stimulus condition is to motivate the selection of unrequested information. However, the unrequested information must *also* satisfy the applicability conditions of the operator, which include coherence constraints on the extra information. (By convention, the name of a satellite operator describes the type of coherence constraint.) In other words, extra unrequested information in a response is licensed *jointly* by the stimulus conditions and applicability conditions of discourse operators. In Table I, for each satellite operator, we give the stimulus conditions included with it. In the rest of this section, we describe each of the stimulus conditions used in our model.

2.1. Definitions

This section gives one or more rules defining sufficient conditions for each stimulus condition in our model, and discusses how a user model contributes to identifying whether the conditions are satisfied. As mentioned above, while these rules provide sufficient conditions for stimulus conditions, a stimulus condition is *not* sufficient by itself to license the inclusion of unrequested information. (The variables in the stimulus conditions also occur in the applicability conditions of the discourse plan operators, which place additional coherence constraints on the information selected. For a proposition to be selected, it must satisfy at least one stimulus condition and all of the applicability conditions of a satellite operator. This process is described in more detail in Section 5.) The stimulus conditions defined in this section are based on the above linguistic studies as well as our corpus analysis. The rules are encoded as Horn clauses in the formalism of the theorem-prover used by the system. In this formalism, symbols prefixed with '?' are variables, all variables are implicitly universally quantified, and the antecedent conditions are implicitly conjoined. To define some of the terms used below, s and h denote the speaker and hearer, respectively. (*wbel agent p*), which we usually gloss as *agent suspects that p*, denotes that *agent* has a degree of belief less than certainty that p. (*unless p*) is true if p is not provable. Further, by convention, in all of the stimulus condition rules below, the variable $?p$ is the header variable of the satellite operator. (Thus, for example, in one of the immediate satellites of the *Answer-yes* or *Answer-no* operators, it would be bound to the questioned proposition of the Yes–No question.)

2.1.1. *Explanation-indicated*

The first stimulus condition, *Explanation-indicated*, triggers various types of causal explanations (e.g., *Use-obstacle*). For example in (4b),[4] which indirectly conveys a No, R gives an explanation of why R won't get a car, namely, because R's inability to drive is an *obstacle* to R's renting a car.

(4a)   Q: *actually you'll probably get a car won't you as soon as you get there*

---

[4] Stenström's (1984) (110)

(4b)   R: *can't drive*

This stimulus condition may contribute to greater dialogue efficiency by anticipating a follow-up request for an explanation (e.g., a follow-up by Q of *Why not?*). Formally, the condition is defined by the following rule.

```
((explanation-indicated s h ?p ?q)
<-
(wbel s (wbel h (not ?p)))
(unless (wbel s (accepts-authority h s)))))
```

This may be glossed as, *s* is motivated to give *h* an explanation *q* for *p*, where *p* is the questioned proposition, if *s* suspects that *h* suspects that *p* is not true, unless it is the case that *s* has reason to believe that *h* will accept *p* on *s*'s authority. In other words, the stimulus condition holds in situations where the hearer is likely to be surprised by the answer, unless the speaker has some reason to believe that the hearer would accept a direct answer without an explanation. In the above example, *p* is the proposition that R will not be getting a car and *q* is the proposition that R cannot drive. The knowledge used to determine whether the first antecedent holds might be old information in the current user model or might be derived on the basis of syntactic clues, e.g., the form of the question in (4a). The knowledge used to evaluate the truth of the second antecedent could be derived from the social roles of the dialogue participants (e.g., it may be inappropriate for Q to pry into R's reasons), or based on R's presumed superior knowledge of the subject (e.g., the current state of R's headache).

2.1.2. *Excuse-indicated*

Although the stimulus condition *Excuse-indicated* often prompts some of the same kinds of causal explanations as *Explanation-indicated*, it represents a different kind of motivation. A Yes–No question may be interpreted as a prerequest (Levinson, 1983) for a request, i.e. as an utterance used as a preface to another request. (In analyses of discourse based on speech act theory, e.g. Perrault & Allen (1980), prerequests are described as surface speech acts of utterances used to perform indirect speech acts.) Prerequests are often used to check whether a related request is likely to succeed, or to avoid having to make the other request directly. Thus, a negative answer to a Yes–No question used as a prerequest might be interpreted as a refusal. To soften the refusal, the speaker may give an explanation of the negative answer, as illustrated in (5).

(5a)   Q: *Can you tell me the time?*

(5b)   R: *No. My watch is broken.*

Formally, the condition is defined by the following rule.[5]

```
((excuse-indicated s h (not ?p) ?q)
<-
(wbel s (prerequest h s (informif s h ?p)))))
```

This may be glossed as, *s* is motivated to give *h* an excuse *q* for *(not p)*, where *p* is the questioned proposition of the Yes–No question, if *s* suspects that the Yes–No question is a prerequest. For example in (5a), *p* is the proposition *R can tell Q the time*, *q* is the proposition *R's watch is broken*, and the Yes–No question could be a prerequest for *What time is it?*. Techniques for interpreting indirect speech acts (Perrault & Allen, 1980; Hinkelman, 1989) can reason with a model of the questioner's beliefs to determine whether the antecedent holds, i.e., whether the Yes–No question can be analyzed as the surface speech act of an utterance used to perform an indirect speech act.

2.1.3. *Answer-ref-indicated*

This stimulus condition motivates the responder to identify a referent that is not explicitly requested by the question, as illustrated by (6),[6]

(6a)   Q: *You're on that?*

(6b)   *[Who's on that?]*

(6c)   R: *no no no*

(6d)   *Dave is.*

In (6), R has interpreted the question in (a) as a prerequest for the wh-question shown in (b). Thus, (d) not only answers the question in (a) but also the anticipated wh-question in (b). Formally, the condition is defined by the following rule.

```
((Answer-ref-indicated s h ?p ?q)
<-
(wbel s (want h (knowref h ?t ?q))))
```

This may be glossed as *s* is motivated to provide *h* with *q*, if *s* suspects that *h* wants to know the referent of a term *t* in *q*, where *q* is the answer to the anticipated wh-question. In (6), *p* is the proposition *R is on that*, and *q* is the proposition *Dave*

---

[5] One of the referees has provided an example which suggests an additional rule for *excuse-indicated* to cover cases in which Q's Yes–No question is a request to be informed whether R has fulfilled an obligation, and the answer is that R has not fulfilled the obligation. While we do not claim that the stimulus condition rules provided in our model are exhaustive, we expect that more rules can be incorporated without changing the overall approach to generating the responses.

[6] Stenström's (1984) example (102). Also, throughout the paper, propositions that are not explicitly stated are enclosed by square brackets.

is on that. As in *Excuse-indicated*, techniques for interpreting indirect speech acts can be used to determine if the antecedent holds.[7]

2.1.4. *Substitute-indicated*

This stimulus condition motivates the responder to identify the referent of a term that may be helpful to the questioner, as in (7c) below. Although Q may not have intended to use (7a) as a prerequest for the question *What vegetarian menu items do you have?*, R suspects that the answer to this wh-question might be helpful to Q.

(7a)   Q: *Do you have veggie burgers?*
(7b)   R: [*no*]
(7c)   *We have vegetarian chili.*

Formally, the condition is defined by the following rule.

```
((Substitute-indicated s h ?p ?q)
<-
(wbel s (need h (knowref h ?t ?q))))
```

This may be glossed as, *s* is motivated to provide *h* with *q*, if *s* suspects that it would be *helpful* for *h* to know the referent of a term *t* in *q*. In the above example, *p* is the proposition *The restaurant has veggie burgers*, and *q* is the proposition *We have vegetarian chili*. The antecedent would hold whenever obstacle detection techniques (Allen and Perrault, 1980), reasoning on an inferred model of *h*'s (the questioner's) plan, determine that *h*'s not knowing the referent of *t* is an obstacle to *h*'s plan.

2.1.5. *Clarify-concept-indicated*

This stimulus condition motivates the responder to elaborate on certain atypical instances of a concept in order to avoid a possible misunderstanding, as illustrated in (8b)[8] below.

(8a)   Q: *Do you have a pet?*
(8b)   R: *We have a turtle.*

In other words, since turtles are not typical pets, Q might not consider a Yes answer to the question in (8a) to be truthful if R's only pet is a turtle. Formally, the condition is defined by the following rule.

---

[7]   The antecedent is stated in terms of the goal of the indirect speech act, rather than in terms of a particular surface speech act (as in the above rule for *Excuse-indicated*) to allow for cases like (6a) where the surface speech act does not have an argument for the term *t*.

[8]   Hirschberg's (1985) example (177).

```
((Clarify-concept-indicated s h ?p ?q)
<-
(concept ?p ?c)
(has-atypical-instance ?q ?c))
```

This may be glossed as, s is motivated to clarify p to h with q, if p has a concept c such that q provides an atypical instance of c. In the above example, p would be the proposition that *we have c* where c is the concept of a pet, and q the proposition that *we have a turtle*. Identifying what would be regarded as an atypical instance requires reasoning on a user model that includes stereotypical beliefs.

2.1.6. *Clarify-condition-indicated*

This stimulus condition motivates the responder to include extra information about conditions that could affect the veracity of the response, as illustrated by (9c).[9]

(9a)   Q: *Um let me can I make the reservation and change it by tomorrow*
(9b)   R: *[yes]*
(9c)   *if it's still available.*

In (9), a truthful Yes answer depends on the truth of (c). Formally, the stimulus condition is defined by the following rules.

```
((Clarify-condition-indicated s h ?p ?q)
<-
(ignorant s ?q))

((Clarify-condition-indicated s h ?p ?q)
<-
(wbel s (not ?q)))
```

These may be glossed as, s is motivated to clarify a condition q for p to h

(1) if s doesn't know if q holds, or
(2) if s suspects that q does not hold.

In the above example, p is the proposition *Q can make the reservation and change it by tomorrow*, and q the proposition *it is available tomorrow*. For this stimulus condition, it is the responder's own beliefs about the condition, not the responder's beliefs about the questioner's beliefs, that trigger the provision of extra information.

---

[9] American Express tape 10ab.

2.1.7. *Clarify-extent-indicated*

This stimulus condition prompts the responder to include extra information that qualifies the extent to which a Yes or No answer holds, as illustrated by (10b).[10]

(10a)   Q: *Have you gotten the letters yet?*

(10b)   R: *I've gotten the letter from X.*

On the strict interpretation of (10a), Q is asking whether R has gotten *all* of the letters, but on a looser interpretation, Q is asking if R has gotten *any* of the letters. Then, if R has gotten some but not all of the letters, a Yes would be untruthful. However, if Q is speaking loosely, then a No might lead Q to erroneously conclude that R has not gotten any of the letters. R's answer circumvents this problem, by conveying the extent to which the questioned proposition (on the strict interpretation) is true. Formally, the condition is defined by the following rules.

```
((clarify-extent-indicated s h (some-truth ?p) ?q)
<-
(wbel s (ignorant h ?q))
(believe s (highest-true-exp ?q ?p)))

((clarify-extent-indicated s h (not ?p) ?q)
<-
(wbel s (ignorant h ?q))
(believe s (highest-true-exp ?q ?p)))
```

These may be glossed as, *s* is motivated to clarify to *h* the extent *q* to which *p* is true, or the alternative *q* to *p* which is true, if *s* suspects that *h* does not know if *q* holds, and *s* believes that *q* is the highest expression alternative to *p* that does hold. In the above example, *p* is the proposition *R has gotten the letters* and *q* is the proposition *R has gotten the letter from X*. According to Hirschberg (1985), sentences p_i and p_j (representing the propositional content of two utterances) are expression alternatives if they are the same except for having comparable components e_i and e_j, respectively. Further, Hirschberg claims that in a particular discourse context, there may be a partial ordering of values which the discourse participants mutually believe to be salient, and that the ranking of e_i and e_j in this ordering can be used to describe the ranking of p_i and p_j. In the above example, (10b) is a realization of the highest true expression alternative to the questioned proposition, *p*, i.e. the proposition that R has gotten all the letters. Once again, *s* must reason on a model of *h*'s beliefs to evaluate whether the first of the above antecedents hold. The truth of the second antecedent involves the speaker's beliefs about the mutually salient set, and his own private belief about particular elements of that set.

---

[10] Hirschberg's (1985) example (59).

2.1.8. *Appeasement-indicated*

This stimulus condition motivates the responder to offer extra information that may alleviate the questioner's possible disappointment that is entailed by the direct answer, as illustrated by (11b).[11]

(11a)   Q: *Did you manage to read that section I gave you?*
(11b)   R: *I've read the first couple of pages.*

In (11b), R conveys that there is some (though not much) truth to the questioned proposition in an effort to soften his answer. Note that more than one stimulus condition may motivate R to include the same satellite. E.g., in (11b), R may have been motivated also by *clarify-extent-indicated*, which was described above. However, it is possible to provide a context for (11) where *appeasement-indicated* holds but not *clarify-extent-indicated*, or a context where the converse is true. Formally, the condition is defined by the following rules.

```
((appeasement-indicated s h (not ?p) ?q)
<-
(wbel s (undesirable h (not ?p)))
(wbel s (desirable h ?q)))

((appeasement-indicated s h (some-truth ?p) ?q)
<-
(wbel s (undesirable h (not ?p)))
(wbel s (desirable h ?q)))
```

This may be glossed as, *s* is motivated to appease *h* with *q* for *p* not holding or only being partly true, if *s* suspects that (*not p*) is undesirable to *h* but that *q* is desirable to *h*. In the above example, *p* is the proposition *R has read the section that Q gave R*, and *q* is the proposition *R has read the first couple of pages of it*. The antecedents to this rule would be evaluated using heuristic rules of rational agency and stereotypical and specific knowledge about *h*'s desires. For example, two heuristics of rational agency that might lead to beliefs about *h*'s desires are

(1) if an agent wants you to perform an action A, then your failure to perform A may be undesirable to the agent, and
(2) if an agent wants you to do A, then it is desirable to the agent that you perform a part of A.

---

[11] Hirschberg's (1985) example (56).

Table II. General principles underlying stimulus conditions

Principle	Stimulus Condition	Reasons
Efficiency	explanation-indicated	explain unexpected answer
	answer-ref-indicated	answer implicit wh-q
Accuracy	clarify-concept-indicated	qualify answer
	clarify-extent-indicated	qualify answer
	clarify-condition-indicated	qualify answer
Politeness	excuse-indicated	social (N1: excuse)
	appeasement-indicated	social (P1: attend to hearer, P6: avoid disagreement)
	substitute-indicated	social (P1: attend to hearer)

2.2. SUMMARY

In summary, the stimulus conditions in our model can be classified according to three general principles, as shown in Table II. In the third column, we show how our taxonomy of stimulus conditions relates to the four reasons listed in the beginning of this section; for category 4 (social reasons), the relevant politeness strategy from (Brown & Levinson, 1978) is given as well.[12] The first principle, efficiency, includes the motivation to provide implicitly requested information as well as to provide an explanation for unexpected information. In other words, giving this type of extra information contributes to the efficiency of the conversation by eliminating the need for follow-up wh-questions or follow-up *why not?* questions, respectively. Under the principle of accuracy, in addition to the reason cited by Hirschberg (which is represented in our model as *clarify-extent-indicated*), we have identified two other reasons for giving extra information which contribute to accuracy. The principle of politeness includes reasons for redressing face-threatening acts using positive and negative politeness strategies.

3. Acquiring Information for the User Model

The above stimulus conditions use information about the questioner's beliefs and the plan that the questioner is pursuing. This information can be obtained from stereotypical beliefs that the questioner is likely to hold, from beliefs that have been explicitly stated by the questioner or inferred from the preceding dialogue, from analysis of the questioner's utterance, and from incrementally inferring the questioner's plan over the course of the dialogue. Although our system requires access to such knowledge, it is not the purpose of our research to investigate techniques

---

[12] *N*1 refers to negative strategy 1, *P*1 refers to positive strategy 1, and *P*6 refers to positive strategy 6.

for obtaining this information. However, in this section, we discuss previous work on user modeling that provides a good basis for acquiring the needed information.

One way to hypothesize a number of user beliefs after only a short interaction with the user is to employ stereotypes. A stereotype is a cluster of related characteristics that can be ascribed to the user based on some triggering mechanism, such as the user's level of expertise in a domain. A number of researchers have investigated the construction of user models based on stereotypes (Rich, 1979; Chin, 1989). Balim & Wilks (1991) developed a nested belief model that captures an agent's beliefs about other agents' beliefs. Their system combines belief ascription based on stereotypes with belief ascription based on perturbations of the system's own beliefs. User modeling shell systems typically provide a facility for defining and employing stereotypes (Kay, 1995; Kobsa & Pohl, 1994).

Although stereotypes provide a rich set of characteristics that might reasonably be attributed to the user, direct analysis of the user's actions can provide evidence of individual knowledge and beliefs. If the user's actions consist of natural language utterances, then an analysis of the syntactic form of each utterance can identify presuppositions that represent beliefs that the user implicitly conveys via the utterance. This was the approach taken by Kobsa (1984) in the VIE-DPM system. For example, from an utterance such as

Which directory did Mary put the latex macros in?

VIE-DPM could identify presuppositions such as

(1) the speaker believes that latex macros exist,
(2) the speaker believes that the latex macros were put into a directory, and
(3) the speaker believes that the hearer knows which directory the macros were placed in.

Kass (1991) developed a set of heuristics based on general features of human behavior for hypothesizing user beliefs. For example, his concept generalization heuristic states that if the user knows of three concepts that are all specializations of a more general concept D, then one can rationally conclude that the user knows about D. Similarly, his agent rule states that if the system believes that the user has performed an action A, then one can rationally conclude that the user knows about A and how to perform A.

Although these models provide a variety of strategies for hypothesizing a model of the user's beliefs, they do not provide a model of uncertain belief which is essential for evaluating some of our stimulus conditions. Galliers (1991; 1992) specified a nonnumeric theory of belief revision which relates strength of belief to persistence of belief. She points out that a belief model for communication must contain a multi-strength model of belief that can be modified as the conversation proceeds. She uses endorsements (Cohen, 1985) in an assumption-based truth maintenance system (ATMS; DeKleer, 1986) to specify a system that orders beliefs according to how strongly they are held. This ordering is used to calculate which beliefs should be revised when beliefs are challenged in the course of conversation. Driankov developed a logic in which belief/disbelief pairs capture how strongly a proposition is believed (Driankov, 1988; Bonarini et al. 1990). Driankov's work is the first formally defined and well-developed logic that models strength of belief. Although his model appears to provide the kind of representational capability needed by our system, it has not as yet been used in acquiring a model of the user's beliefs over the course of a dialogue.

Galliers and Driankov provide mechanisms for reasoning with beliefs of different strengths, but they do not address how the syntactic form of an utterance conveys the strength of the speaker's beliefs. In research on recognizing expressions of doubt (Lambert & Carberry, 1992a; Lambert & Carberry, 1992b), it has been posited that certain utterances, such as surface negative questions of the form *Isn't Dr. Smith on sabbatical?*, convey a strong but uncertain belief in the proposition that Dr. Smith is on sabbatical whereas other utterances such as *I think that Dr. Smith is on sabbatical* convey a weaker belief. Thus a belief reasoning module is needed that takes into account the syntactic form of utterances in modeling the strength of different user beliefs.

A number of researchers have investigated techniques for inferring a model of an agent's plan (Allen & Perrault, 1980; Carberry, 1988b; Litman & Allen, 1987; Lambert & Carberry, 1991; Pollack, 1986). Allen formulated heuristics for identifying obstacles in the inferred domain plan, including knowledge deficits that could be overcome via helpful information from the respondent. In addition, Allen (Perrault & Allen, 1980) showed how plan recognition techniques could be used to recognize the intended meaning of indirect speech acts.

The above strategies form a basic set of techniques for inferring a model of an agent's beliefs and plans. Our system assumes the existence of such a user model that can be accessed in order to evaluate whether stimulus conditions are satisfied.

4. Discourse Plan Operators and Coherence Rules

Our computational model for generating responses to Yes–No questions makes use of discourse plan operators that encode generic programs for expressing what we refer to as a *full answer*. A full answer consists of the direct answer and any additional relevant information which the system decides to provide on its own initiative. For example, the discourse plan operators for constructing full Yes (*Answer-yes*) and full No (*Answer-no*) answers are shown in Figure 1. (All five top-level operators are shown in Appendix II.)

To briefly describe our formalism, variables are denoted by symbols prefixed with '?'. The first line of a discourse plan operator specifies the type of discourse act, the participants, and a propositional variable. For example, (*Answer-yes s h p*) describes the act of speaker *s* giving a Yes answer to the request made by hearer *h* that *h* be informed of *s*'s evaluation of the truth of the questioned proposition, *p*. *Applicability conditions* (Carberry, 1988b) are conditions which must hold for an

```
(Use-contrast s h ?p):              (Use-obstacle s h ?p):
  Existential variable: ?q            Existential variable: ?q
  Applicability conditions:           Applicability conditions:
    (bel s                              (bel s
      (cr-contrast ?q ?p))                (cr-obstacle ?q ?p))
    (Plausible                          (Plausible
      (cr-contrast ?q ?p))                (cr-obstacle ?q ?p))
  Stimulus conditions:                Stimulus conditions:
    (answer-ref-indicated               (explanation-indicated
      s h ?p ?q)                          s h ?p ?q)
    (clarify-concept-indicated          (excuse-indicated
      s h ?p ?q)                          s h ?p ?q)
    (appeasement-indicated
      s h ?p ?q)
    (substitute-indicated
      s h ?p ?q)
  Nucleus:                            Nucleus:
    (inform s h ?q)                     (inform s h ?q)
  Satellites:                         Satellites:
    (Use-cause s h ?q)                  (Use-obstacle s h ?q)
    (Use-elaboration s h ?q)            (Use-elaboration s h ?q)
  Primary goals:                      Primary goals:
    (BMB h s (cr-contrast ?q ?p))       (BMB h s (cr-obstacle ?q ?p))
```

Figure 1. Discourse plan operators for Yes and No answer.

operator to be selected but which the planner will not attempt to bring about. For example, the second applicability condition of *Answer-no* requires that the speaker believe that *p* is false. The primary goals of a discourse plan specify the intended effects of the plan.

The *nucleus* and *satellites*[13] describe communicative acts to be performed to achieve the goals of the plan. *Inform* is a primitive act that can be realized directly. The nonprimitive acts are defined by discourse plan operators themselves. Thus, a discourse plan may have a hierarchical structure. The satellites describe which types of unrequested but relevant information may be included in the response. A full answer may contain zero, one, or more instances of each type of satellite specified in the operator. However, an instance of a satellite may not be included unless at least one of its stimulus conditions and all of its applicability conditions are satisfied. (Also, as discussed in Section 5, the current algorithm does not search for more than one instance of a satellite satisfying the same stimulus condition and applicability conditions.)

---

[13] This terminology was borrowed from Rhetorical Structure Theory (Mann & Thompson, 1987).

```
(Use-contrast s h ?p):              (Use-obstacle s h ?p):
  Existential variable: ?q            Existential variable: ?q
  Applicability conditions:           Applicability conditions:
    (bel s (cr-contrast ?q ?p))         (bel s (cr-obstacle ?q ?p))
    (Plausible (cr-contrast ?q ?p))     (Plausible (cr-obstacle ?q ?p))
  Stimulus conditions:                Stimulus conditions:
    (answer-ref-indicated s h ?p ?q)    (explanation-indicated s h ?p ?q)
    (clarify-concept-indicated s h ?p ?q)  (excuse-indicated s h ?p ?q)
    (appeasement-indicated s h ?p ?q)   Nucleus:
    (substitute-indicated s h ?p ?q)      (inform s h ?q)
  Nucleus:                            Satellites:
      (inform s h ?q)                   (Use-obstacle s h ?q)
  Satellites:                           (Use-elaboration s h ?q)
    (Use-cause s h ?q)                Primary goals:
    (Use-elaboration s h ?q)            (BMB h s (cr-obstacle ?q ?p))
  Primary goals:
    (BMB h s (cr-contrast ?q ?p))
```

Figure 2. Two satellite discourse plan operators.

For example, consider the *Use-contrast* and *Use-obstacle* discourse plan operators, shown in Figure 2, describing possible satellites of *Answer-no*. In general, each satellite operator in our model has applicability conditions analogous to those shown in Figure 2. The first applicability condition of the *Use-obstacle* operator requires that the speaker believe that the relational proposition (Mann & Thompson, 1983) *(cr-obstacle q p)* holds for some propositions q and p instantiating the variables $?q$ and $?p$, respectively. The second applicability condition requires the relational proposition to be *mutually plausible*, so that the hearer will be able to recognize the intended relational proposition.

The truth of the latter type of applicability condition is determined in our model by a set of *coherence rules*. Encoded as Horn clauses, the coherence rules provide sufficient conditions for the mutual plausibility of a relational proposition $(CR\ q\ p)$, where CR is a coherence relation (similar to the informational relations of (Mann & Thompson, 1983)), and q and p are propositions. If the relational proposition is plausible to the system with respect to the beliefs which it presumes to be shared with the questioner, we assume that it would also be plausible to the questioner. The presence of mutual plausibility requirements in the applicability conditions of our satellite discourse plan operators ensures that the proposition realized by the satellite will be interpreted by the questioner as having the intended relationship to its nucleus.

Although domain-specific knowledge may be required for the evaluation of a coherence rule, the rules themselves do not contain domain-specific knowledge. To give an example, one of the coherence rules for *cr-obstacle* is shown below.

```
((Plausible (cr-obstacle (not (in-state ?sq ?tq))
                         (not (occur ?ep ?tp))))
<-
(MB (state ?sq))
(MB (event ?ep))
(MB (timeperiod ?tq))
(MB (timeperiod ?tp))
(MB (before-or-includes ?tq ?tp))
(MB (app-cond ?sq ?ep))
(unless (MB (in-state ?sq ?tq)))
(unless (MB (occur ?ep ?tp))))
```

The rule can be glossed as:

> It is mutually plausible to the speaker and hearer that (*cr-obstacle q p*) holds, where *q* is the proposition (*not* (*in-state sq tq*)) and *p* is the proposition (*not* (*occur ep tp*)), if it is mutually believed that time period *tq* starts before or includes *tp* and that state *sq* is an applicability condition of a typical plan for doing *ep* (unless it is mutually believed that state *eq* does hold during *tq* or that event *ep* does occur during *tp*).[14]

For example in (12), *q* is the proposition *R does not have R's checkbook*, and *p* is the proposition *R is not going to pay by check*, i.e., not having one's checkbook is an obstacle to paying by check.

(12a)   Q: *Are you going to pay by check?*

(12b)   R: *No.*

(12c)   R: *I don't have my checkbook.*

In our model, applicability conditions are necessary but not sufficient for deciding to include a satellite in the response. Each satellite operator also includes *stimulus conditions* (as described in Section 2). In order for an instance of a satellite to be included, all of the applicability conditions and at least one of the stimulus conditions of the satellite operator must be true. In addition to being triggered by the current state of the user model, stimulus conditions may be triggered by the user's anticipated reaction to part of the planned response. This will be described and illustrated in Section 5.

In addition to five top-level discourse plan operators, our model includes ten satellite operators that capture the range of types of extra information that our studies have shown can be realized as an indirect answer to a Yes–No question. The stimulus conditions associated with each of the satellite operators were given in Table 1.

---

[14] The purpose of the antecedent clauses beginning with *unless* is to eliminate candidates during interpretation, and can be ignored for the purposes of this discussion. The interpretation component is described in (Green, 1994).

5. Initiative in the Generation Algorithm

This section describes our generation algorithm, focusing on the computational mechanism for taking the initiative to provide unrequested information in the response. The algorithm is invoked whenever it is the system's turn and the strongest discourse expectation (Carberry, 1989) is that the system will provide an answer to a Yes–No question, that is, to a request to be informed of the truth of some proposition p.

The inputs to generation include

- the semantic representation of p,
- a set of discourse plan operators,
- a set of coherence rules,
- a set of stimulus condition rules, and
- the system's beliefs, including a model of the system's beliefs about the user's beliefs; the system's beliefs may be partitioned into:
    - beliefs which are presumed to be shared with Q (which we refer to as *shared* beliefs). Shared beliefs are required for determining when coherence relations are mutually plausible, and thus constrain what information can be provided as an indirect answer.
    - beliefs which are not presumed to be shared with Q (which we refer to as *non-shared* or *private* beliefs). Non-shared beliefs (including beliefs about the hearer's beliefs) may trigger certain stimulus conditions.

The output of the generation algorithm is a discourse plan which can be realized by a tactical generation component (McKeown, 1985). We assume that when answer generation begins, the system's *only* goal is to satisfy the discourse expectation, and that the system can truthfully provide exactly one of the following answer types based upon its non-shared beliefs: *yes* (that p is true), *no* (that p is false), *partly yes* (that p is partly but not completely true), *maybe yes* (that the system suspects that p is true), or *maybe no* (that the system suspects that p is false).

Our initiative mechanism is used during the first phase of response generation, *content planning*. During content planning the generator creates a discourse plan for a full answer, i.e., a direct answer and extra appropriate information, e.g. (13b) given explicitly, followed by (13c)–(13e).

(13a)   Q: *Can you tell me my account balance?*
(13b)   R: *No.*
(13c)   *I cannot access your account records on our computer system.*
(13d)   *The line to our computer system is down.*
(13e)   *You can use the ATM machine on the corner to check your account.*

In the second phase of generation, *plan pruning*, the generator determines which propositions of the planned full answer are inferrable from the rest of the full answer and thus do not need to be explicitly stated. For example, given an appropriate

INPUT   sat-header: satellite operator header, (Use-CR s h p)
OUTPUT   sat-plans: list of instances of discourse plan operator with
                        header identical to sat-header, or null

1. Set sat-op to operator, (Use-CR s h ?p), with ?p instantiated with p
   from sat-header.
2. Set sat-plans to null.
3. For each stimulus condition SC of sat-op, create formula, PAT, which
   is conjunction of sat-op's applicability conditions and SC:
   3.a. If PAT is provable, then:
        3.a.1. Create instance, I, of sat-op using the assignment for the
               existential variable in PAT,
        3.a.2. Expand I's satellites, and
        3.a.3. Add I to sat-plans.

Figure 3. Algorithm for expanding a satellite.

model of Q's beliefs, our system generates a plan for asserting only the propositions conveyed in (13d) and (13e) as an answer to (13a).

5.1. GENERATION ALGORITHM

Content planning is performed by top-down expansion of an answer discourse plan operator. The process begins by instantiating each top-level answer discourse plan operator with the questioned proposition until one is found such that its applicability conditions hold. Note that since the applicability conditions of each of the top-level operators distinguish alternative possible evaluations of the truth of the queried proposition (that p is true, that p is false, that there is some truth to p, etc.), only one top-level discourse plan operator will be selected. Then, this operator is expanded. A discourse plan operator is expanded by deciding which of its satellites to include in the full answer and expanding each of them (recursively).

The algorithm for expanding satellites is given in Figure 3. Each stimulus condition of a satellite is considered in turn. If a conjunction of the applicability conditions and the current stimulus condition (i.e. the formula PAT in Figure 3) holds for some instantiation of the variables of the satellite, then that instance of the satellite is included in the plan. The same type of satellite (e.g., *Use-contrast*) may be included more than once if more than one stimulus condition of the satellite holds. For example, the speaker may decide to respond to (11a) with (11b) (repeated below) motivated by *Clarify-extent-indicated*, followed by (11c) motivated by *Appeasement-indicated*.[15]

(11a)   Q: *Did you manage to read that section I gave you?*
(11b)   R: *I've read the first couple of pages.*
(11c)   R: *But I've read all the other sections.*

In the current algorithm, only the first instance of a stimulus condition found to satisfy each PAT formula is incorporated into the satellite. An area for future work is to extend the model to account for how a speaker would select among alternatives satisfying the same PAT formula. (For example, if the speaker is motivated to provide an excuse, should he use the first excuse he finds, or search for all possible excuses; in the latter case, how should he choose which one(s) to use?) We assume that, lacking such a mechanism, it is preferable for our current system to include at most one instance satisfying each PAT formula.

The output of the content planning phase, an expanded discourse plan representing a full answer, is the input to the plan pruning phase of generation. The expanded plan is represented as a tree of discourse acts. The goal of this phase is to make the response more concise, i.e., to determine which of the planned acts can be omitted while still allowing Q to infer the full discourse plan. To do this, the generator considers each of the acts in the frontier of the tree from right to left. (This ensures that a satellite is considered before its related nucleus. Also, only a leaf that is a nucleus with a sibling satellite can be pruned.) The generator creates a trial plan consisting of the original plan minus the nodes pruned so far and minus the current node. Then, using the interpretation module (described in (Green, 1994)), the generator simulates Q's interpretation of a response containing the information that would be given explicitly according to the trial plan. If Q could infer the full plan (as the most preferred interpretation), then the current node can be pruned.[16] Otherwise, it is left in the plan and the next node is considered.

Note that plan pruning is a greedy algorithm, in the sense that an exhaustive trial of all possible prunings is not considered. We decided to use a greedy algorithm, in part, because of the time cost of simulating interpretation of each trial plan. (The interpretation component uses the discourse plan operators and coherence rules to recognize the underlying discourse plan. The main cost of discourse plan recognition is the cost of hypothesizing parts of the plan, other than the direct answer,

---

[15] Thus, if the *same* proposition satisfies more than one stimulus condition of the same satellite, then the current algorithm would incorporate the proposition into two satellites of the plan; in that case, e.g., (11b) would be repeated. A solution to this using a greedy approach would be to disallow the incorporation of a proposition that has already been incorporated into the plan by the algorithm. A more general solution would require a more sophisticated planning algorithm that could detect when a step in the plan satisfies multiple goals.

[16] In other words, the goal of pruning is not to *reduce* the information conveyed by the response, since all of the information in the full plan was selected in order to satisfy the request and the stimulus conditions. The goal is only to determine what parts of the response do not have to be explicitly realized by the sentence generator.

which have been pruned.) An area of future research which might eliminate the need to perform exhaustive trials, would be to take advantage of a more powerful planning paradigm such as (Young, 1994) during content planning.

5.2. EXAMPLE

To give a brief example of how unrequested information is selected, consider (13) repeated below. Although the full answer shown in (13b)–(13e) would be selected during the first phase of response generation, the parts of the response appearing in square brackets would not be given explicitly by the system if (during the second phase of response generation) the system determines that they are inferrable from the rest of the response. That is, our complete model accounts for the generation of (13d)–(13e) alone as an indirect answer.

(13a)   Q: *Can you tell me my account balance?*
(13b)   R: [*No.*]
(13c)   [*I cannot access your account records on our computer system.*]
(13d)   *The line to our computer system is down.*
(13e)   *You can use the ATM machine on the corner to check your account.*

First (13b), which provides the requested information, is selected as a consequence of instantiating an *Answer-no* operator (given in Figure 1) in order to satisfy the current discourse expectation. This operator specifies that a coherent No answer may include additional information representing an obstacle to the truth of the questioned proposition, i.e., information resulting from expanding a *Use-obstacle* satellite (given in Figure 2). In order for an instance of *Use-obstacle* to be included in the discourse plan, the system must be able to instantiate the satellite operator's existential variable with a proposition q satisfying the applicability conditions and at least one of the stimulus conditions. A search of the system's knowledge base of beliefs finds a proposition realizable as (13c) for the stimulus condition of *Excuse-indicated*. In other words, (13c) is included because the system suspects that Q said (13a) as a prerequest for a request to be told Q's account balance. The *Use-Obstacle* satellite whose nucleus is realized as (13c) can be expanded further: (13d) is provided as a *Use-Obstacle* satellite of (13c) motivated by the stimulus condition *Explanation-indicated*, i.e., because the system suspects that Q will be surprised by the information given in (13c). (13e) is provided as a *Use-Contrast satellite* of the top-level of the *Answer-No* plan, motivated by the *Substitute-indicated* stimulus condition.

In summary, each of the unrequested pieces of information can be seen as resulting from the system's beliefs about Q and the effect that other parts of the planned response may have on Q. The following imaginary dialogue between Q and R illustrates the role of stimulus conditions in deciding what unrequested information to include.

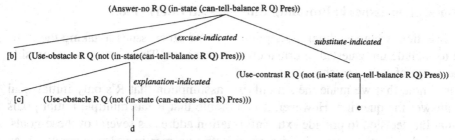

Figure 4. Discourse plan for example (3).

(13a)   Q: *Can you tell me my account balance?*

(13b)   R: *No, I cannot.*

       Q: *Why not?*

(13c)   R: *I cannot access your account records on our computer system.*

       Q: *Why not?*

(13d)   R: *The line to our computer system is down.*

       Q: *How can I check my account balance?*

(13e)   R: *You can use the ATM machine on the corner to check your account.*

In this example, the system has no other information on the subject and so will not provide any other information. Thus the full plan would contain the discourse acts shown in Figure 4, where the stimulus conditions are shown next to the arcs leading to a satellite operator. (The acts in the plan are labelled (b)–(e) corresponding to the part of (13) they represent.) Note that if this plan were output without undergoing plan pruning, it would be realized as a direct answer (13b), and extra information (13c)–(13e). An interesting area for future research is whether, given an agent's shared and non-shared beliefs, the applicability conditions and stimulus conditions sufficiently constrain the amount of unrequested information selected or whether other types of constraints should be incorporated (e.g., attentional, stylistic) into our model. Also, it remains to be seen whether different stimulus conditions should be given different priorities.

In phase two, plan pruning, the generator's overall goal is to make the answer as concise as possible. The plan pruning algorithm considers the primitive acts of the full plan shown in Figure 4 in the order (e), (d), (c), and (b). Since (e) and (d) are not inferrable from any other acts, they would be automatically retained in the plan. Next, a trial plan with (c) pruned from it would be considered. Interpretation of the response consisting of (b), (d), and (e) is simulated. Since the full plan could be inferred, (c) would be pruned. Next, another trial plan would be considered, where, in addition to (c), (b) has been pruned. Since the full plan could again be inferred from the resulting trial response consisting of just (d) and (e), (b) would also be pruned. The output of phase two would be the plan shown in Figure 4 with (b) and (c) marked as pruned.

6. Some other Issues in Providing Unrequested Information

In this section, we give a brief description of some other issues in taking the initiative to include unrequested information in a response. These issues were outside of the scope of our research.

First, note that we made the simplifying assumption that R's only initial goal is to answer the question. However, it is possible that R has multiple initial goals and that his decision to provide extra information addresses several of these goals. For example, R might have decided to give the answer in (14c) not only as an explanation, but also as background for R's request in (14d).

(14a)   Q: *Are you going to the lecture?*
(14b)   R: *[no]*
(14c)   *I have to get my brakes fixed.*
(14d)   *Can you recommend a garage near campus?*

Second, in addition to affecting syntactic and lexical aspects of discourse (Hovy, 1990; Makuta-Giluk, 1991; DiMarco & Hirst, 1993), stylistic goals may affect which and how much information is given. For example, a speaker may take the initiative to elaborate on an answer in order to make it more interesting, as shown in (15).

(15a)   Q: *Do you have a car?*
(15b)   R: *[yes]*
(15c)   *I bought a British-racing-green Austin-Healey 3000 last week.*

On the other hand, a stylistic goal of terseness may override the stimulus conditions we have provided for indirect answers. For example, depending upon the degree of Q's interest in R's affairs, the indirect answer in (16c)–(16f) may provide Q with more than Q cares to know.

(16a)   Q: *Are you going to the movies tonight?*
(16b)   R: *[no]*
(16c)   *I can't afford to.*
(16d)   *I spent $900 on my car last week.*
(16e)   *It needed a new transmission.*
(16f)   *The car is 15 years old.*

7. Implementation and Evaluation

7.1. IMPLEMENTATION

We have implemented a prototype of the model described in the preceding sections. The implementation, which runs on a standard work station, is written in Common Lisp and uses HCPRVR (Chester, 1980), a Horn clause theorem-prover

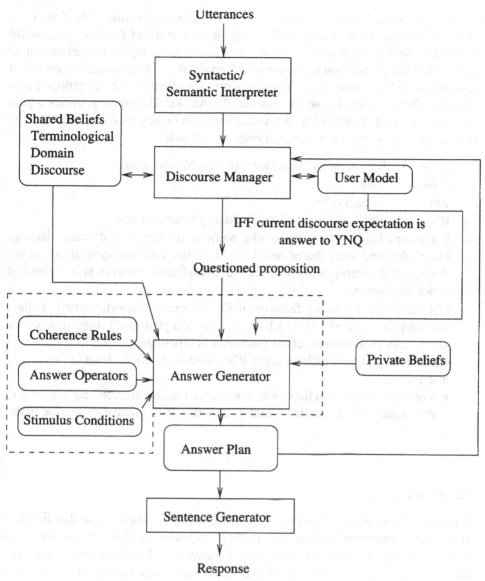

Figure 5. Discourse generation architecture.

also implemented in Lisp. The implemented system can produce all of the types of answers discussed in this paper, and has been tested on a variety of examples. (The results of an evaluation are discussed in the following section.) Figure 5 shows how the system would be integrated into a full discourse generation architecture. In the figure, functional components are enclosed in rectangles, and knowledge sources are enclosed in ovals. Our prototype includes the knowledge sources and components shown within the dashed lines. (For testing and evaluation, we also provided the system with a representation of the other required inputs.)

The Discourse Manager, which is responsible for maintaining the Discourse Model (Carberry, 1990) and providing high-level control of the dialogue, would invoke the Answer Generator whenever the current most highly ranked discourse expectation is a proposition of the form (*informif s h p*), the discourse expectation resulting from Q's asking R the Yes–No question (where *p* is the questioned proposition). If the system knows the answer, the Answer Generator provides a plan describing a direct or indirect answer to the Sentence Generator for realization. The knowledge sources used to generate a response include:

- discourse plan operators for answers to Yes–No questions,
- coherence rules,
- stimulus condition rules,
- R's shared terminological beliefs (including belief axioms),
- R's shared beliefs about the world, namely, stereotypical domain planning knowledge and other shared beliefs (both actual and stereotypical) about the domain, and stereotypical metabeliefs about relations between knowledge and action in planning,
- R's shared beliefs about features of the discourse context, namely, beliefs resulting from assertions which have been accepted in the discourse so far and beliefs about salient sets as discussed in (Hirschberg, 1985),
- the User Model, by which we mean R's non-shared beliefs about Q's beliefs,[17] and
- R's other non-shared beliefs, which includes the information requested by Q and unrequested information which R may take the initiative to provide in the response.

7.2. EVALUATION

Although the linguistic studies discussed in Section 2 clearly show that humans often include additional information in their responses to Yes–No questions, we conducted a brief study to determine how humans would evaluate responses actually produced by our system. For this evaluation, we selected an imaginary domain which had not been used for testing during development of the prototype. In this domain, a laboratory is inhabited by a talking robot and a mouse; outside of the laboratory is a manager who cannot see the laboratory, but the robot and manager can communicate with each other. This domain was selected because it could easily be presented to human subjects with a minimum of description about the beliefs that might motivate the robot's responses. Also, a new domain was used so that our experience with the other domains would not influence the evaluation. The system

---

[17] Although there is disagreement on the proper relationship between User Models and Discourse Models (Schuster et al., 1988), we distinguish the two here on pragmatic grounds, to emphasize the role of R's non-shared beliefs about Q's beliefs in triggering stimulus conditions.

was run to verify that it could actually generate the responses which were evaluated in the study.[18]

The study was conducted by means of a questionnaire (shown in Appendix I) given to ten subjects who were not familiar with our research. The beginning of the questionnaire includes a brief description of the domain, followed by a set of eleven Yes–No questions posed by the manager to the robot. Some of the questions are preceded by a few sentences to establish context. Each question is followed by a set of four possible responses by the robot. The subjects were told that each of the responses was a true statement in that domain, and were asked to select the response that they would view as best. For each question, the choices include a direct response of *Yes* or *No* (depending on the correct answer to the question), the direct response with further emphasis (such as *No, I can't*), and two extended responses that consist of the direct answer with extra information. In nine of the eleven questions, the extra information in one of the extended responses is motivated by one of our model's stimulus conditions (and was the response generated by our system for evaluation), while the extra information in the other extended response is not. In two of the questions, none of the responses contain extra information motivated by one of the stimulus conditions. The purpose of these two *bogus* examples was to make certain that the subjects were not inclined to always select responses with extra information.

The results are shown in Table III. The rows of the table present the results for each question. The second column lists the stimulus condition, if any, that triggers one of the possible responses to the question. Questions 3 and 7 were bogus questions in which none of the responses was motivated by a stimulus condition. The next three columns indicate respectively the number of subjects who selected the response motivated by the listed stimulus condition, the number who selected the direct answer alone or the direct answer with emphasis but no additional information, and the number who selected an extended response not motivated by a stimulus condition. Note that none of the subjects selected a response with extra information for the two bogus questions, indicating that they were not merely inclined to select responses with extra information. Although the overall results demonstrate that responses containing the kind of extra information produced by our system will be viewed favorably by users, questions 8 and 10 warrant further discussion.

The extra information in one of the responses to question 10 was motivated by the *Appeasement-indicated* stimulus condition. In that response, *No. I've put away*

---

[18] Our evaluation did not address the question of whether the system would generate indirect answers with the same frequency as reported in human-human dialogues, e.g., as reported in (Stenström, 1984). It would be difficult to evaluate this since the system's decision whether to provide the answer directly or indirectly depends upon the set of beliefs that are assumed to be shared. Moreover, that decision is independent of the initiative mechanism, since it is made during the plan pruning phase.

Table III. Results of study

	Stimulus Conditions SC	Response SC	Direct Answer Only	Other Extended Response
1.	answer-ref-indicated	10	0	0
2.	substitute-indicated	10	0	0
3.	none	0	10	0
4.	explanation-indicated	9	1	0
5.	clarify-extent-indicated	10	0	0
6.	clarify-condition-indicated	10	0	0
7.	none	0	10	0
8.	excuse-indicated	8	2	0
9.	clarify-concept-indicated	10	0	0
10.	appeasement-indicated	4	5	1
11.	explanation-indicated	9	1	0

most of the balls.,[19] the robot answers that he has not yet done the requested task (putting away the blocks), but attempts to appease the questioner by describing another task that he has completed (putting away most of the balls). Since only four of the ten subjects selected this response, it is possible that the subjects do not view appeasement as an appropriate stimulus condition in human-machine dialogue, despite the fact that it does occur in human-human dialogue. Alternatively, the subjects did not have enough information to recognize the response as attempted appeasement. Also, question 8 was problematic. The original question given to the first four subjects asked whether the robot could give the lab manager the time. The answer generated by the system (*No. There is no clock in here.*) was motivated by the stimulus condition *Excuse-indicated*. However, two of the four subjects selected the direct answer alone (*No.*) and subsequently explained that if the robot could tell time, then certainly he had an internal clock that he could use since all computers have internal clocks and thus the presence or absence of a clock in the room was immaterial. Since the beliefs of these subjects conflicted with the beliefs which were intended as the context for interpreting the robot's response, we altered the question for the remainder of the study to circumvent this problem.

The study supports our system's approach for taking the initiative to provide unsolicited information in response to Yes-No questions. It indicates that our stimulus condition mechanism produces responses containing extra information that users will view more favorably than responses without the extra information. However,

---

[19] Only one ball is shown in the picture. We intended for this response to describe a situation where a group of balls that were in the room had been put away and thus were no longer visible in the picture.

we have not addressed the question of when other stylistic considerations might limit the amount of extra information that is included, or how to choose among multiple instances satisfying the same stimulus condition of a satellite. Also, it would be useful to see whether subjects prefer extra information motivated by some stimulus conditions more than that motivated by other stimulus conditions. These issues will be addressed in future research.

8. Related Research

Some previous work in cooperative response generation describes discourse contexts in which certain types of unrequested information should be given in order to avoid misleading the questioner (Hirschberg, 1985; Joshi et al., 1984; vanBeek, 1987) or to help the questioner overcome obstacles to his inferred plans (Allen and Perrault, 1980). Contexts described in that work relevant to the generation and interpretation of answers to Yes–No questions have been represented in our model as stimulus conditions (e.g., *Clarify-extent-indicated*, *Answer-ref-indicated*). In addition to identifying other important stimulus conditions (e.g., *Explanation-indicated* and *Excuse-indicated*), our approach to providing unrequested information differs from past work in two ways. First, we provide a unified model for taking the initiative to provide this type of unrequested information. That is, use of stimulus conditions has been integrated into a general model for generating responses, and further, this model should be able to accommodate other stimulus conditions as they are discovered. Second, past work was generally limited to generating single-sentence responses sensitive to the actual discourse context. Our model is capable of generating multiple-sentence responses containing unrequested information addressing the actual discourse context as well as anticipating the effect of parts of the planned response on the addressee. Other research has addressed the inclusion of extra information in order to block erroneous inferences in extended explanations (Zukerman & McConachy, 1993), but this work does not address types of information that can be used as an indirect answer.

Our work differs from most previous work in cooperative response generation in that, in our model, the information given in an indirect answer conversationally implicates (Grice, 1975) the direct answer. Hirschberg (1985), who provided general rules for identifying when a scalar conversational implicature is licensed, claimed that speakers may give indirect responses to Yes–No questions in order to block potential incorrect scalar implicatures of a simple Yes or No. She implemented a system which determines whether the Yes/No[20] licenses any unwanted scalar implicatures, and if so, proposes alternative scalar responses which do not. This type of response is similar, in our model, to a speaker's use of *Use-contrast* motivated by *clarify-extent-indicated*, as illustrated in (10). (Our coherence rules for the relation *cr-contrast* as well as our rules for *clarify-extent-indicated* make

---

[20] Hirschberg did not address other possible types of direct answers, represented by the Answer-Hedged, Answer-Maybe, and Answer-Maybe-Not operators in our model.

use of the notion of a salient partial ordering which was elucidated by Hirschberg.) However, Hirschberg's model does not account for quite a variety of types of indirect answers which can be generated using the other operators in our model, nor for other motives for using *Use-contrast.*

Research on misconceptions (McCoy, 1988; Quilici et al., 1988; Pollack, 1990) has resulted in systems that include extra information in a response in order to address the source of a detected misconception. In contrast, our system produces responses that sometimes have the objective of preventing a misconception from occurring. For example, the stimulus condition *clarify-concept-indicated* is triggered when an answer is based on an atypical instance of a concept; the extra information prevents the questioner from drawing an erroneous conclusion from the direct answer. This is similar to Zukerman's work on preventing erroneous inferences in extended explanations (Zukerman & McConachy, 1993). Other stimulus conditions, such as *explanation-indicated*, are related to misconceptions in that they are triggered when the questioner's expectation about the answer is wrong. However, our system has only been concerned with use of *weak* expectations (such as a default expectation that a person will be at work on Monday morning). Although the extra information in its response provides an explanation for the unexpected answer, our system does not perform deep reasoning to identify and address the reasons for the questioner's erroneous expectations. Such deeper reasoning is beyond the scope of the current research.

Rhetorical or coherence relations (Grimes, 1975; Halliday, 1976; Mann & Thompson, 1987) have been used in several text-generation systems to aid in ordering parts of a text (e.g. Hovy, 1988) as well as in content-planning (e.g. Mc Keown, 1985; Moore & Paris, 1993). The discourse plan operators based on coherence relations in our model (i.e. the operators used as satellites of top-level operators) play a similar role in content-planning of an indirect answer. When coherence relations are used for content-planning, it is necessary to constrain the information which thereby may be selected. McKeown (1985) uses discourse focus constraints. In Moore (1995), plan selection heuristics are used that maximize the hearer's presumed familiarity with the concepts in the text, prefer general-purpose to less general operators, and minimize verbosity. Maybury's (1992) system uses 'desirable' preconditions, preconditions that are not necessary preconditions, to prioritize alternative operators. In contrast, by the use of stimulus conditions, our system models the speaker's motivation for taking the initiative in content selection based upon general principles of efficiency, accuracy, and politeness. The discourse operators in Haller's IDP system (Haller & Shapiro, 1996) include optional satellites that can be filled when replanning in response to *why* follow-up questions or when the system is running in anticipatory mode; the potential fillers for the satellites are the propositions that the system used in its reasoning and which the user does not know. Thus, in anticipatory mode, Haller's system acts as if it is checking whether every potential satellite filler satisfies our *explanation-indicated* stimulus condition; but the other motivations covered by our stimulus conditions are not handled.

Finally, the model presented in this paper is relevant to several systems described in this issue. It could be used by the CIRCSIM tutor described by Shah et al. (1998) in generating responses to a student's Yes-No questions. Shah et al. present a classification of student initiative types and tutor responses. Consider for example the following dialogue segment from their paper:

EX. 2.9

K16-st-46-2: *Is sympa stimulation the only factor influencing cc?*
K16-tu-47-1: *It is in the experiment we are discussing today.*

The tutor's response in K16-tu-47-1 can be analyzed as an indirect answer containing extra information motivated by our *Clarify-extent-indicated* stimulus condition. In other words, the tutor's response provides extra information to avoid misleading the student. In addition, once pedagogical agents such as the agent described by Lester et al. (1999) have the ability to engage in a natural language dialogue, strategies such as ours will increase the agent's life-like qualities by producing responses to Yes–No questions that embody the qualities of responses found in naturally occurring dialogue.

9. Conclusion

We have presented a computational model for taking the initiative to provide unrequested but relevant information in responses to Yes–No questions, focusing on the kinds of unsolicited information that may be used in place of or accompanying a direct answer. In our model, stimulus conditions represent types of discourse contexts in which a speaker would be motivated to provide unrequested information. Stimulus conditions can be thought of as situational triggers that give rise to new speaker goals, and that are the compiled result of 'deeper' planning based upon communicative goals. Stimulus conditions are used as part of a discourse-plan-based approach to response generation that enables the generation of coherent multiple-sentence responses. During the content planning phase of response generation, the system reasons on a model of the questioner to determine what stimulus conditions are satisfied as part of the process of deciding what extra information to include in the full answer. A study supports the kinds of responses produced by our system.

Appendix I: Evaluation Study

The following is the domain description and questionnaire used for a study to evaluate the initiative taken by our system. The blocks world diagram presented to the subjects was a color drawing, while we have annotated the objects in the

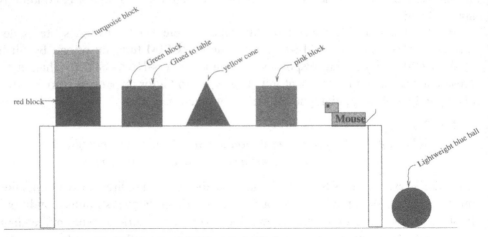

A Blocks World Diagram

Figure 6.

figure to indicate their color. The responses produced by our system were: 1c, 2d, 3d, 4c, 5a, 6b, 7b, 8c, 9c, 10a, 11a.

DOMAIN DESCRIPTION

This picture depicts a room containing a table with some objects on it and on the floor beside it.

- The green block is on the table but is glued to the table.
- The item on the floor is a lightweight blue ball.
- There is a clock in the room. The manager cannot see the clock, and the only way that the robot can know the time is from this clock.
- The room also contains a forklift, which the robot can operate. The forklift is not shown in the picture.
- There is a live mouse on the table who occasionally causes problems.
- A talking robot is in the room. The robot can see the room and knows the status of the objects in the room.
- The lab manager, M, uses the robot to perform tasks. He can talk to the robot. However, he cannot see the room and does not know the status of the objects in the room.

QUESTIONNAIRE

(1)   M: 'I am looking for the blue ball.'
              'Is it on the table?'

A. 'No.'
B. 'No. It's not.'
C. 'No. It's on the floor.'
D. 'No. It cost $5.'

(2) M: 'I need a ball to play catch with my kids.'
'Is there a red ball in the room?'

A. 'No.'
B. 'No. The green block is glued to the table.'
C. 'No. There's not.'
D. 'No. There's a blue ball.'

(3) M: 'Can you stack the cone on the green block?'

A. 'Yes. I can.'
B. 'Yes. The blue ball is on the floor.'
C. 'Yes. The red block is on the table.'
D. 'Yes.'

(4) M: 'I think the green block is fairly light.'
'Can you pick it up?'

A. 'No.'
B. 'No. I can't.'
C. 'No. The green block is glued to the table.'
D. 'No. The blue ball is on the floor.'

(In the following, assume that only one of the balls that was ordered has arrived.)

(5) M: 'I ordered a blue ball and a red ball for you.'
'Have they both arrived?'

A. 'No. I got the blue one.'
B. 'No.'
C. 'No. The green block is glued to the table.'
D. 'No. I haven't.'

(In question 6, assume that the mouse keeps pushing balls off the table but that M doesn't know this.)

(6)   M: 'I'd like to keep the floor clear of objects.'
             'Can you keep the blue ball on the table?'

       A.   'Yes, I can.'
       B.   'Yes, if I can keep the mouse from pushing it off again.'
       C.   'Yes.'
       D.   'Yes. The turquoise block is on the red block.'

(7)   M: 'Is there a cat in the room?'

       A.   'No. The green block is glued to the table.'
       B.   'No.'
       C.   'No. There isn't.'
       D.   'No. I can't pick up the green block.'

Original version of Question 8:

(8)   M: 'Can you tell me the time?'

       A.   'No. I can't.'
       B.   'No.'
       C.   'No. There's no clock in here.'
       D.   'No. The mouse is on the table.'

Revised version of Question 8.

(8)   M: 'Can you tell me the time?'

       A.   'No. I can't.'
       B.   'No.'
       C.   'No. The clock is broken.'
       D.   'No. The mouse is on the table.'

(9)   M: 'Are there any toys in the room?'

       A.   'Yes.'
       B.   'Yes, there are.'
       C.   'Yes. There's a ball and some blocks.'
       D.   'Yes. The table is about three feet tall.'

(10)   M: 'You are such a lazy robot.'
               'Have you put away the blocks?'

           A.   'No. I've put away most of the balls.'
           B.   'No.'
           C.   'No. I haven't.'
           D.   'No. There's a pink block.'

(11)   M: 'The pink block may be too heavy for you to move.'
               'Can you move the pink block?'

           A.   'Yes. I can use the forklift.'
           B.   'Yes. The yellow block is beside the pink block.'
           C.   'Yes.'
           D.   'Yes. I can.'

Appendix II: Top-Level Discourse Plan Operators

```
(Answer-yes s h ?p):              ; Q: Are you going shopping?
  Applicability conditions:
    (discourse-expectation (informif s h ?p))
    (bel s ?p)
  Nucleus:
    (inform s h ?p)              ; R: yes
  Satellites:
    (Use-condition s h ?p)       ;   if I finish my homework.
    (Use-elaboration s h ?p)     ;   I'm going to the mall.
    (Use-cause s h ?p)           ;   I need shoes.
  Primary goals:
    (BMB h s ?p)

(Answer-no s h ?p):               ; Q: Are you going shopping?
  Applicability conditions:
    (discourse-expectation (informif s h ?p))
    (bel s (not ?p))
  Nucleus:
    (inform s h (not ?p))        ; R: no
  Satellites:
    (Use-otherwise s h (not ?p)) ;   I'd not have time to study.
    (Use-obstacle s h (not ?p))  ;   Besides, I'm broke.
    (Use-contrast s h (not ?p))  ;   I'm going shopping on payday.
  Primary goals:
    (BMB h s (not ?p))
```

```
(Answer-hedge s h ?p):                    ; Q: Do you own a house?
   Applicability conditions:
      (discourse-expectation (informif s h ?p))
      (bel s (some-truth ?p))
      (unless (bel s ?p))
   Nucleus:
      (inform s h (some-truth ?p))      ; R: sort of
   Satellites:
      (Use-contrast s h (some-truth ?p));   I own a condo.
   Primary goals:
      (BMB h s (some-truth ?p))


(Answer-maybe s h ?p):                    ; Q: Is Lynn here?
   Applicability conditions:
      (discourse-expectation (informif s h ?p))
      (wbel s ?p)
   Nucleus:
      (inform s h (wbel s ?p))          ; R: I think so.
   Satellites:
      (Use-result s h ?p)               ;   Her backpack is here.
      (Use-possible-cause s h           ;   I think it's her
              (wbel s ?p))              ;      office hour.
      (Use-usually s h ?p)              ;   She's usually here.
   Primary goals:
      (WBMB h s ?p)

(Answer-maybe-no s h ?p):                 ; Q: Is Lynn here?
   Applicability conditions:
      (discourse-expectation (informif s h ?p))
      (wbel s (not ?p))
   Nucleus:
      (inform s h (wbel s (not ?p)))   ; R: I don't think so.
   Satellites:
      (Use-result s h (not ?p))         ;   Her backpack is gone.
      (Use-possible-obstacle s h
              (wbel s (not ?p)))        ;   I think she's sick.
      (Use-usually s h (not ?p))        ;   Also, she's not usually
                                        ;      here now.
   Primary goals:
      (WBMB h s (not ?p))
```

References

Allen, J. F. and C. R. Perrault: 1980, Analyzing intention in utterances. *Artificial Intelligence*, **15**(3) 143–178.

Ballim, A. and Y. Wilks: 1991, Beliefs, stereotypes and dynamic agent modeling. *User Modeling and User-Adapted Interaction*, **1**(1), 33–65.

Bonarini, A., E. Cappelletti, and A. Corrao: 1990, Network-based management of subjective judgements: A proposal accepting cyclic dependencies. *Technical Report Technical Report 90-067*, Dipartimento di Elettronica, Politecnico di Milano, Milano, Italy.

Brown, P. and S. Levinson: 1978, Universals in language usage: Politeness phenomena. In: E. N. Goody (ed.): *Questions and politeness: Strategies in social interaction*. Cambridge: Cambridge University Press, pp. 56–289.

Carberry, S.: 1988, Modeling the User's Plans and Goals. *Computational Linguistics*, **14**(3), 23–37.

Carberry, S.: 1989, A pragmatics-based approach to ellipsis resolution. *Computational Linguistics*, **15**(2), 75–96.

Carberry, S.: 1990, *Plan Recognition in Natural Language Dialogue*. Cambridge, Massachusetts: MIT Press.

Chester, D.: 1980, HCPRVR: An interpreter for logic programs. In: *Proceedings of the First Annual National Conference on Artificial Intelligence*. pp. 93–95.

Chin, D. N.: 1989, KNOME: Modeling what the user knows in UC. In: A. Kobsa and W. Wahlster (eds.): *User Models in Dialog Systems*. Berlin, New York: Springer-Verlag.

Chu-Carroll, J. and M. Brown: 1998, An evidential model for tracking initiative in collaborative dialogue interactions. *User Modeling and User-Adapted Interaction*. **8**(3–4), pp. 215–254.

Cohen, P. R.: 1985, *Heuristic Reasoning about Uncertainty: An Artificial Intelligence Approach*. Pitman Publishing Company.

DeKleer, J.: 1986, An assumption-based TMS. *Artificial Intelligence*, **28**, 269–301.

DiMarco, C. and G. Hirst: 1993, A computational theory of goal-directed style in syntax. *Computational Linguistics* **19**(3), 451–499.

Driankov, D.: 1988, *Towards a Many-Valued Logic of Quantified Belief*. Ph.D. thesis, Linkoping University, Department of Computer and Information Science, Linkoping, Sweden.

Galliers, J. R.: 1991, Belief revision and a theory of communication. *Technical Report Technical Report 193*, University of Cambridge, Cambridge, England.

Galliers, J. R.: 1992, Autonomous belief revision and communication. In: P. Gardenfors (ed.): Belief Revision, *Cambridge tracts in theoretical computer science*. Cambridge, England: Cambridge University Press.

Green, N. L.: 1994, A computational model for generating and interpreting indirect answers. Ph.D. thesis, University of Delaware. Department of Computer and Information Sciences, *Technical Report No. 95-05*.

Grice, H. P.: 1975, Logic and conversation. In: P. Cole and J. L. Morgan (eds.): *Syntax and Semantics III: Speech Acts*. New York: Academic Press, pp. 41–58.

Grimes, J. E.: 1975, *The Thread of Discourse*. The Hague: Mouton.

Guinn, C.: 1998, Principles of mixed-initiative human–computer collaborative discourse. *User Modeling and User-Adapted Interaction*. User Modeling and User Adapted Interaction **8**(3–4), pp. 255–314.

Haller, S. and S. Shapiro: 1996, IDP – an interactive discourse planner. In: *Trends in Natural Language Generation – An Artificial Intelligence Perspective*. Springer-Verlag, pp. 144–167.

Halliday, M.: 1976, *Cohesion in English*. London: Longman.

Hinkelman, E. A.: 1989, Linguistic and pragmatic constraints on utterance interpretation. Ph.D. thesis, University of Rochester. Department of Computer Science, *Technical Report 288*, May 1990.

Hirschberg, J. B.: 1985, *A Theory of Scalar Implicature*. Ph.D. thesis, University of Pennsylvania. Department of Computer and Information Science, MS-CIS-85-56, LINC LAB 21.

Hovy, E. H.: 1988, Planning coherent multisentential text. In: *Proceedings of the 26th Annual Meeting of the Association for Computational Linguistics*, Buffalo, N.Y. pp. 163–169.

Hovy, E. H.: 1990, Pragmatics and Natural Language Generation. *Artificial Intelligence*, **43**, 153–197.

Joshi, A., B. Webber, and R. Weischedel: 1984, Living up to expectations: computing expert responses. In: *Proceedings of the Fourth National Conference on Artificial Intelligence*, Austin, Texas, pp. 169–175.

Kass, R.: 1991, Building a user model implicitly from a cooperative advisory dialog. *User Modeling and User-Adapted Interaction*, **1**(3), 203–258.

Kay, J.: 1995, The UM toolkit for reusable, long term user models. *User Modeling and User-Adapted Interaction*, **4**(3), 149–196.

Kobsa, A.: 1984, VIE-DPM: A user model in a natural language dialogue system. In: *Proceedings of the 8th German Workshop on Artificial Intelligence*, Wingst, Germany pp. 145–153.

Kobsa, A. and W. Pohl: 1994, The user modeling shell system BGP-MS. *User Modeling and User-Adapted Interaction*, **4**(2), 59–106.

Lambert, L. and S. Carberry: 1991, A tripartite plan-based model of dialogue. In: *Proceedings of the 29th Annual Meeting of the Association for Computational Linguistics*, Berkeley, CA pp. 47–54.

Lambert, L. and S. Carberry: 1992a, Modeling negotiation dialogues. In: *Proceedings of the 30th Annual Meeting of the Association for Computational Linguistics*, Newark, DE pp. 193–200.

Lambert, L. and S. Carberry: 1992b, Using linguistic, world, and contextual knowledge in a plan recognition model of dialogue. In: *Proceedings of the 14th International Conference on Computational Linguistics*, Nantes, France pp. 310–316.

Lester, J., B. Stone, and G. Stelling: 1999, Lifelike pedagogical agents for mixed-initiative problem solving in constructivist learning environments. In this issue.

Levinson, S.: 1983, *Pragmatics*. Cambridge: Cambridge University Press.

Litman, D. and J. Allen: 1987, A plan recognition model for subdialogues in conversation. *Cognitive Science*, **11**, 163–200.

Makuta-Giluk, M.: 1991, A computational rhetoric for syntactic aspects of text. *Technical Report CS-91-56*, Department of Computer Science, University of Waterloo, Waterloo, Ontario, Canada.

Mann, W. C. and S. A. Thompson: 1983, Relational Propositions in Discourse. *Technical Report ISI/RR-83-115*, Information Sciences Institute, University of Southern California, Marina del Rey, California.

Mann, W. C. and S. A. Thompson: 1987, Rhetorical structure theory: toward a functional theory of text organization. *Text*, **8**(3), 167–182.

Maybury, M. T.: 1992, Communicative acts for explanation generation. *International Journal of Man-Machine Studies*, **37**, 135–172.

McCoy, K. F.: 1988, Reasoning on a highlighted user model to respond to misconceptions. *Computational Linguistics*, **14**(3) pp. 52–63.

McKeown, K. R.: 1985, *Text Generation*. Cambridge, England, Cambridge University Press.

Moore, J. D.: 1995, *Participating in Explanatory Dialogues*. Cambridge, MA MIT Press.

Moore, J. D. and C. Paris: 1993, Planning text for advisory dialogues: capturing intentional and rhetorical information. *Computational Linguistics*.

Moore, J. D. and M. E. Pollack: 1992, A problem for RST: The need for multi-level discourse analysis. *Computational Linguistics*, **18**(4), 537–544.

Perrault, R. and J. Allen: 1980, A plan-based analysis of indirect speech acts. *American Journal of Computational Linguistics*, **6**(3-4), 167–182.

Pollack, M.: 1986, A model of plan inference that distinguishes between the beliefs of actors and observers. In: *Proceedings of the 24th Annual Meeting of the Association for Computational Linguistics*. New York, New York, pp. 207–214.

Pollack, M.: 1990, Plans as complex mental attitudes. In: P. Cohen, J. Morgan, and M. Pollack (eds.): *Intentions in Communication*. Boston, MA, MIT Press.

Quilici, A., M. Dyer, and M. Flowers: 1988, Recognizing and responding to plan-oriented misconceptions. *Computational Linguistics*, **14**(3), 38–51.

Rich, E.: 1979, User Modelling via Stereotypes. *Cognitive Science*, **3**(4), 329–354.

Schuster, E., D. Chin, R. Cohen, A. Kobsa, K. Morik, K. S. Jones, and W. Wahlster: 1988, Discussion Section on the Relationship between User Models and Discourse Models. *Computational Linguistics*, **14**(3), 79–103.

Shah, F., M. Evens, J. Michael, and A. Rovick: 1998, Classifying Student Initiatives and Tutor Responses: A First Step toward Mixed-Initiative Dialogue. Submitted.

Smith, R. and S. Gordon: 1997, Effects of variable initiative on linguistic behavior in human–computer spoken natural language dialogue. *Computational Linguistics*, **23**(1), 141–168.

SRI: 1992, *Transcripts of audiotape conversations*. Prepared by Jacqueline Kowto under the direction of Patti Price at SRI International, Menlo Park, California.

Stenström, A.-B.: 1984, Questions and Responses in English Conversation. In: C. Schaar and J. Svartvik (eds.): *Lund Studies in English 68*. Malmö, Sweden: CWK Gleerup.

van Beek, P.: 1987, A model for generating better explanations. In: *Proceedings of the 25th Annual Meeting of the Association for Computational Linguistics*, Stanford, CA, pp. 215–220.

Whittaker, S. and P. Stenton: 1988, Cues and control in expert-client dialogues. In: *Proceedings of the 26th Annual Meeting of the Association for Computational Linguistics*, Buffalo, N.Y. pp. 123–130.

Young, M. R.: 1994, A developer's guide to the longbow discourse planning system. *Technical Report ISP TR No. 94-4*, University of Pittsburgh, Intelligent Systems Program.

Zukerman, I. and R. McConachy: 1993, Consulting a user model to address a user's inferences during content planning. *User Modeling and User-Adapted Interaction* **3**(2), 155–185.

Authors' Vitae

Nancy Green

Carnegie Mellon University, School of Computer Science, 5000 Forbes Avenue, Pittsburgh, PA 15213, USA.

Dr. Green received an M.A. in Linguistics from the University of North Carolina in Chapel Hill, an M.S. in Computer Science from the University of Pennsylvania, and a Ph.D. in Computer Science from the University of Delaware. Currently, Dr. Green is a Systems Scientist with the Human-Computer Interaction Institute at CMU performing research on the automatic generation of integrated text and information graphic presentations. Prior to that she was a Postdoctoral Research Fellow in the Computer Science Department at CMU studying machine learning applied to discourse processing. This paper describes part of her dissertation research with Sandra Carberry.

Sandra Carberry

Department of Computer Science, University of Delaware, Newark, DE 19716, USA.

Dr. Carberry is an associate professor in the computer science department at the University of Delaware. She received a B.A. in mathematics from Cornell University, an M.S. in computer science from Rice University, and a PhD in computer science from the University of Delaware. Her current research interests include user modeling, computational linguistics with an emphasis on dialogue systems, and medical informatics. Her book "Plan Recognition in Natural Language Dialogue" was published by MIT Press in 1990.

User Modeling and User-Adapted Interaction **9:** 133–166, 1999.
© 1999 *Kluwer Academic Publishers.*

133

User-Tailored Planning of Mixed Initiative Information-Seeking Dialogues

ADELHEIT STEIN[1], JON ATLE GULLA[2] and ULRICH THIEL[1]

[1]*GMD-IPSI, German National Research Center for Information Technology, Integrated Publication and Information Systems Institute, Darmstadt, Germany. e-mail: stein@darmstadt.gmd.de*
[2]*Norwegian University of Science and Technology, Department of Computer Science, Trondheim, Norway*

(Received 6 November 1997; in revised form 12 May 1998)

Abstract. Intelligent dialogue systems usually concentrate on user support at the level of the domain of discourse, following a plan-based approach. Whereas this is appropriate for collaborative planning tasks, the situation in interactive information retrieval systems is quite different: there is no inherent plan-goal hierarchy, and users are known to often opportunistically change their goals and strategies during and through interaction. We need to allow for mixed-initiative retrieval dialogues, where the system evaluates the user's individual dialogue behavior and performs situation-dependent interpretation of user goals, to determine when to take the initiative and to change the control of the dialogue, e.g., to propose (new) problem-solving strategies to the user. In this article, we present the dialogue planning component of a concept-oriented, logic-based retrieval system (MIRACLE). Users are guided through the global stages of the retrieval interaction but may depart, at any time, from this guidance and change the direction of the dialogue. When users submit *ambiguous queries* or enter *unexpected dialogue control acts*, abductive reasoning is used to generate interpretations of these user inputs in light of the dialogue history and other internal knowledge sources. Based on these interpretations, the system initiates a short dialogue offering the user suitable options and strategies for proceeding with the retrieval dialogue. Depending on the user's choice and constraints resulting from the history, the system adapts its strategy accordingly.

Key words: conversational retrieval, mixed initiative, dialogue planning, dialogue act interpretation, abductive reasoning

1. Mixed Initiative in Retrieval Systems: Why, When, and How?

Artificial intelligence systems which support users of information systems often interpret human–computer interaction as a collaborative dialogue in which both information seeker and provider may take the initiative and control the dialogue. Most current approaches in this area presuppose well-defined tasks, e.g., looking up information for travel planning, where the task and domain levels are closely intertwined. Bunt (1989) coined the term 'information dialogue' for the type of dialogue occurring in simple *factual* information systems, such as electronic services which provide access to phone directories, train schedules and the like.

By contrast, classical information retrieval (IR) systems accessing large textual or multimedia databases have to deal with a different kind of user behavior. In such settings, many users initially have vague information needs: they know they need some information but often cannot specify it. Belkin & Vickery (1985) call this an 'anomalous state of knowledge'. The usual solution in this case is to consult a human intermediary. To obtain a satisfactory result it is crucial that the dialogue partners establish – in addition to a shared notion of what information is desired – a mutual understanding of the *criteria* to be used to decide whether retrieved items constitute a solution to the information problem.

Humans have, of course, a certain repertoire of behavioral patterns for handling problems of this type, and a whole set of retrieval tactics and strategies known to skilled searchers has been identified in IR research (see, e.g., Saracevic et al., 1997). Cooperative systems that aim to support the user in finding and pursuing appropriate retrieval strategies have to internally represent and use knowledge about such behavioral patterns. They must also take into account that users may at any time change their understanding of the information problem and adopt other strategies than those suggested by the system. Hence, we need context-dependent user guidance without presupposing a strict hierarchy of plans and task goals. At the same time, sufficient *dialogue control options* should be available, for example, to force the system to react to changed user strategies.

In order to offer effective dialogue support, any system must rely on an implicit or explicit model of when initiative shifts (or should shift) among the dialogue participants. Engaging in cooperative mixed-initiative dialogues requires the system to apply mechanisms for deciding *when to take or relinquish initiative* depending on the current dialogue situation, and *how to adjust its behavior* accordingly. In mixed-initiative dialogues, the roles of the two participating agents are not predetermined (cf. Allen, 1994). Agents should not only collaborate to solve domain problems, but also to perform 'interaction management' (Bunt, 1996). That is, they should have options for negotiating both dialogue control ('about' dialogue) and problem-solving strategy ('about' task or strategy).

The type of information-seeking interaction we are considering in this paper requires an inference process which reasons about both the *information problem* and the *dialogue situation*. Typically, the information problem tends to be 'open-ended' in the sense that the user's information need is underspecified at the beginning, and both dialogue partners contribute to a constructive solution based on additional assumptions or hypotheses about the information need, which then may be negotiated and clarified. Hence, it is crucial that the system is capable of showing initiative at the task level, i.e., by attempting to transform the originally vague information problem into a solvable one. This is accomplished by an abductive reasoning system analyzing the user's queries (cf. Müller & Thiel, 1994).

The focus of this paper, however, is at the level of dialogue, where the system needs to be highly flexible in detecting and interpreting the user's initiative – be it a rejection of the system's hypotheses or a change of interest. As dialogue management imposes logical requirements different from those encountered in the retrieval task, we employ two different abductive inference engines for the system's retrieval and dialogue components (cf. Thiel et al., 1996, and Stein et al., 1997a).

Starting with a general model of information-seeking dialogue, our approach identifies dialogue situations in which the system should seize initiative to act cooperatively. Given a repertoire of retrieval strategies (represented as abstract dialogue plans, called 'scripts'), a set of dialogue control rules, and the abductive inference mechanism, the system is able to initiate negotiations about the current strategy based on an evaluation of the dialogue history. Although certainly superior to an automated system, even a human intermediary has only a limited understanding of the user's actual information need. Thus, the intermediary must rely on obvious, observable features of the dialogue situation, for example, when a query yields no or too many results, is too ambiguous, etc. The skilled searcher – or a system endowed with an equivalent behavioral repertoire – can then suggest helpful strategies to circumvent the problem. Users may follow the suggested strategies or perform specific dialogue controlacts to change the direction of the dialogue whenever they want, e.g., if a certain aspect of their information need turns out to be ambiguous and they decide to follow a newly detected thread.

In the remainder of this article, we outline our approach to mixed-initiative dialogue in the framework of an intelligent IR system, discussing how the system uses this model to actively engage in the dialogue and to adapt its behavior to the current situation. Our experimental prototype MIRACLE and some interaction examples are described in Section 4. We employ a comprehensive dialogue model (see Section 5) to represent various facets of the user's behavior and the system's reactions in a structured dialogue history. The dialogue component described in Section 6 uses abduction to make sense of ambiguous user inputs, evaluating the history. It generates situation-dependent interpretations of these inputs, infers possible follow-up actions, and – taking individual user preferences into account – offers the user suitable options for proceeding in the dialogue.

2. Related Research

Recently, issues of mixed initiative and dialogue control have been increasingly addressed in research on *intelligent human-computer collaboration* (see Terveen, 1995, for an overview). Relevant AI-oriented approaches concentrate on collaborative activity focusing on the agents' beliefs, goals, and plans. Most computational models of collaborative discourse in AI follow a 'plan-based approach' (Taylor et al., 1996), where the agents are seen to have goals to achieve plans on the level of the domain of discourse. Typical application areas are transportation or travel planning (e.g., Rich & Sidner, 1998). Some existing discourse models (e.g., Traum & Allen, 1994; Jameson & Weis, 1995; McRoy & Hirst, 1995) also address social factors, such as conversational conventions, expectations, and obligations.

Most of the numerous research prototypes concerned with discourse planning and adaptive user modeling concentrate on natural language applications (see Wahlster & Kobsa, 1989, for an early survey, and Schuster et al., 1988, for a discussion of the relationship between user models and discourse models). As typical examples we refer to explanation dialogue systems (e.g., Moore & Paris, 1993; Chu-Carroll & Carberry, 1995; Stock et al., 1997; McRoy et al., 1997), intelligent presentation systems (see a selection in Maybury & Wahlster, 1998), and task-oriented spoken dialogue systems (see, e.g., Maier et al., 1997, for a recent collection). User modeling components are generally construed as a means to enhance a system's reactiveness to user needs. Whereas most approaches concentrate on user stereotypes and characteristics such as background knowledge, other valuable approaches rely on 'short-term individual user models' built up incrementally (Rich, 1989). For the latter one needs to decide what entities are to be represented in the *dialogue history* (e.g., only the topics/concepts addressed during the discourse or, additionally, intentional structures as described by Grosz & Sidner, 1986, 1990). Also, the system must employ an active component which exploits the history or user model in order to generate cooperative user support.

Research relevant to our application context stems from the field of *information retrieval (IR)* and, more specifically, intelligent multimedia IR (see Ruthven, 1996 and Maybury, 1997, for recent collections). Information retrieval involves a variety of reasoning tasks, ranging from problem definition to relevance assessment. Some researchers in IR established a *retrieval-as-inference* approach following a proposal put forward by van Rijsbergen (1989). Here, a document is assumed to be relevant if its contents (as a set of logical propositions) allow the query to be inferred. Several logics have been proposed in order to formalize this relationship. A complementary view of the retrieval process relies on cognitive models, trying to capture the interactive nature of IR (e.g., Logan et al., 1994). Cognitive approaches attempt to represent the mental state of users, e.g., their knowledge, intention, and beliefs. The dialogue contributions are modeled as dialogue acts which exert certain well-defined effects on these representations.

Early online information systems like online library catalogues and bibliographical databases offered only very few interaction facilities and little user support. They simply processed submitted queries. The shortcomings of this 'matching' paradigm (cf. Bates, 1986) were soon recognized, and information retrieval was more and more regarded as a process involving cycles of query refinements following inspection of results. Simple document-oriented *relevance feedback* facilities were employed in early experimental systems (cf. Salton & McGill, 1983), allowing the users to accept or reject individual documents retrieved. Although this kind of interaction was more reminiscent of a *dialogue* (cf. Oddy, 1977) than a programming activity (as suggested by the matching paradigm), the effectiveness of the interaction was impeded by the insufficient means of dialogue control available to the user.

Relevance is usually decided upon in terms of meaning and use. Hence, more advanced IR systems not only refer to retrieved objects/documents but also to the *concepts* the user has in mind when formulating a query. Using tools like domain models, thesauri, and certain inference mechanisms, concept-based IR systems can enhance the conceptual coherence of the retrieval process decisively. However, even if a system can determine the intended meaning of a user's conceptual query, its relevance to the user's information need can only be inferred from the user's reactions during interaction. Contemporary IR systems that provide additional user support, such as automatic query expansion and relevance feedback facilities, treat such facilities as *extra-dialogic functions* – usually as additional operations on the query or result set, which are regarded as data objects but not as dialogue contributions. In most cases, these systems do not incorporate any elaborate dialogue models or dialogue planning components. We believe, however, that methods derived from dialogue modeling, intelligent information retrieval, and user modeling, should be *combined* to improve a system's capability to actively participate in a dialogue and deal with vague and changing user goals.

Following a *retrieval-as-interaction* point of view (see, e.g., Belkin & Vickery, 1985 and Ingwersen, 1992), the notion of 'conversational IR' was introduced, and it was suggested to model the entire interaction as a complex web of mode-independent 'conversational acts' based on a multi-layered model of conversational tactics and information-seeking strategies (see Stein & Thiel, 1993, and Belkin et al., 1995). In this article, we refer to the theoretical framework proposed there, describe some recent extensions and the formal specifications of the dialogue model we developed for integration in MIRACLE, and finally discuss a dialogue planning approach which enables the system to detect problematic dialogue situations and suggest solutions. Similar to the underlying retrieval procedure, the dialogue planning component employs abductive reasoning as its inferential framework.

3. 'Initiative' and 'Control'

In our dialogue system, we use the COnversational Roles (COR) model (Sitter & Stein, 1992, 1996) as a general model of information-seeking dialogue and combine it with a number of abstract dialogue plans (called 'scripts') in order to allow both dialogue flexibility and goal-directed user guidance. Whereas COR describes all of the possible interchanges of dialogue moves and acts that may occur at the various states of a dialogue, scripts are used to guide the user through the global stages of retrieval interaction. Both the COR model and scripts are domain and application independent, COR covering the illocutionary aspects and flexible conversational tactics of the dialogue and the scripts representing useful strategies and 'recommended' actions for solving different types of retrieval tasks.

The integrated dialogue model (see Section 5) is made explicit in a declarative notation, which is sufficient for purposes of dialogue analysis and the construction of a hierarchically structured dialogue history. For dialogue planning purposes, however, we need an additional, active mechanism which enables the system to generate cooperative dialogue contributions and hence to *engage in a mixed-initiative interaction*. To achieve this goal, our dialogue planning component (see Section 6) exploits its internal knowledge sources, i.e., the dialogue model, a number of dialogue control rules, and the dynamically created dialogue history, in order to manage the user–system interaction and be able to actively participate in the dialogue. The system reacts immediately to unexpected situations (user actions not covered in scripts or plans); it uses abductive inference in order to compute suitable follow-up actions which are not pre-specified in the current script for this specific situation or dialogue state and offers the user the resulting set of options for continuing the dialogue.

In the context of our view of mixed initiative, we introduce below some specific definitions of '*taking initiative*' and related terms, and then discuss the distinctions between *initiative – control* and *task initiative – dialogue initiative* in our model (see Section 5.1 for a more concrete discussion of how these definitions are used and interpreted in the COR dialogue model).

Turn taking (choice/change of speaker) may be an important indicator for shifts in initiative or control, but surely is not identical with taking the initiative. Agents are seen to **take the initiative** when they take the turn to start a new dialogue segment (COR dialogue cycle or embedded subdialogue) determining the dialogue focus and the 'conditions of action' for the subsequent moves. Typical examples of moves/acts which initiate a new dialogue cycle or subdialogue are requests for information, such as queries or help requests, and voluntary offers to do some specific action (e.g., to change the presentation mode or to provide a detailed explanation).

Referring to interpersonal aspects, the term 'condition of action' is used to denote one of several possible functions of a dialogue act. We regard the dialogue as a 'cooperative negotiation' where both agents have discourse obligations and expectations. When performing an act, the speaker enters upon a commitment or tries to fulfill a pending commitment, or, if this is impossible, withdraws or rejects it in a way that can be understood by the addressee. As will be discussed in more detail in Section 5.1, *initiating* acts like 'request' and 'offer' usually do introduce new conditions of action, specifying which agent is to perform what action. *Responding* acts like 'accept', 'promise', and 'inform', on the other hand, adopt or fulfill the conditions from a preceding turn. An inform act, for example, does not define any new conditions of action (although it might be uttered with the general expectation that the addressee will/should give some feedback). From what has been said above it follows that the agent that initiates a new dialogue cycle *holds the initiative* until the requested/offered information is presented, or the request/offer is withdrawn, rejected, or countered by either agent.

Initiative and control are not equivalent from our point of view. Agents are seen to **take control** of the dialogue when they attempt to 'change the direction' of the dialogue. This may happen either when an unexpected act is performed (e.g., an act not included in the current plan/script, such as rejecting an offer or refusing to answer a question) or when the current dialogue course is suspended (e.g., by initiating a clarification subdialogue). In the latter case the agent controls the direction but *also* takes over the initiative, at least until the subdialogue is finished. We use the term 'dialogue control act' when an unexpected/non-recommended act is performed without taking over the initiative, i.e., without specifying which agent should do what action next. Typical examples are withdrawals (of previously made commitments), rejections (of a commitment or suggestion of the other agent), and negative evaluations (of information provided by the dialogue partner).

Some of the existing models of mixed initiative in AI-based dialogue systems (cf. Cohen et al., 1998, for an extended review) address different *types* of initiative/control, on different levels of the discourse. Chu-Carroll & Brown (1998), for example, make an explicit distinction between 'task initiative' and 'dialogue initiative', claiming that both must be modeled in order to account for complex behavior and interaction patterns. As mentioned above, most existing IR systems do not provide sufficient user support at the dialogue level, and retrieval tasks are mainly supported by providing extra-dialogic functions or tools to the user (e.g., thesauri or other terminological aids). In the MIRACLE system, we try to couple the retrieval and dialogue functionalities more closely in an integrated framework, distinguishing, as do Chu-Carroll and Brown, between dialogue and task initiative.

In our view, taking the *dialogue initiative* means to start a dialogue cycle, determining a new dialogue focus and condition of action, as described above. We speak of *task initiative* when the agent not only initiates a new cycle but also proposes some problem-solving action(s) for a given task. In principle, our model allows each dialogue partner to take the dialogue initiative, the task initiative, and the control of the dialogue (there exist some examples of each form in MIRACLE). However, taking into account specific differences between user and system, the implementation in MIRACLE clearly favors or restricts some of these options. For example, the user takes the dialogue initiative whenever submitting a query or clarification request and is completely free to take control and change the current direction of the dialogue, whereas the system should only do so if it can, at the same time, propose ways of how to best proceed or at least explain why the current strategy or direction failed.

Knowing what kind of dialogue acts have actually been performed, the system is able to track initiative shifts and then decide whether it needs to seize initiative itself, and in which way. When the user directly responds to some system initiative, e.g., accepts an offer, the system keeps the initiative and continues as expected. When users take the dialogue initiative or control and their input (request/query or control act) is unambiguous, the system responds by providing the retrieved results or simply executing what the user wanted – while the user is still holding the initiative. If the user's request or control act is ambiguous, however, the system needs to take the initiative back in order to cooperate, for instance, in the task of finding a good/better query or next step, rather than leaving this to the user alone. Using abduction, the system is usually able to generate a number of different

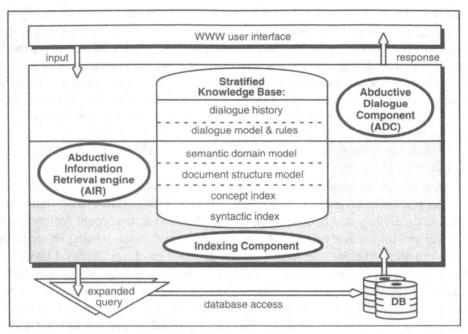

Figure 1. Architecture of MIRACLE.

interpretations of the ambiguous user act and to actively suggest suitable problem-solving actions (although the system does not propose domain actions or plans).

According to our definitions above, the system is taking the *task initiative* (which 'includes' dialogue initiative) whenever it presents the generated query and control act interpretations to the user. In both cases, the system does not just initiate a simple clarification dialogue, e.g., asking users to specify the input themselves, but offers its own interpretations and suggestions of how the user could proceed. This may be regarded as initiating the establishment of mutual beliefs about what the user actually intended – not only concerning the user's current information need or dialogue control act (trying to identify the act type), but also inferring the user's future intention, e.g., to change the current strategy. This model is discussed in detail in Section 6.

4. Retrieval Interaction in MIRACLE

Most contemporary IR systems concentrate on the efficient processing of queries, whereas the user–system interaction is not in the focus of the system design. Our rationale (cf. Thiel et al., 1996) takes a different point of view and regards both aspects as equally important. This is reflected in the baseline architecture of our system prototype (see Figure 1). MIRACLE (MultImedia concept Retrieval bAsed on logiCaL query Expansion) allows concept-based retrieval in large multimedia databases and is implemented in C, Smalltalk, and Prolog. The system integrates

Deduction			
from:	a → b	All artists have created a work of art.	(rule)
	a	Christo Javacheff is an artist.	(fact)
infer:	b	Christo Javacheff has created a work of art.	(conclusion)
Abduction			
from:	a → b	All works of art have a creation date.	(rule)
	b	Michelangelo's Pietà has a creation date.	(observation)
infer:	a	Probably, Michelangelo's Pietà is a work of art.	(hypothesis)

Figure 2. Two kinds of inference.

three active components: a probabilistic *indexer* for texts and images (Müller & Kutschekmanesch, 1996) (or, alternatively, the full text retrieval system INQUERY, cf. Callan et al., 1992); an abductive *retrieval engine* (Müller & Thiel, 1994; and the abductive *dialogue component* discussed in this article. Currently, the system interfaces two applications, a subset of Macmillan's Dictionary of Art in electronic form and a relational database with information about European-funded research projects (ProCORDIS). The arts databases consist of SGML-structured full text documents (biographies of artists, reference articles, etc.), factual knowledge about the artists and their works of arts, and a sample of photographs of the art objects. All examples dicussed in the following are taken from the arts application domain.

Both the retrieval engine and the dialogue manager employ abductive reasoning to make sense of ambiguous user inputs – the retrieval engine when dealing with the interpretation of user *queries*, and the dialogue component with other ambiguous user acts, i.e., *dialogue control acts*, such as withdraw, reject, request for clarification. The dialogue component will be described in later sections; below we briefly outline MIRACLE's retrieval functionality so as to illustrate the wider application context of the dialogue planning.

4.1. QUERY EXPANSION USING ABDUCTION

Queries are entered via a query form, which allows the specification of restrictions on the attributes of objects to be retrieved. The system retrieves relevant parts of artists' biographies or other documents related to the query concepts, together with factual information from a database (see Stein et al., 1997a, for a number of illustrative examples). However, the retrieval process is not confined to keyword matching but employs a concept model to establish the relationship between query concepts and access paths to the database. If a user query is ambiguous with respect to the semantic domain model, the abductive inference mechanism (see Figure 2) generates query reformulations considering the available information structures. A query like 'Search for artists with style *Impressionism* in country *France*' might be interpreted in several ways, depending on the actual domain model. The country attribute, for instance, can either be mapped onto the artists' nationality, place of birth or death, the location of one/most of their works of art, etc.

Abduction can be roughly characterized as a process which *generates explanations for a given observation.* Unlike deductive inference (see Figure 2), abduction allows not only truth-preserving but also hypothetical reasoning. In our context, the observation to be explained is the user's query (or any other ambiguous dialogue act of the user, as discussed in Section 6 below). In general, abduction will find *all* possible 'explanations' with respect to a given set of data and a query formulation (for more detailed discussions of abductive retrieval see Müller & Thiel, 1994 and Thiel et al., 1996). As not all of the explanations need to be valid altogether, we refer to each explanation as a feasible hypothesis. The system presents these hypotheses to the user as *query interpretations,* and in the next step the user may select the appropriate interpretation(s) for searching the database. Thus, the interpretations are negotiated interactively, and the user's choices are stored in the dialogue history and used as constraints to prevent the system from producing inappropriate query interpretations in subsequent steps.

4.2. INTERACTION EXAMPLES

Consider the example dialogue displayed in Figure 3. To improve readability it is given in natural language, although in MIRACLE the user performs a dialogue act by direct graphical manipulation, for example, filling in query forms and manipulating graphical interface objects.

After an introductory sequence, where the global task and strategy are negotiated, the user submits a query which can be paraphrased as: 'Search for *painters* in *Paris* who were concerned with *Madonna* as a subject of work of art'. Since this query is ambiguous, the retrieval engine generates four query interpretations (Figure 4 shows the second, # 2 of 4). These interpretations differ from one another mainly with respect to the interpretation of the query attributes 'town' and 'subject', whereas 'profession' is unambiguous in MIRACLE. Concerning the town attribute, for example, the system offers to either look for artists who were born in Paris or died there; as to subject (a free text field), the interpretations differ depending on the search method applied, e.g., partial string matching versus probabilistic fulltext retrieval.

Concerning the structure of the example dialogue, there are four *global* phases (an analysis showing more fine-grained structures and the types of dialogue moves and acts will be given in Figure 7 in the next section). In the introductory phase the user is offered several options, and she chooses to search the domain database rather than looking at the available meta-information sources. The system instantiates a script for *retrieval* interaction (see Section 5.2), whereas it would use different scripts for *browsing* in the meta-information resources, e.g., a thesaurus.

S: You may (1) search DB, (2) check DB structure, (3) check thesaurus.
U: chooses (1) to search the database
S: displays the query form

U: enters query: profession "painter", subject "Madonna", town "Paris"   [Q1]
S: Which query interpretation do you want:
       (1) The artist is related to Paris because ... and the subject Madonna is ...,
       (2) ..., (3) ..., (4) ...
U: selects query interpretation (4)
U: clicks on "withdraw"
S: Do you want to
       (1) choose another query interpretation
       (2) modify your previous query
       (3) enter a completely new query
U: chooses (2)
S: OK.
S: displays the last query (filled–in query form)

U: adds in the subject field "OR Maria"   [Q1a]
S: Which query interpretation do you want: (1) ..., (2) ..., (3) ..., (4) ...
U: chooses (2)
S: Here are the retrieved hits: ... (displays table)
U: clicks on "reject"
S: Do you want to
       (1) save the results (yes – no) and then
       (2) choose another query interpretation
       (3) modify your previous query
       (4) enter a completely new query
       (5) forget your query and restart the session ?
U: selects (1) to save and (3) to modify previous query
S: displays the previous query

U: replaces in the subject field "Maria" by "Mother and child"   [Q1b]
S: informs user that query interpretation (2) is used to search the DB and shows results
U: ...

Figure 3. Example dialogue.

According to the retrieval script the user is expected to submit a query as a first step. In our example the user fills in three slots of the query form (profession, subject, and town) and then hits the search DB button. This initial query (Q1) is refined in the following two phases: the user enters the operator OR and an additional search term (Maria) in the subject field (Q1a) and replaces one of the search terms in her last query (Q1b). Note that all of the three queries use the same three attributes and differ from one another only in the search term specifications. Hence, the *structure* of the interpretations generated by the retrieval engine is identical for all queries in our example.

Figure 4. MIRACLE screen (query interpretation state).

As shown in Figure 4, a query interpretation is presented to the user in the form of a list of the internal rules relevant to each of the interpretations, highlighting the currently active rules (black bullets) but also showing the non-active ones (the light-colored bullets 7 and 10 in Figure 4). Both after Q1 and Q1a the user is asked/gets the option to choose among four query interpretations: the system presents the first interpretation, a 'slider' for inspection of the other interpretations, and a button (search DB) for selecting the one query interpretation to be executed. It is only in the last dialogue cycle, after Q1b, that the system does not 'ask' the user again to select a query interpretation but immediately shows the retrieved results, additionally informing the user that query interpretation # 2 has been used again (i.e., the same interpretation the user selected for the previous query). This change of the system's strategy is based on the *dynamic user model* built up as the dialogue develops. We will show in Section 6 how this is accomplished by using constraints stored in the dialogue history.

Dialogue control options are represented in the upper part of the MIRACLE screen (see Figure 4). The buttons request, withdraw, and reject are generally available but may invoke different functions, depending on the current dialogue situation and the previous history. Although the button labels are similar to the names of the generic dialogue acts defined by the COR model (Section 5.1), they do not exactly match the act definitions. When the user, for instance, clicks on reject, this is internally represented as a `reject_offer` or a negative `evaluate_inform` act, thus as an immediate reaction to the system's preceding offer/inform. Even if the user by mistake presses the 'wrong' button (e.g., *reject* if she wants to revise an *own* decision), the dialogue component – consulting the dialogue model and history – is able to either identify the correct act or to generate a number of plausible interpretations, then asking the user which one she actually intended.

At a closer look it is obvious that both user and system take the initiative and change the direction of the dialogue at several points: (1) after any ambiguous user query the system initiates a subdialogue asking the user to choose among the generated query interpretations; (2) the user takes the initiative and changes the direction of the dialogue any time she does not follow the recommended dialogue course, e.g., clicking the withdraw and reject buttons in our example; (3) if such a dialogue control act is ambiguous, the system takes the initiative back and offers the user reasonable continuations of the dialogue (the latter will be explained in detail throughout the next sections). In some cases the subdialogues initiated by the system may be quite short and have the character of simple clarifications. However, depending on the number and 'difficulty' of the system-generated interpretations or suggestions, the dialogue may become quite complex. Experiences with test users of the retrieval component of MIRACLE showed, for example, that for certain types of (non-trivial) queries a rather large number of query interpretations were generated. In such cases the users took the time for inspecting and comparing the interpretations in peace, asking for additional explanations to be able to make their choice or to learn more about the retrieval method.

5. Modeling Information-Seeking Dialogue

To allow for mixed-initiative interaction, where both user and system may actively engage in the negotiation of dialogue goals, a good dialogue system must provide both the necessary *flexibility* and dialogue *guidance*. In our system we deal with these issues by employing a dialogue model which consists of two interrelated tiers. The *COnversational Roles (COR)* model describes all dialogue acts and interaction options available at any state of a dialogue, allowing for symmetric changes of initiative between the agents. *Scripts* represent prototype classes of dialogues for particular goal-directed information-seeking strategies. Modeling the recommended dialogue steps/acts (a subset of the available COR acts) for a given strategy, scripts are used to guide the user through the various stages of a retrieval session. Whereas the scripts decide who should take the turn in which situation and what are useful actions, the user may at any time depart from the current script by performing an act not included there, i.e., a COR 'dialogue control act'. Thus, users may decide on their own whether (and for how long) they want to follow the guided mode or suspend it and take the initiative themselves.

We will show in the next sections how the two tiers of our dialogue model represent mixed initiative and dialogue control at the descriptive level. Section 6 then describes in detail how the dialogue component uses this model to monitor the interaction, construct the dialogue history, and control changes in initiative depending on the actual dialogue course.

5.1. CONVERSATIONAL ROLES (COR) MODEL

We developed the COR model (Sitter & Stein, 1992) as a general model of cooperative information-seeking dialogue between two agents that alternately take the roles of information seeker (A) and information provider (B). The contributions of A and B are categorized as generic dialogue acts based on their main illocutionary point, similar to the 'Conversation for Action' model proposed by Winograd & Flores (1986). As such, COR abstracts away from both the specific semantic content and the modality (linguistic vs. non-linguistic) and concentrates on the *interpersonal function of dialogue acts* and the role assignments. COR covers all kinds of information-seeking dialogue, e.g., simple factual information dialogues as well as more complex negotiations. The model has later been refined and used in various research prototypes developed at our institute (MIRACLE being the only one using abductive dialogue planning) and elsewhere (e.g., Hagen, 1999).

Comparable dialogue models or grammars (e.g., Fawcett et al., 1988, and Traum & Hinkelmann, 1992) are mostly concerned with natural language and specific kinds of dialogue, e.g., exchange of factual information within well-defined task settings, such as most of the approaches presented in this issue. To account for the requirements of natural language they cover a variety of linguistic aspects, e.g., rhetorical and textual structures. The COR model itself does not rely on such linguistic knowledge, but it was used in natural language dialogue systems (e.g., 'SPEAK!', see Grote et al., 1997, and Stein, 1997) for monitoring the dialogue, whereas the linguistic resources were constituted by other strata representing the semantics and grammar.

COR uses recursive state-transition networks as the representation formalism. Figure 5 displays the main network for representing *dialogues* (the top-level dialogue as well as embedded subdialogues and meta-dialogues). Circles and squares depict the dialogue states; arcs/transitions between them generic dialogue moves. A dialogue consists of dialogue *cycles*, i.e., sequences of moves starting in state 1 and leading back to it. Note that in the simplest case, a *move* (Figure 6) consists

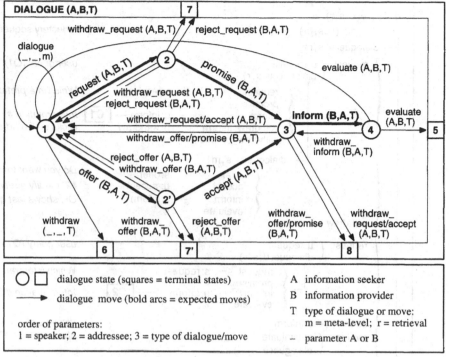

Figure 5. COR net for DIALOGUES.

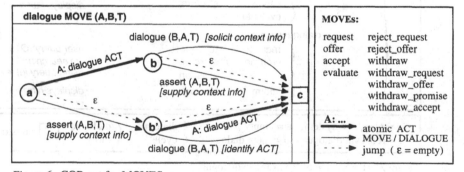

Figure 6. COR net for MOVES.

of a single atomic dialogue *act* (e.g., a request act in the request move). Moves may also include additional elements (e.g., subdialogues) or may even be entirely omitted (empty). A COR analysis of our example dialogue is given in Figure 7 in the form of a complex history tree. It shows the COR acts assigned to the single contributions and illustrates the resulting dialogue structure consisting of dialogue *acts*, *moves*, and *cycles*.

The dialogue network (Figure 5) visualizes different types and functions of moves by graphical means. The arcs pointing to the right-hand side, for example, denote a goal-directed (ideal) course of action consisting of so-called 'expected

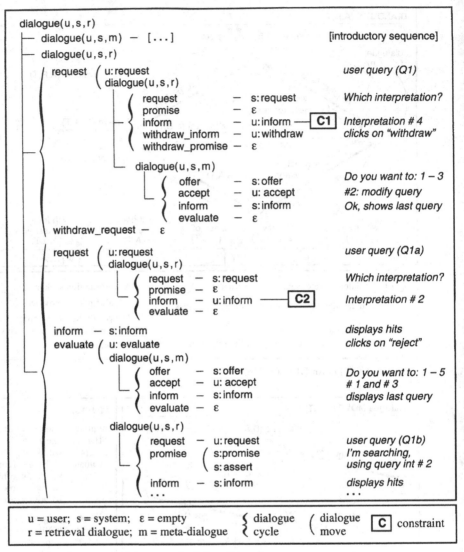

Figure 7. History tree of the example dialogue.

moves', i.e., a move complies with the expectation expressed by the preceding move (e.g., acceptance of an offer). Arcs that point back to state 1 or a terminal state represent deviations from the expected course (these moves being, however, a legitimate and useful means for controlling the dialogue).

Each dialogue cycle may either be initiated by A with a `request` for information or by B with an `offer` to look up some specific piece of information. These *initiating moves/acts* of a cycle or whole (sub-)dialogue have a special status in terms of our definitions of initiative and dialogue control given in Section 3 above. They are instrumental in determining the dialogue focus and at the same time may have a pronounced dialogue control function. The respective speaker takes the dialogue initiative, determining both the global topic of the following dialogue cycle and new ('forward-directed') conditions of action. By contrast, inform (giving requested information) and other statements (volunteered information, such as explanations) do not define new conditions of action.

Aside from inform, *responding moves/acts* have mainly dialogue control functions. They are 'backward directed' in that they refer to previous acts and the conditions of action expressed there, whether in the affirmative or negative (for instance, adopting or rejecting/withdrawing these conditions). Some of them may contribute to the topical progression, for example, when a topic is specified or selected from a list of options offered (accept). However, their primary function is not giving information or introducing new discourse topics, but to either keep the dialogue going or change its direction.

Responding moves that follow the expected dialogue course (promise and accept) neither introduce new conditions of action nor aim to change the direction of the dialogue. An exception is the evaluate move: it is certainly responding, as some information presented is evaluated (relevance assessment); on the other hand, if the evaluation expressed is negative, the move may have a similar function as a rejection. The speaker may not only mean to tell that the information given was irrelevant but may intend to change the direction of the dialogue, possibly in order to shift the global topic. The multi-functionality of acts is quite obvious in this case.

As discussed in Section 3 above, there are basically two ways of changing the direction and *taking control* of the dialogue: withdrawing/rejecting some previous act or initiating an embedded subdialogue. In the withdraw/reject case this does not mean a change in initiative, since these are responding 'control acts'. They may be performed, however, precisely with the aim to take the initiative right after, e.g., when rejecting an offer first and then coming up with a counteroffer or a request for information/action. Initiating a subdialogue, on the other hand, certainly means a change in initiative, since new dialogue topic is being raised, be it a request for help on topic X or an offer to provide an explanation of Y.

Figure 6 shows that an atomic dialogue act (e.g., A: request) may be preceded or followed by optional transitions, i.e., an additional statement (assert) of the speaker (A) or a subdialogue initiated by the addressee (B). The atomic act determines the main illocutionary function of the whole move and is called its 'nucleus', whereas the subdialogues and assert moves are optional 'satellites' (cf. Mann & Thompson, 1987).

Analyses of transcripts of real dialogues between human information seekers and information brokers showed (cf. Sitter & Stein, 1992, Fischer et al., 1994) that in many cases certain moves/acts were explicitly made/uttered but were often skipped in quite similar situations in other states of the dialogue. Usually, information requests and offers were explicit but even these were sometimes missing, for instance, when the specification of the requested/offered information could be inferred from the context or was anticipated. Only inform acts providing requested information/retrieved results (if available), were hardly ever skipped and may hence be used as fix-points for analyzing the dialogues. (These analyses also showed that it was often the human intermediary who took the conversational lead and suggested new ways of how to interpret and solve the information problem.)

Therefore, COR allows in theory any move/act in a retrieval dialogue – except inform – to be omitted, i.e., be a tacit transition (empty acts (ϵ) are also stored in the dialogue history at their respective position in the tree, see Figure 7). For a given application, however, one might need to simplify the COR model somewhat in order to facilitate the generation of the history and reduce its complexity, e.g., avoiding large numbers of empty transitions in a row. In MIRACLE, for example, we have allowed at most two moves per dialogue cycle to be entirely jumped (typically, these are promise and evaluate, but *not* request and inform), and the scripts described below decide which single acts must not be jumped within a move. For other (types of) applications one might disallow the omission of certain moves, globally or for particular dialogue situations. This can be done by specifying variants of networks for different types of moves and dialogues, e.g., considering the domain of discourse (object-level vs. meta-level) and the general function of moves for a dialogue cycle (task-oriented vs. dialogue control function).

Using the COR model we can analyze and represent the complex interchange of dialogue acts – including their propositional content – in a hierarchical dialogue history (see Figure 7). Representing the act type of each individual input action and locating it in the larger structure of the dialogue history (e.g., within moves and subdialogues), the system is in a position to know in which specific situations the user took the initiative and/or tried to change the direction of the dialogue. This builds an important knowledge source for the dialogue component for planning the subsequent interaction.

5.2. SCRIPTS FOR INFORMATION-SEEKING STRATEGIES

Whereas the COR model addresses mixed initiative on the 'dialogue level', scripts address the 'task level' (see also Chu-Carroll & Brown, 1998). COR accounts for possible continuations in any dialogue state but does not place restrictions on the selection of moves, e.g., to determine which of the possible moves should be preferred for a particular task or strategy. The latter is achieved by scripts which give us structured guidelines for tasks like querying a database or browsing in a meta-information resource.

Based on a multi-dimensional classification of information-seeking strategies, the scripts proposed by Belkin et al. (1995) implement *prototypical* interaction patterns corresponding to the various strategies. In MIRACLE they are used as 'tentative' global plans for guiding the user through a session. Here, a script is an executable representation of those types of acts that are useful to fulfill a given task and related goals. That is, a script contains forward-directed, *recommended* user

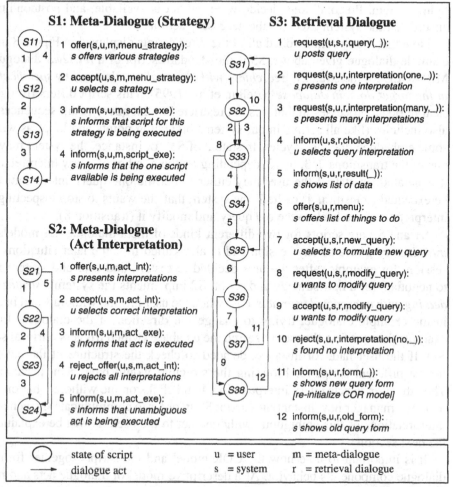

Figure 8. Structure of scripts S1, S2, and S3.

actions and *possible* system reactions at the various stages of a retrieval dialogue. A script may call other sub-scripts to deal with smaller tasks.

Compared to plan operators in traditional planning systems, the scripts are more like *sequences of connected plan operators* that implement typical information-seeking strategies. Although plan operators could give us the same functionality as scripts, the scripts make it easier to relate the dialogue to real information-seeking strategies, and these can be inspected and selected by the end-users without problems.

A recursive transition network (RTN) formalism is used to represent scripts, the transitions containing references to COR dialogue acts (see Figure 8). An additional and unique parameter is added to the COR acts so that the dialogue component can distinguish between the different instances of the acts in the reasoning system. Preconditions decide when an act is available, and postconditions ensure that the system executes the necessary actions.

Note that the system invoked all of the three scripts displayed in Figure 8 in the example dialogue given above. S3 is the standard script of a *retrieval* dialogue in MIRACLE for the strategy *'searching, with the goal of selection, by specification, in the target domain database'* (Belkin et al., 1995). This script differs from classical retrieval processes in that it is not restricted to flat query-result sequences but also includes (like all scripts in our system) branching points and loops as well as some embedded dialogue cycles. In state 2 of S3, for instance, the system may use one of the transitions 2, 3, or 10, depending on the number of query interpretations it generated; in state 3 the user may either select the one query interpretation to be executed (transition 4) or 'tell' the system that she wants to stop inspecting the interpretations, go back to the old query and modify it (transition 8).

S1 and S2 are scripts for two different kinds of meta-dialogue. S1 models the *introductory phase* of any session and is also called in some later situations in a session, for example, after the user decided to restart, and user and system need to negotiate for a new strategy and script. S2 implements the system's *strategy for dealing with unexpected user acts*, e.g., when the user hits the withdraw and buttons in the example dialogue, trying to change the direction of the dialogue. In our example the user first chooses to search the database (which triggers retrieval script S3). If the user had, for instance, decided to check the structure of the database first, a different script for browsing the structure would have been instantiated. Then the user selects query interpretation 4 and clicks on the withdraw button. The dialogue manager now instantiates script S2 in order to communicate the generated interpretations of this ambiguous withdraw act to the user, as will be explained in the next section.

It is important to note how the COR model and the scripts together form the dialogue component's behavior. As a descriptive model of dialogue acts and roles, the COR model allows a mixed-initiative strategy to be adopted without deciding on how the strategy should be realized. Within a script describing a particular task, there is no room for changing the direction of the dialogue. However, letting the user select a dialogue control act (e.g., reject or withdraw), which is a COR act that forces her out of the active script, we take advantage of a change of initiative at the dialogue level in order to reconsider the whole task. When this dialogue control act is then interpreted by the system, the user gets the chance to choose another task, choose another strategy for doing the task, choose other constraints or search terms for the task, etc. Even though the task-oriented scripts are not designed for mixed-initiative problem solving, the change of initiative at the dialogue level combined with a comprehensive reasoning about the user's actions and intentions do also have profound effects at the task level.

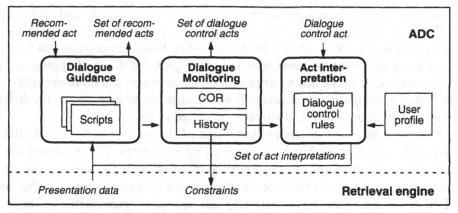

Figure 9. Architecture of the Abductive Dialogue Component (ADC).

6. Abductive Dialogue Planning

The Abductive Dialogue Component (ADC) forms a separate component in MIR-ACLE and provides an interface to the retrieval component. The ADC is implemented in SWI-Prolog using Flach's (1994) abduction engine, and it combines the COR model, the scripts, and other internal knowledge sources into an executable system with reasoning capabilities. With reference to the architecture shown in Figure 9, we first explain the functional aspects of the dialogue component. After going through the use of abduction to interpret ambiguous user acts, we discuss how dynamic and static user models fit into the logical framework and are used to tailor the dialogues to certain characteristics of the user.

6.1. FLEXIBILITY AND GUIDANCE IN RETRIEVAL DIALOGUES

A dialogue starts out with the COR model in its initial state, an empty dialogue history, and a script invoked by the system after the user has selected a task and/or information-seeking strategy from a list or menu offered in the introductory phase of the dialogue. As the dialogue develops, ADC executes the COR model and the script in parallel. For every act in the dialogue, the corresponding transition in the script is fired, and the state of the retrieval session changes. The acts recommended to the user at a certain stage of the dialogue are all the dialogue acts leading out from the active state of the script. By firing script transitions and presenting these recommended acts, the Dialogue Guidance module shown in Figure 9 helps the user to select the actions that are appropriate for satisfying her information needs. The script also includes the system acts that are linked to the transitions and call routines in the underlying retrieval engine.

Since every transition in the script is assigned a generic COR act, like `request` or `inform`, the Dialogue Monitoring module can fire transitions in the COR model and build up a structured dialogue history while the script is being executed. COR acts missing in the current script (e.g., jumps and substructures such as subdialogues) are identified by searching the COR networks. The search yields a list of possible COR transitions leading to the script transition just fired, and a ranking based on complexity is used to pick out the most appropriate one. The resulting tree-like history of primitive dialogue acts and more abstract moves reveals the dialogue structure and tells us what has happened earlier in the dialogue. The history of our example dialogue is sketched in Figure 7.

Now, as long as the user performs one of the recommended acts in the active script, the dialogue history is not used by the system. The recommended acts currently available from the script pop up on the MIRACLE screen as interactive objects (e.g., in Figure 4 the slider for the four query interpretations and the 'search DB' button for executing the currently selected query interpretation). This shows the user what she is supposed to do at the various stages of the retrieval session. Even though these acts are intended to help the user, there might be situations in which the user would like to deviate from the recommendations. She might, for example, change her mind about her query or suddenly realize that she should have chosen another script in the first place. Since we cannot anticipate these deviations in advance, the user needs a set of *generic dialogue control* acts that at least indicate in what direction she might like to change the course of the dialogue. These dialogue control acts are found as backward-directed acts leading out from the active state of the COR model (see dialogue net in Figure 5). They are represented on the MIRACLE screen as generally available dialogue control buttons (as shown in the upper part of Figure 4). Presenting these acts to the user as alternatives to the recommendations from the script, the system gets more flexible and the user can take control of the dialogue when needed.

If the user selects one of the dialogue control acts from the COR model, the Act Interpretation module uses abduction to interpret the act in light of the current dialogue context. In the remaining sections, we have a look at the abduction system and its use in dealing with vague or ambiguous user acts. We first explain the principles of abductive reasoning and then show how the dialogue component works for our example dialogue.

6.2. THE PRINCIPLE OF ABDUCTIVE DIALOGUE PLANNING

As shown in Figure 2, abductive reasoning assumes that there is already a *conclusion* or *observation* available. The task of the abduction engine is to find potential facts that together with a *rule base* would logically imply the conclusion at hand. In MIRACLE the conclusion comes in the form of an observation of user behavior (e.g., a user's query or a dialogue control act), whereas the potential facts are referred to as a *hypothesis* explaining this behavior. The rule base defines the concepts found in the observation and the logical relationships between these and other concepts. Some concepts are not defined at all in the rule base – these are called *abducibles* and are the concepts that can be included in the hypotheses

1. $resume(X) \rightarrow change\_act(X)$
   If the user intends to completely reformulate the propositional content of an act, she changes the original act.

2. $modify(request(X, Y, Z, query(Q))) \rightarrow change\_act(request(X, Y, Z, query(Q)))$
   If the user wants to modify a previous query, she changes the original query.

3. $request(X, Y, Z, W) \wedge change\_act(request(X, Y, Z, W)) \rightarrow change\_input(X, Y, Z)$
   If the user intends to change her previous request, she changes her inputs.

4. $inform(X, Y, Z, W) \wedge change\_act(inform(X, Y, Z, W)) \rightarrow change\_input(X, Y, Z)$
   If the user intends to change her previous inform act, she changes her inputs .

5. $suppress(X) \wedge change\_session \rightarrow evaluate(X, neg)$
   If the user wants to suppress the system act and change to another session, she hits the reject button.

6. $suppress(inform(X, Y, Z, W)) \wedge change\_input(Y, X, Z) \rightarrow evaluate(inform(X, Y, Z, W), neg)$
   If the user wants to suppress the data presented and change her inputs to the system, she hits the reject button.

7. $inform(X, Y, Z, W) \wedge change\_input(X, Y, Z) \rightarrow withdraw(inform(X, Y, Z, W))$
   If the user has given some information and wants to change the inputs, she withdraws her inform act.

8. $inform(X) \wedge delete\_or\_store(inform(X, Y, Z, W)) \rightarrow suppress((inform(X, Y, Z, W))$
   If the user wants to delete or store some presented data for later use, she suppresses them in the current context.

Figure 10. Some dialogue control rules.

explaining the observation. If there are several hypotheses that imply the observed phenomenon, each hypothesis forms an *interpretation* of the observation. The user can then choose the interpretation she finds closest to her intentions.

There are a number of recent approaches that also deal with the disambiguation of dialogue acts or misconceptions using abductive inference (e.g., Hobbs et al., 1993, and McRoy & Hirst, 1995). The fundamental difference to our approach is that they focus on linguistic ambiguities in natural language discourse, whereas we deal with contextual (dialogue-dependent) ambiguity.

In ADC the dialogue control act chosen from the COR model is the observation, and the rule base is made up of certain dialogue control rules (see Figure 10). The rules map from concrete actions and properties of the dialogue history to these backward-directed control acts from COR. When a dialogue control act is chosen by the user, a part of the dialogue history together with the dialogue control rules provide the logical basis for interpreting this ambiguous act. We look for a hypothesis that allows the dialogue control act to be inferred according to the following logical relationship:

$$Dialogue\_context \cup Dialogue\_control\_rules \cup Hypothesis \vdash$$
$$Dialogue\_control\_act$$

The dialogue context is a subset of the complete dialogue history. It contains the list of atomic system acts and atomic user acts that are found relevant on the basis of the history tree. An act α in the history tree is deemed relevant to a dialogue control act β if the two acts do not belong to different (high-level) dialogue cycles at the same level in the dialogue tree and if there is no other dialogue control act γ between α and β. The content of these dialogue contexts will become clearer when we explain the reasoning behind the example dialogue.

Some of the dialogue control rules are shown in Figure 10. Note that these rules contain atomic acts (but not *moves*), and the logical representation used here corresponds to the prefix notation for atomic acts used in the COR nets and the dialogue history, e.g., request(A ,_,_,_) would correspond to A: request. The concrete actions included in the hypothesis explain what the user intended to do when she chose the dialogue control act in that particular context. When there are many hypotheses that imply the dialogue control act of the user, each of them is referred to as an *interpretation of the act*. The rules are set up on the basis of some initial system testing and are to be refined and extended as the system is evaluated with real users.

Looking at the dialogue control rules in Figure 10, we see that a negative evaluate act can be interpreted either as a user's intention to change her previous input (Rule 6) or as a dissatisfaction with the current script (Rule 5). A withdraw act is only interpreted as the intention to change the previous input (Rule 7). The predicates resume/1, modify/1, change_session/0, and delete_or_store/1 are abducibles and are offered to the user as possible interpretations of her ambiguous dialogue act. Each of them is linked to a function in the IR system that the user might be interested in running. The atomic dialogue acts referred to in the rules, like inform/4, count as facts if they are found in the dialogue context.

6.3. INTERPRETING DIALOGUE CONTROL ACTS

Consider the example dialogue presented in Figure 3, in which the user is searching for some information about painters in the database. She enters a query using the fields profession, subject, and town, and the retrieval engine presents four interpretations of the query. So far, the dialogue is a simple execution of script S3. After choosing one of the query interpretations generated and displayed on the screen as shown in Figure 4, however, the user suddenly hits the *withdraw button*. This act is not anticipated in script S3, but is one of those dialogue control acts made available from the COR model. Since it is not clear what the user wants to do next, the abduction process is triggered, and ADC tries to figure out how the act should be understood and what dialogue continuations are possible and can be recommended in this situation.

At this moment, there is a dialogue context H1 containing the following three acts (see also the COR history tree in Figure 7):

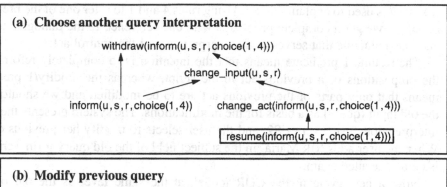

(a) Choose another query interpretation

withdraw(inform(u,s,r,choice(1,4)))

change_input(u,s,r)

inform(u,s,r,choice(1,4))   change_act(inform(u,s,r,choice(1,4)))

resume(inform(u,s,r,choice(1,4)))

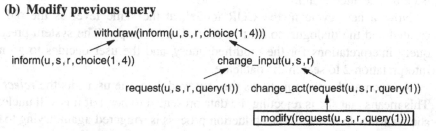

(b) Modify previous query

withdraw(inform(u,s,r,choice(1,4)))

inform(u,s,r,choice(1,4))   change_input(u,s,r)

request(u,s,r,query(1))   change_act(request(u,s,r,query(1)))

modify(request(u,s,r,query(1)))

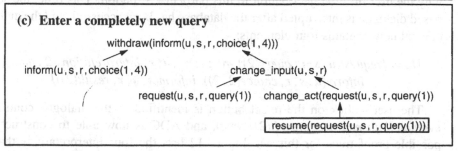

(c) Enter a completely new query

withdraw(inform(u,s,r,choice(1,4)))

inform(u,s,r,choice(1,4))   change_input(u,s,r)

request(u,s,r,query(1))   change_act(request(u,s,r,query(1)))

resume(request(u,s,r,query(1)))

Figure 11. Interpretations of the withdraw act (proof trees).

$$H1 = \{request(u,s,r,query(1)), request(s,u,r,interpretations(1,many)),$$
$$inform(u,s,r,choice(1,4))\}$$

The first predicate in H1 is the user's query (request), the second is the system's presentation of query interpretations (request, asking the user which one she prefers), and the last is the user's answer (inform), i.e., her choice of the one interpretation to be used for searching in the database. The observation to be explained is the subsequent withdrawal of the user, which is stored in ADC as *withdraw_inform(u,s,r,choice(1,4))*. The abduction engine uses the dialogue control rules in the reverse direction to find possible proofs for the observation (see the proof trees in Figure 11).

A proof tree is valid when all non-proven predicates are either abducibles or come from the dialogue trace. In our example dialogue three interpretations of the withdraw act are inferred. The starting point of the proof trees shown in Figure 11 is the dialogue control act *withdraw_inform(u,s,r,choice(1,4))*. In the first proof

(a) rule 7 is used to explain this act. Using rules 4 and 1 to infer one of the premises of rule 7, we get a complete proof tree with one reference to the dialogue history and one abducible that serves as the interpretation of the control act.

The resume/1 predicate means that the intention is to completely reformulate the propositions of a previous act in the script, whereas the modify/1 predicate means that only parts of the previous act are to be modified and we should keep the old input (query) as a basis for the modifications. The system presents the three interpretations using script S2, and the user selects to modify her previous query. When the user adds 'OR Maria' in the subject field of the old query form, script S1 is being executed again.

Now, a new cycle in the COR model, at the same level as the old one, is created and the dialogue context is defined to be empty. The system presents the query interpretations for the modified query, and the user decides to go now for interpretation 2 to search the database.

As soon as the system shows the retrieved data, the user hits the *reject button*. This means that she is rejecting the data presented to her, but it is still unclear what she wants to do instead. The abduction process is triggered again, trying to explain why the user hit the reject button in this particular situation. This time, the script-based dialogue is interrupted after the database has been accessed, and the dialogue context now contains four elements:

$$H2 = \{request(u, s, r, query(2)), request(s, u, r, interpretations(2, many)),$$
$$inform(u, s, r, choice(2, 2)), inform(s, u, r, result(2))\}$$

The user's click on the reject button is identified as the dialogue control act *evaluate(inform(s, u, r, result(2)), neg)*, and ADC is now able to construct four possible proof trees for this act. Figure 12 lists the four interpretations that are presented as alternative actions to the user. Since the system has presented some data to the user, the user is given a chance to save the data before she starts doing something else (the delete_or_store predicate). She is then given the choice between choosing another interpretation, creating a new or modified query, or starting a new retrieval session.

In this way the dialogue component is able to deal with ambiguous user acts that take the initiative in the dialogue and change its direction. The dialogue component tries to explain ambiguous acts on the basis of the context and maps them to possible concrete actions that are presented to the user. At the same time, executing the script makes it possible for the ADC to guide the user and help her work efficiently with the system. The logical foundation ensures the extensibility and reliability of the component, and – as we will see in the next section – it enables the system to use two very powerful user-tailoring mechanisms.

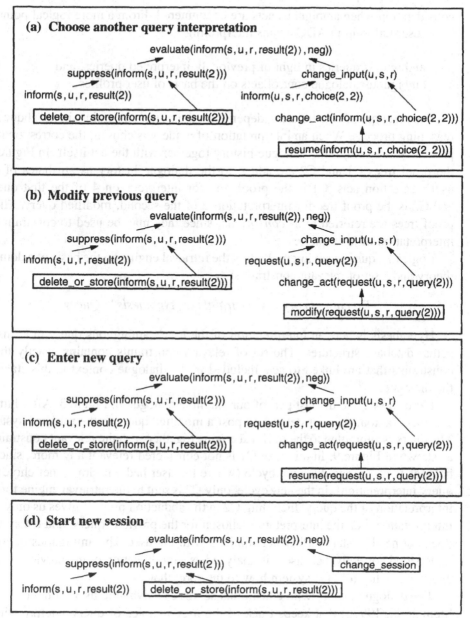

Figure 12. Interpretations of the evaluate act (proof trees).

6.4. USER-TAILORING OF DIALOGUES

User-tailoring in ADC is possible both at the retrieval level and at the dialogue act level. As far as retrieval is concerned, the component dynamically adapts the retrieval engine's behavior according to the user's previous choices. User-tailoring at the dialogue level is more static, but implies that user profiles are taken into consideration when ambiguous acts are encountered. From a more logical point of view, user-tailoring in ADC means interpreting

- ambiguous queries in light of previously interpreted queries, and
- ambiguous dialogue control acts on the basis of user profiles.

The first type of user-tailoring depends on the use of constraints in the abductive reasoning process. When an interpretation of a query is chosen, the corresponding proof tree is added to the dialogue history together with the act itself. In Figure 7, the proof trees C1 and C2 are added to the dialogue history as attributes of the user's selection acts. C1 is the proof tree for interpretation 4 of the first query, and C2 is the proof tree for interpretation 2 of the second, modified query. These proof trees are referred to as *constraints*, since they may be used to constrain the interpretation of later queries.

Logically, queries are interpreted by the retrieval engine on the basis of a domain theory and a set of relevant constraints:

$$Domain\_theory \cup Constraints \cup Hypothesis \vdash Query$$

Hypothesis is here an interpretation of the user's ambiguous query in terms of actual database structures. The set of relevant constraints contains exactly those constraints that are linked to acts included in the dialogue context at this stage of the dialogue.

Let us now go to the last part of our example dialogue in Figure 3. After hitting the reject button, the user decides to post a modified query to the retrieval system. The query is submitted to the retrieval engine together with the relevant constraints, as shown in Figure 9. In this case C1 is not considered relevant any more, since it belongs to a separate dialogue cycle (where the user had withdrawn her choice of query interpretation). In the new cycle, only C2 is sent to the retrieval engine for the interpretation of the query. Including C2 in the abduction process gives us only one interpretation, i.e., the interpretation chosen for the previous query, and the system does not need to start further negotiations with the user. The ambiguous query is understood correctly, because it is analyzed as a modification of the previous query and the user has told the system how to interpret that one.

The dialogue history with constraints serves as a dynamic user model (see also Stein et al., 1997b) that keeps track of the user's choice of query interpretations. Using the constraints, the retrieval engine gradually builds up an understanding of how the user wants her queries to be interpreted. The COR analysis of the dialogue (see Figure 7) indicates which of the user's previous choices are relevant to the new queries. If the COR analysis of the dialogue structure is wrong, important constraints may be lost and the user would be forced to specify the same choices several times.

Now, the second form of user modeling deals with the user's choice of dialogue acts. Without user-tailoring, the dialogue context decides which dialogue control rules can be used to construct a proof tree. It is, however, possible to specify a *user profile* that further restricts the abductive reasoning process. Such a profile is a set of facts that determines the desirability of certain dialogue acts. For taking user profiles into consideration, the abduction process has to be modified as follows:

$$Dialogue\_context \cup Dialogue\_control\_rules \cup User\_profile \cup Hypothesis \vdash$$
$$Dialogue\_control\_act$$

The system now looks for an interpretation that takes the dialogue context as well as the specific preferences of the user into account. If the user as a rule prefers not to modify old queries, she would simply specify a user profile P like this: $P = \{\neg\, modify(\_,\_,\_,\_)\}$. This profile would rule out all act interpretations that assume the user to modify an existing query. The interpretations involving the posting of completely new queries would be allowed, as would interpretations that do not directly address any previous queries. If this user profile had been specified before the withdraw act in the example dialogue above, for instance, only the interpretations (a) and (c) would have been presented: 'Do you want to (1) choose another query interpretation or (2) enter a completely new query?'.

The user profile helps us set up a personalized user interface. Only actions preferred by the user are made available to the act interpretation process, and the user can change the profile at any time during the dialogue. In theory, the user profile can also include dialogue control rules that are relevant only to one person or a group of persons. Such rules have to be formulated with care, though, since they have to be consistent with the other dialogue control rules available. Automatic update of the profile on the basis of the ongoing dialogue is feasible, though it is hard to say how useful that is.

The kernel of ADC is the abduction engine that constitutes a platform for combining different kinds of dialogue information. User profiles, constraints, dialogue histories, and rules for interpreting dialogue acts all fit into the same logical framework. As a whole, this system allows us to infer observable dialogue control acts from properties of the user and the dialogue context by making assumptions about the user's real intentions. The assumptions come in the form of system functions that may change the direction of the dialogue and the whole purpose of the retrieval session. Logically speaking, thus, mixed-initiative dialogues at the task level arise when

– the user triggers the abduction process with a dialogue control act,
– the user's real intentions cannot unambiguously be inferred, and
– the relevant dialogue control rules address task-oriented concepts.

As such, mixed-initiative dialogues come into play when the user suspends the current dialogue course, e.g., rejecting a system's suggestion, or when she does not precisely formulate her information need, e.g., entering an ambiguous query. In both kinds of situations the system is able to engage in a cooperative dialogue with the user. Making assumptions about the user's actual information need, the system takes the initiative and offers the user interpretations of her query based on the domain model of the database and the dialogue context (i.e., constraints stored in the dialogue history). The dialogue manager, on the other hand, analyzes the intentional structure of the dialogue history and is thus able to identify situations where the users tries to change the current dialogue strategy. It acts cooperatively in such situations, suggesting suitable continuations of the retrieval dialogue in such a way that the user can easily switch to the newly suggested dialogue course and does not need to activate complicated sequences of interface functions.

7. Conclusions

The model of mixed-initiative retrieval dialogues presented in this article relies on knowledge about users which is incrementally acquired from their interactive behavior during a session with an IR system. The Abductive Dialogue Component (ADC) of the MIRACLE system uses a comprehensive dialogue model to construct a complex dialogue history, part of which is used as a dynamic user model. The dialogue history explicitly represents both the intentional structure of the discourse and knowledge about the user's preferences for particular retrieval strategies and query interpretations.

Whereas the retrieval interaction is roughly guided by dialogue scripts, the user may change the direction of the dialogue at any time. The dialogue model allows her to perform certain 'dialogue control acts', such as reject and withdraw, in order to depart from the initial script. If such a dialogue control act is ambiguous in a given situation, the dialogue component uses abduction to generate plausible 'interpretations' of the act based on a number of dialogue control rules and the dialogue history/context. The interpretations show the user which concrete retrieval functions and strategies are available in this situation. Aside from just informing the user about these options, the system takes the initiative and *recommends* suitable dialogue continuations to the user, i.e., in this case, actions that are not pre-specified by scripts. Based on the user's choice of action, the system adapts its subsequent behavior, updating the initial script or instantiating a new one. A specific interpretation may also include an abducible that assumes certain characteristics of the user, and if this interpretation is selected, the assumption is found valid and used to filter the interpretations of later user acts.

Given the dialogue model and the abductive reasoning mechanism, the next task for the dialogue component is to extend the set of dialogue control rules, i.e., formulate adequate rules that have the necessary generality. The rules must refer to the functionality of the given retrieval system but also take the short-term conditions of the dialogue into account. A larger number of dialogue control rules will allow us to gradually dispense with the dialogue scripts and to achieve more flexibility in the handling of mixed-initiative retrieval dialogues.

Acknowledgements

We would like to thank Adrian Müller for the design and implementation of the abductive retrieval component of the MIRACLE system, and the three anonymous reviewers for their comments on earlier drafts of this paper.

References

Allen, J. F.: 1994, *Mixed Initiative Planning: Position Paper*. Paper presented at ARPA/Rome Labs Planning Initiative Workshop. Also available from http://www.cs.rochester.edu/research/trains-/mip/home.html.

Bates, M.: 1986, An exploratory paradigm for online information retrieval. In: B. Brookes (ed.): *Intelligent Information Systems for the Information Society*. Amsterdam: North-Holland, 91–99.

Belkin, N. J., Cool, C., Stein, A. and Thiel, U.: 1995, Cases, scripts, and information seeking strategies: On the design of interactive information retrieval systems. *Expert Systems and Applications* 9(3), 379–395.

Belkin, N. J. and Vickery, A.: 1985, *Interaction in Information Systems: A Review of Research from Document Retrieval to Knowledge-Based Systems*. London: The British Library.

Bunt, H. C.: 1989, Information dialogues as communicative action in relation to partner modeling and information processing. In: M. M. Taylor, F. Neel, and D. G. Bouwhuis (eds.): *The Structure of Multimodal Dialogue*. Amsterdam: North-Holland, 47–73.

Bunt, H. C.: 1996, Interaction management functions and context representation requirements. In: S. LuperFoy, A. Nijholt, and G. van Zanten (eds.): *Dialogue Management in Natural Language Systems. Proceedings of the Eleventh Twente Workshop on Language Technology*. Enschede, NL, 187–198.

Callan, J. P., Croft, W. B. and Harding, S. M.: 1992, The INQUERY Retrieval system. In: *Proceedings of the 3rd International Conference on Database and Expert Systems Application*. Berlin and New York: Springer, 78–83.

Chu-Carroll, J. and Brown, M. K.: 1998, An Evidential Model for Tracking Initiative in Collaborative Dialogue Interactions. *User Modeling and User-Adapted Interaction* 8(3-4), 215–254.

Chu-Carroll, J. and Carberry, S.: 1995, Generating information-sharing subdialogues in expert-user consultation. In: C. S. Mellish (ed.): *Proceedings of the 14th International Joint Conference on Artificial Intelligence (IJCAI '95)*. San Mateo, CA: Morgan Kaufmann, 1243–1250.

Cohen, R. et al.: 1998, What is Initiative?. *User Modeling and User-Adapted Interaction* 8(3-4), 171–214.

Fawcett, R. P., van der Mije, A. and van Wissen, C.: 1988, Towards a systemic flowchart model for discourse. In: *New Developments in Systemic Linguistics*. London: Pinter, 116–143.

Fischer, M., Maier, E. A. and Stein, A.: 1994, Generating cooperative system responses in information retrieval dialogues. In: *Proceedings of the Seventh International Workshop on Natural Language Generation (INLG '94), Kennebunkport, ME*. 207–216.

Flach, P.: 1994, *Simply Logical: Intelligent Reasoning by Example*. Chichester: John Wiley.

Grosz, B. J. and Sidner, C. L.: 1986, Attention, intentions and the structure of discourse. *Computational Linguistics* 12(3), 175–204.

Grosz, B. J. and Sidner, C. L.: 1990, Plans for discourse. In: P. R. Cohen, J. Morgan, and M. E. Pollack (eds.): *Intentions in Communication*. Cambridge, MA: MIT Press, 417–444.

Grote, B., Hagen, E., Stein, A. and Teich, E.: 1997, Speech production in human-machine dialogue: A natural language generation perspective. In: E. Maier, M. Mast, and S. LuperFoy (eds.): *Dialogue Processing in Spoken Language Systems. ECAI'96 Workshop, Budapest, Hungary*. Berlin, Heidelberg and New York: Springer, 70–85.

Hagen, E.: 1999, *An Approach to Mixed Initiative Spoken Dialogue*. In this issue.

Hobbs, J. R., Stickel, M. E., Appelt, D. E. and Martin, P.: 1993, Interpretation as abduction. *Artificial Intelligence* **63**(1-2), 69–142.

Ingwersen, P.: 1992, *Information Retrieval Interaction*. London: Taylor Graham.

Jameson, A. and T. Weis: 1995, How to juggle discourse obligations. In: *Proceedings of the Symposium on Conceptual and Semantic Knowledge in Language Generation*. Heidelberg. (Also available as Report No. 133, SFB378 (READY), University of the Saarland, Oct. 1996).

Logan, B., Reece, S. and Sparck Jones, K.: 1994, Modelling information retrieval agents with belief revision. In: W. Croft and C. van Rijsbergen (eds.): *Proceedings of the 17th Annual International Conference on Research and Development in Information Retrieval (SIGIR '94)*. Berlin: Springer, 91–100.

Maier, E., Mast, M. and LuperFoy, S. (eds.): 1997, *Dialogue Processing in Spoken Language Systems. ECAI'96 Workshop, Budapest, Hungary*. Berlin and New York: Springer.

Mann, W. C. and Thompson, S. A.: 1987, Rhetorical structure theory: A theory of text organization. In: L. Polanyi (ed.): *The Structure of Discourse*. Norwood, NJ: Ablex, 85–96.

Maybury, M. T. (ed.): 1997, *Intelligent Multimedia Information Retrieval*. Menlo Park, CA: AAAI Press/MIT Press.

Maybury, M. T. and Wahlster, W. (eds.): 1998, *Readings in Intelligent User Interfaces*. San Mateo, CA: Morgan Kaufman.

McRoy, S. W., Haller, S. and Ali, S. S.: 1997, Uniform knowledge representation for language processing in the B2 system. *Natural Language Engineering* **3**(2–3), 123–145.

McRoy, S. W. and Hirst, G.: 1995, The repair of speech act misunderstandings by abductive inference. *Computational Linguistics* **21**(4), 435–478.

Moore, J. D. and Paris, C. L.: 1993, Planning text for advisory dialogues: capturing intentional and rhetorical information. *Computational Linguistics* **19**(4), 651–694.

Müller, A. and Kutschekmanesch, S.: 1996, Using abductive inference and dynamic indexing to retrieve multimedia SGML documents. In: I. Ruthven (ed.): *MIRO 95. Proceedings of the Final Workshop on Multimedia Information Retrieval*. Berlin and New York: Springer (eWiC, electronic Workshops in Computing series).

Müller, A. and Thiel, U.: 1994, Query expansion in an abductive information retrieval system. In: *Proceedings of the Conference on Intelligent Multimedia Information Retrieval Systems and Management (RIAO '94), Vol. 1*. New York, 461–480.

Oddy, R.: 1977, Information retrieval through man-machine-dialogue. *Journal of Documentation* **33**(1), 1–14.

Rich, C. and Sidner, C. L.: 1998, COLLAGEN: A Collaboration Manager for Software Interface Agents. *User Modeling and User-Adapted Interaction* **8**(3-4), 315–349.

Rich, E.: 1989, Stereotypes and user modeling. In: A. Kobsa and W. Wahlster (eds.): *User Models in Dialogue Systems*. Berlin and New York: Springer, 35–51.

Ruthven, I. (ed.): 1996, *MIRO 95. Proceedings of the Final Workshop on Multimedia Information Retrieval*. Berlin and New York:, Springer (eWiC, electronic Workshops in Computing series).

Salton, G. and McGill, M. J.: 1983, *Introduction to Modern Information Retrieval*. New York: McGraw-Hill.

Saracevic, T., Spink, A. and Wu, M.-M.: 1997, Users and intermediaries in information retrieval: What are they talking about?'. In: A. Jameson, C. Paris, and C. Tasso (eds.): *User Modeling: Proceedings of the Sixth International Conference, UM '97*. Vienna and New York: Springer Wien New York, 43–54.

Schuster, E., Chin, D., Cohen, R., Kobsa, A., Morik, K., Sparck Jones, K. and Wahlster, W.: 1988, Discussion section on the relationship between user models and dialogue models. *Computational Linguistics* **14**(3), 79–103.

Sitter, S. and Stein, A.: 1992, Modeling the illocutionary aspects of information-seeking dialogues. *Information Processing & Management* **28**(2), 165–180.

Sitter, S. and Stein, A.: 1996, Modeling information-seeking dialogues: The conversational roles (COR) model. *RIS: Review of Information Science (online journal)* **1**(1). Available from http://www.inf-wiss.uni-konstanz.de/RIS/...

Stein, A.: 1997, Usability and assessments of multimodal interaction in the SPEAK! system: An experimental case study. *New Review of Hypermedia and Multimedia (NRHM), Special Issue on Evaluation of Multimedia IR Systems* **3**, 159–180.

Stein, A., Gulla, J. A., Müller, A. and Thiel, U.: 1997a, Conversational interaction for semantic access to multimedia information. In: M. T. Maybury (ed.): *Intelligent Multimedia Information Retrieval.* Menlo Park, CA: AAAI/The MIT Press, 399–421.

Stein, A., Gulla, J. A. and Thiel, U.: 1997b, Making sense of user mouse clicks: Abductive reasoning and conversational dialogue modeling. In: A. Jameson, C. Paris, and C. Tasso (eds.): *User Modeling: Proceedings of the Sixth International Conference, UM '97.* Vienna and New York: Springer Wien New York, 89–100.

Stein, A. and Thiel, U.: 1993, A conversational model of multimodal interaction in information systems. In: *Proceedings of the 11th National Conference on Artificial Intelligence (AAAI '93), Washington D.C.* Menlo Park, CA: AAAI Press/ MIT Press, 283–288.

Stock, O., Strapparava, C. and Zancanaro, M.: 1997, Explorations in an environment for natural language multi-modal information access. In: M. T. Maybury (ed.): *Intelligent Multimedia Information Retrieval.* Menlo Park, CA: AAAI Press/The MIT Press, 381–398.

Taylor, J. A., Carletta, J. and Mellish, C.: 1996, Requirements for belief models in cooperative dialogue. *User Modeling and User-Adapted Interaction* **6**(1), 23–68.

Terveen, L. G.: 1995, Overview of human-computer collaboration. *Knowledge-Based Systems. Special Issue on Human-Computer Collaboration* **8**(2-3), 67–81.

Thiel, U., Gulla, J. A., Müller, A. and Stein, A.: 1996, Dialogue strategies for multimedia retrieval: Intertwining abductive reasoning and dialogue planning. In: I. Ruthven (ed.): *MIRO 95. Proceedings of the Final Workshop on Multimedia Information Retrieval.* Berlin and New York: Springer (eWiC, electronic Workshops in Computing series).

Traum, D. R. and Allen, J. F.: 1994, Discourse obligations in dialogue processing. In: *Proceedings of the 32nd Annual Meeting of the Association for Computational Linguistics (ACL '94),* 1–8.

Traum, D. R. and Hinkelman, E.: 1992, Conversation acts in task-oriented spoken dialogue. *Computational Intelligence* **8**(3), 575–599.

van Rijsbergen, C. J.: 1989, Towards an information logic. In: N. Belkin and C. van Rijsbergen (eds.): *Proceedings of the SIGIR '89.* New York: ACM Press, 77–86.

Wahlster, W. and Kobsa, A.: 1989, User models in dialogue systems. In: A. Kobsa and W. Wahlster (eds.): *User Models in Dialogue Systems.* Berlin and New York: Springer, Chapt. 1, 4–34.

Winograd, T. and Flores, F.: 1986, *Understanding Computers and Cognition.* Norwood, NJ: Ablex.

Authors' vitae

Dr. Adelheit Stein

GMD-IPSI, German National Research Center for Information Technology, Integrated Publication and Information Systems Institute, D-64293 Darmstadt

Dr. A. Stein has been a senior researcher at GMD-IPSI since 1988. She received her M.S. degree in Philosophy, Sociology, and Psychology and her Ph.D. in Social Sciences from the University of Constance in 1980 and 1983, respectively. She worked as a researcher at the University of Constance until 1984 in the fields of social interaction theory, human development, and family studies. Until 1987 she was deputy manager of a German association of online information providers in Frankfurt. Her current research interests include human–computer collaboration, dialogue modeling and planning, and intelligent interfaces for information retrieval. The present article describes joint research initiated during Dr. Gulla's research stay at GMD-IPSI.

Dr. Jon Atle Gulla
Norsk Hydro, Av. de Marcel Thiry 83, 1200 Brussels, Belgium.
Also: Norwegian University of Science and Technology, Department of Computer Science, N-7034 Trondheim, Norway

Dr. J. A. Gulla is a senior consultant at Norsk Hydro and also a part-time associate professor at the Norwegian University of Science and Technology. He received his M.S. and Ph.D. degrees in Computer Science from the Norwegian Institute of Technology in 1988 and 1993, respectively. He received his M.S. degree in Linguistics from the University of Trondheim in 1995. From 1995 to 1996 he was a guest researcher at GMD-IPSI. Dr. Gulla has worked in several areas of software engineering and artificial intelligence, including conceptual modeling, knowledge representation, text generation, and dialogue systems. He is now focusing on change management issues in software engineering projects.

Dr. Ulrich Thiel
GMD-IPSI, German National Research Center for Information Technology, Integrated Publication and Information Systems Institute, D-64293 Darmstadt

Dr. U. Thiel is head of the research division 'Advanced Retrieval Support for Digital Libraries' at GMD-IPSI. He received his M.S. (diploma) in Computer Science from the University of Dortmund in 1983 and his Ph.D. in Information Science from the University of Constance in 1990. Until 1988 he was a researcher and lecturer of Information Science at the University of Constance. Since 1990 he has been manager of several projects and research groups in GMD-IPSI. His primary research interests are in multimedia information retrieval, intelligent interfaces, and discourse and user modeling. Current projects of the division focus on digital library systems, information filtering, recommender systems, multimedia retrieval, intelligent retrieval and dialogue management.

User Modeling and User-Adapted Interaction **9:** 167–213, 1999.
© 1999 *Kluwer Academic Publishers.*

An Approach to Mixed Initiative Spoken Information Retrieval Dialogue

ELI HAGEN*
Simon Fraser University, Burnaby, BC, Canada; Deutsche Telekom Berkom, Darmstadt, Germany;
e-mail: hagen@cs.sfu.ca

(Received: 12 November 1997; accepted in revised form 17 July 1998)

Abstract. We present an approach to mixed initiative dialogue in acoustic user interfaces to databases. First, we discuss how we distinguish between initiative and control in mixed initiative information retrieval dialogue and how the notions of taking, keeping, and relinquishing initiative and control are reflected in our approach. Based on this discussion, we develop a dialogue planning algorithm. This algorithm distinguished between resources and routines and between the type and the content of an utterance; type and content are calculated separately by routines that reason on the resources – a dialogue model, a dialogue history, and an application description. Through this division we achieve a dialogue where the system adapts to the user's attempts at changing the direction of a dialogue. Finally, we argue that automatic segmentation of the dialogue and automatic tracking of initiative and control is inherent to our approach.

Key words: dialogue management, dialogue planning, mixed initiative dialogue, spoken dialogue systems

1. Introduction

Our main goal is to develop fully automatic spoken information retrieval systems with which a person can speak close to naturally. Over the years, many dialogue systems have been researched (Baekgaard et al., 1994; Sadek et al., 1994; Ball & Ling, 1994; Blomberg et al., 1993; Peckham, 1993; Oerder & Aust, 1993; Glass et al., 1995) and currently there is industrial interest in the field – notably from the phone companies (Spiegel & Kamm, 1997). Companies partly introduce new services in order to gain competitive advantage and partly to automate existing services in order to reduce cost. Directory assistance and switch board services (Whittaker & Attwater, 1994; Kaspar et al., 1995; Naito et al., 1994) are typical examples.

The speech technology in dialogue systems consists of a speech recognition/ interpretation module that analyses and interprets user utterances and a text generation/speech synthesis module that generates and produces system utterances.

---

* The author is a visiting researcher in the research group, Interaktionssysteme, Deutsch Telekom Berkom, D-64307 Darmstadt, Germany. The research described here was developed as part of their TESADIS project (see Feldes et al. 1998).

Additionally, we need a dialogue manager that coordinates these modules,[1] it decides when the system shall speak, what it shall say, when the system shall listen, and what it shall listen for. The dialogue manager works on an abstract level, i.e. it produces abstract representation that are transformed into low level representations by the other modules; the text generator produces a text (our language is German) and the speech recognizer a recognition grammar and vocabulary.

On the recognition side, we need to overcome the problem of imperfect speech recognition, thus we chose a predictive approach. If the dialogue manager predicts what the user might say, the recognizer can adjust its recognition grammars and vocabularies accordingly, such that the recognition rate increases. Predictive approaches have also been suggested by Bilange (1991), Dahlbäck & Jönsson (1992), and Young et al. (1990).

On the synthesis side, the dialogue manager must choose the type of the next utterance (e.g. ask for a new value or ask for confirmation of a previously recognized value), it must choose the content of the next utterance, and it must decide whether to produce a complex utterances with several communicative goals or not (e.g. implicit confirmation).

A central theme on both the recognition and the synthesis side is that utterances may contain several communicative goals. We argue that a dialogue system should be able to understand complex user utterances (e.g. over-answering) and to produce its own complex utterances since they can lead to more efficient and less annoying dialogues between user and system.[2] The two dialogues below illustrate this point. In Dialogue 1 several communicative goals are understood and produced, while Dialogue 2 shows the single goal alternatives of these utterances. (The $_T$, $_K$, $_R$ notation will be explained in Section 2.3. Please ignore it here.)

Dialogue 1: Mixed initiative dialogue

    A.   Sys: $_T$Welcome to TESADIS.$_R$
    B.   Usr: ⟨No response⟩$_R$
    C.   Sys: $_T$Do you want the rate$_K$ or the total cost of a call?$_R$
    D.   Usr: $_T$The rate$_K$ of a call to Frankfurt, please.$_R$
    E.   Sys: $_T$Do you want the rate$_K$ of a call to Frankfurt am Main$_K$ or Frankfurt an...?[3]
    F.   Usr: $_T$Am Main.$_R$
    G.   Sys: ⟨Long pause⟩$_R$
    H.   Usr: $_T$On a holiday.$_R$

Dialogue 2: Question/answer dialogue

    A.   Sys: $_T$Welcome to TESADIS.
    B.   Do you want the rate of a call?$_R$
    C.   Usr: $_T$Yes, to Frankfurt, please.$_R$
    D.   Sys: $_T$What is the destination of your call?$_R$
    E.   Usr: $_T$Frankfurt!$_R$

---

[1] In this paper, the terms dialogue manager, dialogue planner, and dialogue planning algorithm are used synonymously.

[2] In (Hagen & Grote, 1997), we presented some ideas of how to deal with the production side.

F. Sys: $_T$ Is the destination of your call Frankfurt? $_R$
G. Usr: $_T$ Yes!! $_R$
H. Sys: $_T$ Do you want Frankfurt an der Oder? $_R$
I. Usr: $_T$ NOOOOO! FRANKFURT AM MAAAAIIIN!! $_R$
J. Sys: $_T$ Do you want Frankfurt am Main? $_R$

All examples in this paper are taken from one of TESADIS' test applications – a system that customers can call and ask questions about the cost of telephone calls between various locations at various times, i.e. the system needs to acquire inform- ation about the zone (local or long distance) and the time of a call. This application is described in more detail in Section 4.1.

The issues discussed above can be summarized under the heading of *mixed ini- tiative dialogue*, and using the mixed initiative terminology, they can be rephrased as: A dialogue manager must know when to take, keep, and relinquish initiative and control. It must recognize when the user takes, keeps, and relinquishes initi- ative and control. It must adapt to the user's behaviour and react appropriately to unexpected changes in initiative.

In this paper, we develop a mixed initiative dialogue planning algorithm and show how initiative and control are reflected in our approach. Our algorithm dis- tinguishes between resources and routines and between the type and the content of an utterance; type and content are calculated separately by routines that reason on the resources – a dialogue model, a dialogue history, and an application description. Through this division we achieve a dialogue where the system adapts to the user's attempts at changing the direction of a dialogue.

The paper is organized as follows. In Sections 2 and 3, we discuss initiative and control and how the notions of taking, keeping, relinquishing, and taking back initiative and control are reflected in our approach. We define, control in terms of the dialogue model and the dialogue history, thus before defining control in Section 3, we present these two resources. In Sections 4 and 5, we discuss how the ideas in the previous sections are realized computationally in a mixed initiative dialogue manager. In the remainder of this section, we present an overview of the dialogue manager and how it interacts with the other modules in a dialogue system.

1.1. OVERVIEW OF THE APPROACH

Several approaches to dialogue management have been proposed in the literature, e.g. plan recognition based approaches (Allen & Perrault, 1980; Litman & Al- len, 1987; Carberry, 1990; Lambert & Carberry, 1991; Chu-Carroll & Carberry, 1995), logic based approaches (Sadek, 1990), form filling approaches (Goddeau et al., 1996), script based approaches (Stein et al., 1999), application dependent dialogue grammar approaches (Kaspar et al., 1995), and functional grammar ap- proaches (O'Donnell, 1990). The plan based, logic based, and functional grammar approaches do not cover all mixed initiative phenomena in our domain and sev- eral approaches were developed for task oriented dialogues and typed input. The script, form filling, and grammar dependent approaches were too inflexible for our applications. Thus we have chosen not to apply any of the above mentioned approaches and instead to use an application independent dialogue grammar as basis for our dialogue manager. See (Smith and Hipp, 1994) for a good review of these approaches.

Another line of research is linguistic discourse theories (Grosz & Sidner, 1986; Kamp & Reyle, 1993; Mann & Thompson, 1988). One reason for not using linguistic theories is speed of computation. Since our conversations take place over the telephone, our main acceptance criteria is speed. If the computations take too long, the user will not accept the system and in the worst case hang up. Another reason is that our speech recognizer (from Lernout and Hauspie) uses phrase spotting techniques, thus there would not be much of a sentence to parse. Eventually, dialogue research must move in this direction, but until we have overcome the above mentioned problems, simplified theories must suffice. An additional goal of our research is to explore how far you can get without elaborate linguistic theories (at the syntactic, semantic, and discourse levels).

Our approach to dialogue management is to factor out all the procedural knowledge about how to continue a dialogue from the dialogue model[3] and to hide this information in reasoning routines. The dialogue manager calculates the type and the prepositional content of an utterance separately. A *type* (or illocution) is, for instance, request for a new value, while the content is *which* value to request. These two kinds of knowledge depend strongly on what has already happened in a dialogue, hence as a dialogue develops, we build up a sophisticated dialogue history. Further, an application description defines an application's data-needs, i.e. which knowledge has already been acquired and which is missing. We say that the dialogue history and the application description provide the context in which the dialogue manager calculates how a dialogue can continue. The calculations are done by application independent procedures that reason on these structures.

The dialogue history is a tree-like structure and the first step of the planning is to examine the tree and to decide where to continue the dialogue. From each applicable node a set of possible dialogue continuations is calculated in accordance with a dialogue model. The node from which the continuations were calculated is called a continuation's parent node. A continuation defines the type of the next utterance. A type can be, for instance, requesting something, withdrawing from the conversation, rejecting a previous utterance, evaluating a previous utterance, promising to do something, or giving information.

Given a certain context, the continuations are interpreted into dialogue hypotheses with propositional content. The current context is the local structure around a continuation's parent and the state of the domain model (the current data-needs). A continuation might result in several hypotheses. A hypothesis records the con-

---

[3] In this paper, the dialogue manager is the module concerned with speech input and output. A dialogue model or a dialogue grammar is a model of how an information retrieval dialogue can develop.

tinuation from which it originated such that it can be added to the dialogue history if the hypothesis is realized (by either user or system).

The result of the dialogue planning phase is a set of dialogue hypotheses. A hypothesis is an abstract representation of a possible next turn that is passed as input to other modules. If the hypotheses represent a system utterance, the text generation module chooses a subset and transforms these into a German text. If they represent a user utterance, the interpretation module transforms them into an appropriate low level recognition grammar and vocabulary. In either case, the dialogue planner gets back the chosen hypotheses from which it extracts the continuations. Starting from the continuations' parent node, it builds the continuation into the dialogue history. Further, the domain model is updated in accordance with the realized hypotheses. The extended dialogue history and new status of the domain model serve as the context from which a new set of continuations is calculated.

Through the natural division of the knowledge into type and content, we achieve a flexible dialogue manager that adapts to the user's behaviour. Moreover, the reasoning routines and the dialogue grammar are application independent, which makes it easy to reuse this dialogue manager in new applications.

2. Mixed Initiative Information Retrieval Dialogue

In the literature on mixed initiative, the terms *control* and *initiative* have been used synonymously (Whittaker & Stenton, 1988; Walker & Whittaker, 1990; Lester et al., 1999). But, following Jordan & Di Eugenio (1997) and Cohen et al. (1999), we would like to distinguish between these two terms. Below we discuss how our view on initiative and the notions of *taking, keeping,* and *relinquishing* differ from what is commonly seen in the literature. The discussion on control will be postponed to Section 3.3 since we first need to explain a few technical concepts.

2.1. TAKING THE INITIATIVE EQUALS TAKING THE TURN

Previous research on initiative tends not to consider replying to a question as a way of taking initiative. Thus a distinction between taking the turn and taking the initiative is achieved. According to these approaches, the following dialogue, for instance, has two turns but the initiative remains with the system.

Dialogue 3: Answering question

   A. Sys: Where do you want to phone from?
   B. Usr: Frankfurt.

We, however, do consider replying as taking initiative and consequently the distinction between turn and taking initiative disappears. In the following, we present our arguments why we equate the two. First, an intuitive argument. In our dialogues, we have identified three situations in which we argue that a speaker takes the initiative.[4] These are exemplified with the following dialogues.

Dialogue 4: Ignoring question

    A.   Sys: Where do you want to phone **from**?
    B.   Usr: **To** Frankfurt.

Dialogue 5: Over-answering question

    A.   Sys: Where do you want to phone from?
    B.   Usr: From Frankfurt around nine.

Dialogue 6: Interrupting question (barge-in)

    A.   Sys: Where do you want to...?
    B.   Usr: Frankfurt.

We argue that a speaker takes the initiative if she introduces new topics into a conversation, i.e., if she answers another question than the one asked, as in Dialogue 4, or if she over-answers a question, as in Dialogue 5. Further, we argue that a speaker takes the initiative if she interrupts the other speaker before the content of her utterance is clear (barge-in, see Kaspar et al. 1997). In Dialogue 6, utterance A could continue with either '...phone *to*?' or '...phone *from*?' If a speaker barges-in and guesses at what she wanted to say, she must take the initiative.

Second, we argue that the user in Dialogue 3 also takes the initiative. If we compare Dialogue 3 with Dialogue 6, we see that the difference does not so much lie in the answers but rather in the questions. What we consider different in the barge-in and non-barge-in situations is whether the system relinquishes the initiative or not – not whether the user takes the initiative. We say that in Dialogue 6, the system did not relinquish the initiative before the user replied, while if the system gets to finish its utterance as in Dialogue 3, we say that it relinquishes the initiative. Obviously, if we let the system relinquish the initiative, we also have to grant the next speaker taking of the initiative. Thus we argue that the user in Dialogue 3 takes the initiative and consider normal replies as taking initiative. The four dialogues above are typical of information retrieval dialogues and since we in all four situations have argued that the second speaker also takes the initiative, we say that in our type of dialogue, taking the initiative is equal to taking the turn.

2.2. KEEPING THE INITIATIVE

With keeping the initiative, we mean that a speaker produces a complex utterance with more than one communicative goal. Implicit confirmation techniques, for instance, fall into this category. (Utterance E in Dialogue 1 is representative of this category.) A user who is familiar with the domain and knows which parameters the system needs might use this type of turn to provide more information than asked

---

[4] These are intuitions that need empirical validation.

for in one go (e.g., utterance B in Dialogue 5). See (Green & Carberry, 1999) for an interesting discussion on over-answering and the conditions under which it takes place.

2.3. TURNS

Based on the above discussion on taking, keeping, and relinquishing the initiative, we divide the turns in our dialogues into four different types. (These are all seen from a system's point of view). We use the following notation: $X+Y+\ldots$, where X and Y are either *take, keep,* or *relinquish*, means that a turn contains the initiatives X, Y, etc in the given order. X^* means zero or more occurrences of initiative X. X^+ means one or more occurrences of initiative X. In the examples we use the following notation:

$_T$Utterance (turn) with one$_K$ and two communicative goals.$_R$

where the subscript T means taking initiative, K means keeping initiative, and R means relinquishing initiative.

In the type definitions below, 'one thing' means that a turn or part of a turn is mapped onto one communicative goal, where a communicative goal *is defined by the application.* The utterance 'I want to call my friend who lives in Munich.' contains (at least) two communicative goals, but as far as the system is concerned, the utterance is mapped onto the single goal inform(destination = Munich). The information about who lives in Munich is discarded since in this example the system could not map this information onto a goal.

Since we equate taking the initiative with taking the turn, we can assume that 'beginning to speak' signals 'taking of initiative' and conversely, 'stopping to speak' signals 'relinquishing of initiative'. Mixed initiative interaction implies knowing *when* to take, keep, and relinquish the initiative, but since we can only *control* when the system takes, keeps, and relinquishes the initiative, the system listens to the user and *assumes* that the user has taken/relinquished the initiative when the speech recognition system does/does not hear anything.

We define three types of *complete* turns. The first two describe simple turns that are mapped onto zero or one communicative goal, while the last one describes turns that are mapped onto several goals.

- *relinquish*

   Not saying anything over some period of time implies relinquishing the initiative and conversely relinquishing the initiative implies not saying anything. For example,

   Usr: '$_R$'

- *take + relinquish*

Saying one thing implies taking and relinquishing the initiative and conversely, taking and relinquishing the initiative implies saying one thing. For example,

Sys: $_T$Where do you want to phone to?$_R$
Usr: $_T$Munich.$_R$

− *take* + *keep** + *relinquish*
Saying more than one thing implies keeping the initiative and conversely, keeping the initiative implies saying more than one thing. For example,

Sys: $_T$Where do you want to phone to$_K$ and from?$_R$
Usr: $_T$I'm calling from Munich$_K$ to Darmstadt.$_R$

Assuming that the user is co-operative (if she starts talking about something irrelevant, this is detected as speech. Recall that we are using phrase spotting techniques, hence proper linguistic analysis is unavailable to us), we can use our turn definitions to distinguish between the following two replies to the question 'Where do you want to call to?'

Usr: '$_R$'
Usr: $_T$I want to call ⟨long pause⟩$_R$ Hamburg.

In the first case, the user ignores the question, while in the second case, she pauses too long such that the recognizer thinks that she has stopped speaking and thus relinquished the initiative. In both cases, the system cannot map the utterance onto a communicative goal, hence both utterances are interpreted as reject request. If we combine this interpretation with the initiative information, however, we are able to distinguish between them. In the first case, the user only relinquished the initiative, hence the system could repeat the previous question. In the second case, the system should respond differently since the user did take the initiative and started answering the question. It was the fault of the system that it did not understand and it could respond 'I did not understand you. Please repeat.'

We define *incomplete* turns as turns that were interrupted, i.e. turns without relinquish:

− *take* + *keep**
The speaker can say zero or more things depending on where she is interrupted. For example,

Sys: $_T$Where do you want to...
Sys: $_T$Where do you want to phone to$_K$...?

If we compare these examples to the *take* + keep* + relinquish ones, we see that the speaker was interrupted before the utterance is complete and was not allowed to relinquish the initiative.

[358]

In an information retrieval system, we can use the different characterizations as an indication of whether the user answered the intended question or not.

2.4. TAKING BACK THE INITIATIVE

So far we have discussed initiative in terms of individual utterances but in a mixed initiative system, we also need to look at initiative *between* utterances. The system relinquishes the initiative after every complete turn and the user may or may not take the initiative and react to what the system said. The system is assumed to be co-operative and consequently never allowed not to take the initiative when expected to; it shall take the initiative in response to user utterances and if the user chooses to relinquish and not to say anything, it shall take it back and continue the dialogue intelligently. The following dialogue illustrates two such situations.

Dialogue 7: Reply expected or not

A. Sys: $_T$ Welcome to TESADIS. $_R$
B. Usr: (No response) $_R$
C. Sys: $_T$ Do you want the rate $_K$ or the total cost of a call? $_R$
D. Usr: (No response) $_R$
E. Sys: $_T$ Do you want the rate $_K$ or the total cost of a call? $_R$

Different dialogue acts build up different expectations for how a dialogue can continue. For instance, after request and offer the speaker expects a reply, while after inform and evaluate her expectations are neutral and she is prepared to continue the dialogue after for a short time having given the hearer the opportunity to take the initiative. We say that a speaker can *expectedly* or *unexpectedly* take and relinquish the initiative. In utterance B in Dialogue 7, relinquishing the turn is expected since in utterance A, the system provided information, which is not an encouragement to speak. In utterance D, however, relinquishing the turn is unexpected since the system asked a direct question. If the user had said something in B, she would have taken the initiative unexpectedly, while in D the taking of initiative is expected. Based on these observations, we divide dialogue acts into two groups: *neutral* and *reply expected*.

This grouping allows us to distinguish between the sequences A+B+C and C+D+E although both have similar initiative pattern:

A, C: *take + keep* + relinquish*

B, D: *relinquish*

C, E: *take + keep + relinquish*

Since utterance A is neutral and C expects a reply, we know that after C the system utterance was not successful and hence when taking back the initiative in E, the system should take that into consideration, i.e. the grouping allows us to interpret and to react to identical user responses differently.

We also use the grouping to control how long to wait for a user utterance in the planning algorithm; the speech recognizer listens for a shorter time after neutral utterances than after reply expected utterances. In the planning algorithm, this type of initiative is accounted for together with the definition of taking and relinquishing the dialogue; if the system does not hear anything, it assumes that the user has not taken the initiative and hence it takes it back.

Relinquishing of initiative is only reflected in the dialogue history when it is unexpected since unexpected relinquishing changes the direction of a dialogue, while expected relinquishing does not. Taking of initiative, however, is always reflected in the dialogue history, since it implies deciding (but not necessarily changing) the direction of a dialogue, and this decision must be taken into account when planning the next step.

2.5. MIXED INITIATIVE

We require of a mixed initiative information retrieval system that it be able to deal with all the types of initiative described in the previous sections.

- Both participants should be able to keep the initiative, i.e., the system should understand and produce *take* + *keep*$^+$+ *relinquish* type turns.
- Further the system should be able deal with barge-in. The system itself should not barge-in on the user but as illustrated in Section 2.3, the system may mistakenly think that the user has relinquished the initiative if she pauses too long. It should detect this and do its best to repair.
- Finally, the system must be able to take back the initiative after relinquish type turns from the user.

These requirements are captured by the following four pairs of turns. We define a system to be a mixed initiative system if it can deal with any combination of these pairs. Recall that the turn types are defined form the system's point of view. Since not saying anything over some period of time is defied as relinquish and the system is not allowed to barge-in, there are no user utterances without relinquish.

(1) Sys: *take* + *keep**+ *relinquish*
    Usr: *relinquish*

(2) Sys: *take* + *keep**+ *relinquish*
    Usr: *take* + *keep**+ *relinquish*

(3) Sys: *relinquish*
    Usr: *take* + *keep**+ *relinquish*

(4) Sys: *take* + *keep**
    Usr: *take* + *keep**+ *relinquish*.

Following these definitions, Dialogue 1 in Section 1 consists of the four pairs $1 + 2 + 4 + 3$ and is thus, representative of a mixed initiative system. The system can take back the initiative (C), it can deal with barge-in (F) and it understands utterances in which the user keeps the initiative (D). Further, in utterances C and E the system keeps the initiative with '...or the total cost of a call?' and '...Frankfurt an der Oder?'

Dialogue 2 shows the non-keeping alternatives of some of the utterances in Dialogue 1 . It consists of only *take* + *relinquish* type utterances, which result in a question answer type system. We see that a dialogue feels more natural and can be more efficient if the system is able to convey several of its information needs in one utterance and if it can understand complex user utterances with more than one communicative goal.

3. Control Defined in Terms of the Dialogue History

One building block in our system is a model of information retrieval dialogue at the illocutionary level (Sitter & Stein, 1992). The term *illocution* is part of speech act theory as introduced by Austin (1962). We gloss the term as 'an abstract representation of an utterance's type', e.g. the illocution of the utterance 'What time did the phone call take place?' is request information. Please see (Austin, 1962) for a proper definition of this term and other speech act terminology.

The dialogue model itself cannot account for mixed initiative interaction. First, the dialogue history originally proposed only allows the forward computation to continue from the point of the last utterance, which would lead to a question–answer system. We will expand on this point in Section 3.2. Second, the model has previously only been used in graphical user interfaces where user responses are restricted to having one communicative goal. Further, since the answers are in response to a prompt (e.g. an empty field in a form, dialogue box), the context of the response is known. In a spoken system, however, users' behaviour is not so well defined since, for instance, they over-answer questions, ignore questions and answer something that was not asked, or change their mind and correct information they provided previously. In order to account for this erratic behaviour, we need to be able to map individual utterances onto several communicative goals. A novel contribution of the work presented here is a method for mapping utterances onto multiple communicative goals based on our domain model.

Third, the model is only concerned with the illocution of utterances and thus needs to be combined with a component that is concerned with the content. In previous systems (Hagen & Stein, 1996; Stein et al., 1999), the content model was provided by scripts. Scripts, however, are inflexible since they define system and user behaviour prior to compilation, which makes it difficult to adapt the behaviour as a dialogue develops. We developed a dialogue manager that consists of several resources and algorithms that reason on these dynamically changing resources. Illocution and content are calculated separately and finally the information is combined into communicative goals. Thus we no longer need to employ the script formalism for the context.

In this section, we present two of the resources in our system – the dialogue model and the dialogue history and then we define our view on having control of a dialogue in terms of these resources.

3.1. THE DIALOGUE MODEL

We use a dialogue grammar as our dialogue model. A dialogue grammar describes regularities in dialogue in much the same way as a syntactic grammar describes the syntax of a sentence. A syntactic grammar rule states that 'verb follows subject', for instance. On the dialogue level, rules are of the type 'answers follows questions' or if the grammar is recursive, 'questions can be followed by clarification questions'. These two observations can be represented by the following grammar rules:

(1) dialogue = question + answer
(2) dialogue = question + dialogue

Through empirical studies, the regularities of different types of dialogue are discovered and for a given dialogue type, a dialogue grammar with rules covering as many phenomena as possible is developed.

We have chosen a grammar based approach to dialogue modelling for two reasons. First, it is computationally tractable. (With a context free grammar, parsing can be done in polynomial time). In the domain of information retrieval over the telephone, computation time is crucial for the system's acceptance by users. Second, a grammar can be used to parse a dialogue in order to obtain a highly structured dialogue history. Several dialogue grammars have been proposed over the years (e.g. Bennacef et al., 1995; Bilange, 1991; Eckert et al., 1992; Jönsson, 1993; Polanyi & Scha, 1984; Reichman, 1985; Sinclair & Coulthard, 1975; Traum & Hinkelman, 1992) but since none of these have sufficient coverage for our purpose and some have never been tested in a computational setting, we have chosen to work with the grammar presented below.

In Figure 1, we present a simplified version of our speech act oriented dialogue model. (See Sitter & Stein, 1992, for a detailed discussion and Stein et al., 1999 for an alternative representation). We use the following notation: (Sub)-dialogues and dialogue moves begin with an upper case (e.g. Request), while dialogue acts are all lower case (e.g. request). (The dialogue/move/act terminology is explained in the following paragraph). Moves in square brackets ([ ]) are optional and X^+ means one or more instances of constituent X.

In our model, a *dialogue* is defined recursively. The top level dialogue contains everything that happens in one phone call, i.e., it is the unit in which a conversation is initiated and completed. For example, a user poses questions, the system offers a list of tasks that it can solve, a user receives answers to her questions, or a user hangs up because the system has made too big a mess. A dialogue is organized into a sequence of dialogue *cycles*, which consist of a sequence of dialogue *moves*

1. Dialogue(S,K) → (Cycle(S,K))$^+$
2. Cycle(S,K) → Request(S,K), Promise(K,S), Inform(K,S), Evaluate(S,K).
3. Cycle(S,K) → Request(S,K), [Promise(K,S)], WithdrawRequest(S,K).
4. Cycle(S,K) → Request(S,K), Promise(K,S), WithdrawPromise(K,S).
5. Cycle(S,K) → Request(S,K), RejectRequest(K,S).
6. Cycle(S,K) → Offer(K,S), Accept(S,K), Inform(K,S), Evaluate(S,K).
7. Cycle(S,K) → Offer(K,S), [Accept(S,K)], WithdrawOffer(K,S).
8. Cycle(S,K) → Offer(K,S), Accept(S,K), WithdrawAccept(S,K).
9. Cycle(S,K) → Offer(K,S), RejectOffer(S,K).
10. Cycle(S,K) → Withdraw(user,system).
11. Cycle(S,K) → Withdraw(system,user).
12. Request(S,K).
13. Request(S,K) → request(S,K), [Dialogue(K,S)].
14. Request(S,K) → request(S,K), [Assert(S,K)].
15. Request(S,K) → Dialogue(K,S).
16. Request(S,K) → Assert(S,K), [request(S,K)].
17. Request(S,K) → Assert(S,K), [Dialogue(K,S)].
18. Offer(K,S).
19. Offer(K,S) → offer(K,S), [Dialogue(S,K)].
20. Offer(K,S) → offer(K,S), [Assert(K,S)].
21. Offer(K,S) → Dialogue(S,K).
22. Offer(K,S) → Assert(K,S), [offer(K,S)].
23. Offer(K,S) → Assert(K,S), [Dialogue(S,K)].
24. Promise(K,S).
25. Promise(K,S) → promise(K,S), [Dialogue(S,K)].
26. Promise(K,S) → promise(K,S), [Assert(K,S)].
27. Promise(K,S) → Dialogue(S,K).
28. Promise(K,S) → Assert(K,S), [promise(K,S)].
29. Promise(K,S) → Assert(K,S), [Dialogue(S,K)].
30. Inform(K,S) → inform(K,S), [Dialogue(S,K)].
31. Assert(user,system) → assert(user,system), [Dialogue(system,user)].
32. Assert(system,user) → assert(system,user), [Dialogue(system,user)].

Figure 1. A simplified grammar representation of the dialogue model. Notation: Dialogue moves begin with an upper case (e.g. Request), while dialogue acts are all lower case (e.g. request). Moves in square brackets ([ ]) are optional and X$^+$ means one or more instances of constituent X.

(e.g., Offer + Accept + Withdraw Offer = a cycle).[5] We organize the cycles such that only one topic is negotiated within one cycle. At the top level of a dialogue, the topic is a query and its answer and if a user wants to know the answer to several queries in one phone call, they are modelled as several cycles. At lower levels, the topic of a cycle is a parameter (e.g. in our test application, time and duration of a phone call).

Dialogue moves are complex units that organize the negotiation of individual illocutions within a cycle, e.g., a request for information is clarified or further specification of an ambiguous is requested. Normally a move contains an atomic dialogue *act* of its own type, e.g., a Request move contains a request act. The negotiation within a move is accounted for through additional moves and subdialogues. We summarize: Dialogue moves are decomposed into a sequence of dia-

---

[5] In the text we often leave out the parameters in order to enhance readability.

logue acts, moves (Assert) and (sub)-dialogues (e.g. Request(K,S) → request(K,S), Dialogue(S,K)).

Each constituent has two parameters for which we choose the names *S* and *K* – representing information *seeker* and information *knower*. The first parameter represents the initiator, or speaker, of a particular constituent, the second the hearer. The initiator of a Dialogue is assigned the seeker role, hence these parameters define which moves are open to information seeker and knower at any point of a dialogue. During execution, the parameters are instantiated to either 'user' or 'system', i.e., if we start the grammar with Dialogue(user, system), the user would be assigned the seeker role, and hence at the top level, only seeker moves would be open to her, e.g. Request, Evaluate, Withdraw request, and conversely, Offer, Promise, Inform, Reject request, etc. would be open to the system. In every move the hearer can initiate a sub-dialogue and within this sub-dialogue, the hearer's role changes from knower to seeker, since it is initiated by the hearer. Hence the hearer of a dialogue has access to seeker moves through the initiation of a sub-dialogue. The recursive representation of a dialogue together with role switching serves as the illocutionary basis from which we address mixed initiative interaction where both information seeker and information knower can employ, for instance, retraction, correction, and clarification tactics.

The presentation in Figure 1 is simplified in the sense that we only present selected dialogue moves in detail, (i.e. Request, Offer, Promise, Inform, and Assert) since all the other dialogue moves have the same structure as these. One only has to exchange the labels. For instance, exchanging Offer for Accept in rule 19 yields the rule Accept(K,S) → accept(K,S), [Dialogue(S,K)].

The grammar is used to parse dialogues into a dialogue history. Our dialogue grammar is over-generative, i.e. if in a cycle only the inform act is actually articulated, empty Request and Promise moves appear in the dialogue history (see Section 3.2). To account for this situation, we could have added a rule Cycle → Inform. Instead, we chose to use the over-generative grammar since in the dialogue history we wish to keep an explicit representation of speech acts that were not articulated. For example, when the user over-answers a question, we consider the over-answering an answer to a question that the system has not yet asked. This explicit representation of unexpressed speech acts is essential in order to account for certain phenomena in mixed initiative interaction, as we will explain in Section 3.2.

Another reason for using an over-generative grammar, is that we in future work wish to generate user models automatically from the dialogue history. A user who is familiar with the domain might frequently over-answer questions and hence the dialogue history would contain many empty Requests from which we can deduce that the user is experienced.

3.2. THE DIALOGUE HISTORY

From the above grammar description, a tree-like dialogue history (or parse tree) is dynamically constructed as a dialogue develops. The structure of the dialogue history is the basis of our approach to mixed initiative, hence we will spend some time on explaining it and comparing our choice to other possible choices. Consider the following dialogue. (The speech acts are shown in parentheses).

Dialogue 8:

A. Sys: Which city do you want to call? (request)
B. Usr: I want to call a friend in Hamburg
   around six. (inform, inform)
C. Sys: Did you say Homburg? (request)

D. Usr: No. Hamburg. (inform, inform)
E. Sys: Oh, sorry. (assert)
F. Sys: You mean Hamburg? (request)
G. Usr: Yes (inform)
H. Usr: ...and change that to five o'clock (inform)

In utterance B, the user over-answers the question in that she additionally provides the time of her call. In terms of the dialogue history there are several ways of dealing with this situation:

(1) Throw away the additional information, but this does not facilitate mixed initiative dialogue, so we will not consider this option further.
(2) Map the utterance onto a single inform (the (Sitter & Stein, 1992) solution).
(3) Map the utterance onto several informs. We first consider option two.

3.2.1. *One Speech Act per Utterance*

We first consider option number two. Mapping utterance B onto one speech act would result in the following dialogue history of utterances A and B. In the diagram, only one parameter – the initiator – is included since the second parameter is a function of the first. The parameters are shown instantiated: u = user and s = system. To the right of the dialogue history, we list the rules (from Figure 1) that were applied.[6] A letter in parentheses after the rule number denotes the utterance in which the rule was introduced.

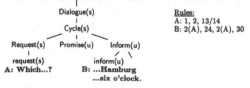

```
            |
        Dialogue(s)                    Rules:
            |                          A: 1, 2, 13/14
         Cycle(s)                      B: 2(A), 24, 2(A), 30
         __|_____
        /      |        \
  Request(s) Promise(u) Inform(u)
      |                 /  \
  request(s)        inform(u)  \
  A: Which...?      B: ...Hamburg
                      ...six o'clock.
```

---

[6] Note on the rules: As utterance A was articulated, it was not known that rule 2 was used. It could be either 2, 3, 4, or 5. For clarity, we do not list all the rules when it later in the dialogue becomes clear which rule was used. Further, Figure 1 is only a grammar *representation*. The dialogue model was *implemented* as a network, hence in the system these ambiguities are not present.

The dialogue history is built dynamically, i.e., the representation of utterance C would be appended to the above structure. In prior approaches (Sitter & Stein, 1992; Hagen & Stein, 1996), the rules were applied strictly sequentially, hence in these approaches the point where to append utterance C was limited to the move node above the last utterance (acts are atomic), i.e. Inform in the current example. We say that the Inform node is *open* or *incomplete*. Open nodes are points from which the computation of future utterances can start, hence the above dialogue history has only one open node from which the dialogue could continue. In the diagrams, open nodes are indicated by a line without a child. A move is *closed* if the end of a rule describing the given move is reached or if the node is above the current recursion level. For example, a Request move is closed if the end of one of the rules 12–17 is reached. In the current example, the Request node was closed by rule 13 (or 14, the Dialogue is optional) and Promise by rule 24. The Dialogue and Cycle nodes are closed because they are above Inform – the current level of recursion.

The representation of future utterances is computed by applying the dialogue rules to the open nodes in the dialogue history. Consider utterance C: After utterance B, the computation stopped just after Inform in rule 30. In this particular case, we would continue with the optional Dialogue in rule 30, which takes the computation back to rule 1, and so on. This computation of future utterance types we call *forward computation*.

The dialogue model has previously only been used in graphical user interfaces with serial input channels (e.g. prompt + mouse click), thus it was sufficient to build a dialogue history that restricted the forward computation to the node representing the last action. When working in the spoken modality, the interaction is not so well structured. In utterance B, for instance, the user provided more information than was requested. In the following we will justify why the old style dialogue history is inadequate for the spoken modality.

It is unclear how to incorporate utterance C into the above tree since it only refers to the destination. Since C is a follow-up question to the user's answer, it should be part of the Inform sub-tree, but if we hang a sub-dialogue that only refers to the destination off the Inform node, we need an additional mechanism for deciding that the sub-dialogue only refers to a part of the parent utterance.

Users do not only provide additional information. They also do not answer all questions. Consider the following situation in which utterance C refers to both the destination and the time:

Dialogue 9:

    B.   Usr: I want to call a friend in Hamburg around six. (inform)
    C.   Sys: That was Homburg at six o'clock? (request)
    D.   Usr: No. Hamburg. (inform)

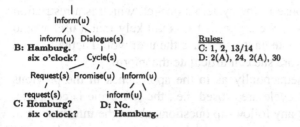

In the above dialogue history, we have no explicit representation of the fact that the user ignored one of the questions, so again, we would need an additional mechanism that reasons on the dialogue history in order to discover the implicit information that the user did not answer all the questions. We will discuss how we deal with this situation in Section 3.2.3.

The situations above show that a dialogue history in which an entire utterance is mapped onto one speech act – regardless of how many communicative goals it contains – is unintuitive and troublesome since useful information is only implicitly available. Thus we discard the option of mapping complex utterances onto single speech acts and move on to the third option.

3.2.2. *Several Speech Acts per Utterance*

If we map the utterance onto several speech acts, we can build three different structures. In the first solution, we keep the notion of having only one open node from which the dialogue can continue and this solution is illustrated in the diagram below. In the rules, a move name in parentheses after a rule number means that the exact rule is not listed in Figure 1 but it can be constructed through substitution of the name in parentheses in the given rule.

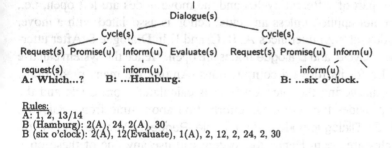

Rules:
A: 1, 2, 13/14
B (Hamburg): 2(A), 24, 2(A), 30
B (six o'clock): 2(A), 12(Evaluate), 1(A), 2, 12, 2, 24, 2, 30

For the second inform act, we chose the cycle Request(s) + Promise(u) + Inform(u) instead of Offer(u) + Accept(s) + Inform(u) since it is unlikely that the moves in the latter are skipped. Consider the following dialogue.

Dialogue 10: An Offer-Accept-Inform cycle

- A. Usr: I have a choice between early and late afternoon. (offer)
- B. Sys: Late afternoon is cheaper. (Accept)
- C. Usr: Six o'clock, then. (inform)

We see that the inform is a response to the system's accept, which is a restriction on the choices offered by the user. We argue that it is unlikely that a user would skip her own offer and then articulate an inform since the user would actually need the information in the Accept before she can articulate the inform.

Since the rules are applied sequentially as in the approaches in the previous section, all the nodes in the left cycle are closed, i.e., the left cycle is complete. Consequently, one could not ask any follow-up questions about the information in this cycle. We discard this solution, since in a spoken system one must have the possibility to ask confirmation questions about all answers from the user.

To get around the problem with the complete cycle, one could include only one inform in the dialogue history and store the other information somewhere else, as illustrated

This solution could, however, not deal with utterance H (at least not in a uniform way) since the information about the time of the call would not yet be in the dialogue history, i.e., we would not have a context from which we could predict that the user could possibly change this information. Consequently we discard this solution too.

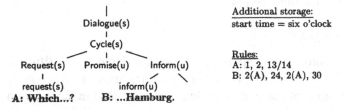

The last and preferred solution is to consider the first inform in Utterance B in Dialogue 8 an answer to the question in A and the second inform an answer to an unasked question about the destination of the call. Technically, this translates into: the speech acts are part of different cycles and the move nodes are left open, i.e., the move rules are not applied unless an actual action is associated with a move. We illustrate our idea through utterances A, B, C, and H in Dialogue 8. After utterance A, the Request, Cycle, and Dialogue nodes are open. Hence the system can use all these three nodes for its forward computations. Among the many predictions, the hypothesis for answering the question in A is calculated from Cycle and the one that the user provides the additional information about time from Dialogue. After utterance B, the Dialogue node and the Cycle, Request, Promise, and Inform nodes in both cycles are open. Hence the system can use any one of these open nodes for its forward calculations. In the current example the responses C and H are represented as sub-dialogues of the first and the second Inform.

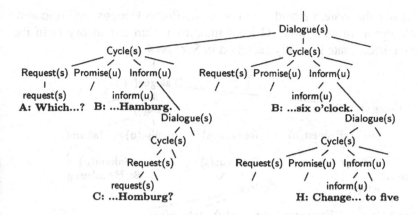

Rules:
A: 1, 2, 13/14
B (Hamburg): 2(A), 30
B (six o'clock): 1(A), 2, 30
C: 1, 2, 13/14
H: 1, 2, 30

The increased number of open nodes increases the systems ability to predict future utterances from the user. We can, for instance, predict normal answers, over-answering, changes to previous answers, user ignorance, or worse that the user hangs up. For user prediction almost all open nodes are used and almost all resulting predictions are handed over to the speech recognizer. For the system's own utterances, the situation is a bit different. The increased number of open nodes gives the system more flexibility in calculating its own responses, but since there are many more open nodes and predictions than the system can use for a single utterance, the increased flexibility introduces the new problem of choosing which open nodes to use. In the above example, the second part of B introduces a cycle with an incomplete Request that the system could have picked up and continued the dialogue with. In Dialogue 8 it chose not to, but consider the following one:

Dialogue 11:
- A. Sys: What time do you want to make your call? (request)
- B. Usr: I want to call a friend in Hamburg. (reject request + inform)
- C. Sys: Why didn't you answer my question? (request)
-     Sys: I didn't ask you where you want to call yet. (inform)

Here the user ignores the system's request completely and introduces the destination of her call into the conversation, i.e. after B, the dialogue history would have an open Reject Request in the first Cycle and open Request and Promise in the second Cycle. In its reply, the system decided to pick up both these nodes from which it calculated utterance C.

Our node choosing strategies are based on Grice's maxims for co-operative communication (Grice, 1975). In the above example utterance C violates the Relevance Maxim, hence the system would not choose the Reject Request and Request nodes. Our attempt at implementing Grice's maxims within our theory is in its infancy and the current state is briefly sketched in Section 4.5.

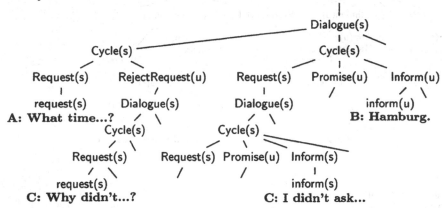

Rules:
A: 1, 5, 13/14
B: 1(A), 2, 30
C (Why...?): 1, 2, 13/14
C (I didn't...?): 1, 2, 30

Among all the nodes that are deemed appropriate by Grice's axioms, we additionally use the temporal structure of a dialogue to guide the choice. The above examples show that the temporal structure of a dialogue is not preserved by our dialogue history, thus the above structures are complemented by a linear structure with pointers to the sub-structures that represent real utterances. The temporal structure also keeps track of which utterances belong to which turn. We use the temporal structure to guide the choice of which topic to process next when calculating system utterances such that the user perceives the resulting dialogue as coherent. Coherent dialogue is essential for the quality of spoken dialogue systems since topic jumping may confuse the users such that they become uneasy and produce more 'hmm' and 'haas', which degrade the performance of the speech recognition such that the system will have to ask for the same information repeatedly.

3.2.3. *Multi-functional Utterances*

As mentioned in Section 3.2.1 and shown in the previous example, we wish to keep an explicit representation of situations in which the user does not answer a question from the system. These utterances are multi-functional in that they are described by two (or more) different speech acts. An old argument against grammar based approaches to dialogue modelling can be summarized as follows: A dialogue grammar can be rephrased as a state machine where the speech acts become the state transition labels. Typically only one state can result from a transition and a state machine can only be in one state at a time. But since utterances can be multi-

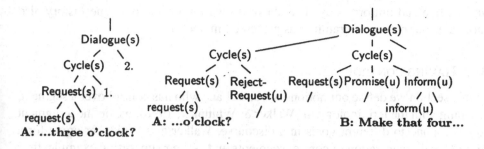

Rules:
A1,A2: 1, 5, 13/14
B1,B2: 1(A), 2, 30

Figure 2. A dialogue history for multi-functional utterances.

functional (e.g., both a rejection and an assertion), a traditional state machine would need to be in several states simultaneously, which is normally not allowed. Consequently grammar based systems cannot account for multi-functional utterances (Cohen, 1998).

Our system, however, does not have this problem since we do not rely on individual states in the state machine to define the state of a dialogue; the dialogue history determines the state of a dialogue. Further the functionality of an utterance is not defined through a single transition from one state to another, but rather the *combination* of predictions from several of the open nodes in the dialogue history, i.e., the mechanism is the same as for utterances that contain several speech acts of the same type (previous section). We illustrate with the following dialogue:

Dialogue 12: Multi-functional utterances

    A. Sys: Did you say three o'clock? (request)
    B. Usr: Make that four o'clock please. (reject request + inform)

After the system utterance, the dialogue history would look like the left hand-side of the diagram in Figure 2. The following *combination* of paths through the dialogue model accounts for the user utterance: From open node one, the prediction [RR(u), rr(u)] (rules 5, 13/14(Reject Request)) is calculated and from open node two [Cycle(s) R(s), P(u), I(u), i(u)] (rules 2, 30). Together these predictions account for utterances B and the resulting dialogue history is shown in the right hand side of Figure 2. The two purposes of utterance B – in this example, reject request and inform – have been accounted for in terms of two dialogue cycles.

In this section we have presented for a novel way of organizing the dialogue history. This includes mapping utterances onto several speech acts and building these into the dialogue history as several incomplete dialogue cycles with several open nodes. The concept of several open nodes provides the system with more flexibility in how to continue a dialogue, and allows us to account for many naturally occurring mixed initiative phenomena. Further, we can represent these in an intuitive and uniform way. The above discussion on the dialogue history also motivates our choice of grammar as presented in Section 3.1.

3.3. HAVING CONTROL

In this section we define our notions of control and who has control over a segment. Keeping with the terminology in (Walker & Whittaker, 1990), we define a segment to correspond to different goals in a discourse. Walker and Whittaker argue for a hierarchical organization of control segments and as their supporting example, they present a sub-dialogue where the topic of the sub-dialogue is completed during the sub-dialogue, i.e., the control segment for the sub-dialogue is completely embedded in the first one. In our domain, we additionally need to allow for overlapping control segments since, for example, the user might take the initiative and introduce a new topic as in Dialogue 13 and the system might continue these topics after the completion of the segment in which it was introduced. In these situations, the control segments are not strictly embedded but overlapping. Walker and Whittaker did not report any results on how to deal with segments that are not strictly embedded in another segment and in the remainder of this section, we will discuss how we can use our dialogue history to organize control segments and how this approach enables the system to account for overlapping segments. Consider the following dialogue and dialogue history:

Dialogue 13:

    A.   Sys: Which city do you want to call? (request)
    B.   Usr: I want to call a friend in Hamburg
                around six. (inform, inform)
    C.   Sys: Did you say Hamburg? (request)
    D.   Usr: Yes. (inform)
    E.   Sys: Before six o'clock?

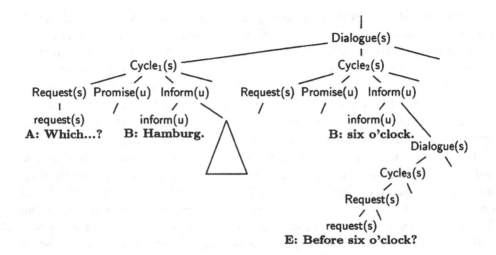

We keep the terminology from (Grosz & Sidner, 1986; Walker & Whittaker, 1990): ICP = initiating conversational participant, i.e., the initiator of the discourse segment, OCP = other conversational participant, and the discourse segment purpose must be the purpose of ICP. Walker & Whittaker (1990) place a segment boundary whenever the roles of the participants change. As explained above, this does not work when the segments overlap, hence we do not use role change but rather cycles in the dialogue history to mark segment boundaries. Further, we say that a speaker controls a segment if she has control over a cycle, i.e., the ICP controls the cycle and the cycle's purpose is the purpose of the ICP. In the above example, cycles one and three are controlled by the system, while cycle two is controlled by the user. In cycle one, it was the system's purpose to acquire the destination of the call and in cycle two, it was the user's purpose to provide the system with the time of the call.

Linear topic shifts (i.e., no embedding) *with* change in control is represented as adjacent cycles with different ICP. Linear topic shifts *without* change in control is represented as adjacent cycles with the same ICP. The above structure also allows for an elegant representation of multi-functional utterances as shown in the dialogue history of Dialogue 12, where the multi-functional utterance is split over two cycles.

Since the control segments need not be strictly adjacent anymore, we need to include the temporal ordering of the utterances into the description of a control segment if we want to be able to reproduce a dialogue from the representation.

4. Dialogue Hypotheses

In Sections 4 and 5, we show how the theories in the previous sections are incorporated into our algorithms. In our system, the illocutionary aspect and the content aspect of utterances are calculated separately. We calculate how a dialogue can continue illocutionary by applying the grammar rules to the relevant open nodes in the dialogue history. The resulting structures are called *continuations* (Subsection 4.2). The content is calculated by interpreting these continuations with respect to the dialogue history and the state of an application description (or domain model, see Subsection 4.1). These structures, we call *hypotheses* (Subsection 4.3). A hypothesis is an abstract representation of a possible next turn (or part of turn) that is passed as input to other modules. If they represent a system utterance, a text generation module transforms them into a German text. If they represent a user utterance a speech recognizer transforms them into its internal format.

In this section, we concentrate on how to calculate continuations and hypotheses for individual turns. We will first discuss simple hypotheses with one communicative goal, i.e., *take* + *relinquish* type utterances. In Subsection 4.4, we continue with *take* + *keep** + *relinquish* type utterances and discuss how these are represented by sets of hypotheses. In Section 5, we will move to the inter-turn level and discuss how we achieve the mixed initiative interaction defined in Subsection 2.5. Before

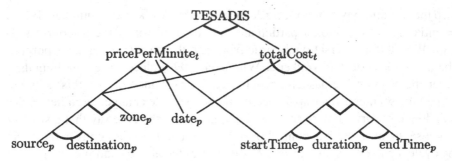

Figure 3. A simplified version of the application description for the TESADIS telephone rate inquiry system. Notation: The subscripts *t* and *p* identify nodes as task or parameter nodes respectively. ∪ is logical AND and ∨ is logical OR.

discussing the algorithms we present the application description – the last resource needed for the content computations.

4.1. THE APPLICATION DESCRIPTION

The application description is a declarative description of a domain organized as an AND-OR tree. Similar hierarchical structures were presented in (Young et al., 1990) for a naval domain and in (Caminero-Gil et al., 1996) for an e-mail assistance domain. The structure in Figure 3 shows a simplified version of our telephone rate inquiry application as introduced in Section 1. The AND-OR connections (∪ = logical AND, ∨ = logical OR) define obligatory parameters and alternative ways of describing parameters. Our tree has two types of nodes. *Task* type nodes define the tasks solvable by the application (e.g. totalCost). *Parameter* type nodes define the parameters needed to solve a task (e.g., duration). The function *Type(n)* returns the type of a node *n*, where the domain of *Type()* is {param, task}. In our test domain, *Type*(duration) = param and *Type*(totalCost) = task.

The structure in Figure 3 is interpreted as follows: The application TESADIS can solve two types of tasks: pricePerMinute or totalCost of a call. In order to solve the task pricePerMinute, for instance, the system needs to acquire values for the parameters startTime and date and either zone or source and destination. The knowledge in the tree is purely declarative and it is assumed that the underlying database knows how to calculate the zone from source and destination.[7]

The state of the application description is defined as the combination of the state of all the nodes. A node can be in one of three states: Open/closed nodes are nodes for which the system has not/has acquired a confirmed value. Topic nodes are nodes for which either the system has requested a value or for which the user has provided a value, but it is not yet a confirmed value. The state of the application description (partially) determines the system's behaviour. The system

---

[7] In future work, the application description will be extended with the relations IS-A, HAS-A, PART-OF, etc.

Table I. Some continuations from open node number one in Figure 2. Notation: X/Y means rule X or Y.

Continuation	Rules applied
Promise(u,s), promise(u,s)	2/3/4, 25/26
Promise(u,s), Assert(u,s), assert(u,s), promise(u,s)	2/3/4, 28, 31, 28
Promise(u,s),promise(u,s),Assert(u,s),assert(u,s),Inform(s,u)	2, 26, 31, 2
Promise(u,s), Inform(u,s)	2
Promise(u,s), Inform(u,s), inform(u,s)	2, 30
Promise(u,s), Dialogue(s,u), Cycle(s,u), Withdraw(u,s)	2/3/4, 27, 1, 10
Promise(u,s), WithdrawPromise(u,s)	4
RejectRequest(u,s)	5
WithdrawRequest(s,u)	3

Table II. Some continuations from open node number two in Figure 2. Due to space restrictions, some of the names have been shortened. Notation: X/Y means rule X or Y.

Continuation	Rules applied
Cycle(s,u), Request(s,u), request(s,u)	1, 2/3/4/5, 13/14
Cycle(s,u), Request(s,u), Dialogue(u,s)	1, 2/3/4/5, 15
Cycle(s,u), Request(s,u), Assert(s,u)	1, 2/3/4/5, 16/17
Cycle(s,u), Request(s,u), Promise(s,u), WithdrawReq(s,u)	1, 3
Cycle(s,u), Request(s,u), RejectRequest(s,u)	1, 5
Cycle(s,u), Request(s,u), WithdrawRequest(s,u)	1, 3
Cycle(s,u), Offer(s,u), offer(s,u)	1, 6/7/8/9, 19/20
Cycle(s,u), Withdraw(s,u)	1, 11
Cycle(s,u), Request(s,u), Dialogue(u,s), Cycle(u,s)	1, 2/3/4/5, 15, 1
Cycle(s,u), Request(s,u), Promise(s,u), Inform(u,s), Inf(u,s)	1, 2, 30

will, for instance, never request a value for a node that is closed, while the user, of course, is allowed to change her mind and provide new values for closed nodes. The function *Status(n)* returns the status of a node *n*, where the domain of *Status( )* = {open, closed, topic}.

4.2. ILLOCUTIONARY CONTINUATIONS OF A DIALOGUE

The dialogue model is used generatively to calculate the possible illocutionary continuations of a dialogue, and the dialogue history defines the context in which to calculate the continuations, i.e., from the open nodes. We illustrate with an example using the dialogue history in Figure 2 as the current context. Some of the possible continuations (of length ≤ 4) from the open nodes in Figure 2 are shown in Tables I and II.

Since the model is recursive, we had to determine the longest continuation ever needed such that the expansion procedure would not continue indefinitely. With the current dialogue model and dialogue history, it can be shown that the critical measure is the distance from a move node to an inform. We summarize the argument from (Hagen & Stein, 1996): We assume that all actions are represented by a dialogue act, hence we only calculate continuations that end with an act. The only move – and consequently act – that a speaker cannot skip is Inform and Assert, i.e., we have to identify the longest continuation ending with inform. The longest continuation *after* an inform is [Dialogue, Cycle, Request, Promise, Inform, inform] (e.g. utterance H, in Dialogue 8) and the longest continuation *before* an inform is [Dialogue, Cycle, Request, Promise, Inform, inform] (e.g., second part of utterance C, in Dialogue 11).[8] Thus this is longest continuation ever needed and we use this as our measure for when to terminate the rule expansion.

We say that a continuation is typed and the function *Type(c)* returns the type of a continuation c. The type is determined by the last constituent of a continuation, e.g., *Type*([Cycle, Request, Promise, Inform, inform]) = inform. The function *Parent(c)* returns a pointer to the open node from which continuation c originated.

Currently, we calculate the continuations dynamically as a dialogue develops. If we experience performance problems when we extend the system's dialogue coverage or want the system to engage in long conversations, we could, however, move the whole calculation process off-line and store pre-calculated continuations in a table. Hence the time spent per open node could be reduced to the time it would take to access the table.

4.3. INTERPRETATION OF CONTINUATIONS

The type of a dialogue continuations defines the illocution of an utterance and in order to assign content to an utterance, the continuations are interpreted in a given dialogue context. The context is made up of the local structure around the open node from which the continuation was generated, the state of the application description at the time of interpretation, and the state of various other information sources. An interpreted continuation we call a *hypothesis*. A hypothesis is a structure with fields name, param, value, noOfMentions, and continuation.

- A hypothesis has a name, e.g., requestValue, inform, evaluate, requestConfirmation
- param is one of the nodes in the application description (e.g., zone, duration, startTime) or one of the symbols task, cancel, repeat, forward, back, repeatall, first, second, third, last.

---

[8] Recall argument from Section 3.2.2 why we do not consider [Dialogue, Cycle, Offer, Accept, Inform, inform]

- value is the current value of param, e.g., if param = zone, value could be 'long distance', or if param = source, value could be 'Hamburg'.

- noOfMentions records the number of times a hypothesis has been articulated (only relevant for system hypotheses, this value guides the text generation system in the generation of alternative utterances).

- continuation records the illucutionary continuation. It is needed to update the dialogue history (see sub-routines *Update*( ) and *UndoUpdate*( ) in Section 5).

A hypothesis with the following values is glossed as 'ask for the second time whether the destination is Hamburg'.

```
name = requestConfirmation,
param = destination,
value = Hamburg,
noOfMentions = 2,
continuation = [Dialogue(s,u),Cycle(s,u),Request(s,u),request(s,u)]
```

In the text, the continuation is not shown and the above hypothesis would be denoted requestConfirmation(destination = Hamburg, 2). The fields are left out if equal to NULL, e.g., requestValue(source, 1) (gloss: ask for the first time where the user is calling from).

Hypotheses are passed as input to other modules. If they represent a system turn, text generation transforms them into a German text that is synthesized. If they represent a user turn, the interpretation module transforms them into an appropriate recognition grammar and vocabulary. After recognition, it chooses the hypotheses that were most likely realized by the user and fills in the value field if appropriate. The dialogue planner gets back the chosen hypotheses from which it extracts the continuations. Starting from the continuations' parent node, it builds these into the dialogue history. Further, the dialogue model is updated in accordance with the realized hypotheses. The extended dialogue history and new status of the domain model serve as the context from which a new set of continuations is calculated.

A summary of the hypotheses that we can currently calculate are shown in Tables III and IV. In the following, we will explain our interpretation algorithms through several examples. A more mathematical representation is given in Appendix A.

Our first example is a situation in which the last system utterance was the first request for a value for the parameter date, but the user did not provide a satisfactory answer – either she ignored the question or the recognition score was low. We assume that the task is pricePerMinute (ppm), in the application description, the task nodes are closed, the date node has status topic, and all other nodes are open. In both situations, we assume that the system has chosen the node and continuation for how to continue the dialogue. In the diagrams, continuations are underlined. In Section 3, we drew the parse trees as if the actual utterances were

Table III. List of hypotheses that the system can articulate.

Name of hypothesis	Function
requestValue	request a parameter value
requestConfirmation	request confirmation of a parameter value
requestDisambiguation	request disambiguation of a parameter value
withdrawOffer	withdraw from the conversation because of an error
withdrawPromise	withdraw from the conversation because of an error
rejectRequest	withdraw from the conversation because of an error
inform	provide the answer to the query
evaluate	evaluate information from the user

attached to the act nodes but this is not quite right. The *hypothesis* representing an utterance is attached to the node.

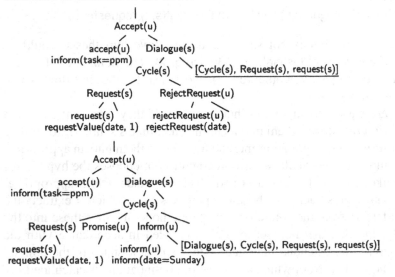

In both scenarios, the system analyses the local structure around the continu-ation's parent node. First, it checks the context above the parent node: The hypo-thesis is inform(task=pricePerMinute) and since the status of pricePerMinute is closed, the system reasons that the negotiation of the task is complete, and hence it will not build a hypothesis in this situation.

Next, the system checks the parent node. In the first scenario, this is Dialogue. No hypotheses are associated with Dialogue nodes so it goes on to investigate the neighboring cycle. Here it discovers that the previous question was unsuccessful and that not even a preliminary value for date is available. Thus the continuation is interpreted as requestValue with the same param as in the neigbouring cycle and with noOfMentions increased by one. The resulting hypothesis is request-Value(date, 2). A variable defines how many times to ask for the same value.

Table IV. List of hypotheses that the user can articulate and the system understand.

Name of hypothesis	Function
promise	promise to answer question
inform	provide a value
disambiguate	choose one value from a set
informPositive	provide positive answer to a yes no question
informNegative	provide negative answer to a yes no question
back	repeat previous answer
forward	tell next answer
repeat	repeat current answer
repeatAll	repeat all answers
rejectRequest	not answer a question
rejectOffer	not answer a question
withdrawAccept	withdraw from conversation
changeValue	change a value provided previously
clarifyRequest	ask question about a question

In the second scenario, the parent node is an Inform, hence the system retrieves the associated hypothesis inform(date = Sunday). In the application description, the system sees that the status of date is topic, so it checks with the other knowledge sources what the reason could be why the date node is not closed. In our example, it discovers that the recognition score was too low. Thus it interprets the continuation as requestConfirmation with param and value equal to those of the context Inform. noOfMentions is set to one since this is the first sub-dialogue of Inform. The resulting hypothesis is requestConfirmation(date = Sunday, 1).

In our next example, we consider how the system calculates how the user can respond to the request for confirmation in the previous example. We will limit our discussion to one continuation. In the following section, we show how hypotheses from several open ends are combined in order to compute complex user utterances.

Since the parent node of the continuation is Cycle, the system checks what happened at the beginning of the cycle. Since the type of the hypothesis is request, it decides to interpret the continuation as the direct answer to this question. The hypothesis associated with the request is requestConfirmation, hence the continuation results in two hypotheses informPositive(date = Sunday) and informNegative (date = Sunday), i.e., the user can confirm or contest that the system has recognized Sunday correctly.

4.4. MIXED INITIATIVE WITHIN TURNS

In the remainder of this section, we show some examples of how our dialogue planner understands and produces complex utterances of the *take + keep* +* relinquish type. Complex utterances are represented by a set of hypotheses, i.e., all continuations from all relevant open nodes are calculated and interpreted into hypotheses and then these are combined according to certain rules. In information retrieval dialogues two types of utterances dominate – questions and answers, hence the examples are concerned with requestValue and inform hypotheses.

In the first example, we show how to predict complex answers. Consider a situation in which the task has been negotiated to pricePerMinute (ppm), the user does not know whether the call is local or long distance (zone), the system does not know any other parameter values, and it has asked for one of the missing ones, say, source. In the application description, all task type nodes are closed, zone is closed, source has status topic and all other parameter nodes have status open. The relevant part of the dialogue history looks as follows:

```
                    |
               Accept(u)
             ⁄        ╲
       accept(u)     Dialogue(s)
  inform(task=ppm)      ⁄  ╲
                  Cycle(s)   `5. [Cycle(s),Request(s),request(s),Inform(u), inform(u)]
                ⁄  ╲
         Request(s)    `2. [Promise(u), Inform(u), inform(u)]
        ⁄  ╲           3. [Promise(u),promise(u)]   4. [RejectReq(u),rejectReq(u)]
    request(s)   `1. [Dialogue(u),Cycle(u),Request(u),request(u)]
requestValue(source, 1)
```

The interpretations are shown in Table V. Hypothesis A predicts that the user could ask for clarification of the system's question. Hypothesis B predicts that the user might answer the question. Hypothesis C predicts that the user cannot immediately answer the question, but promises to search for the answer. D predicts that the user might ignore the question. E–H predict that the user might provide extra information that the system did not ask for. *Which* extra information is calculated from the application description after the heuristic: the user might in any utterance provide a value for nodes in the application description that are not closed. In the above example, continuation number five results in three inform hypotheses, since the nodes destination, date and startTime are open. Continuation five also

[380]

Table V. Continuations and their interpretations in a situation in which the system has requested a parameter value.

No.	Hypotheses	Continuation
A	requestClarification(request = source)	1
B	inform(source)	2
C	promise(source)	3
D	rejectRequest(source)	4
E	inform(destination)	5
F	inform(date)	
G	inform(startTime)	
H	changeValue(pricePerMinute)	

results in a hypothesis that predicts that the user might change a value that she has provided previously, here the task.

In our example, the five continuations resulted in a total of eight hypotheses. These eight are further combined according to certain rules to form sets. We list some examples:

inform(source) + inform(date) = 'From Frankfurt on a working day'.
inform(source) + inform(destination) = 'From Frankfurt to Munich'.
inform(source) + inform(startTime) = 'From Frankfurt at noon'.
inform(source) + inform(date) + inform(startTime)
    = 'From Frankfurt to Munich around noon').
inform(source) + inform(destination) + changeValue(task)
    = Sorry. I want the total cost of a call from Frankfurt to
      Munich. Not the rate'.

The eight hypotheses plus the sets would be sent to the speech recognizer, which transforms them into phrase spotting patterns. Depending on what the user chooses to do, one or more of the hypotheses would be sent back to the planner such that their continuations can be built into the dialogue history. For example, if the user answers 'From Frankfurt to Munich', inform(source) and inform(destination) would be returned and continuations two and five would be added to the dialogue history.

In the next example, we show how the dialogue planner can support the speech recognizer in predicting the sequence in which to search for phrases. In utterance C in Dialogue 8, the system pursues the goal of acquiring confirmation of an already recognized destination (requestConfirmation(destination = Homburg)). The dialogue history for utterances A, B (first part), and C in Dialogue 8 is shown below. The resulting hypotheses are listed in Table VI.

Table VI. Continuations and their interpretations in a situation in which the system has asked for confirmation of a parameter value.

No.	Hypothesis	Continuation
A	requestClarification(param=source)	1
B	informPositive(source)	2
C	informNegative(source)	
D	promise(source)	3
E	rejectRequest(source)	4
F	inform(source)	5
G	changeValue(destination)	
H	inform(destination)	7
I	inform(date)	
J	inform(startTime)	
K	changeValue(pricePerMinute)	

We see that the direct answer to the system's question can be either to confirm or to contest the destination (hypotheses B and C). Empirical studies show that the user might contest and correct in the same utterance, e.g., 'No. Hamburg'. Hence we can instruct the recognizer to only look for the combination of informNegative(source) + inform(source), in that order. Unfortunately this type of support is not always possible as illustrated with the following utterances 'No. Hamburg, not Homburg.' vs. 'No. Not Homburg, Hamburg'.

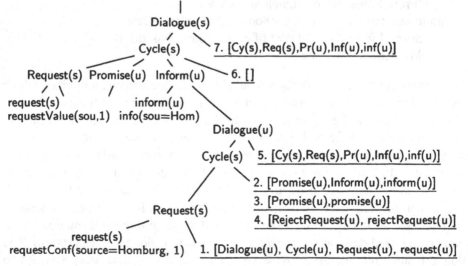

In the above examples, the system utterances contained only one communicative goal but it is, of course, also possible for the system to combine several hypotheses into one utterance. We use Dialogue 1 to illustrate. The dialogue history for utterances C and D is shown below and the resulting hypotheses are listed in Table VII. We assume that the speech recognition score for both task and destination are medium and that a geographical reasoner has discovered that Frankfurt is ambiguous.

First we discuss how the system chooses which hypotheses to realize acoustically. Hypothesis D allows the system to evaluate the destination value, but since the system only evaluates values that do not need further negotiation (i.e., the associated node in the application description is closed), this hypothesis is not considered at this point. Hypothesis F lets the system end the conversation, but the system is only allowed to use this option in cases of technical difficulty. We assume no technical difficulty in our example, hence this continuation is not considered either. Hypothesis G lets the system answer the user's query, but since it does not have all the parameter values yet, this continuations is not considered. That leaves hypotheses A, B, C, and E for further consideration.

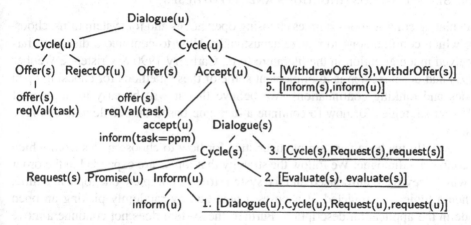

All four hypotheses allow the system to ask for clarification of the values that the user provided, i.e., 'Frankfurt' and 'rate'. The type of clarification depends on the information provided by the system's other knowledge sources and reasoning modules. Both values need to be confirmed since the speech recognition score was not high enough. Additionally Frankfurt is ambiguous. In this case the system can try to implicitly confirm its recognition result by asking the user to disambiguate between the two values. Consequently it drops the confirmation hypothesis. Further, it decides to combine the remaining hypotheses requestDisambiguation (destination = Frankfurt am Main), requestDisambiguation(destination = Frankfurt an der Oder), and requestConfirmation(task = pricePerMinute) into one utterance, e.g., 'Do you want the rate of a call to Frankfurt am Main or Frankfurt an der Oder?' If the recognition score had been low, it would have realized the goals separately since the probability of an incorrect result would be too high.

Table VII. Continuations and their interpretations in a situation in which the system asks a complex question.

No.	Hypothesis	Continuation
A	requestDisambig(source = Frankfurt am M.)	1
B	requestDisambig(source = Frankfurt an d. O.)	
C	requestConfirm(source = Frankfurt)	
D	evaluate(source)	2
E	requestConfirmation(task = pricePerMinute)	3
F	withdrawOffer(pricePerMinute)	4
G	inform(pricePerMinute)	5

4.5. SELECTING CONTINUATIONS AND HYPOTHESES

Calculating continuations implies choosing open nodes and for system turns, choosing which continuations to realize acoustically. How to continue a discourse has received much attention in the literature (e.g., Carberry 1990 & Cristea & Webber 1997) and our next step is to implement some of these methods for choosing open nodes and ranking continuations. We believe that it will be easy to implement different strategies for how to continue a dialogue based on our flexible dialogue history.

Currently we have very simple heuristics for how to choose nodes from which to continue a dialogue. We follow the strategy that topics are expanded in the order in which they were introduced and the system tries to complete one topic at a time. When a topic is completed, it chooses a new one by randomly picking an open node in the application description. Further, the system does not continue a move that does not have an act as a child, i.e., in the interest of generating efficient and user friendly dialogues, we don't allow dialogues like the one in Dialogue 11. The system is also not allowed to pick up nodes that are to the left of the last node in a cycle, e.g., if the user skipped Promise, the system cannot ask why she did that.

After having chosen open nodes, the system chooses which continuations from a given node to realize acoustically. For this part, we have implemented heuristics such as choosing requestConfirmation or requestDisambiguation, (Hypotheses are listed in Tables III and IV), before say, promise, or that the system is not allowed to reject or withdraw unless there is a technical problem. In Section 4.4, we presented one example of how the system chooses continuations to realize acoustically.

5. Mixed Initiative between Turns

In the previous section we discussed mixed initiative on the turn level. In Subsection 2.5, we defined our notion of mixed initiative *between* turns and in this section,

Algorithm: MixedInitiativePlanner(DS)
    loop
        UH_1 := CalculateHypotheses(usr, *DS*)
        send UH_1 to speech recognizer
        SH := CalculateHypotheses(sys, *DS*)
        SH' := choose system hypotheses from SH
        DS := Update(SH', *DS*)
        UH_2 := CalculateHypotheses(usr, *DS*)
        if user said something
            SRresult := speech recognition result, where SRresult $\subset UH_1$
            DS := UndoUpdate(SH', *DS*)
            DS := Update(SRresult, *DS*)
        else
            send UH_2 to speech recognizer
            realize SH' acoustically
            if user says something
                SRresult := speech recognition result, where SRresult $\subset UH_2$
                DS := Update(SRresult, *DS*)
            end if
        end else
    end loop
End

Subroutine: CalculateHypotheses(speaker, DS)
    C := continuations for *speaker* from open nodes in dialogue history
    if (*speaker* = usr)
        return InterpretUsrContinuations(C, *DS*)
    else
        return InterpretSysContinuations(C, *DS*)
End

Subroutine: Update(Hypotheses, DS)
// Update( ) takes a set of hypotheses as input and updates the dialogue
// history and the application description accordingly.
    loop for all H in *Hypotheses*
        update status of H.param in application description
        incorporate H.continuation into dialogue history
    end loop
End

Subroutine: UndoUpdate(Hypotheses, DS)
// UndoUpdate( ) takes a set of hypotheses as input and undoes the work
// done by Update( ) on the dialogue history and the application description
    loop for all H in *Hypotheses*
        remove H.continuation from dialogue history
        reset status of H.param in application description
    end loop
End

Figure 4. The dialogue planning algorithm. Notation: *DS* = dialogue state. UH/SH = user/system hypotheses. H.fieldname denotes field *fieldname* of hypothesis H.

we present a top level dialogue planning algorithm that adheres to this definition. A resulting sample dialogue is shown in Appendix B. We conclude the section with some remarks on the implementation and future system evaluation.

5.1. THE DIALOGUE PLANNING ALGORITHM

The following description of our planning algorithm is accompanied by the pseudo code in Figure 4. The algorithm takes a dialogue state as input, i.e., a dialogue history and an application description. To ensure that the speech recognition and the speech synthesis units are properly coordinated, the algorithm calculates user and system hypotheses in pairs – a system initiative and a set of possible user responses. This approach does, however, not lead to a question–answer system since before calculating the next system turn, it first calculates possible *user* hypotheses in the current state. These are sent to the speech recognizer and prepare the system to recognize additional information that the user might provide while the system calculates what its next turn should be, e.g., utterance H in Dialogue 1.

The system calculates the user hypotheses anew instead of reusing those from the previous recognition stage. This is to be prepared to recognize changes to the values provided last, i.e., if utterance H in Dialogue 1 had been 'Sorry. I mean Frankfurt an der Oder', a changeValue(destination) hypothesis is needed to understand this utterance. Since this value is newly recognized, the previous set of hypotheses did not contain a changeValue(destination) hypothesis, rather an inform(destination) hypothesis, which is now redundant.

The routine *CalculateHypotheses( )* takes a dialogue state and the speaker for which it shall calculate hypotheses as input. As explained in Section 4, hypotheses are calculated in two steps – first the continuations (illocution) and then these are assigned content and interpreted into hypotheses. The interpretation routines were informally described in Subsections 4.3 and 4.4, and more details are given in Appendix A.

After having calculated how the user might amend the previous utterance, the expected pair of turns is calculated: calculate system hypotheses and from this set, choose some to realize acoustically. The dialogue state is updated accordingly. From this new state, calculate how the user can respond to the chosen system hypotheses.

When the calculations are complete, the system checks whether the user said something while it was busy. If yes, the system hypotheses are *not* realized acoustically, and the dialogue history is reset to the one that was valid at the beginning of the loop. This history is then updated with the speech recognition result. If the user did not say anything while the system was busy, the second set of user hypotheses are sent to the recognizer, and the system hypotheses are realized acoustically. After the recognition is finished, the results are incorporated into the dialogue state.

Our algorithm can deal with all four pairs of turns that we defined in Subsection 2.5. Type one is dealt with implicitly through recognition timeouts whose values depend on the type of the system utterances. Type two describes a normal question–answer pair and are dealt with through the sets SH' and UH_2. Type three is dealt with through the calculation of UH_1 as described above. Type four describes barge-in and is dealt with on the turn level. The user is not allowed to barge-in until *relinquish* or at least one *keep* has been synthesized.

The above algorithm cannot deal with utterances like 'I want to call ⟨long pause⟩ Hamburg', if the pause is too long. In this case, this answer would be interpreted as rejectRequest(destination) since the speech recognizer cut of recognition before the content word 'Hamburg'. If we want to account for this type, we need to modify the algorithm as follows: after having recorded the current recognition result, open up the speech recognition again with the same UH_1. In the 'if user said something clause', check if I_u originated from the current or the previous UH_1. If I_u is from the previous UH_1, *UndoUpdate*(I_s) and *UndoUpdate*(previous I_u) and then go to the beginning of the loop. Currently our underlying speech recognition system can not deal with this situation, hence we will not implement this modification of the planning algorithm until the underlying speech recognition system can deliver this type of results to the planner.

5.2. IMPLEMENTATION AND EVALUATION

The algorithm has been implemented in C++ under Visual C++. Empirical studies in our sample domains have shown that the approach has low computational complexity and runs fast enough to be used in telephone interfaces to information retrieval systems. The time taken to calculate hypotheses on a Pentium 166 with 64 MB memory is much less than one second throughout the entire dialogue.

The algorithms were implemented and tested in the telephone inquiry domain illustrated through the dialogues in this article. In a laboratory setting, it has been ported to several other domains of comparable structure and size. If no additional capabilities are required, the time needed for porting *of the dialogue planner* is the time needed to change the application description. This time does not include the time needed adapt the speech recognizer and the speech synthesizer, i.e., development of new vocabularies and low level interpretation routines.

Although the planner has not yet been formally evaluated, informal test runs and porting in a laboratory setting gave encouraging results. As a step towards a fully automatic directory assistance system, the dialogue planner will be built into a prototype system at Deutsche Telekom Berkom in the summer of 1998. This whole system will be formally evaluated in a large field trial in 1999 with real customers. A large factor in this evaluation is the performance of the dialogue planner. For the evaluation we are considering several approaches, e.g., (Walker et al., 1997; EAGLES, 1997).

6. Discussion

We have discussed how we distinguish between initiative and control in mixed initiative information retrieval dialogue and how these theoretical notions are reflected in our algorithms. Further, we have identified the structure of the dialogue history as the most important part of our planning algorithm; it represents the context in which we calculate how a dialogue can continue and we define control and organize control segments in terms of the dialogue history. We have argued for a certain organization of the dialogue history such that we in a system without proper linguistic analysis can account for many mixed initiative phenomena in a uniform way.

We have presented a predictive dialogue planner for mixed initiative information retrieval dialogue. It employs a modular architecture where the resources have been divided into application independent and application dependent modules with clearly defined interfaces between them. The division nicely corresponds to the linguistic concepts of illocution and propositional content.

Automatic segmentation of dialogues and automatic tracking of control and initiative are inherent to our approach. (See (Chu-Carroll & Brown, 1998) for a model on how to track initiative in collaborative dialogues.) The hierarchical organization of the control segments in the dialogue history keeps track of who has control of a segment since the speaker of the leftmost utterance in a cycle controls the segment to which it belongs.

Since we equate taking the initiative with taking the turn, the temporal component of the dialogue history also tracks who takes the initiative, i.e., a change in speaker indicates a new turn and hence a change in initiative. The same mechanism is used to track keeping and taking back initiative. By knowing who the initiating conversational participant (ICP) of a turn is and then following the temporal ordering, we know that as long as the turn is the same and the speaker does not change, the ICP of the turn is keeping the initiative. The second type is characterized as follows. By knowing who the ICP of a turn is and then following the temporal ordering, we know that if the speaker does not change but the turn is different, then the ICP kept the initiative between turns. This situation also describes that the other conversational participant relinquished the initiative between the turns.

The dialogue grammar approach has been considered a weak approach to dialogue management since a grammar alone cannot function as a dialogue manager. Cohen (1998) writes that dialogue grammars need to function together with a planning mechanism that chooses an appropriate system response and that chooses the content of the response in order to function as a cooperative conversant. We consider this an asset, since it allows us to calculate the type and the content of utterances separately. We consider the grammar as a resource similar to the application description and the dialogue history and for these resources, we developed reasoning routines that deliver different kinds of knowledge needed to produce and understand utterances. From the dialogue grammar, we calculate the type of an utterance, from the dialogue history and the application description, we calculate its context, and from the status of the application description, we calculate its content. Finally, these three kinds of knowledge are combined to form one abstract representation. Through the division of knowledge into type and content, we achieved a flexible dialogue manager that can easily adapt to the user's behaviour. Moreover, the reasoning routines and the dialogue grammar are application independent, hence it is easy to reuse this dialogue manager in new applications.

Appendix. A. Interpretation Algorithms

In Figures 5 and 6, we present simplified versions of the sub-routines that calculate hypotheses from continuations, i.e., *InterpretSysContinuations*( ) and *InterpretUsrContinuations*( ). We only include a few of their sub-routines, since they are all based on the same principles. Their associated sub-routines are explained below. In the illustrations below, the continuations are written between [and]. The local context in the dialogue history that is relevant for the interpretation is shown as a partial tree.

ParentContext(c) searches upwards in the tree from *Parent*(c) until it finds a move, *m*. If *m* has an act as a child *ParentContext*(c) returns the hypothesis attached to this act, otherwise *ParentContext*(c) returns NULL. In all three situations below, *ParentContext*(c) returns the hypothesis inform(p = v,1).

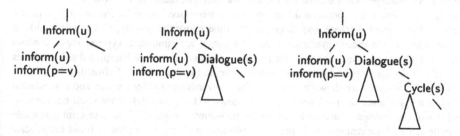

NoOfSiblingHypotheses(c, *test*) returns the number of hypotheses in the same sub-dialogue that pass *test*. In the following situation *NoOfSiblingHypotheses*(c, {name = requestConfirmation ∧ param = parentContext(c).param}) returns one.

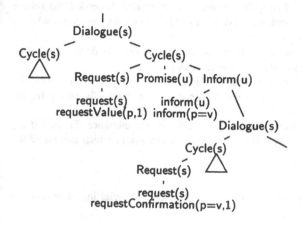

CycleInitialContext( ) calculates what happened initially in a cycle. If *Parent*(c) = Dialogue, as in the example immediately above, *CycleInitialContext*(c) returns NULL. Otherwise *CycleInitialContext*(c) searches upwards in the tree until it finds a cycle y. If the leftmost child of y has an act as child, *CycleInitialContext*(c) returns the hypothesis attached to this act, otherwise *CycleInitialContext*(c) returns NULL. In both situations below, *CycleInitialContext*(c) would return requestValue ($p = v$,1).

```
        |                                    |
   Dialogue(s)                           Cycle(s)
     /    \                               /    \
Cycle(s)  Cycle(s)                   Request(s)
  △        /   \                          |
      Request(s)                     request(s)
          |                        requestValue(p,1)
      request(s)
    requestValue(p,1)
```

B. Sample Dialogue with the Planner

The theoretical considerations presented in the previous sections have been implemented in a prototype dialogue manager, and we illustrate some of the dialogue manager's current capabilities with a transcript of an interaction between a user and our system (see Figure 7). For testing purposes, we hand coded a small database and since for the time being the prototype is running without speech recognition and speech synthesis, input and output are simulated; system output consists of system hypotheses and the user types in her replies as keywords that are interpreted as hypotheses with respect to the database and current dialogue situation (as described in Subsection 4.3). In the transcript, the hypotheses are shown on the left. The keywords entered by the user and a translation of the system hypotheses potential utterances are shown to the right. Below we point out some of the features of our dialogue manager based on the transcript in Figure 7. This transcript was made to illustrate some of the dialogue manager's capabilities, so please ignore the at times rather stale dialogue. Below we comment on the individual turns in the dialogue.

A+OO. Currently greetings and goodbyes are not calculated automatically.

B–C. If the user does not take the initiative after the greeting, the system does and asks what task it can solve for the user.

D–E. If the recognition result is good enough such that no confirmation is needed, the system starts asking for the values that it needs in order to solve the task, but the user does not know whether the call she wants to make is local or long distance.

F. The system confirms if it means to have understood the user. A variable defines how often these 'OKs' shall be generated. In the example it was set to 'always'.

G. If the application description defines alternative ways of acquiring parameter values, the system continues by asking for one of the alternative values instead of repeatedly asking for the original one.

I–K. The user can provide more information than asked for in one utterance. Further, if the recognition of context words (here: to, from) is bad, the system can ask to which parameter the recognized value belongs.[9]

---

[9] This clarification is obviously irrelevant for this application, but is crucial in, for instance, a ticket booking system.

Subroutine: InterpretSysContinuations(C, DS)

    Hyps := ∅

    loop for all c in C

        if (Type(c) = request)

            Hyps := Hyps ∪ InterpretSysRequest(c)

        else if (Type(c) = promise)

            Hyps := Hyps ∪ InterpretSysPromise(c)

        else if (Type(c) = inform)

            Hyps := Hyps ∪ InterpretSysInform(c)

             ⋮

    end loop

    return Hyps

End

Subroutine: InterpretSysRequest(a continuation c)

    parentHyp := ParentContext(c)

(1) **if** (parentHyp = NULL)

        return requestValue(p ∈ AD st. Type(p) = task, NULL, 1,c)

(2) **else if** (parentHyp.name = inform) ∧

        (Status(parentHyp.param) ≠ closed) ∧

        (RecognitionScore(parentHyp.param) < high) ∧

        (n := NoOfSiblingCycles(c, {name = requestConfirmation,

        param = parentHyp.param}) < max)

        return requestConfirm(parentHyp.param, parentHyp.value, n+1, c)

(3) **else if** (parentHyp.name = inform) ∧

        (Status(parentHyp.param = closed) ∧

        (Type(parentHyp.param) = task)

(4) **if** (∃ p ∈ AD st. Status(p) = topic)

        currentTopic := PreviousSystemContext(Status(param) = topic)

        if (n := NoOfSiblingCycles(c, {name = requestValue,

        param = currentTopic}) < max)

        return requestValue(currentTopic, NULL, n+1, c)

    else if (∃ p ∈ AD st. Status(p) = open)

        return requestValue(p ∈ AD st. Status(p) = open, NULL, 1, c)

End

Subroutine: InterpretSysInform(a continuation c)

    leftHyp := LeftContext(c)

    if (parentContext(c) = NULL) ∧ (∀ p ∈ AD status(p) = closed)

        return inform(leftHyp.value, NULL, 1, c)

End

Figure 5. The sub-routine calculating system hypotheses from continuations. Notation: AD is the application description. C is a set of continuations. DS is a dialogue state. H.fieldname denotes field *fieldname* of hypothesis H.

Subroutine: InterpretUsrContinuations(C, DS)
    Hyps := ∅
    loop for all c in C
        if (Type(c) = request)
            Hyps := Hyps ∪ InterpretUsrRequest(c)
        else if (Type(c) = inform)
            Hyps := Hyps ∪ InterpretUsrInform(c)
           ⋮

    end loop
    return Hyps
End

Subroutine: InterpretUsrRequest(a continuation c)
    parentHyp := ParentContext(c)
    if (parentHyp.name = inform) ∧ (Type(parentHyp.param) = task)
        ∧ (parentHyp.value = all)
        return repeatAll(parentHyp.param, all, _, c)
    else
        return { repeat(parentHyp.param, parentHyp.value, _, c),
                next(parentHyp.param, parentHyp.value+1, _, c),
                back(parentHyp.param, parentHyp.value-1, _, c) }
End

Subroutine: InterpretUsrInform(a continuation c)
    parentHyp := parentContext(c)
    initialHyp := cycleInitialContext(c)
(1) **if** (initialHyp = NULL) ∧ (parentHyp.name = inform)
    if (Type(parentHyp.param) = task)
        return { changeValue(parentHyp.value, NULL, _, c),
            inform(p, _, _, c) ∀ p ∈ AD st. Status(p) = open}
    else
        return changeValue(parentHyp.param, NULL, _, c) ∪
(2) **else if** (initialHyp.name = requestValue)
        return inform(initialHyp.param, NULL, _, c)
(3) **else if** (initialHyp.name = requestConfirmation)
        return { informPositive(initialHyp.param, initialHyp.value, _, c),
            informNegative(initialHyp.param, initialHyp.value, _, c) }
End

Figure 6. The sub-routine calculating user hypotheses from continuations. Notation: AD is the application description. C is a set of continuations. DS is a dialogue state. H.fieldname denotes field *fieldname* of hypothesis H. An underscore indicates that noOfMentions is irrelevant for user hypotheses.

A.	SYS:		'Welcome to TESADIS...'
B.	SYS:	requestValue(aTask=price/min, 1)	'Do you want a rate
		requestValue(aTask=totalCost, 1)	or the total cost of a call?'
C.	USR:	accept(aTask=pricePerMinute)	rate
		rejectOffer(aTask=totalCost)	
D.	SYS:	requestValue(zone=local, 1)	'Local
		requestValue(zone=long d., 1)	or long distance?'
E.	USR:	informNegative(zone=unknown)	dont know
		informNegative(zone=unknown)	
F.	SYS:	evaluate(zone, 1)	'Ok'.
G.	SYS:	requestValue(source, 1)	'Where will you be calling from?'
H.	USR:	inform(unknown=Munich)	mumble mumble Munich
		inform(unknown=Frankfurt)	to Frankfurt
I.	SYS:	requestDisambig(dest.=M., 1)	'*To*
		requestDisambig(source=M., 1)	or *from* Munich?'
J.	USR:	inform(source=Munich)	from
		rejectRequest(dest.=M.)	
K.	SYS:	evaluate(source)	'Ok'.
L.	SYS:	requestConfirm(destination, 1)	'And you are calling Frankfurt?'
M.	USR:	informPositive(destination)	yes
		inform(startTime=afternoon)	afternoon.
N.	SYS:	requestDisambig(dest.=F. am Main, 1)	'Frankfurt am Main
		requestDisambig(dest.=F. an der Oder, 1)	or Frankfurt an der Oder?'
O.	USR:	inform(destination=Oder)	Oder
		rejectRequest(dest.=am Main)	
P.	SYS:	evaluate(destination, 1)	'Ok'.
Q.	SYS:	requestDisambig(startTime=12-3, 1)	'Is your call between 12 and 3
		requestDisambig(startTime=3-6, 1	or between 3 and 6?'
R.	USR:	inform(startTime=unknown)	dontknow
		inform(startTime=unknown)	
S.	SYS:	evaluate(startTime, 1)	'Ok'.
T.	SYS:	requestValue(date, 1)	'What day of the week is your call?'
U.	USR:	rejectRequest(date)	(return)
V.	SYS:	requestValue(date=workday, 2)	'Is your call on a working day?'
W.	USR:	rejectRequest(date=workday)	(return)
X.	SYS:	inform(aTask, 1)	'There are three answers:'
Y.	SYS:	inform(aTask=1st answer, 1)	'Before 3 on a weekday: 0.60 DM'.
Z.	USR:	request(repeat)	repeat
AA.	SYS:	promise(repeat, 1)	'One moment'.
BB.	SYS:	inform(aTask=1st answer, 2)	'Before 3 on a weekday: 0.60 DM'.
CC.	USR:	request(forward)	next
DD.	SYS:	promise(forward, 1)	'One moment'.
EE.	SYS:	inform(aTask=2nd answer, 1)	'After 3 on a weekday: 0.30 DM'.
FF.	USR:	request(back)	previous
GG.	SYS:	promise(back, 1)	'Ok'.
HH.	SYS:	inform(aTask=1st answer, 3)	'Before 3 on a weekday: 0.60 DM'.
II.	USR:	—	
JJ.	SYS:	inform(aTask=3rd answer, 1)	'Between 12 and 6 on a holiday':...
KK.	USR:	request(first)	first
LL.	SYS:	promise(first, 1)	'One moment'.
MM.	SYS:	inform(aTask=1st answer, 4)	'Before 3 on a weekday: 0.60 DM'.
NN.	USR:	—	
OO.	SYS:		'Thank you for calling...'

Figure 7. Transcript of a dialogue.

L. The system picks up old topics before it starts asking for new parameter values. In utterance H, the user provided the source value, but the recognition result was not convincing enough, hence the confirmation question.

M. The user has the opportunity of combining confirmation of values with mention of new information.

N–P. At this point the system has recognized two ambiguities: there are two cities called Frankfurt and the afternoon is divided into two time slices. By using the temporal information in the dialogue history, the system chooses to continue with disambiguation of the topic that it was already working on instead of the new one.

Q–S. The system tries to disambiguate values, but when unsuccessful, it goes on to the next parameter.

T–W. If the user chooses to ignore the request (or the speech recognition can not map her utterance to a phrase that it knows), the system tries a second time, maybe with another version of the question. How many times the system requests the same information is predefined through a variable setting.

X–NN. When there are no more parameters values to acquire, the system evaluates the query with respect to the database. If the cardinality of the answer set is less than some predefined value, the answers to the query are presented one by one. Otherwise it tries acquire more specific parameter values from the user. The user has the possibility of navigating between the answers, e.g. 'repeat' in utterance Y, 'forward' in utterance BB, 'back' in FF, and 'first' in JJ. If the user does not take the initiative and there are still answers that have not been mentioned, the system automatically continues with the next one (utterances HH and II). If after the last answer the user does not take the initiative, the system assumes that the user is satisfied and completes the dialogue.

Acknowledgments

The author thanks Fred Popowich, Susan Haller, and the three anonymous reviewers for their comments on earlier drafts of this paper. Without the co-operation with the colleagues at Deutsche Telekom Berkom, this work could not have been developed. The author also acknowledges usage of the infrastructure in the Natural Language Lab at Simon Fraser University. Financial support from the Norwegian Research Council, project number 116578/410 is greatly appreciated.

References

Allen, J. and C. Perrault: 1980, Analyzing intention in utterances. *Artificial Intelligence* **15**(3), 143–178.

Austin, J.: 1962, *How to Do Things with Words*. London: Oxford University Press.

Baekgaard, P., O. Bernsen, T. Brøndsted, P. Dalsgaard, H. Dybkjær, L. Dybkjær, J. Kristiansen, L. Larsen, B. Lindberg, B. Maegaard, B. Music, L. Offersgaard, and C. Povlsen: 1994, The danish spoken language dialogue project – A general overview. In: *Proc. ESCA Wshp. on Spoken Dialogue Systems; Theories and Applications*. pp. 89–92.

Ball, J. E. and D. T. Ling: 1994, Spoken language processing in the persona conversational assistant. In: *Proc. ESCA Wshp. on Spoken Dialogue Systems; Theories and Applications*. pp. 109–112.

Bennacef, S., F. Néel, and H. Maynard: 1995, An oral dialogue model based on speech acts categorization. In: *Proc. ESCA Wshp. on Spoken Dialogue Systems; Theories and Applications*. pp. 237–240.

Bilange, E.: 1991, A task independent oral dialogue model. In: *Proc. of 5th Euro. Conf. of the ACL*. pp. 83–87.

Blomberg, M., R. Carlson, K. Elenius, B. Granström, J. Gustafson, S. Hunnicutt, R. Lindell, and L. Neovius: 1993, An experimental dialogue system: WAXHOLM. In: *Proc. European Conf. on Speech Communication and Technology (Eurospeech'93)*. pp. 1867–1870.

Caminero-Gil, J., J. Alvarez-Cercadillo, C. Crespo-Casas, and D. Tapias-Merino: 1996, Data-driven discourse modeling for semantic interpretation. In: *Proc. of 1996 Intl. Conf. on Acoustics, Speech, and Signal Processing (ICASSP'96)*. pp. 401–404.

Carberry, S.: 1990, *Plan Recognition in Natural Language Dialogue*. Cambridge, MA. London, England: MIT Press.

Chu-Carroll, J. and M. Brown: 1998, An evidential model for tracking initiative in collaborative dialogue interactions. *User Modeling and User-Adapted Interaction*. **8**(3–4) pp. 215–254.

Chu-Carroll, J. and S. Carberry: 1995, Response generation in collaborative negotiation. In: *Proc. of the 33th Annual Meeting of the ACL*. Also available as http://xxx.lanl.gov/cmp-lg/9505001.

Cohen, P.: 1998, Dialogue modeling. In: R. Cole, J. Mariani, H.Uszkoreit, G. Varile, A. Zaenen, and A. Zampolli (eds.): *Survey of the State of the Art in Human Language Technology*. Cambridge University Press, Cambridge, Chapt. 6.3. Also available at http://www.cse.ogi.edu/CSLU/HLTsurvey/.

Cohen, R., C. Allaby, C. Cumbaa, M. Fitzgerald, K. Ho, B. Hui, C. Latulipe, F. Lu, N. Moussa, D. Pooley, A. Qian, and S. Siddiqi: 1998, What is initiative?. *User Modeling and User-Adapted Interaction*. **8**(3–4) pp. 171–214.

Cristea, D. and B. Webber: 1997, Expectations in incremental discourse. In: *Proc. of the 35th Annual Meeting of the ACL and the 8th Conf. of the European ACL*. pp. 88–95.

Dahlbäck, N. and A. Jönsson: 1992, An empirically based computationally tractable dialogue model. In: *Proc. of the 14th Annual Conference of the Cognitive Science Society (COGSCI-92)*. Bloomington, Indiana.

EAGLES: 1997, *Handbook of Standards and Resources for Spoken Language Systems*. http://coral.lili.uni-bielefeld.de/EAGLES/eagbook/eagbook.html.

Eckert, W., G. Fink, A. Kießling, R. Kompe, T. Kuhn, F. Kummert, M. Mast, H. Niemann, E. Nöth, R. Prechtel, S. Rieck, G. Sagerer, A. Scheuer, G. Schukat-Talamazzini, and B. Seestaedt: 1992, EVAR: Ein sprachverstehendes Dialogsystem. In: *KONVENS 92*. pp. 49–58.

Feldes, S., G. Fries, E. Hagen, and A. Wirth: 1998, A novel service creation environment for speech-enabled database access. In: *Proc. of 4th IEEE Workshop on Interactive Voice Technology for Telecommunications Applications (IVT-TA'98)*.

Glass, J., G. Flammia, D. Goodine, M. Phillips, J. Polifroni, S. Sakai, S. Seneff, and V. Zue: 1995, Multilingual spoken-language understanding in the MIT voyager system. *Speech Communication* **17**(1–2), 1–18.

Goddeau, D., H. Meng, J. Polifroni, S. Seneff, and S. Busayapongchai: 1996, A form-based dialogue manager for spoken language applications. In: *Proc. of the 1996 Intl. Conf. on Spoken Language Processing (ICSLP'96)*.

Green, N. and S. Carberry: 1999, A computational mechanism for initiative in answer generation'. *User Modeling and User-Adapted Interaction*. This issue.

Grice, H.: 1975, Logic and conversation. In: P. Cole and J. Morgan (eds.): *Syntax and Semantics, Vol. 3: Speech Acts*. Academic Press, pp. 41–58.

Grosz, B. and C. Sidner: 1986, Attention, intentions, and the structure of discourse. *Computational Linguistics* **12**(3), 175–204.

Hagen, E. and B. Grote: 1997, Generating efficient mixed initiative dialogue. In: *Proc. ACL Workshop Interactive Spoken Dialog Systems: Bringing Speech and NLP Together in Real Applications*. pp. 53–56.

Hagen, E. and A. Stein: 1996, Automatic generation of a complex dialogue history. In: *Proc. 11th Canadian Conference on Artificial Intelligence (AI96)*. pp. 84–96.

Jönsson, A.: 1993, A dialogue manager using initiative-response units and distributed control. In: *Proc. of 6th Euro. Conf. of the ACL*.

Jordan, P. and B. Di Eugenio: 1997, Control and initiative in collaborative problem solving dialogues. In: *Working Notes of the AAAI-97 Spring Symposium on Computational Models for
Mixed Initiative Interaction*. pp. 81–84.

Kamp, H. and U. Reyle: 1993, *From Discourse to Logic*, vol. 42 of *Studies in Linguistics and
Philosophy*. Kluwer Academic Publisher, Dordrecht.

Kaspar, B., G. Fries, K. Schuhmacher, and A. Wirth: 1995, Faust – A directory assistance demon-
strator. In: *Proc. European Conf. on Speech Communication and Technology (Eurospeech'93)*.
pp. 1161–1164.

Kaspar, B., K. Schuhmacher, and S. Feldes: 1997, Barge-in revised. In: *Proc. European Conf. on
Speech Communication and Technology (Eurospeech'97)*.

Lambert, L. and S. Carberry: 1991, A tripartite plan-based model of dialogue. In: *Proc. of the 29th
Annual Meeting of the ACL*. pp. 47–54.

Lester, J., B. Stone, and G. Stelling: 1999, Lifelike pedagogical agents for mixed-initiative problem
solving in constructivist learning environments. *User Modeling and User-Adapted Interaction*.
This issue.

Litman, D. and J. Allen: 1987, A plan recognition model for subdialogues in conversations. *Cognitive
Science* **11**, 163–200.

Mann, W. and S. Thompson: 1988, Rhetorical structure theory: Toward a functional theory of text
organization. *Text* **8**(3), 243–281.

Naito, M., S. Kuroiwa, K. Takeda, and S. Y. F. Yato: 1994, A real-time speech dialogue system for a
voice activated telephone extension service. In: *Proc. ESCA Wshp. on Spoken Dialogue Systems;
Theories and Applications*. pp. 129–132.

O'Donnell, M.: 1990, A dynamic model of exchange. *Word* **41**(3), 293–327.

Oerder, M. and H. Aust: 1993, A realtime prototype of an automatic inquiry system. In: *Proc. of the
1994 Intl. Conf. on Spoken Language Processing (ICSLP'94)*. pp. 703–706.

Peckham, J.: 1993, A new generation of spoken dialogue systems: Results and lessons from the
SUNDIAL project. In: *Proc. European Conf. on Speech Communication and Technology (Eurospeech'93)*.

Polanyi, R. and R. Scha: 1984, A syntactic approach to discourse semantics. In: *Proc. of the 10th
Intl. Conf. on Computational Linguistics (COLING'84)*. pp. 413–419.

Reichman, R.: 1985, *Getting Computers to Talk Like You and Me*. Cambridge, MA: MIT Press.

Sadek, M.: 1990, Logical task modelling for man-machine dialogue. In: *Proc. of the Natl. Conf. on
Artificial Intelligence (AAAI'90)*. pp. 970–975.

Sadek, M., Bretier, V. Cadoret, A. Cozannet, P. Dupont, A. Ferrieux, and F. Panaget: 1994, A cooperative spoken dialogue system based on a rational agent model: A first implementation on the AGS
application. In: *Proc. ESCA Wshp. on Spoken Dialogue Systems; Theories and Applications*. pp.
145–148.

Sinclair, J. and R. Coulthard: 1975, *Towards an Analysis of Discourse: The English Used by Teachers
and Pupils*. London: Oxford University Press.

Sitter, S. and A. Stein: 1992, Modelling the illocutionary aspects of information-seeking dialogues.
Information Processing and Management **8**(2), 165–180.

Smith, R. and D. Hipp: 1994, *Spoken Natural Language Dialog Systems; A Practical Approach*. New
York, Oxford: Oxford University Press.

Spiegel, M. and C. Kamm: 1997, Special issue on interactive voice technology for telecommunica-
tion applications (IVTTA'96). *Speech Communication* **23**(1–2).

Stein, A., J. A. Gulla, and U. Thiel: 1999, User tailored planning of mixed initiative information
seeking dialogues. *User Modeling and User-Adapted Interaction*. This issue.

Traum, D. and E. Hinkelman: 1992, Conversation acts in task-oriented spoken dialogue. *Computational Intelligence* **8**(3), 575–599.

Walker, M., D. Litman, C. Kamm, and A. Abella: 1997, PARADISE: A framework for evaluating spoken dialogue agents. In: *Proc. of the 35th Annual Meeting of the ACL and the 8th Conf. of the European ACL.* pp. 271–280.

Walker, M. and S. Whittaker: 1990, Mixed initiative in dialogue: An investigation into discourse segmentation. In: *Proc. of the 28th Annual Meeting of the ACL.* pp. 70–78.

Whittaker, S. and D. Attwater: 1994, Advanced speech applications – The integration of speech technology into complex services. In: *Proc. ESCA Wshp. on Spoken Dialogue Systems; Theories and Applications.* pp. 113–116.

Whittaker, S. and P. Stenton: 1988, Cues and control in expert-client dialogues. In: *Proc. of the 26th Annual Meeting of the ACL.* pp. 123–130.

Young, S., A. Hauptmann, W. Ward, E. Smith, and P. Werner: 1990, High level knowledge sources in usable speech recognition systems. In: A. Waibel and K. Lee (eds): *Readings in Speech Recognition.* San Mateo, CA: Morgan Kaufman, pp. 538–549.

Author's Vita

Eli Hagen
School of Computer Science, Burnaby BC, Canada V5A 1S6
Eli Hagen is a Ph.D. candidate in Computer Science as Simon Fraser University. She received her B.Sc. in Computer Science from Queen's University, Ontario in 1989 and her M.Sc. in the same field from Simon Fraser University in 1991. Her primary research interests lie in spoken dialogue systems and text generation and text analysis in the context of spoken dialogue. Previous research has included work on automatic generation of intonation markers for synthesis. Her contribution is based on her Ph.D. work and her experiences gained at Deutsche Telekom Berkom while integrating her theoretical work into real world dialogue systems.